# The Economics of the Middle East

# The Economics of the Middle East

*A Comparative Approach*

JAMES E. RAUCH

Oxford University Press is a department of the University of Oxford. It furthers
the University's objective of excellence in research, scholarship, and education
by publishing worldwide. Oxford is a registered trade mark of Oxford University
Press in the UK and certain other countries.

Published in the United States of America by Oxford University Press
198 Madison Avenue, New York, NY 10016, United States of America.

© Oxford University Press 2020

All rights reserved. No part of this publication may be reproduced, stored in
a retrieval system, or transmitted, in any form or by any means, without the
prior permission in writing of Oxford University Press, or as expressly permitted
by law, by license, or under terms agreed with the appropriate reproduction
rights organization. Inquiries concerning reproduction outside the scope of the
above should be sent to the Rights Department, Oxford University Press, at the
address above.

You must not circulate this work in any other form
and you must impose this same condition on any acquirer.

Library of Congress Cataloging-in-Publication
Data Names: Rauch, James E., author.
Title: The economics of the Middle East :
a comparative approach / James Rauch.
Description: New York, NY, United States of America :
Oxford University Press, 2020. |
Includes index.
Identifiers: LCCN 2018059969 | ISBN 9780190879181 (hardcover : alk. paper) |
ISBN 9780190879198 (pbk. : alk. paper)
Subjects: LCSH: Middle East—Economic conditions—21st century. |
Economic development—Middle East. | Middle East—Economic policy. |
Middle East—Social conditions—21st century. | Middle East—Social policy
Classification: LCC HC415.15 .R38 2020 | DDC 330.956—dc23
LC record available at https://lccn.loc.gov/2018059969

1 3 5 7 9 8 6 4 2

Paperback printed by Sheridan Books, Inc., United States of America
Hardback printed by Bridgeport National Bindery, Inc., United States of America

*To Doris, without whom this book could not and would not have been written*

# Contents

*Acknowledgments*   xi
*Using This Book*   xiii

1. Introduction   1
   The Scope of This Book   1
   The Human Development Index   6
   Three Arab Worlds   17
   Human Development in the Three Arab Worlds
   on the Eve of the "Arab Spring"   22
   Human Development in the Three Arab Worlds after
   the "Arab Spring"   29
   A Note on Country Groups   33
2. Historical Perspective   35
   Introduction   35
   Extensive versus Intensive Growth   36
   The Division of the World   42
   The Great Divergence   51
3. International Trade, Natural Resource Rents, and Foreign
   Direct Investment   55
   Introduction   55
   International Trade and Industrialization of the Arab
   Mediterranean and Turkey   57
   Manufactured Exports to High-Income Consumers   67
   Service Exports to High-Income Consumers: Tourism   71
   Natural Resource Rents and OPEC   76
   Foreign Direct Investment   84
4. Human Resources   91
   Introduction   91
   Education   93
   Health   103
   The Demographic Transition   112

## viii CONTENTS

5. Gender Gaps   121
   - Introduction   121
   - Education   122
   - Labor Force Participation   125
   - Health   132
6. Income Inequality, Poverty, Migration, and Unemployment   139
   - Introduction   139
   - Income Inequality as Measured by the Gini Index   140
   - Poverty Headcounts   145
   - Migration and Remittances   151
   - Public and Private Sector Expenditure to Reduce Poverty   162
   - Unemployment and Self-Employment   166
7. Environmental Challenges   171
   - Introduction   171
   - Water Scarcity and Lack of Access to Basic Drinking Water and Sanitation Services   173
   - Air Pollution   180
   - Municipal Waste and Greenhouse Gas Emissions   185
   - The Consequences of Global Warming for the Arab Countries, Iran, and Turkey   191
8. Government Spending: Urban Infrastructure, Energy Subsidies, and the Military   195
   - Introduction   195
   - Urbanization and Strain on Public Finance   196
   - Urban Primacy   200
   - Energy Subsidies   204
   - Military Spending   210
   - Slums   213
   - Infrastructure Quality   219
9. Political Economy   223
   - Introduction   223
   - Corruption, GDP Per Capita, and Bureaucratic Inefficiency   224
   - Bureaucratic Performance with Regard to Starting a Business and Enforcing Contracts   229
   - Politically Connected Firms in Egypt and Tunisia   236

10. Conclusion: Some Modest Proposals for Policy 251

*Appendix* 257
*References* 281
*Index* 289

# Acknowledgments

There are many people I would like to thank, without implicating them in any views I express or mistakes I might have made. I apologize to anyone I have forgotten. Lisa Anderson, Prashant Bharadwaj, and David Lagakos read drafts of various chapters and provided helpful feedback. Ying Feng, Scott Kostyshak, Adam Soliman, and especially Kye Lippold supplied valuable research assistance. I received useful suggestions from Shanta Devarajan, Raymond Fisman, Tarek Hassan, Paul Niehaus, and anonymous reviewers. The students at the University of California, San Diego in my classes on the economics of the Middle East have helped me to refine my ideas over the years. I would also like to thank the Economics Department of the NYU Stern School of Business for hosting me during the sabbatical when I wrote much of this book.

Special thanks are due to my editor, David Pervin. David went far beyond the usual editorial duties, helping to shape this book and repeatedly challenging me to do more. The book is far better as a result.

Above all I thank my wife, Doris Bittar, for her constant encouragement. I owe my entire interest and experience in the Middle East to her.

# Using This Book

This book places great emphasis on data. Data facilitate comparisons across countries. Data also check any tendency to make unsubstantiated claims, because we can examine whether the claims are backed by evidence. These features of data are helpful when we study a part of the world about which people have very strong opinions, though it would be naïve to think that any scholarly approach can eliminate all biases.

Data need to be organized and presented well to be useful. The Human Development Index (HDI) of the United Nations Development Program provides a starting point for our data organization. We describe the HDI in the section titled "The Human Development Index" in Chapter 1. In this section we also show interested readers exactly how the HDI is computed; others can skip over the technical details of its computation without loss of continuity.

The only math used in this book beyond arithmetic is logarithms. These are used to compute the HDI and to make some figures easier to read. Everything one needs to know about logarithms for these purposes is explained using arithmetic in Box 1.2.

Chapter 1 provides the foundation for the remainder of this book. Chapters 2 and 3 should be read together. Both of these chapters primarily examine production at the firm, sector, and country levels. Chapters 4 and 5 should also be read together. The main focus of both chapters is the actions of individuals and households. Each of Chapters 6, 7, 8, and 9 is more capable of standing alone.

# The Economics of the Middle East

# 1
# Introduction

### The Scope of This Book

In this book we study the economies of the Arab world, Iran, and Turkey. In line with contemporary practice of economists, we take a broad approach to the study of the economy, encompassing subjects such as education, health, and the environment. The population of the Arab world is more than five times larger than the population of Iran or Turkey, so the Arab economies will receive more space. Fortunately, the economic issues facing Iran and Turkey are sufficiently similar to the issues facing some of the Arab countries that we will usually be able to discuss them together.

We define the Arab world as consisting of all United Nations (UN) member states belonging to the Arab League. Figure 1.1 shows the countries we will study, labeled with dark letters. The twenty-one Arab countries are solid light gray, contrasted with the solid dark gray of Iran and Turkey. It is important to note that Palestine is a member of the Arab League but not a UN member state. The situation of Palestine is unique and therefore does not fit into the comparative framework used in this book.

Language rather than ethnicity is the chief determinant of membership in the Arab League. The Arab League includes all countries in which (a dialect of) Arabic is the spoken language of the majority. The Arab League also includes Comoros, Djibouti, and Somalia, in which Arabic is widely used but not the dominant spoken language. These three countries account for only 4 percent of 2016 Arab UN member state population (see Table 1.6).

Ethnic Arabs are from the Arabian peninsula. How did their language spread to the enormous area shown in Figure 1.1? The explanation lies in events that began early in the seventh century. At that time the Persian and Roman empires that dominated the areas that became the Arab world were both in weakened conditions. A new religion, Islam, arose in the Arabian peninsula. Energized by their new religion, Arabs spread out of the Arabian peninsula and conquered the Persian Empire and the southern part of the Roman Empire, bringing Islam all the way to the Atlantic Ocean in the west and to the Indus River (in present-day Pakistan) in the east. The Arabic

2 THE ECONOMICS OF THE MIDDLE EAST

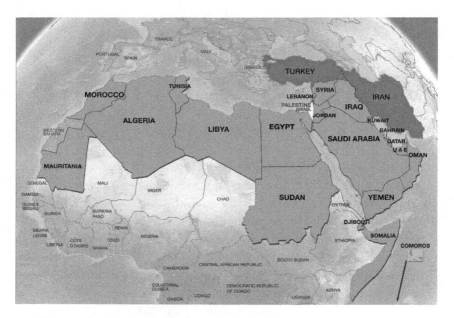

**Figure 1.1.** The Scope of This Book

*Note:* This map is for illustrative purposes and does not imply the expression of any opinion on the part of the author concerning the legal status or name of any country or territory or concerning the delimitation of frontiers or boundaries.

*Source:* Doris Bittar.

language spread with the Arab conquest for several reasons. People of the Islamic faith, called Muslims, believe that the *Qur'an*, the holy book of Islam, was directly dictated by God (*Qur'an* means "recitation"), so one has to learn Arabic to understand God's message to humankind. This could not have been the only reason to learn Arabic, however, since Christians and Jews who did not convert to Islam but lived under Arab rule also became Arabic speakers. Because the rulers spoke Arabic, there was a strong incentive to learn Arabic in order to communicate with them. There was also intermarriage between the conquering Arab armies and local women, giving rise to Arabic-speaking children.

A revival of Persian language and culture in the ninth century stopped the eastern spread of Arabic, so that Persians adopted Islam but not Arab identity. Today Persian is written in Arabic script, adding some letters that are not in Arabic. As the successor to a later revival of the Persian Empire, Iran defines the eastern boundary of the Arab world (see Figure 1.1). Similarly, the northern spread of Arabic was checked by the Turks, who adopted Islam and Arabic script but not the Arabic language. (Turkey switched from Arabic script to a Latin-based script beginning in 1923.) As the successor to the Ottoman Empire, the last of a series of Turkish empires, Turkey (and the Mediterranean Sea) defines the northern boundary of the Arab world. The southern spread of both Islam and Arabic was hindered by the Sahara Desert, leading to the irregular southern boundary of the Arab world seen in Figure 1.1. From this brief overview we see that the histories and cultures of Iran, Turkey, and the Arab world are intertwined, providing a reason, in addition to their economic similarities, to study them together.

### Box 1.1

**Do Arabs Speak Arabic?** The Arab world is unified by language and culture. Yet if an Iraqi and a Moroccan speak to each other in the language they speak at home, they will probably not be able to understand each other. As the Arabic language spread from the Arabian peninsula, it became grammatically simplified and mixed with native languages. Regional dialects of Arabic evolved. As noted in the section titled "Education" in Chapter 4, the existence of dialects complicates the question of whether students are best served by education in Arabic or a colonial language. Kees Versteegh (2001) distinguishes five groups of regional dialects: Arabian peninsula, Iraqi, Syro-Lebanese, Egyptian, and North African. Note that this list omits some dialects, such as Sudanese. It is very likely that two Arabs from the same dialect region will be able to understand each other's speech. There does not appear to be any systematic study of the ability of Arabs from different dialect regions to understand each other. Casual observation indicates that Arabs speaking dialects from Egypt, Israel/Palestine, Jordan, Lebanon, and Syria can understand each other, whereas Arabs speaking dialects from the Arabian peninsula or Iraq cannot understand Arabs speaking North African dialects.

Starting in the nineteenth century, Modern Standard Arabic (MSA) was developed for formal written and spoken communication. MSA is an updated version of the Arabic used in the *Qur'an* and other texts from the seventh through ninth centuries. Arabs who attend public schools or most private schools learn to speak, read, and write MSA. Returning to the original example, if the Iraqi and Moroccan are

> educated, they can shift their speech toward MSA and be able to communicate successfully.
>
> MSA is used for government documents, newspapers, and textbooks, and often for their spoken equivalents (political speeches, media broadcasts, and lectures). This means that an Arab who did not study MSA and listens to a political speech, media broadcast, or lecture in MSA will usually not be able to understand it.

Over time the empire that Arabs established in the seventh and eighth centuries weakened, and Arabs came to be ruled by other peoples, though they retained their Arabic language and identity. From the sixteenth through eighteenth centuries the Ottoman Empire, based in Istanbul, ruled all of the Arab world except parts of the Arabian peninsula, the Sudan, and Morocco. In the nineteenth century France and the United Kingdom took over sections of the Arab world from the Ottoman Empire, beginning with the French colonization of Algeria. After the defeat of the Ottoman Empire in World War I, all of the Arab world except parts of the Arabian peninsula was controlled by Europeans, chiefly France and the United Kingdom but also Italy. Decolonization began before World War II, accelerated after World War II, and was completed by 1977.

It was during the period of European colonialism that the boundaries of today's Arab states shown in Figure 1.1 were established. For each Arab UN member state, Table 1.1 lists the short version of its official name that we will use in this book, its official name, the year in which it became politically independent, and its former colonial power. Table 1.1 also lists the official names of Iran and Turkey, which were never colonized. We shall see in Chapter 3 that the ability of the Arab countries, Iran, and Turkey to make economic policy independent of European control was in some cases of great importance. Political independence enabled countries to make decisions in what they perceived to be their own economic interests, even when these decisions were not economically advantageous for the former colonial powers.

In the section of this chapter titled "Three Arab Worlds," we will organize the twenty-one Arab economies into three groups. We will then provide an overview of recent socioeconomic development in these three Arab country groups in the sections titled "Human Development

**Table 1.1.** The Arab World, Iran, and Turkey

**Official Country Names, Dates of Political Independence, and Former Colonial Powers**

| Country | Official Name | Date of Political Independence | Former Colonial Power |
|---|---|---|---|
| Algeria | People's Democratic Republic of Algeria | 1962 | France |
| Bahrain | Kingdom of Bahrain | 1971 | United Kingdom |
| Comoros | Union of the Comoros | 1975 | France |
| Djibouti | Republic of Djibouti | 1977 | France |
| Egypt | Arab Republic of Egypt | 1922/1956 | United Kingdom |
| Iraq | Republic of Iraq | 1932 | United Kingdom |
| Jordan | Hashemite Kingdom of Jordan | 1946 | United Kingdom |
| Kuwait | State of Kuwait | 1961 | United Kingdom |
| Lebanon | Republic of Lebanon | 1943 | France |
| Libya | Libya | 1951 | Italy |
| Mauritania | Islamic Republic of Mauritania | 1960 | France |
| Morocco | Kingdom of Morocco | 1956 | France |
| Oman | Sultanate of Oman | | none |
| Qatar | State of Qatar | 1971 | United Kingdom |
| Saudi Arabia | Kingdom of Saudi Arabia | 1930 | none |
| Somalia | Federal Republic of Somalia | 1960 | Italy and United Kingdom |
| Sudan | Republic of the Sudan | 1956 | United Kingdom |
| Syria | Syrian Arab Republic | 1946 | France |
| Tunisia | Republic of Tunisia | 1956 | France |
| UAE | United Arab Emirates | 1971 | United Kingdom |
| Yemen | Republic of Yemen | 1967/1990 | United Kingdom |
| Iran | Islamic Republic of Iran | | none |
| Turkey | Republic of Turkey | 1923 | none |

*Notes*: The United Kingdom ended its protectorate over Egypt in 1922. However, the United Kingdom maintained control over the Suez Canal until 1956. The Kingdom of Saudi Arabia was established in 1930. In 2011, South Sudan seceded from Sudan. The United Kingdom ended its protectorate over the port of Aden in Yemen in 1967. In 1990, the Yemen Arab Republic (North Yemen) and the People's Democratic Republic of Yemen (South Yemen) unified to become the Republic of Yemen. Turkey is the successor to the Ottoman Empire. The Republic of Turkey was established in 1923.

*Source*: Wikipedia.

in the Three Arab Worlds on the Eve of the 'Arab Spring'" and "Human Development in the Three Arab Worlds after the 'Arab Spring,'" leaving Iran and Turkey in the background. Starting in Chapter 2, and continuing for the remainder of this book, we will study Iran and Turkey alongside the Arab world.

The section titled "Human Development in the Three Arab Worlds on the Eve of the 'Arab Spring'" covers the period 1970–2010 and the section titled "Human Development in the Three Arab Worlds after the 'Arab Spring'" covers the years 2011–2016. The reason for the break between 2010 and 2011 is that on December 17, 2010, a political uprising began in Tunisia that spread with varying force to most Arab countries, in what became known as the "Arab Spring." By the end of February 2012, autocrats in Egypt, Libya, Tunisia, and Yemen, who had collectively held power for 127 years, had been deposed, and Syrian President Bashar al-Assad was fighting a war to remain in power, which he continues to do at time of writing. The upheaval associated with the Arab Spring led to a major break in the trend of socioeconomic development for many Arab countries, and to reduced availability of data for the countries that descended into civil war. For both these reasons it will often be useful throughout this book to distinguish the period through 2010 from the period after 2010.

Our organization of the Arab countries and overview of their socioeconomic development will be guided by the data used to construct the Human Development Index (HDI). The HDI was introduced by the UN Development Program in 1990. It is designed to provide a broad measure of socioeconomic development, and is thus very much in the spirit of this book. We describe the HDI thoroughly in the next section, which includes many technical details. Fortunately, this section is not representative of the rest of the book.

## The Human Development Index

The HDI gives equal weight to three dimensions of human development: "Long and healthy life" (health), "Knowledge" (education), and "A decent standard of living" (income). For our purposes, the main value of the HDI is that it provides indicators to use to measure health, education, and income. We are less concerned with the specific HDI values for the countries we study, but for completeness we show how to compute those.

"Long and healthy life" is measured by life expectancy at birth. This is the "number of years a newborn infant could expect to live if prevailing patterns of age-specific mortality at the time of birth stay the same throughout the infant's life," according to the notes to Table 1 of the 2016 *Human Development Report* (http://hdr.undp.org/en/composite/HDI).

"Knowledge" is measured by an average of mean years of schooling and expected years of schooling. Mean years of schooling equals the average number of years of education attained by people aged 25 and older. Expected years of schooling equals "number of years of schooling that a child of school entrance age can expect to receive if prevailing patterns of age-specific enrollment rates persist throughout the child's life" (http://hdr.undp.org/en/composite/HDI).

"A decent standard of living" is measured by Gross National Income (GNI) per capita. GNI per capita equals aggregate income of a country divided by its midyear population. Income is counted for all of the country's workers and owners of capital, whether the workers or capital are located in the country or located abroad. By the same token, income earned in the country by foreign workers or foreign-owned capital is not counted in GNI. That is, income earned in the country by foreigners is not "national" income because it is not earned by the citizens of the country. The HDI measures GNI in *international dollars*, which are "dollars" that have the same purchasing power in every country. Later in this section we will explain how income measured in US dollars is converted to international dollars.

Each of the data for the HDI is converted into an index by making it a fraction of the distance from a minimum to a goal or maximum. Table 1.2 shows the data for Egypt in 2015, along with the minima and maxima,

Table 1.2. Human Development Index Data, Egypt 2015

| Dimension | Indicator | Minimum | Egypt | Maximum |
| --- | --- | --- | --- | --- |
| Health | Life expectancy (years) | 20 | 71.3 | 85 |
| Education | Mean years of schooling | 0 | 7.1 | 15 |
|  | Expected years of schooling | 0 | 13.1 | 18 |
| Income | GNI per capita (2011 P$) | 100 | 10,064 | 75,000 |

*Note*: The choices of minima and maxima are explained in the Technical Notes to the 2016 Human Development Report (http://hdr.undp.org/sites/default/files/hdr2016_technical_notes.pdf).
*Source of data*: http://hdr.undp.org/en/composite/HDI.

for life expectancy, mean years of schooling, expected years of schooling, and GNI per capita. The units of GNI per capita are 2011 P$ (P$ denotes international dollars, also known as purchasing power parity dollars). P$ have been converted from US$ using domestic price data that were collected from countries in 2011. The indices for mean and expected years of schooling are averaged to obtain an education index, and then the health, education, and income indices are geometrically averaged to obtain the HDI. (The geometric average of n numbers equals the product of the numbers raised to the power 1/n, whereas the arithmetic average equals the sum of the numbers divided by n.) The income index uses the natural logarithm of GNI per capita, which is a way of capturing the intuition that a thousand dollars of additional income is worth much less to a rich person than to a poor person. (Economists call this "diminishing marginal utility of income.") Box 1.2 explains why logarithms are useful for many purposes in this book in addition to the HDI.

We now use the data in Table 1.2 to compute the HDI for Egypt in 2015:

$$\text{Health index} = \frac{71.3 - 20}{85 - 20} = 0.789$$

$$\text{Mean years of schooling index} = \frac{7.1 - 0}{15 - 0} = 0.473$$

$$\text{Expected years of schooling index} = \frac{13.1 - 0}{18 - 0} = 0.728$$

$$\text{Education index} = \frac{0.473 + 0.728}{2} = 0.601$$

$$\text{Income index} = \frac{\ln(10,064) - \ln(100)}{\ln(75,000) - \ln(100)} = 0.697$$

Human Development Index = $(0.789)^{1/3}(0.601)^{1/3}(0.697)^{1/3} = 0.691$.

Use of the geometric instead of the arithmetic average to compute the HDI favors countries that perform relatively equally across the three indices. Consider two hypothetical countries, $A$ and $B$. $A$ has indices 0.7, 0.7, and 0.7, and $B$ has indices 1, 1, and 0.3. The reader can verify that $\text{HDI}_A = 0.700 > 0.669 = \text{HDI}_B$, whereas if the HDI were computed using the arithmetic average, we would have $\text{HDI}_A = 0.700 < 0.767 = \text{HDI}_B$.

Because the HDI is the average of three indices, each of which ranges from 0 to 1, it must also range from 0 to 1. The 2016 *Human Development Report* assigns countries to four categories of human development based on their HDI scores: "low," HDI < 0.550; "medium," 0.550 ≤ HDI < 0.700; "high," 0.700 ≤ HDI < 0.800; and "very high," HDI ≥ 0.800. The Arab world contains countries in every human development category. Iran and Turkey are both in the "high" human development category.

### Box 1.2

**Why Use Logarithms?** The HDI uses the logarithm of per capita income to capture the idea that equal increments to income contribute less to well-being the higher income is. Thus if we increase by P$1,000 the income of an individual with an initial income of P$10,000, the logarithm of her income increases more than if we increase by P$1,000 the income of an individual with an initial income of P$20,000. Other functions such as the square root also have this property. What is special about logarithms is that equal *percentage changes* in incomes yield equal increases in well-being. In our example, the income of the poorer individual increases 10 percent but the income of the richer individual increases only 5 percent. In order for the logarithms of the individuals' incomes to increase equally, the income of the richer individual must also increase 10 percent, or P$2,000.

Logarithms work this way because the difference between the logarithms of two numbers equals the logarithm of the ratio of the two numbers. In mathematical notation, $\log(x_2) - \log(x_1) = \log(x_2/x_1)$. Since a percentage change corresponds to a ratio, the same percentage change corresponds to the same difference in the logarithms. In our example, 11,000/10,000 = 22,000/20,000, so $\log(11,000) - \log(10,000) = \log(22,000) - \log(20,000)$.

This property of logarithms makes them extremely useful for graphing. Let us call the variable on the horizontal axis $x$ and the variable on the vertical axis $y$. If $\log(x)$ is plotted on the horizontal axis, a straight line in the graph shows a constant change in $y$ with respect to percentage changes in $x$. We will use this property of logarithms throughout this book, starting with Figure 1.2, where we plot the logarithm of Gross Domestic Product (GDP) per capita on the horizontal axis. Similarly, if log($y$) is plotted on the vertical axis, a straight line in the graph shows a constant percentage change in $y$ with respect to changes in $x$.

The UN Development Program chooses to use the *natural logarithm* of per capita income when computing HDI. Per capita incomes with natural logarithms that are one unit apart have the ratio $e$, the exponential constant, which equals approximately 2.7. (The most popular alternative to the natural logarithm is the common logarithm. Per capita incomes with common logarithms that are one unit apart have the ratio 10.) Henceforward we will use *logarithm* as a synonym for *natural logarithm*, and write ln($x$) instead of log($x$). In Figure 1.2, Djibouti (DJI) and Jordan (JOR) have logarithms of 2015 GDPs per capita that are one unit apart (8.05 versus 9.05). Hence their 2015 GDPs per capita in 2011 P$, 3,139 and 8,491, respectively, have a ratio equal to 2.7. Note that in Figure 1.2, ln(GDP per capita) lies between 6 and 12. This means that no country has a GDP per capita less than P$$e^6$ = P$403 or more than P$$e^{12}$ = P$162,755.

The next-to-last column of Table 1 in the 2016 *Human Development Report* gives the difference between country ranking by GNI per capita and country ranking by HDI (http://hdr.undp.org/en/composite/HDI). There are many reasons to believe the two rankings will be highly correlated, not least that richer countries can afford better health care and more education. Nevertheless, there are many countries ranked much higher (positive number) or much lower (negative number) by HDI than by GNI per capita. Of the ten countries ranked thirty or more places lower by HDI than by GNI per capita, four belong to the Arab world: Iraq, Kuwait, Qatar, and UAE. This reflects the fact that countries with high endowments of oil and natural gas per capita can achieve high incomes without achieving long lives or high levels of education, because their high incomes are based on physical rather than human wealth. These four Arab countries will be among those classified as "fuel-endowed" in the next section. We can also compare countries that would be ranked nearly the same by GNI per capita but very differently by HDI. Egypt and Jordan have nearly the same GNI per capita in 2015 (P$10,064 versus P$10,111), but Jordan is ranked twenty-five places higher than Egypt by HDI, placing Jordan in the "high" human development category, whereas Egypt is in the "medium" human development category. Despite having the same average incomes, the average Jordanian lives 2.9 years longer than the average Egyptian and has 3.0 more years of education. The education difference is especially striking: The average Jordanian has 42 percent more schooling.

We conclude this section with an explanation of how and why income measured in US dollars is converted to international dollars. The easiest way to compare incomes across countries is to convert their GNIs per capita from their currencies to US dollars. One can find GNI per capita in US dollars for the vast majority of the world's countries in the World Development Indicators (http://databank.worldbank.org/data/source/world-development-indicators). Unfortunately, conversion to US dollars is a demonstrably inaccurate way to compare standards of living across countries. The reason is that prices, converted to US dollars, tend to be lower in poor countries than in rich countries. In other words, the US dollar typically "goes farther" in poor countries than in rich countries, so that comparisons between US dollar incomes exaggerate the true differences between the standards of living in poor and rich countries.

To adjust for the differences in prices across countries, the International Comparison Program (ICP) collects prices for thousands of goods and services in as many countries as possible. Most recently the program collected price data for 199 countries in 2011. The ICP aggregates these data into national price indices, which are used to convert incomes in US dollars to "international dollars" by dividing each country's US dollar income by its ICP price index. The ICP sets the value of the US price index to one, so that US income measured in international dollars is the same as US income measured in US dollars. Countries with ICP price indices that are lower than one therefore have higher P$ incomes than US$ incomes, and countries with ICP price indices that are higher than one have lower P$ incomes than US$ incomes.

As Jagdish Bhagwati (1984) and others have shown, the main reason that prices in poor countries are lower than in rich countries is that services (such as health care, housing, and transportation) are cheaper, rather than that goods (such as clothing, electronics, and furniture) are cheaper. International trade tends to equalize the prices of goods across countries, but most consumer services cannot be shipped across borders. Box 1.3

provides a more detailed explanation for why prices of services tend to rise relative to prices of goods as countries grow richer.

> **Box 1.3**
>
> **Why Are Services Cheap Relative to Goods in Poor Countries?** Let us first see why prices of goods tend toward equality across countries. Suppose that (1) the price of good $i$ in the United States equals $P_i^{US}$, measured in US dollars; (2) the price of good $i$ in country $j$ equals $P_i^j$, measured in the currency of country $j$; and (3) the exchange rate equals $x$, measured in US dollars per unit of currency of country $j$. Then the dollar price of good $i$ is the same in the United States and in country $j$ if $P_i^{US} = xP_i^j$. For example, at the end of 2017 a Tunisian dinar was worth about 40 cents (US$0.40). If the price of a shirt in Tunisia were 50 dinars, its dollar price would be (0.40)(50) = US$20, so the equation would hold if the price of the same shirt in the United States were 20 dollars.
>
> The equation $P_i^{US} = xP_i^j$ is known as the *law of one price*. We would expect this "law" to hold if international trade were completely free, that is, if there were no transport costs, tariffs, or other trade barriers. Suppose the law did not hold. If $P_i^{US} > xP_i^j$, then one could buy good $i$ in country $j$, resell it in the United States, and make a guaranteed profit. This process, known as *international goods arbitrage*, will bid up the price of good $i$ in country $j$ and bid down the price of good $i$ in the United States until the law of one price holds. International goods arbitrage also rules out $P_i^{US} < xP_i^j$.
>
> Although international trade is not completely free in the real world, containerization and the World Trade Organization have sufficiently lowered transport costs and government trade barriers, respectively, so that international arbitrage can keep the dollar prices of goods fairly close across countries. However, international arbitrage does not work for most services. If haircuts are cheaper in country $j$ than in the United States, it is impossible for an arbitrageur to buy haircuts in country $j$ and resell them in the United States, and extremely expensive for a consumer to fly from the United States to country $j$ to get a cheap haircut. Housing and local transportation are similar to haircuts in this regard, though many business services such as accounting can be cheaply transported electronically.
>
> Now that we see why goods prices tend toward equality across countries and service prices do not, it remains to be shown why service

> prices are lower in poor countries. The key is that wages are lower in poor countries. Since labor is a major input to production of services, and technology for producing most consumer services does not differ dramatically across countries, lower wages translate into lower costs of production. Returning to the haircut example, the technology used by a barber is not much different in a poor country than in a rich country, but the poor-country barber is willing to cut hair for much less because the wages in alternative occupations are much lower.

Figure 1.2 plots the ICP price index against the logarithm of GDP per capita for the year 2015. We use 2015 because too many countries are missing GDP per capita data in later years. GDP equals the value of goods and services produced inside a country, which in turn equals the income of

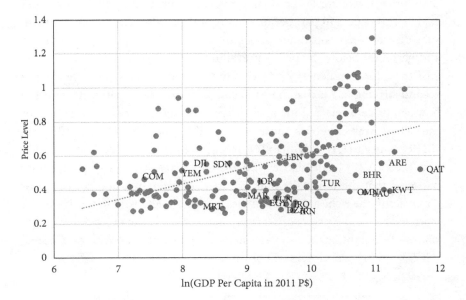

**Figure 1.2.** Price Level by GDP Per Capita, 2015

*Note:* Data are provided as "price level ratio of PPP conversion factor (GDP) to market exchange rate." Price level is expressed relative to the United States price level, which is set equal to one. List of included countries available on request.

*Source of data:* World Development Indicators.

workers and owners of capital earned inside that country. Unlike GNI, GDP does not add income earned abroad or subtract income sent abroad. Except in Tables 1.4 and 1.5, we will use GDP instead of GNI for the remainder of this book because it is available for more countries and years and because it reflects the productivity of a country better than GNI. For most countries GDP and GNI differ very little, and for almost all countries growth of GDP tracks growth of GNI very closely.

Figure 1.2 confirms that there is a strong positive relationship between country price levels and country incomes. All but one country with ln(GDP per capita) less than 10 (approximately 2011 P$22,000) has a price level lower than in the United States (i.e., lower than one). Figure 1.2 also reveals two striking facts about the countries we study in this book. First, consider the line that best fits the data. This positively sloped line shows the average relationship between price levels and (the logarithms of) GDPs per capita for all the countries for which we have data in 2015. For any given GDP per capita it provides the best prediction of the country price level we should expect. We see that most of the countries we study fall below this line, so their price levels are lower than we would expect given their GDPs per capita. This occurs in part because many of these countries use government subsidies to keep consumer prices for food and energy (e.g., electricity and gasoline) below the prices prevailing in other countries. We will discuss these food and energy subsidies in Chapters 6 and 8, respectively. The second striking fact is that the Arab countries defy the positive relationship between price levels and incomes. It appears that the prices of services for the richest Arab countries, those in the Gulf Cooperation Council (Bahrain (BHR), Kuwait (KWT), Oman (OMN), Qatar (QAT), Saudi Arabia (SAU), and UAE (ARE)), fail to rise with their incomes. The most likely explanation is that the unusually high numbers of migrant workers from poor countries in the richest Arab countries keep the wages paid to service sector workers, hence the prices of services, at a low level. The exceptionally high shares of migrant labor, Arab and non-Arab, in Gulf Cooperation Council (GCC) country workforces will be discussed in Chapter 6.

### Box 1.4

**Measuring GDP per Capita in Constant Versus Current Units of Account.** We have seen that, in order to compare GDPs per capita across countries, we need to use international dollars (P$) instead of

US dollars as our unit of account. We also want to be able to compare GDPs per capita within the same country over time. This comparison is made more difficult by price inflation. Let us define *real GDP* as GDP adjusted for price inflation, and *nominal GDP* as GDP not adjusted for price inflation. Consider a country with a constant population, and suppose that all prices in this country double between 2015 and 2016, without any change in actual production of goods and services. In this country real GDP per capita is unchanged from 2015 to 2016, but nominal GDP per capita doubles. It is clear that if we want to use GDP per capita as an indicator of average standard of living or economic productivity, we should prefer real GDP per capita to nominal GDP per capita to measure changes over time.

To convert nominal GDP per capita to real GDP per capita we need to use a price index to measure inflation. This requires that we choose a base year for the index, that is, a year in which the index is set equal to 1. We now call the units of account (such as P$) in which we measure real GDP per capita *constant base-year* units of account, and the units of account in which we measure nominal GDP per capita *current* units of account. We then use this formula:

$$\text{real GDP per capita in constant base-year units of account} = \text{nominal GDP per capita in current units of account} \div \text{price index}.$$

Note that, in the base year itself, real GDP per capita = nominal GDP per capita. Returning to our example in which prices double between 2015 and 2016, let us choose 2015 as the base year. The price index then equals 1 in 2015 and 2 in 2016. We have:

$$\text{2016 real GDP per capita in constant 2015 units of account} = \text{2016 nominal GDP per capita in current units of account} \div 2.$$

Since nominal GDP per capita doubles from 2015 to 2016, we obtain the correct result that real GDP per capita does not change from 2015 to 2016.

For the remainder of this book, we measure real GDP per capita in constant 2011 P$, unless stated otherwise. We choose 2011 as our base year because this is the most recent year in which the ICP measured prices, and it is the base year used for constant P$ by international organizations such as the UN and World Bank. For simplicity we will use the words "GDP per capita in 2011 P$" for "real GDP per capita in constant 2011 P$."

Table 1.3 illustrates the difference between (real) GDP per capita in 2011 P$ and (nominal) GDP per capita in current P$. The table shows the following data for Egypt: GDP per capita in 2011 P$, GDP per capita in current P$, and the price index used to convert current P$ to 2011 P$. These data are shown for the base year 2011, the three preceding years, and the three following years. We see that, in the base year, GDP per capita in 2011 P$ equals GDP per capita in current P$. We also see that the price index always increases from one year to the next, indicating that inflation was always positive during this period in Egypt. The last column of Table 1.3 shows that, from 2008 to 2014, Egyptian GDP per capita grew by 6.2 percent measured in 2011 P$ and by 16.2 percent measured in current P$. The 10 percent difference between growth measured in current and constant P$ is approximately equal to the 9.4 percent growth in the price index during this period. (To obtain the growth of GDP per capita in 2011 P$ exactly from the growth of GDP per capita in current P$ and the growth in the price index, divide 1.162 by 1.094.)

Table 1.3 demonstrates clearly the importance of adjusting for price inflation. Looking only at GDP per capita in current P$, we miss the fall in output of goods and services that occurred in Egypt with the Arab Spring in 2011. Real GDP per capita did not recover its 2010 level

Table 1.3. Egypt 2008–2014 GDP Per Capita, 2011 P$ and Current P$

|  | 2008 | 2009 | 2010 | 2011 | 2012 | 2013 | 2014 | 2014÷2008 |
|---|---|---|---|---|---|---|---|---|
| GDP per capita, 2011 P$ | 9305 | 9562 | 9857 | 9824 | 9822 | 9814 | 9880 | 1.062 |
| GDP per capita, current P$ | 8939 | 9255 | 9658 | 9824 | 10,003 | 10,156 | 10,387 | 1.162 |
| Price index | 0.961 | 0.968 | 0.980 | 1.000 | 1.018 | 1.035 | 1.051 | 1.094 |

Note: Price index computed by dividing GDP per capita, 2011 P$ by GDP per capita, current P$.

Source of data: World Development Indicators.

until 2014.

## Three Arab Worlds

Study of the economies of the Arab world has been hindered by its tremendous socioeconomic diversity. In Table 1.4 we compare the human development diversity of the Arab world to that of Latin America, another vast geographic area defined by language and culture. To be consistent, we use a linguistic definition of Latin America, including all Western Hemisphere countries in which a language from the Iberian Peninsula (Portuguese or Spanish) is predominant, but excluding countries such as Haiti. This gives us nineteen Latin American countries, listed at the bottom of Table 1.4, compared to twenty-one Arab League countries. For each indicator (except expected years of schooling) used to compute the HDI, we compare the range for Arab League countries to the range for Latin American countries in 2010. We choose the year 2010 because indicators for Libya, Syria, and Yemen are often missing after the Arab Spring started in 2011. We see that the range of Arab values is nearly double the range of Latin American values for life expectancy, more than 20 percent higher for mean years of education, and more than seven times greater for income measured by GNI per capita in 2011 P$.

**Table 1.4.** Range of Human Development Index Indicators: Arab World versus Latin America, 2010

| Indicator | Arab World Maximum | Arab World Minimum | Range | Latin America Maximum | Latin America Minimum | Range |
|---|---|---|---|---|---|---|
| Life expectancy (years) | 78.5 (Lebanon) | 54.0 (Somalia) | 24.5 | 78.9 (Cuba) | 66.4 (Bolivia) | 12.5 |
| Mean years of schooling | 9.2 (Jordan) | 2.6 (Yemen) | 6.6 | 9.7 (Chile) | 4.3 (Guatemala) | 5.4 |
| GNI per capita (2011 P$) | 114,051 (Qatar) | 1410 (Comoros) | 112,641 | 19,187 (Chile) | 3787 (Honduras) | 15,400 |

*Notes:* Latin America includes Argentina, Bolivia, Brazil, Chile, Colombia, Costa Rica, Cuba, Dominican Republic, Ecuador, El Salvador, Guatemala, Honduras, Mexico, Nicaragua, Panama, Paraguay, Peru, Uruguay, and Venezuela. Comoros, Djibouti, Lebanon, Oman, and Somalia are missing data for schooling. Somalia is missing data for GNI per capita. GNI per capita for Chile is for 2011; value for 2010 is missing.

*Sources of data:* World Development Indicators, www.barrolee.com v. 2.1, February 2016.

From a socioeconomic point of view, then, the Arab world is not a useful aggregate, because the average over such dissimilar countries does not reveal a central tendency. Our strategy in this book, therefore, is to disaggregate the Arab world into smaller groups of countries, each of which is more socioeconomically homogeneous than the entire Arab world. We will now decide the nature and number of these country groups.

Let us start from the fact that some Arab countries are located in sub-Saharan Africa. This region is well known for poor socioeconomic performance. On the subject of growth in GDP per capita, for example, William Easterly and Ross Levine (1997) have written about "Africa's Growth Tragedy" and Paul Collier and Jan Willem Gunning (1999) ask, "Why Has Africa Grown So Slowly?" (By "Africa," both articles mean "sub-Saharan Africa.") The causes of poor socioeconomic performance in sub-Saharan Africa are controversial. One cause for which there is substantial evidence is tropical diseases. In particular, John Gallup and Jeffrey Sachs (2001) developed a malaria index that has proved to be a powerful explanatory variable for socioeconomic performance. Since data for the HDI indicators and related measures of socioeconomic performance started to become available for sub-Saharan Africa in the 1960s, we examined the values of the malaria index in 1965. Except for Djibouti, every Arab sub-Saharan country was in the highest category for malaria intensity, as were all non-Arab sub-Saharan countries except Lesotho, South Africa, and Swaziland. Yemen, which is at the same latitude as the Arab sub-Saharan countries and separated from the African continent only by a strait less than thirty kilometers wide, was also in the highest intensity category for malaria. Given the similarities in geographic location and disease environment between Comoros, Djibouti, Mauritania, Somalia, Sudan, and Yemen, we will group them together as Arab sub-Saharan Africa. This country group is shown in Figure 1.3.

Our next grouping of Arab countries is motivated by the well-known abundance of oil and natural gas resources in the Arab world. The surprising negative consequences of fossil fuel endowments for economic growth and political stability of countries both inside and outside the Arab world has become known as the "oil curse" (Gelb 1988). We will discuss the possible causes for the oil curse in Chapter 3. At the same time, countries like Qatar have clearly escaped the oil curse and become fabulously wealthy as a result of their fuel endowments. In either case, exceptionally high fuel endowments per capita set countries apart, shaping their economies and societies in defining ways.

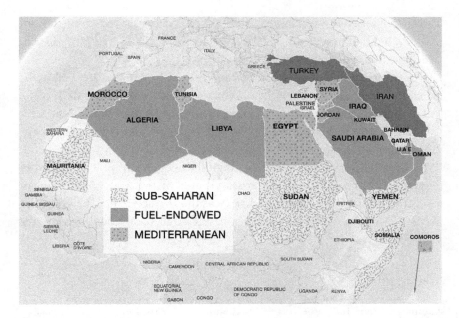

**Figure 1.3.** The Three Arab Worlds

*Note:* This map is for illustrative purposes and does not imply the expression of any opinion on the part of the author concerning the legal status or name of any country or territory or concerning the delimitation of frontiers or boundaries.

*Source:* Doris Bittar.

In order to decide which countries belong in the fuel-endowed group, we need to determine what counts as "exceptionally high" fuel endowments per capita. We rank all countries in the world from highest to lowest proven fuel reserves per capita. As with the malaria index, we wanted to use data on fuel reserves per capita at the beginning of the period when data for the HDI indicators and related measures of socioeconomic performance started to become available for the relevant countries. The authoritative data source is the *BP Statistical Review*, which publishes cross-country comparable estimates of oil and natural gas reserves dating back only to 1980, so that is the earliest year we can use. A minor issue arises regarding how to aggregate oil and natural gas reserves. We converted the oil and natural gas into BTUs (British thermal units) using standard conversion factors and computed 1980 BTU reserves per capita. This procedure yielded a ranking with a clean break at Algeria, which has 69 percent more reserves per capita than the next country down and nearly 5 times more reserves per capita than the next Arab country down. We will call Algeria and all countries ranked above it "fuel-endowed countries." The Arab fuel-endowed countries are Algeria, Bahrain, Iraq, Kuwait, Libya, Oman, Qatar, Saudi Arabia, and UAE. We show this country group in Figure 1.3.

The Arab countries that are neither fuel-endowed nor in Arab sub-Saharan Africa are Egypt, Jordan, Lebanon, Morocco, Syria, and Tunisia. All of these countries except Jordan border on the Mediterranean Sea. A related fact is that, prior to the Arab Spring, international tourism was exceptionally important for all of their economies, as will be shown in Chapter 3. We will call this group of countries the Arab Mediterranean. It is marked in Figure 1.3. Although the characteristics shared by the Arab Mediterranean countries do not define them as sharply as the characteristics shared by the Arab sub-Saharan African countries or the Arab fuel-endowed countries

**Table 1.5.** Range of Human Development Index Indicators: Three Arab Worlds, 2010

| Country Group | Indicator | Maximum | Minimum | Range |
|---|---|---|---|---|
| Arab sub-Saharan Africa | Life expectancy (years) | 63.5 (Yemen) | 54.0 (Somalia) | 9.5 |
| | Mean years of schooling | 3.8 (Mauritania) | 2.6 (Yemen) | 1.2 |
| | GNI per capita (2011 P$) | 3534 (Yemen) | 1410 (Comoros) | 2124 |
| Arab fuel-endowed countries | Life expectancy (years) | 77.6 (Qatar) | 68.5 (Iraq) | 9.1 |
| | Mean years of schooling | 8.9 (UAE) | 6.0 (Algeria) | 2.9 |
| | GNI per capita (2011 P$) | 114,051 (Qatar) | 12,876 (Algeria) | 101,175 |
| Arab Mediterranean | Life expectancy (years) | 78.5 (Lebanon) | 70.3 (Egypt) | 8.2 |
| | Mean years of schooling | 9.2 (Jordan) | 4.2 (Morocco) | 5.0 |
| | GNI per capita (2011 P$) | 16,231 (Lebanon) | 6353 (Morocco) | 9878 |

*Notes*: Arab sub-Saharan Africa includes Comoros, Djibouti, Mauritania, Somalia, Sudan, and Yemen. Arab fuel-endowed countries include Algeria, Bahrain, Iraq, Kuwait, Libya, Oman, Qatar, Saudi Arabia, and UAE. Arab Mediterranean includes Egypt, Jordan, Lebanon, Morocco, Syria, and Tunisia. Comoros, Djibouti, Lebanon, and Somalia are missing data for schooling. Somalia and Syria are missing data for GNI per capita. GNI per capita for Yemen is for 2011; value for 2010 is missing.

*Sources of data*: World Development Indicators, www.barrolee.com v. 2.1, February 2016.

define these groups, the Arab Mediterranean countries are still more homogeneous than Latin America in their levels of human development.

Table 1.5 imitates Table 1.4, showing the range of the three human development indicators for each of the three Arab worlds separately rather than for the Arab world as a whole. A comparison of Table 1.5 to Table 1.4 shows that the ranges for Arab sub-Saharan Africa and the Arab Mediterranean are smaller than in Latin America for all three human development indicators. Moreover, the ranges for life expectancy and mean years of schooling are smaller than in Latin America for all three Arab country groups. Only the range of GNI per capita for the Arab fuel-endowed countries is too large by the standard of Latin America. For this reason we will sometimes find it useful to distinguish the GCC countries as a group separate from the other Arab fuel-endowed countries. Another point to note from Table 1.5 is that for all three human development indicators the maxima for Arab sub-Saharan Africa are below the minima for both other country groups, confirming that Arab sub-Saharan Africa displays the poor socioeconomic performance for which sub-Saharan Africa overall is known.

Table 1.6 shows the populations of the three Arab worlds in 2016, the most recent year available at time of writing. This table shows that Figure 1.3

**Table 1.6.** Population of Arab UN Member States, 2016 (in millions; total is 401.9 million)

| Sub-Saharan | | Fuel-Endowed | | Mediterranean | |
|---|---|---|---|---|---|
| Comoros | .796 | Algeria | 40.606 | Egypt | 95.689 |
| Djibouti | .942 | Bahrain | 1.425 | Jordan | 9.456 |
| Mauritania | 4.301 | Iraq | 37.203 | Lebanon | 6.007 |
| Somalia | 14.318 | Kuwait | 4.053 | Morocco | 35.277 |
| Sudan | 39.579 | Libya | 6.293 | Syria | 18.430 |
| Yemen | 27.584 | Oman | 4.425 | Tunisia | 11.403 |
| | | Qatar | 2.570 | | |
| | | Saudi Arabia | 32.276 | | |
| | | UAE | 9.270 | | |
| Total | 87.5 | Total | 138.1 | Total | 176.3 |
| Share | 22% | Share | 34% | Share | 44% |
| Non-Arab countries of interest | | Iran | 80.277 | Turkey | 79.512 |

*Source of data*: World Development Indicators.

is potentially misleading, in that the Arab Mediterranean contains 44 percent of the Arab population but only 14 percent of Arab land area. A smaller fraction of the land area in the Arab Mediterranean is sparsely inhabited or uninhabited desert than in the other two Arab worlds. Table 1.6 also lists the populations of the other two countries we study in this book, Iran and Turkey. Iran's fuel reserves per capita fit our criterion for classification as a fuel-endowed country. Turkey borders on the Mediterranean Sea and international tourism is exceptionally important for its economy. Together the populations of the Arab countries, Iran, and Turkey sum to over 560 million.

## Human Development in the Three Arab Worlds on the Eve of the "Arab Spring"

Now that we have divided the Arab world into three relatively homogeneous country groups, we are ready to put these country groups in context. We will compare Arab sub-Saharan Africa to non-Arab sub-Saharan Africa, the Arab fuel-endowed countries to the non-Arab fuel-endowed countries, and the Arab Mediterranean to the rest of the non-Arab world that is not in sub-Saharan Africa and not fuel-endowed. This last comparison group of countries, however, is simply too diverse to make a satisfactory comparison group for the Arab Mediterranean on its own. We therefore supplement it with two narrower country groups: Latin America (minus its fuel-endowed country, Venezuela) and Southern Europe, in which we include the UN Geographic Region of the same name minus Albania and the countries that formerly made up Yugoslavia. Southern Europe, chiefly Greece, Italy, Portugal, and Spain, represents the human development aspirations of the Arab Mediterranean. Both country groups were part of the Roman Empire. More importantly, all of the Arab Mediterranean countries have concluded Euro-Mediterranean Association Agreements with the European Union (except Syria whose agreement is only initialed). The clear intention of the "Barcelona Process," of which these agreements are a part, is to extend the developmental pull of the European Union across to the south side of the Mediterranean in the hopes of repeating the earlier developmental success with the countries on the north side.

We will evaluate Arab socioeconomic progress over the four decades from 1970 to 2010 by comparing the changes in life expectancy, years of schooling, and income for the three Arab country groups to the changes for their non-Arab counterparts. As stated in the section titled "The Human

Development Index," we will measure income by GDP per capita in 2011 P$ instead of GNI per capita because more data for GDP are available and the changes in GDP track the changes in GNI very closely for almost all countries. We choose 1970 as our start date because data before 1970 are too scarce. We choose 2010 as our end date because starting in 2011 the data for the three Arab worlds reflect the Arab Spring. We will evaluate Arab socioeconomic progress post-Arab Spring in the next section of this chapter.

For each human development indicator and country group we compute the population-weighted averages in 1970 and 2010, and the change or growth rate between the two years. Countries are included in the statistics only if they have data for both years. The countries included in all population-weighted averages computed in this book are listed in the Appendix. Non-Arab fuel-endowed countries are identified using the same fuel reserves criterion used to identify Arab fuel-endowed countries.

---

**Box 1.5**

**Why Do We Use Population-Weighted Averages?** We can explain the use of population-weighted averages with a simple example. Suppose that Algeria and Qatar were the only fuel-endowed Arab countries, and consider the data in Table 1.7. In this simple example, [36.118 ÷ (36.118 + 1.780)] × 100 = 95.3 percent of the population of the Arab fuel-endowed countries lives in Algeria. It follows that the GDP per capita of Algerians is much more representative of the GDPs per capita of residents of the Arab fuel-endowed countries than is the GDP per capita of Qataris. The average GDP per capita that we compute for

Table 1.7. 2010 GDPs Per Capita and Populations of Algeria and Qatar

| Country | GDP per capita (2011 P$) | Population (millions) |
|---|---|---|
| Algeria | 12,871 | 36.118 |
| Qatar | 125,141 | 1.780 |

*Source of data*: World Development Indicators.

> the residents of the Arab fuel-endowed countries should therefore be much closer to the GDP per capita of Algerians than to the GDP per capita of Qataris.
>
> Suppose we use a simple average of Algerian and Qatari GDPs per capita to represent the average GDP per capita of residents of the Arab fuel-endowed countries. The simple average equals (12,871 + 125,141) ÷ 2 = (0.5)(12,871) + (0.5)(125,141) = 69,006. By giving equal weights of 0.5 to the Algerian and Qatari GDPs per capita, the simple average yields a very misleading number, one that is halfway between the GDPs per capita of Algerians and Qataris instead of much closer to the GDP per capita of Algerians. If we instead use a population-weighted average, we replace the weights 0.5 and 0.5 with 36.118 ÷ (36.118 + 1.780) = 0.953 for Algerian GDP per capita and 1.780 ÷ (36.118 + 1.780) = 0.047 for Qatari GDP per capita. The population-weighted average then equals (0.953)(12,871) + (0.047)(125,141) = 18,148, which is much closer to the Algerian GDP per capita than is the simple average.
>
> Note that the population-weighted average GDP per capita is equal to the total GDP of Algeria and Qatar divided by the total population of Algeria and Qatar. We can see this as follows. Recall that GDP per capita = GDP ÷ population. The formula for the population-weighted average is then [Algerian population ÷ (Algerian + Qatari populations)](Algerian GDP ÷ Algerian population) + [Qatari population ÷ (Algerian + Qatari populations)](Qatari GDP ÷ Qatari population) = (Algerian + Qatari GDPs) ÷ (Algerian + Qatari populations). This result generalizes to the population-weighted average GDP per capita for any number of countries.

We begin with life expectancy. Table 1.8 shows that life expectancy in each of the three Arab worlds increased more than in the comparison country groups between 1970 and 2010. In Arab sub-Saharan Africa, life expectancy was 2.7 years higher than in non-Arab sub-Saharan Africa in 1970 and 4.7 years higher in 2010. In the Arab fuel-endowed countries and the Arab Mediterranean, life expectancies were lower than in the comparison country groups in both 1970 and 2010, but the differences were reduced. Life expectancy in the Arab fuel-endowed countries was 2.9 years less than in the non-Arab fuel-endowed countries in 1970 but only 1.3 years less in 2010. Life expectancy in the Arab Mediterranean caught up to life expectancies in the comparison country groups more

**Table 1.8.** Life Expectancy in the Three Arab Worlds and Comparison Country Groups

|  | Life Expectancy at Birth (Years) | | |
|---|---|---|---|
|  | 1970 | 2010 | Change 1970–2010 |
| Arab sub-Saharan Africa | 47.0 | 61.5 | 14.5 |
| Non-Arab sub-Saharan Africa | 44.3 | 56.7 | 12.4 |
| Arab fuel-endowed countries | 53.9 | 72.8 | 18.9 |
| Non-Arab fuel-endowed countries | 56.7 | 74.1 | 17.4 |
| Arab Mediterranean | 53.5 | 72.0 | 18.5 |
| Rest of non-Arab world | 60.1 | 72.7 | 12.6 |
| Latin America | 60.2 | 74.5 | 14.2 |
| Southern Europe | 71.3 | 81.5 | 10.2 |

*Notes:* Due to rounding errors, some "change" column figures may appear to be inconsistent with the other figures in corresponding table rows. The population-weighted averages for each country group include the countries listed in the Appendix. The excluded countries were missing data.

*Source of data:* World Development Indicators.

dramatically. Between 1970 and 2010, the Arab Mediterranean closed its life expectancy gap with the non-Arab world that is not sub-Saharan or fuel-endowed, with Latin America, and with Southern Europe by 5.9, 4.3, and 8.3 years, respectively.

Next we compare progress in education. We see in Table 1.9 that in 1970 all three Arab worlds had lower average years of schooling than their counterparts in the rest of the world. Unlike in the case of life expectancy, only for the Arab Mediterranean did mean years of schooling increase more between 1970 and 2010 than for the comparison country groups. By 2010, the Arab Mediterranean had reduced its education gaps with the non-Arab world excluding fuel-endowed countries and sub-Saharan Africa, with Latin America, and with Southern Europe by 1.6, 1.3, and 1.0 years, respectively. In contrast, by 2010 Arab sub-Saharan Africa fell behind non-Arab sub-Saharan Africa in mean years of schooling by an additional 0.3 years, and the Arab fuel-endowed countries fell behind the non-Arab fuel-endowed countries in mean years of schooling by an additional 0.5 years.

Although Arab progress in education relative to the comparison groups of countries is less impressive than Arab progress in health, it is remarkable

Table 1.9. Education in the Three Arab Worlds and Comparison Country Groups

| Country Group | Average Years of Schooling Population Age 25 and Older | | |
|---|---|---|---|
| | 1970 | 2010 | Change 1970–2010 |
| Arab sub-Saharan Africa | 0.7 | 3.9 | 3.2 |
| Non-Arab sub-Saharan Africa | 2.3 | 5.8 | 3.5 |
| Arab fuel-endowed countries | 2.1 | 7.5 | 5.4 |
| Non-Arab fuel-endowed countries | 2.7 | 8.6 | 5.9 |
| Arab Mediterranean | 1.6 | 7.2 | 5.7 |
| Rest of non-Arab world | 4.6 | 8.6 | 4.0 |
| Latin America | 3.8 | 8.1 | 4.3 |
| Southern Europe | 5.3 | 9.9 | 4.6 |

The population-weighted averages for each country group include the countries listed in the Appendix. The excluded countries were missing data.
*Source of data*: www.barrolee.com v. 2.1, February 2016.

in percentage terms. Over the four decades from 1970 to 2010, mean years of schooling increased by a factor of 5.6 for Arab sub-Saharan Africa, 3.6 for the Arab fuel-endowed countries, and 4.5 for the Arab Mediterranean. This enormous expansion of schooling from very low initial levels raises the issue of whether educational quality was maintained, which we will address in Chapter 4.

The last indicator we examine is GDP per capita in 2011 P$. Rather than report the change in the levels of GDP per capita between 1970 and 2010, as we did with life expectancy and mean years of schooling, we report the average annual growth rates over these forty years, computed using the formula 2010 GDP per capita = $(1 + \text{growth rate} \div 100)^{40}$(1970 GDP per capita). Remember that the HDI uses the logarithm of GNI per capita instead of the level of GNI per capita. Recalling the properties of logarithms noted in Box 1.2, equal changes in the logarithm of GDP per capita correspond to equal percentage changes in GDP per capita rather than equal changes in the level of GDP per capita. We could report the percentage change in GDP per capita over the entire period 1970–2010 (that is, 100[(2010 GDP per capita) ÷ (1970 GDP per capita) − 1]), but we report the average annual percentage change (growth rate) instead because it is a more familiar measure of economic performance.

Table 1.10 shows that in 1970 the population-weighted average GDPs per capita in all of the three Arab worlds were lower than the population-weighted average GDPs per capita in their respective comparison country groups. Table 1.10 also shows that growth of GDP per capita from 1970 to 2010 was faster in all three Arab worlds than in their respective comparison country groups. As a result, by 2010 the three Arab worlds had closed the gap with or overtaken the standards of living of their counterparts. GDP per capita in Arab sub-Saharan Africa increased from 59 percent of GDP per capita in non-Arab sub-Saharan Africa in 1970 to 90 percent in 2010. GDP per capita in the Arab fuel-endowed countries was 13 percent lower than in the non-Arab fuel-endowed countries in 1970 but 17 percent higher in 2010. GDP per capita in the Arab Mediterranean increased from 45 percent of GDP per capita in the rest of the non-Arab world in 1970 to 63 percent in 2010, from 40 percent of GDP per capita in Latin America to 66 percent in 2010,

Table 1.10. GDP Per Capita in the Three Arab Worlds and Comparison Country Groups

| Country Group | GDP Per Capita in 2011 P$ | | |
|---|---|---|---|
| | 1970 | 2010 | Average Annual Growth Rate |
| Arab sub-Saharan Africa | 1971 | 3361 | 1.3 |
| Non-Arab sub-Saharan Africa | 3305 | 3681 | 0.3 |
| Arab fuel-endowed countries | 15,289 | 23,007 | 1.0 |
| Non-Arab fuel-endowed countries | 17,639 | 19,712 | 0.3 |
| Arab Mediterranean | 2821 | 9036 | 3.0 |
| Rest of non-Arab world | 6225 | 14,332 | 2.1 |
| Latin America | 7081 | 13,646 | 1.7 |
| Southern Europe | 15,776 | 33,441 | 1.9 |

Notes: GDP per capita in 2011 P$ is not available prior to 1990 from the World Development Indicators, so for each country we construct the 1970 GDP per capita in 2011 P$ by applying the ratio of the 1970 to 1990 GDP per capita in 2010 US$ to the 1990 GDP per capita in 2011 P$. The population-weighted averages for each country group include the countries listed in the Appendix. The excluded countries were missing data.
Source of data: World Development Indicators.

and from 18 percent of GDP per capita in Southern Europe to 27 percent in 2010. Note that GDP per capita figures for Arab sub-Saharan Africa and the Arab Mediterranean must be treated with caution because the population-weighted averages are each missing a relatively large country due to lack of data: Yemen for Arab sub-Saharan Africa, and Syria for the Arab Mediterranean.

In the previous section of this chapter we noted that sub-Saharan Africa and fuel-endowed countries were known for slow economic growth. This is confirmed by Table 1.10: GDP per capita for Arab sub-Saharan Africa and the Arab fuel-endowed countries grew more slowly than for the Arab Mediterranean from 1970 to 2010, and GDP per capita for non-Arab sub-Saharan Africa and the non-Arab fuel-endowed countries grew more slowly than for the rest of the non-Arab world (or for Latin America or Southern Europe) from 1970 to 2010.

Let us summarize the progress in human development made by the three Arab worlds relative to their natural comparison country groups over the four decades from 1970 to 2010, the eve of the Arab Spring. On the positive side, Arab sub-Saharan Africa increased its lead over non-Arab sub-Saharan Africa in life expectancy, and almost caught up to non-Arab sub-Saharan Africa in GDP per capita. The Arab fuel-endowed countries surged ahead of the non-Arab fuel-endowed countries in GDP per capita, and closed the gap in life expectancy with the non-Arab fuel-endowed countries to 1.3 years. The Arab Mediterranean closed its gap in life expectancy with the rest of the non-Arab world to only 0.7 year, closed its gap in education to 1.4 years of schooling, and substantially reduced its percentage gap in GDP per capita. On the negative side, mean years of schooling in Arab sub-Saharan Africa are nearly two years lower than in non-Arab sub-Saharan Africa. More fundamentally, every country in Arab sub-Saharan Africa remains in the lowest category of the HDI. For the Arab fuel-endowed countries, achievements in life expectancy and education lag behind achievements in standard of living. That is, although GDP per capita for the Arab fuel-endowed countries is much closer to that of Southern Europe than the Arab Mediterranean, life expectancy and mean years of schooling for the Arab fuel-endowed countries are much closer to the Arab Mediterranean than Southern European levels. The Arab Mediterranean itself is far from its Southern European aspirations for all three human development indicators.

# Human Development in the Three Arab Worlds after the "Arab Spring"

Each of the three Arab worlds contains one country that, after the Arab Spring, descended into civil war: Yemen in Arab sub-Saharan Africa, Libya in the Arab fuel-endowed countries, and Syria in the Arab Mediterranean. We expect that inclusion of these countries in the population-weighted averages for the three Arab worlds will worsen their human development performance post-Arab Spring relative to their counterparts in the rest of the world. Rather than examine these population-weighted averages, we will look within each of the three Arab worlds and compare the human development performances of the countries that were most affected by the Arab Spring to those that were relatively unaffected. For consistency with the previous section, we will use exactly the same data sources. Unfortunately, at time of writing the source of education data (www.barrolee.com) does not report any data post-2010. We therefore examine only two of the indicators used in the previous section, life expectancy at birth and GDP per capita. At time of writing, the latest data available for life expectancy and GDP per capita are for 2016. In Table 1.11 we compare the change in life expectancy post-Arab Spring (2010–2016) to the corresponding pre-Arab Spring period (2004–2010), and in Table 1.12 we compare the average annual growth of GDP per capita post-Arab Spring to the corresponding pre-Arab Spring period.

In Arab sub-Saharan Africa, only one country was strongly affected by the Arab Spring. Yemen changed its head of state, and descended into civil war beginning in 2015. Table 1.11 shows that life expectancy continued to increase throughout Arab sub-Saharan Africa post-Arab Spring, including in Yemen, though in most countries the increase slowed slightly relative to the corresponding pre-Arab Spring period. (Unfortunately, once more recent data for life expectancy in Yemen become available they are likely to show a decline in life expectancy due to the civil war.) In contrast, the data in Table 1.12 show a collapse in Yemen's GDP per capita to about half of its 2010 value. This mostly reflects the impact of the civil war, though Yemen's GDP per capita had already declined by 16 percent to 2011 P$3,767 by 2014. Elsewhere in Arab sub-Saharan Africa GDP per capita continued to grow or at least remain stable.

Among the Arab fuel-endowed countries, both Bahrain and Libya experienced severe political turmoil during the Arab Spring, but only in

**Table 1.11.** Life Expectancy in Arab Countries, Pre- and Post-Arab Spring

|  | Life Expectancy at Birth (Years) | | | Change | |
|---|---|---|---|---|---|
| Country | 2004 | 2010 | 2016 | 2004–2010 | 2010–2016 |
| **Arab sub-Saharan Africa** | | | | | |
| Comoros | 59.9 | 61.9 | 63.7 | 2.0 | 1.8 |
| Djibouti | 57.7 | 60.4 | 62.5 | 2.7 | 2.1 |
| Mauritania | 60.5 | 62.0 | 63.2 | 1.5 | 1.2 |
| Somalia | 52.0 | 54.0 | 56.3 | 1.9 | 2.3 |
| Sudan | 60.0 | 62.6 | 64.5 | 2.6 | 1.9 |
| **Yemen** | **61.5** | **63.5** | **65.0** | **2.0** | **1.4** |
| **Arab fuel-endowed** | | | | | |
| Algeria | 72.3 | 74.7 | 76.1 | 2.4 | 1.4 |
| Bahrain | 75.2 | 76.1 | 76.9 | 0.9 | 0.8 |
| Iraq | 68.5 | 68.5 | 69.9 | −0.1 | 1.4 |
| Kuwait | 73.4 | 74.0 | 74.7 | 0.5 | 0.7 |
| **Libya** | **71.2** | **71.6** | **71.9** | **0.5** | **0.3** |
| Oman | 73.9 | 75.7 | 77.0 | 1.8 | 1.3 |
| Qatar | 76.7 | 77.3 | 78.2 | 0.6 | 0.9 |
| Saudi Arabia | 73.0 | 73.6 | 74.6 | 0.5 | 1.0 |
| UAE | 75.2 | 76.3 | 77.3 | 1.1 | 0.9 |
| Arab Mediterranean | | | | | |
| **Egypt** | **69.3** | **70.4** | **71.5** | **1.1** | **1.1** |
| Jordan | 72.4 | 73.4 | 74.3 | 1.0 | 0.9 |
| Lebanon | 76.4 | 78.4 | 79.6 | 2.1 | 1.2 |
| Morocco | 70.9 | 74.0 | 75.8 | 3.1 | 1.8 |
| **Syria** | **74.3** | **72.1** | **70.3** | **−2.1** | **−1.8** |
| **Tunisia** | **74.0** | **74.8** | **75.7** | **0.8** | **0.9** |

*Note:* Post-Arab Spring, heads of state changed or civil wars began in countries in **bold**. Due to rounding errors, some "change" column figures may appear to be inconsistent with the other figures in corresponding table rows.
*Source of data:* World Development Indicators.

Libya was there a change in head of state, and ultimately civil war. Table 1.11 shows that life expectancy continued to increase for the Arab fuel-endowed countries post-Arab Spring, increasing faster in some countries and slower in others relative to the corresponding pre-Arab Spring period.

**Table 1.12.** GDP Per Capita in Arab Countries, Pre- and Post-Arab Spring

|  | GDP Per Capita in 2011 P$ ||| Avg. Annual Growth (Percent) ||
| Country | 2004 | 2010 | 2016 | 2004–2010 | 2010–2016 |
|---|---|---|---|---|---|
| **Arab sub-Saharan Africa** | | | | | |
| Comoros | 1465 | 1413 | 1411 | −0.6 | 0.0 |
| Djibouti | 2260 | 2635 | 3139 | 3.1 | 3.6 |
| Mauritania | 2819 | 3317 | 3572 | 2.7 | 1.2 |
| Sudan | 2593 | 3366 | 4385 | 4.4 | 4.5 |
| **Yemen** | 4047 | 4479 | 2325 | 1.7 | −10.4 |
| **Arab fuel-endowed** | | | | | |
| Algeria | 11,797 | 12,871 | 13,921 | 1.5 | 1.3 |
| Bahrain | 43,202 | 40,571 | 43,927 | −1.2 | 1.6 |
| Iraq | 10,711 | 12,718 | 16,087 | 2.9 | 4.0 |
| Kuwait | 87,555 | 75,204 | 68,862 | −2.5 | −1.5 |
| **Libya** | 23,640 | 29,630 | 11,193 | 3.8 | |
| Oman | 41,458 | 45,335 | 40,139 | 1.8 | −2.4 |
| Qatar | 11,6418 | 12,5141 | 11,8207 | 1.2 | −0.9 |
| Saudi Arabia | 44,391 | 45,421 | 50,458 | 0.4 | 1.8 |
| UAE | 98,640 | 57,580 | 67,133 | −8.6 | 2.6 |
| **Arab Mediterranean** | | | | | |
| **Egypt** | 7800 | 9857 | 10,319 | 4.0 | 0.8 |
| Jordan | 8399 | 9473 | 8390 | 2.0 | −2.0 |
| Lebanon | 12,325 | 16,452 | 13,268 | 4.9 | −3.5 |
| Morocco | 5252 | 6443 | 7266 | 3.5 | 2.0 |
| **Tunisia** | 8578 | 10,436 | 10,752 | 3.3 | 0.5 |

*Notes:* Countries in **bold** all changed heads of state post-Arab Spring. Somalia and Syria are omitted due to missing data. For Bahrain, Djibouti, and Oman, data are for 2005 and 2015 instead of 2004 and 2016. GDP per capita listed for Libya in 2016 is actually for 2011, the last year for which data are available.
*Source of data:* World Development Indicators.

In Libya the increase in life expectancy almost stopped. Table 1.12 shows that in the year of the Arab Spring GDP per capita in Libya collapsed to 38 percent of its 2010 value; after 2011 there are no reliable data. The largest Arab fuel-endowed countries, Algeria, Iraq, and Saudi Arabia, show continued growth in GDP per capita, with growth in Iraq and Saudi Arabia accelerating and growth in Algeria slowing slightly post-Arab Spring relative to the corresponding pre-Arab Spring period. The smaller GCC countries, Bahrain, Kuwait, Oman, Qatar, and UAE, all show periods of negative GDP per capita growth before or after the Arab Spring or both. Except for Qatar, these periods correspond to surges in immigration of relatively low-wage workers, who bring down average incomes. UAE is the most dramatic case: The 42-percent decrease in GDP per capita during 2004–2010 corresponds to a 102-percent increase in population, and the 17-percent increase in GDP per capita during 2010–2016 corresponds to a 12-percent increase in population. In Chapter 6 we will cover migration to the GCC in detail.

Of the three Arab worlds, the impact of the Arab Spring was most widespread in the Arab Mediterranean. Heads of state changed in Egypt and Tunisia, Syria descended into civil war, and hundreds of thousands of refugees from Syria's civil war flowed into Jordan and Lebanon. Nevertheless, Table 1.11 shows that life expectancy in Egypt, Jordan, and Tunisia continued to increase post-Arab Spring at roughly the same rate as in the corresponding pre-Arab Spring period, and life expectancy in Lebanon and Morocco increased substantially though at a slower rate. In Syria, life expectancy decreased by 3.9 years from 2004 to 2016. (Table 1.11 divides this decrease roughly equally between 2004 and 2010 and between 2010 and 2016, which probably reflects adjustment of 2010 life expectancy to reflect the higher future mortality resulting from the civil war.) Table 1.12 shows that growth of GDP per capita was much more strongly affected by the Arab Spring than was increase in life expectancy. GDP per capita growth turns negative for Jordan and Lebanon and slows dramatically for Egypt and Tunisia. GDP per capita growth also falls for Morocco, but by much less. GDP per capita in Syria has probably suffered a collapse similar to what occurred in Libya and Yemen, but there are no reliable data.

In Chapter 3 we discuss the heavy dependence of the Arab Mediterranean economies on tourism. A decrease in tourism, especially relative to pre-Arab Spring upward trends, very likely accounts for a substantial part of the slowdown in GDP per capita growth shown in Table 1.12. In Chapter 9 we discuss the connections between many large businesses in Egypt and Tunisia and the families and political allies of their former heads of state. Disruption of these businesses may account for some of the decrease in GDP per capita growth in these countries. The 19-percent decrease in Lebanon's GDP per capita during 2010–2016 corresponds to a 39-percent increase in population, compared to a 12-percent increase in population during 2004–2010. Jordan also experienced very high population growth post-Arab Spring due to the inflow of Syrian refugees, but its population growth was similarly very high during the corresponding pre-Arab Spring period. A possible explanation for why Jordan's GDP per capita growth remained positive during 2004–2010 but turned negative during 2010–2016 is that the very high population growth in Jordan during 2004–2010 was caused by an inflow of Iraqi refugees who were much wealthier than the 2010–2016 Syrian refugees. A 2009 study of Iraqi adults registered with the UN High Commissioner for Refugees (http://www.unhcr.org/4acb0ed49.pdf) found that 35 percent had a university degree or higher, and three times more were employed as professionals than as manual laborers.

In sum, Tables 1.11 and 1.12 tell us that the Arab Spring did not much affect human development progress in Arab sub-Saharan Africa or the Arab fuel-endowed countries, outside of the two countries that descended into civil war, Yemen and Libya. These two countries represent 32 and 5 percent of the 2016 populations of Arab sub-Saharan Africa and the Arab fuel-endowed countries, respectively. For the Arab Mediterranean, on the other hand, the negative impact of the Arab Spring on progress in standard of living (income growth) has been widespread, though the negative impact on life expectancy has so far been confined to Syria.

## A Note on Country Groups

In the remainder of this book we will analyze in depth a wide range of issues pertaining to the economies of the Arab world, Iran, and Turkey. We will draw on research by many scholars of the region, some of it focused on individual countries and some of it focused on groups of countries. Much of the latter research uses the World Bank country group Middle East and North Africa (MENA). MENA consists of the countries shown in Figure 1.1 and listed in Table 1.1, subtracting Comoros, Mauritania, Somalia, Sudan, and Turkey, and adding West Bank and Gaza (Palestine).

Table 1.13 should help readers keep track of the various country groups used in this book. For each of the twenty-three countries we study, Table 1.13 shows its classification as sub-Saharan, fuel-endowed, or Mediterranean, and whether it is a member of the Arab League, MENA, or the GCC. Table 1.13 also lists the three-letter World Bank country codes for all the countries we study, which we have already used in Figure 1.2 and will use again in later figures. It is hoped that Table 1.13 will be a useful reference going forward.

**Table 1.13.** Classification of Countries by Groups

|  | World Bank Code | Arab League | MENA | GCC |
|---|---|---|---|---|
| Arab Sub-Saharan Africa | | | | |
| Comoros | COM | x | | |
| Djibouti | DJI | x | x | |
| Mauritania | MRT | x | | |
| Somalia | SOM | x | | |
| Sudan | SUD | x | | |
| Yemen | YEM | x | x | |
| Arab fuel-endowed | | | | |
| Algeria | DZA | x | x | |
| Bahrain | BHR | x | x | x |
| Iraq | IRQ | x | x | |
| Kuwait | KWT | x | x | x |
| Libya | LBY | x | x | |
| Oman | OMN | x | x | x |
| Qatar | QAT | x | x | x |
| Saudi Arabia | SAU | x | x | x |
| UAE | ARE | x | x | x |
| Arab Mediterranean | | | | |
| Egypt | EGY | x | x | |
| Jordan | JOR | x | x | |
| Lebanon | LBN | x | x | |
| Morocco | MAR | x | x | |
| Syria | SYR | x | x | |
| Tunisia | TUN | x | x | |
| Other fuel-endowed | | | | |
| Iran | IRN | | x | |
| Other Mediterranean | | | | |
| Turkey | TUR | | | |

*Notes:* MENA = Middle East and North Africa; GCC = Gulf Cooperation Council.

# 2
# Historical Perspective

## Introduction

In the previous chapter we examined the convergence of the three Arab worlds toward their respective counterparts during the period from 1970 to 2010. This convergence raises the question of how the Arab countries fell behind in the first place. This chapter provides the relevant economic history.

Data for Arab countries are scarce before 1960, and before 1950 there are almost no useful data at all. The same is true for Iran and Turkey. As a result, in this chapter we will rely heavily on something we try to minimize throughout the rest of this book: informed speculation. We focus on how developing countries in general fell behind today's developed countries. It will then become apparent why the Arab countries fell behind even relative to other developing countries. Much of the analysis of the Arab countries could be applied equally well to Iran, but Turkey did not fall behind other developing countries and remains more developed than the Arab Mediterranean countries to the present day.

In the section titled "Extensive versus Intensive Growth," we discuss the period prior to the Industrial Revolution. A key aspect of the Industrial Revolution was replacement of human, animal, water, and wind power by steam power and, later, by diesel/gasoline and electric power. In the absence of modern power-driven machinery, the artisanal cores that remain at the centers of many of the important cities in the countries we study developed during this period. The section titled "The Division of the World" describes how, when the Industrial Revolution began in Great Britain, the world divided into countries that imitated the Industrial Revolution and countries that participated in the Industrial Revolution through exchange of primary products for machine-produced manufactures. The Arab world, Iran, and Turkey fell into the latter group, like nearly all countries outside Western Europe that were not settled by Western Europeans. However, the Arab countries and (to a lesser extent) Iran lagged behind their counterparts in the latter group because they did not have abundant arable land and because their earnings from mineral resources were primarily captured by foreigners. In the section titled "The Great Divergence," we document the great divergence that occurred between the standards of living in the countries that industrialized and those that did not.

## Extensive versus Intensive Growth

It is useful to begin our discussion of the period prior to the Industrial Revolution with the distinction between extensive and intensive growth introduced by Lloyd Reynolds (1983):

> **Extensive growth**: Growth in population matched by growth in output. Output per capita does not change.
>
> **Intensive growth**: Growth in output that exceeds population growth. Output per capita increases.

For most of recorded human history, extensive growth was the only kind of growth that occurred. Only with the Industrial Revolution that began in Great Britain at the end of the eighteenth century did intensive growth take hold on a sustained basis. One might surmise, then, that in the era preceding the Industrial Revolution the world economy simply became bigger without any changes in organization or technology. The logic behind this thinking is that any production process should be able to achieve *constant returns to scale*: If all inputs are increased by the same proportion, output should increase by the same proportion, because one can simply replicate what one was doing before. Suppose, for example, that labor is the only input to production. If labor (population) increases by 10 percent, output must also increase by 10 percent if there are constant returns to scale. Since output and population both increase by 10 percent, output per capita does not change. Growth in population matched by growth in output thus sounds like mere replication, without innovation in the form of important changes in technology or economic organization.

However, with more than one input to production it was often, or even typically, not possible to increase *all* inputs in the same proportion. The most important output whose growth had to match the growth in population was food. The most important input whose growth had to match the growth in population, therefore, was land. People could, of course, spread out onto more land as their numbers grew. However, the land onto which they spread would tend to be of decreasing quality, not able to produce as much as the land already being farmed. Once people began to provide for their food needs primarily through agriculture rather than hunting and gathering, they naturally settled on the land that was best suited for growing crops. This might have been the land with the richest soil, or with the best access to water through rainfall or irrigation. It is no accident that the densest concentration of population in the Arab world is in the Nile delta, which has both rich soil and abundant water through irrigation.

When population growth forced people to spread onto lower quality land, constant returns to scale in agriculture did not apply: Land *of constant quality* did not increase in the same proportion as population. As a result, output could not increase in the same proportion as population unless there were innovative changes in technology or economic organization that allowed more output to be produced for a given amount of inputs. A surprising feature of extensive growth, then, is that it required an increase in what economists call *total factor productivity*: the amount of output that is produced for given quantities of all inputs (also called "factors of production") such as labor, land, and machinery.

> **Box 2.1**
>
> **The Malthusian Equilibrium.** In connection with extensive growth, it is natural to ask, "What happens if food production does *not* grow proportionally to population, so that output per capita falls?" One answer, inspired by the work of Thomas Malthus (1798), is that reduced food per capita and consequent poor nutrition make people more vulnerable to disease and less able and willing to have children. The higher death rate and lower birth rate will drive population back to its original level. More controversially, the Malthusian view asserts that *intensive* growth will tend to reverse itself: If output per head increases, the death rate will fall and the birth rate will rise, causing population growth to increase sufficiently to catch up with output growth. In other words, extensive growth is the only *possible* form of growth. The inability of output per capita to rise above (or fall below) a subsistence level is called the *Malthusian equilibrium*, because any departure from subsistence in either direction is always reversed. Because of the Malthusian equilibrium hypothesis, economics became known as "the dismal science." Ironically, Malthus developed his theory just as the Industrial

> Revolution was making it possible for growth of output to *permanently* outstrip growth of population.

To understand how technology and economic organization changed during the era of extensive growth, both in the region we study and in much of the rest of the world, we can start from the fact that 80 to 90 percent of the population lived in rural areas, according to Reynolds (1983). Most of these people were engaged in subsistence farming, that is, growing food for their own consumption. These subsistence farm households did not spend all of their time farming, however—after all, "man does not live by bread alone." The typical farm family also produced most of its own clothing and housing, plus services such as education, healing, recreation, and religious observance. Reynolds estimates that agricultural activities absorbed 50 to 60 percent of the time of a typical subsistence farming family.

If, as a result of population growth, a farm household settled on lower quality land, family members needed to spend more time on agricultural activities in order to grow the same quantity of food—more time fetching water, planting, weeding, or collecting animal dung for fertilizer. Over the centuries, this intensification of cultivation was aided by a number of technological innovations. For example, it was discovered that certain crops increased rather than reduced the fertility of the soil. Instead of letting the soil lie fallow for a period, a farm household could plant a crop that regenerated the soil. Often this crop was fed to livestock. In the Arab world, there were innovations in irrigation methods that allowed water to be carried farther away from rivers. The most impressive of these innovations was the development of giant water-wheels or *norias*.

### Box 2.2

**The Norias of Hama, Syria.** The Orontes River flows from south to north almost the entire length of Syria. Because it is the northern-most extension of the Great Rift Valley that begins in Mozambique, its water lies exceptionally far below the level of the surrounding land. Reaching this water therefore requires water-wheels of exceptional size. Such water-wheels (*norias*) and their accompanying aqueducts are especially numerous in the city of Hama, where the largest noria has a diameter of 21 meters (69 feet). Since the development of modern pumps the norias have been maintained more to attract tourists than to provide irrigation. They create the impression of a permanent carnival snaking through Hama. Though norias require no fuel, they are very inefficient, in part because of the leakage of water back down to the river before it is carried up to the aqueducts (see Figure 2.1). Readers who would like to learn more about the Norias of Hama can see the fine study by Annette Delpech, François Girard, Gérard Robine, and Muhammad Roumi, *Les Norias de L'Oronte* (1997).

Of course, planting a second crop or building and maintaining waterwheels required farm households to spend more time on agricultural activities. Farming on lower-quality land thus required more work, whether aided by technological innovations or not. This meant that farm households had less time to devote to their other activities, such as producing clothing. How was overall output per capita maintained?

During the era of extensive growth, the primary answer was increased *specialization*. Instead of making their own clothing, for example, farm

**Figure 2.1.** Loss of Water from a Noria as It Is Elevated to an Aqueduct
*Source:* Bernard Gagon, Wikimedia Commons, https://upload.wikimedia.org/wikipedia/commons/0/07/Noria_in_Hama_02.jpg.

households purchased clothing from specialized clothing producers. These specialized producers did not necessarily use a technology superior to the one used by the farmers. Rather, they were better at using the same technology because they trained and practiced more. Economists describe this benefit of specialization as "moving down the learning curve" or *learning by doing*. Specialization and accompanying learning by doing provided the increase in productivity necessary for overall output to keep up with population growth.

In a process spanning generations the specialized artisans gathered into towns, which grew into cities. Farmers brought their produce to these cities and towns in exchange for manufactured goods such as clothing, cooking and eating utensils, and agricultural tools. Today, many cities in the region we study have retained these artisanal cores. A famous example is Fez, Morocco, whose artisanal core has been declared a UNESCO World Heritage Site (see Figure 2.2).

This change in economic organization that stimulated trade between town and country also increased the need for security. Farmers and artisans

**Figure 2.2.** An Eleventh-Century Tannery in the Old City of Fez, Morocco
*Source:* Photo by Rosino, Flickr, https://www.flickr.com/photos/rosino/85707688/in/photolist-8zgUL-8zgUM-8ziZk.

needed to be confident their goods would not be stolen on the road. Moreover, if commercial disputes arose, an authority was needed to resolve them. In Europe, nation-states gradually formed that could provide security and enforce contracts. In the Arab world these services were provided by various Muslim empires, most importantly the Ottoman Empire. Morocco was never incorporated into the Ottoman Empire and was perhaps the Arab entity most closely resembling a European nation-state during the extensive growth period.

There was also long-distance trade between various cities during the period of extensive growth. Overland trade in the Arab world and Persia (present-day Iran) was conducted by camel or mule caravan. Overseas trade relied on sailing ships. These transportation methods were extremely expensive, so long-distance trade was largely confined to goods with very high ratios of value to weight, such as silk and spices. Taxation of this trade allowed surprisingly large accumulations of wealth. The Mamluk empire (1250–1517) based in Cairo was financed by trade in spices, and the Safavid empire (1501–1722) based in Esfahan was financed by trade in silk. Rulers and traders built richly decorated palaces and religious edifices. The palaces have largely disappeared, but most of the major religious buildings remain and can be seen in Cairo and Esfahan today.

The most profitable long-distance trade extended beyond imperial boundaries, hence beyond the abilities of the empires to provide contract enforcement or security. To some extent, empires were substituted in providing these services by *trade diasporas*: ethnic or religious groups with settlements at endpoints and transshipment points of a trade route. In the western Arab world (North Africa), Jews were the key trade diaspora. In the eastern Arab world and Persia, Armenians were the key trade diaspora. Many documents pertaining to the North African Jewish trade diaspora were deposited in the Ben Ezra synagogue in Cairo. The wealth accumulated by the Armenian trade diaspora is evident in the churches of the New Julfa quarter of Esfahan (see Figure 2.3). Why were trade diasporas able to operate so successfully in the absence of any authority with the legal power to resolve disputes? One hypothesis is that members of trade diasporas refrained from cheating each other because the diasporas practiced collective punishment: if a member of a diaspora cheated another member, the entire diaspora would refuse to do business with him. Readers wishing to know more about trade diasporas can start with James Rauch (2001, section 3).

**Figure 2.3.** Cathedral Ceiling in the New Julfa Quarter of Esfahan, Iran
*Source:* Photograph by Diego Delso, Wikimedia Commons, https://commons.wikimedia.org/wiki/
File:Catedral_Vank,_Isfah%C3%A1n,_Ir%C3%A1n,_2016-09-20,_DD_115-117_HDR.jpg.

To summarize, during the period of extensive growth many of the characteristics of a modern economy developed in the absence of modern technology. There was growth in artisanal manufacturing production outside of farm households, trade between these artisans and the households that were ever more specialized in farming, development of cities that were manufacturing and trading centers, long-distance trade between these cities, and evolution of institutions to govern and secure commercial exchange. When modern technology arrived with the Industrial Revolution, the preconditions were in place for extensive growth to become intensive growth.

## The Division of the World

The industrial revolution that began in Great Britain in the late eighteenth century offered the rest of the world two opportunities: to industrialize through imitation, or to trade food and raw materials for the now-cheaper manufactures. The countries that followed the first route became today's more developed countries, and most of the countries that followed the second route became today's less developed (or "developing") countries. This division of the world occurred mainly during the first great "world economic boom" from 1850 to 1914. What determined which countries took the first versus the second route?

This is the most important question in economic history. Our answer will mostly follow the argument of W. Arthur Lewis, a Nobel Prize-winning economist born on the island of St. Lucia in what was then the British West Indies (see Figure 2.4). We must emphasize that competing answers are available, and that it is impossible to know with anything approaching certainty which is the "correct" answer. We briefly discuss the most popular alternative to Lewis's argument in Box 2.3. An advantage of following Lewis's argument is that, in working through the details, we will learn a great deal about the obstacles to development that the Arab world, Iran, and Turkey needed to overcome.

Lewis notes that the industrial revolution introduced "new ways of making the same old things" (1978, p. 10) such as clothing, housewares, and agricultural implements. Here we emphasize the technological aspect of "new." The use of human, animal, water, and wind power in manufacturing

**Figure 2.4.** W. Arthur Lewis
*Source:* Robert Matthew, Princeton University, Office of Communications.

was replaced by steam power and, much later, by diesel/gasoline and electric power. We will call the use of these new power sources in manufacturing "industrialization" and use the term "industrial sector" to describe manufacturing using power-driven equipment.

Lewis writes, "The distinguishing feature of the industrial revolution at the end of the eighteenth century is that it began in the country with the highest *agricultural productivity*—Great Britain . . . . The revolution spread rapidly in other countries that were also revolutionizing their agriculture, especially in Western Europe and North America" (1978, p. 10, emphasis added). Why was agricultural productivity so important? Lewis explains:

> Agriculture has to be capable of producing the *surplus food and raw materials* consumed in the industrial sector, and *it is the affluent state of the farmers that enables them to be a market* for industrial products. If the domestic market is too small, it is still possible to support an industrial sector by exporting manufactures and importing food and raw materials. But *it is hard to begin industrialization by exporting manufactures*. Usually one begins by selling in a familiar and protected home market and moves on to exporting only after one has learnt to make one's costs competitive. (1978, pp. 9–10, emphasis added)

We will now unpack the key points in italics in Lewis's argument. By "agricultural productivity" Lewis means output per worker rather than output per acre, so that higher agricultural productivity implies higher incomes for the farmers. Lewis sees differences in agricultural productivity as caused by countries that were "revolutionizing their agriculture." He is referring to agricultural innovations such as improved seed varieties, greater use of animal fertilizer, and planting regenerative crops instead of letting land lie fallow. In our discussion of extensive growth we described these kinds of innovations as allowing farmers to maintain food output when population pressure pushed them onto lower-quality land, but it was certainly possible for farmers to adopt some of these innovations on land of constant quality, thereby raising food output and their incomes.

Recent research has also emphasized climatological differences as causes of differences in agricultural productivity. John Luke Gallup and Jeffrey D. Sachs (2000, p. 734) state, "High temperature and humidity cause organic matter in the soil to break down quickly, robbing the soil of nutrients as well as the structure needed to absorb fertilizers and slow erosion. . . . The lack of freezing temperatures in the tropics causes a much greater number of agricultural pests in the tropics, including veterinary diseases like trypanosomiasis. Human tropical diseases such as malaria reduce agricultural labor productivity." We noted in Chapter 1 that malaria continues to plague Arab sub-Saharan Africa. Its eradication from the rest of the Arab world, and from Iran and Turkey, is a recent development. Agricultural productivity in the Arab world and Iran is also hampered by lack of water.

One reason to emphasize climatological factors rather than differences in agricultural innovation is that differences in per capita incomes today are highly correlated with differences in per capita incomes as far back as 1500, as we can see from Figure 2.5. In each plot in the figure, income per capita in the later period tends to be positively related to income per capita in the earlier period, though the relationship becomes looser as the length of time between periods increases (compare the plot of 1700 versus 1500

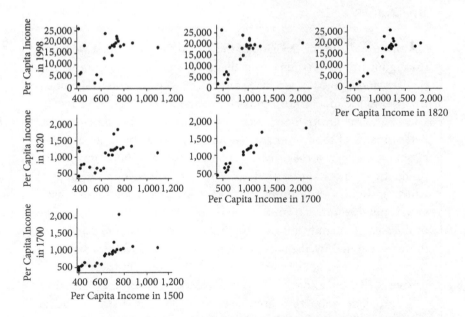

**Figure 2.5.** Scatterplot of Incomes Per Capita in 1500, 1700, 1820, and 1998

*Notes:* Included countries are, from Western Europe, Austria, Belgium, Denmark, Finland, France, Germany, Italy, Netherlands, Norway, Sweden, Switzerland, and United Kingdom, and from the rest of the world, Brazil, Mexico, China, India, Indonesia, Japan, Philippines, Iran, Iraq, Turkey, Egypt, and Morocco. The original source for these data is Madison, Angus. 2001. *The World Economy, Vol. I: A Millennial Perspective.* Paris: OECD.

*Source:* Voigtlander and Voth (2013, Figure 1), copyright American Economic Association. Reproduced with permission of the *Journal of Economic Perspectives.*

to the plot of 1998 versus 1500). Since all countries or regions were primarily agricultural in 1500, agricultural productivity would be the main cause of their differences in per capita incomes at that time. If, as Lewis argues, today's differences in per capita incomes have their roots in differences in agricultural productivity, it appears that those differences in agricultural productivity go back at least to 1500. One can doubt whether differences in the extent to which countries or regions were "revolutionizing their agriculture" were so pronounced in 1500, though it is possible.

Five countries that we study are included in Figure 2.5: Egypt, Iran, Iraq, Morocco, and Turkey. Their incomes through 1820 are described as "conjectures" in the study that is the source for the per capita income data plotted in the figure. Throughout this chapter we must remind ourselves that we lack reliable data, unlike in the rest of this book.

## Box 2.3

**"Institutions" and the Division of the World.** In this chapter we follow the argument of W. Arthur Lewis that productivity in agriculture, particularly food, was the key determinant of whether countries industrialized in the nineteenth and early twentieth centuries. We augment Lewis's argument with more recent research showing the climatological determinants of food productivity. An alternative argument accepted by many (perhaps a majority of) economists is that both agricultural productivity and industrialization were determined by the extent to which a country's institutions provided incentives for productivity-enhancing investment by protecting property rights. That is, farms and businesses would only innovate if they believed they would capture the profits generated by their innovations, and they could not have this confidence unless governments not only enforced contracts between private parties but also refrained from taking the profits for themselves.

A problem with this argument is that it is hard to define "institutions." Are they specific laws? If so, laws that protect property rights do not necessarily translate into actual protection of property rights. Dani Rodrik, Arvind Subramanian, and Francesco Trebbi (2004, p. 157) make this point by comparing China to Russia: "China still retains a socialist legal system, while Russia has a regime of private property rights in place. Despite the absence of formal private property rights, Chinese entrepreneurs have felt sufficiently secure to make large

> investments, making that country by far the world's fastest growing economy over the last two decades. In Russia, by contrast, investors have felt insecure, and private investment has remained low."
>
> A celebrated article by Daron Acemoglu, Simon Johnson, and James Robinson (2001) illustrates this problem. The article provides statistical evidence that in countries where European settlers experienced high mortality they established "extractive" institutions rather than institutions that protected property rights, leading to lower per capita incomes in the present. However, institutions are not defined. Gallup and Sachs (2001) point out that both settler mortality and lower incomes can be explained by prevalence of malaria, with institutions playing no role.

Returning to Lewis's argument, we note that higher agricultural productivity raises both agricultural output and farmer income. This will yield "surplus food" to be consumed by industrial workers if the richer farmers do not consume all of the additional food they are producing. The key is for the "income elasticity of demand" for food to be less than one: if farmers produce 10 percent more food, causing their incomes to increase 10 percent, their consumption of food must increase less than 10 percent. In fact, it is a well-established empirical regularity (known as Engel's Law) that farmers' and other consumers' income elasticity of demand for food is less than one.

Lewis's statement that "it is the affluent state of the farmers that enables them to be a market for industrial products" omits an important detail. The same total farm income could be accounted for by a few wealthy farmers or many middle-class farmers. A small group of wealthy plantation owners might generate a demand for sterling silver cooking utensils, say, that is too small to justify investment in a factory to make them, but the same income spread over a middle class of owner-cultivators may generate a volume of demand for flatware sufficient to support factory production. The number of consumers is thus as important as the total income available. Stanley Engerman and Kenneth Sokoloff (2002) have argued that climate and soil conditions in the temperate and tropical parts of the New World led to agricultural practices that generated a relatively equal distribution of income in the former (Canada and the United States) and a relatively unequal distribution of income in the latter (Latin America). However, even temperate countries in Latin America such as Argentina had relatively high income inequality, whereas Southern-hemisphere temperate countries in the British

Empire such as Australia had relatively low income inequality. This shows the limits of any hypothesis based on one cause, in this case climate and soil conditions, to completely explain the division of the world into industrialized and non-industrialized countries.

With the aid of a diagram inspired by the work of Kevin Murphy, Andrei Shleifer, and Robert Vishny (1989), we can gain a deeper understanding of why both high agricultural productivity and a relatively equal distribution of agricultural income promote the introduction of modern manufacturing techniques (industrialization) in place of traditional handicrafts. The key is that modern manufacturing, unlike handicrafts, requires a large investment in power-driven equipment. As shown in Figure 2.6, this overhead or fixed cost must be spread out over a large quantity of output in order to reduce costs per unit (average costs) below the level of handicraft production. The area to the left of the intersection of the downward-sloping curve and solid horizontal line is where handicrafts can be produced, whereas the area to the right is where power-driven manufacturing replaces handicrafts. This occurs because the "marginal cost," meaning the cost of one *additional* unit of output, is much lower using power-driven equipment. Power-driven equipment saves on labor input (and sometimes on materials input), so once the power-driven equipment is in place the labor (and sometimes the materials) cost of an additional unit of output is lower than for handicraft production. Figure 2.6 shows how the different technological characteristics of factory and handicraft production led to a minimum market

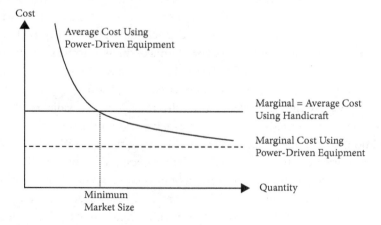

**Figure 2.6.** Increasing versus Constant Returns to Scale

size needed for the former to out-compete the latter. This minimum market size requirement could be satisfied by many middle-class farmers but not by a few wealthy farmers. Expressed differently, because factory production displays *increasing* returns to scale (unit costs fall with the number of units produced), whereas handicraft production displays *constant* returns to scale (unit costs do not change with the number of units produced), a larger market (demand for more units) favors factory production.

Once long-distance transportation costs fell with the introduction of railroads and steam-driven ships in the nineteenth century, the possibility arose that countries that did not meet the minimum market size requirement could industrialize by exporting to foreign markets. Lewis states, "it is hard to begin industrialization by exporting manufactures. Usually one begins by selling in a familiar and protected home market and moves on to exporting only after one has learnt to make one's costs competitive" (1978, p. 10). Let us focus on the word *familiar*. It is one thing to export a homogeneous product like sugar. If a trader sees that the price differential between the home and foreign market is sufficient to cover the customs and transportation costs, he ships the product. Prices convey all the relevant information. It is another thing to export a heterogeneous product like garments or shoes. A trader cannot act on the price differential between domestic and foreign shoes because they bundle together different characteristics. Your shoes may be a poor fit (so to speak) for foreign consumers and thus sell (if they sell at all) for a price well below your expectations.

Learning about foreign markets is an expensive process, and a continuous one, because styles and specifications are always changing. This point is best illustrated by Japan, the only country *not* populated by Western Europeans to successfully industrialize during the world economic boom period 1850–1914. Japan began economic growth as a raw silk exporter, but by 1900 its exports were dominated by cotton textiles. Japan solved the problem of breaking into foreign markets by developing the general trading companies known as the *sogo shosha*. These trading companies were unique, among both developed and less developed countries, in both their size and their scope, until imitations began in South Korea and Turkey in the 1970s and 1980s, respectively. In their book on the *sogo shosha*, M. Y. Yoshino and Thomas B. Lifson (1986, p. 23) write of their operation in the late nineteenth and early twentieth centuries:

> Particularly important . . . was the role the sogo shosha played in providing export opportunities for the myriad small Japanese firms in cottage industries, which, like their counterparts in developing countries today, faced many problems in trying to break into the world market. The sogo shosha fed them market information, helped them design products, extended credit, and, most important, developed foreign outlets for their products.

Japan was ultimately able to catch up to Western European levels of GDP per capita in the 1980s. Its export-oriented strategy was successfully imitated by later industrializers such as South Korea that caught up to Western Europe in the twenty-first century.

An alternative to expensive cultivation of foreign markets is to establish export-oriented manufacturing by domestic factories built and operated by foreign firms based in those markets. Writing about industrialization of the British West Indies, Arthur Lewis (1950) advised, "since it is difficult and expensive to break into a foreign market by building up new distribution outlets, this is most likely to succeed if the islands concentrate on inviting manufacturers who are already well established in foreign markets." Since Lewis wrote these words there has indeed been substantial foreign investment in export-oriented manufacturing in developing countries, and in fact many smaller developing countries could be said to have begun industrialization in this manner. Often such foreign manufacturing investment begins with assembly of components imported from the country that is the source of the investment. More integrated manufacturing in the country that hosts the investment comes later, if at all.

In the next chapter we will show the more recent importance of export-oriented manufacturing, some of it owned and operated by foreign firms, for the Arab Mediterranean countries and Turkey. Could such an industrialization strategy have worked during the 1850–1914 period? There is reason for doubt. First, the difference in wages between the host and source countries was much smaller than it is now, and transportation costs were much larger, so foreign investment in export-oriented assembly operations may not have lowered total costs relative to assembly in the source countries. Second, the returns to foreign investments in agro-processing, mining, and infrastructure (especially railroads) associated with primary-product exports may have seemed like such good bets that few foreigners willing to risk their capital in far-off countries could have been persuaded to try export-oriented manufacturing instead. We conclude that, at least during the late nineteenth and early twentieth centuries, it is reasonable to take the size of the domestic market to be a key variable determining the ability of countries to industrialize.

## The Great Divergence

Arthur Lewis addresses how the tropical countries fared once they settled into the pattern of development through exports of primary products, including cash crops such as cocoa, rubber, and tea, and minerals such as copper and tin. He focuses on the tropical countries of Latin America and the Caribbean, Southeast Asia, and sub-Saharan Africa. He begins by noting that their development attracted immigration of about fifty million people from China and India to work on plantations, in mines, or in construction projects. He argues that the prices of tropical primary products could therefore not rise above the level that supported a Chinese or Indian standard of living, so that increasing productivity in cash crop or mineral exports was not a way out of the trap of low tropical food productivity. For example, suppose that output of rubber per worker increased. Rubber farmers would become richer, and this would attract Chinese and Indian immigrants to grow rubber. The supply of rubber would expand until its price is driven low enough to return the rubber farmers to the Chinese or Indian income level in their home countries, eliminating the incentive for further immigration. This argument assumes that the land needed to grow tropical cash crops was abundant, so that tropical farmers could not get rich from the rent on their land. In other words, if they tried to charge high rents to Chinese and Indian immigrants, the immigrants would simply clear other land for planting. Mineral-bearing lands were not necessarily abundant, but the rents on these lands went to foreign investors.

In contrast, the prices of primary product exports such as wool and frozen meat from the temperate countries of recent European settlement, Canada, Argentina, Chile, Australia, New Zealand, and South Africa, had to sustain a European standard of living in order to attract immigrants from Europe. Immigration to these countries from China and India, on the other hand, was in some cases explicitly restricted. For example, the Immigration Restriction Act of 1901 required a person seeking entry to Australia to write out a passage of fifty words dictated to them in any European language, not necessarily English, at the discretion of an immigration officer. Arthur Lewis writes, "The working classes [in the temperate settlements and in the United States] were always adamant against Indian or Chinese immigration into their countries because they realized that, if unchecked, it would drive wages down close to Indian and Chinese levels" (1978, p. 20).

Despite low prices for tropical cash crops and capture of rents on mineral-bearing lands by foreigners, large-scale exports of primary products generated considerable socioeconomic development in tropical countries. Lewis writes, "countries such as Ceylon [Sri Lanka], Thailand, Burma [Myanmar], Brazil, Colombia, Ghana, or Uganda were transformed during these thirty years before the First World War. They built themselves roads, schools, water supplies, and other essential infrastructure" (1978, pp. 12–13), to which we can add ports and railways. The inclusion of schools and water supplies in this list is important. The colonial powers that controlled the tropical countries saw some benefit in education and disease control to improve worker productivity. For example, Melissa Dell and Benjamin Olken (2017) carefully document the positive impact on educational attainment in Indonesian villages of the presence of Dutch colonial sugar processing factories.

We can now see why the Arab world lagged behind other regions that did not industrialize, not only in income but also in education and health. Large-scale exports of cash crops were not feasible due to lack of rainfall and limited possibilities for irrigation, with some exception for Egypt and (later) Sudan which became significant exporters of cotton. Oil did not become an important export for the Arab fuel-endowed economies (and Iran) until after World War I, and they did not gain control of the rents on their oil-bearing lands until about 1950, as will be discussed in the next chapter. Earnings from primary product exports were therefore not available to pay for the investments in socioeconomic infrastructure that were being made in other developing countries. Bad as reliance on large-scale exports of primary products was for other developing countries, reliance of the Arab world on small-scale exports of primary products was even worse.

The poor economic performance of tropical primary product exporters relative to the industrializing countries led to a huge divergence in per capita incomes between the latter and the former. This divergence has been documented by Lant Pritchett (1997). He begins with the seventeen countries for which we have reasonably reliable estimates of GDP per capita dating back to 1870. These are the core industrialized countries: Western

Europe, former British colonies such as the United States, and Japan. He calculates that in 1990, the ratio of the average GDP per capita of these countries to the average GDP per capita of all other countries is 4.5. If there had been divergence since 1870, this ratio would have been smaller then. Lacking reliable data for the other countries in 1870, how can we compute this ratio?

Pritchett does not "conjecture" per capita incomes for the countries for which he does not have data, as was done in Figure 2.5. Instead, he relies on the technique illustrated in Figure 2.7. In this figure Pritchett plots the logarithm of GDP per capita in 1985 P$ on the vertical axis against time on the horizontal axis (1985 P$ are constructed using the ICP price index for 1985, instead of the ICP price index for 2011 used in Figure 1.2). Recall from Box 1.2 that the properties of logarithms imply that a straight line in this graph shows a constant percentage change in the vertical axis variable with respect to changes in the horizontal axis variable. It follows that a straight line in Figure 2.7 shows a constant rate of growth of GDP per capita over time. Parallel straight lines therefore imply equal growth rates of GDP per capita, so that the ratio of the GDPs per capita stays constant over time.

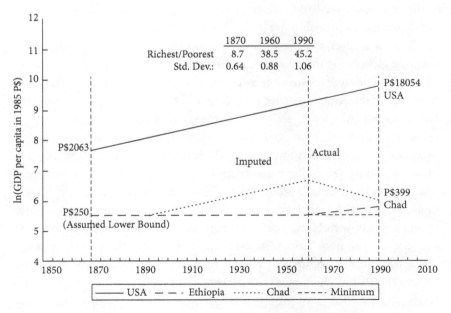

**Figure 2.7.** Simulation of Divergence of GDP Per Capita, 1870–1990
*Source:* Lant Pritchett (1997, Figure 1), *Journal of Economic Perspectives.*

The solid line in Figure 2.7 connects actual data for the United States in 1870 to actual data for the United States in 1990. Pritchett then considers two of the world's poorest countries, Chad and Ethiopia, for which he has actual data in 1960 and 1990 but not in 1870. The dotted and dashed lines for Chad and Ethiopia, respectively, show actual GDPs per capita for 1960 to 1990 but "imputed" GDPs per capita for 1870 to 1960. The key to the imputation is the assumption that GDP per capita cannot fall below 1985 P$250. This lower bound on GDP per capita is based on both the lowest GDPs per capita ever observed and computation of the lowest GDPs per capita that can sustain human life. Because of this lower bound we cannot extend the GDPs per capita of Chad and Ethiopia backward from 1990 to 1870 parallel to US GDP per capita, hence the ratios of US GDP per capita to the GDPs per capita of Chad and Ethiopia must have increased from 1870 to 1990. Using this technique, Pritchett estimates that the ratio of average GDP per capita of the seventeen core industrialized countries to the average GDP per capita of all other countries was 2.4 in 1870, so that it nearly doubled when it reached 4.5 in 1990. This computation assumes that Chad and Ethiopia and other poor countries were at the lower bound of 1985 P$250 in 1870. If they were richer in 1870, their divergence from the United States and the other core industrialized countries was even greater, so Pritchett's estimate of divergence is probably less than what actually occurred.

This great divergence resulted from a combination of a later start of intensive growth for the countries other than the seventeen core industrialized countries and slower intensive growth thereafter. It seems likely that the reason the Arab countries lagged behind their counterparts among the other countries was primarily that they began intensive growth later, rather than that their intensive growth was slower. Reynolds (1983) considers the onset of intensive growth for forty-one countries with 1980 population exceeding ten million: eleven from sub-Saharan Africa, fifteen from Asia, eight from Latin America, and seven from "North Africa and Middle East"—Algeria, Egypt, Iran, Iraq, Morocco, Sudan, and Turkey (Reynolds groups Sudan with North Africa though the World Bank and others group it with sub-Saharan Africa). He estimates that twenty-three of these countries began intensive growth before the end of the first world economic boom in 1914. Only one of these twenty-three, Algeria, is from the North Africa and Middle East group. This was long before Algeria's growth was led by exports of natural gas, and Reynolds attributes its intensive growth to exports of wheat, fruits, and wine, mostly grown by French colonists.

# 3
# International Trade, Natural Resource Rents, and Foreign Direct Investment

## Introduction

At the end of the previous chapter we noted that Lloyd Reynolds (1983) estimated the years in which intensive growth began for forty-one countries with 1980 population exceeding ten million. The years that he gave for the beginning of intensive growth for the seven countries we study with population greater than ten million in 1980 are as follows: Algeria, 1880; Egypt, 1952; Iran, 1950; Iraq, 1950; Morocco, 1920; and Turkey, 1950. As of 1980, Reynolds estimated that Sudan had not begun intensive growth.

For Egypt, Morocco, and Turkey, the beginning of intensive growth is clearly associated with industrialization. The same is very likely true for two smaller Arab Mediterranean countries, Syria and Tunisia. The beginnings of intensive growth in the smallest Arab Mediterranean countries, Jordan and Lebanon, are more likely attributable to foreign aid and tourism, respectively, though there has also been substantial industrialization in Jordan. For Iran and Iraq, the beginning of intensive growth is clearly associated with capturing and increasing profits generated by oil and natural gas exports. The same is certainly true for the smaller, fuel-endowed Arab countries, Bahrain, Kuwait, Libya, Oman, Qatar, Saudi Arabia, and UAE. According to World Bank data, intensive growth finally began in Sudan in 1990, and began in Yemen at about the same time. Increased oil exports are the most likely cause in both cases. Since these are the two largest Arab sub-Saharan African countries, they dominate the population-weighted averages discussed in Chapter 1. None of the four smaller Arab sub-Saharan African countries has begun intensive growth. GDP per capita in Comoros was lower in 2016 than it was in 1980, GDP per capita in Djibouti was about the same in 2016 as in 1990, and GDP per capita in Mauritania was about the same in 2016 as in 1970. There are no reliable data for GDP per capita for Somalia, but it is safe to assume that a sustained rise in average standard of living has not begun there.

In almost all of the countries we study, international trade played a key role in the onset of intensive growth. This is obvious when growth was led by fuel exports or tourism. (Tourism is a service export rather than a goods export—both types of export involve receipt of money from foreigners.) When growth was led by industrialization, the role of international trade was indirect. By 1914 the international trade of the countries we study consisted mainly of exports of primary products in exchange for mostly European manufactures that were now cheaper thanks to the introduction of mass production using power-driven equipment. As some of these countries began their own industrialization, it was natural for them to produce domestic substitutes for the manufactures they were importing. This is known as *import-substituting industrialization*, or ISI for short.

In the larger Arab Mediterranean and fuel-endowed countries and many of the smaller ones, and in Iran and Turkey, the beginnings of intensive growth were aided by government interventions. Governments accelerated ISI by protecting domestic manufacturers from import competition, and governments renegotiated contracts with foreign oil companies to gain a larger share of revenues. These actions were contrary to the interests of the countries that supplied the imported manufactures or owned the oil companies, which in some cases were colonial or former colonial powers. It is therefore important that by 1962 not only Iran and Turkey but all of the Arab Mediterranean countries and the larger Arab fuel-endowed countries were politically independent (see Table 1.1).

The next three sections of this chapter will focus on the international trade of the Arab Mediterranean countries and Turkey. The section titled "International Trade and Industrialization of the Arab Mediterranean and Turkey" shows that, as the limits of import-substituting industrialization were reached, most of these countries turned to export-oriented industrialization. The importance of trade agreements with the European Union to the export-oriented industrialization of the Arab Mediterranean and Turkey is noted in the section titled "Manufactured Exports to High-Income Consumers." Export-oriented industrialization allowed countries to transcend the limits of their domestic markets and learn better technology from foreign buyers. Meeting the quality standards of foreign markets required a combination of skilled labor and improved supply-chain management. After Turkey, Tunisia has had the greatest success in moving from exports based solely on low wages to more skill- and technology-intensive products. The section titled "Service Exports to High-Income Consumers: Tourism" discusses the exceptional dependence of all of the Arab Mediterranean countries and Turkey on tourism for their export revenues. After a boom period, the Arab Spring and terror attacks on tourists caused a sharp downturn in tourism revenues for many countries. That section concludes with a discussion of how, as tourism revives, its positive economic impact could be increased.

We turn to the Arab fuel-endowed countries and Iran in the section titled "Natural Resource Rents and OPEC," which ends with a brief discussion of Sudan and Yemen. With the help of their organization into a price-fixing cartel, the Organization of Petroleum Exporting Countries (OPEC), some of the fuel-endowed Arab countries became wealthy through trade. We discuss the need for diversification of exports away from fuel, and the prospects for success in exporting other goods or services. We conclude this chapter with an analysis of foreign investment in the section titled "Foreign Direct Investment," covering the Arab Mediterranean countries, Arab fuel-endowed countries, and Iran. The data indicate persistence of the historical pattern in which investment from outside the region is concentrated in production of oil and natural gas for export. A new element is the importance of investment flows within the region, especially from the GCC countries to the Arab Mediterranean countries. In contrast to investment from outside the region, these intra-regional investment flows have been concentrated in finance, infrastructure, real estate development, and tourism.

## International Trade and Industrialization of the Arab Mediterranean and Turkey

We can gain a deeper understanding of ISI and subsequent developments in international trade for the Arab Mediterranean countries and Turkey with the aid of diagrams based on the work of Gustav Ranis (1984). The key to these diagrams is recognition that all the countries we study lack the technological sophistication to produce their own capital equipment, that is, the power-driven machinery used in agro-processing, drilling and mining, or manufacturing processes. Whether countries want to expand their production of cash crops and minerals or begin industrialization, they need to import this equipment. In order to earn the foreign exchange (e.g., dollars) needed to pay for imported equipment, they need to export goods and services. As we shall see, over time the goods exported changed from primary products to manufactures such as cotton textiles. The key service export is tourism, discussed in the section titled "Service Exports to High-Income Consumers: Tourism."

We start with the pre-industrialization panel of Figure 3.1, which provides a schematic representation of an economy exporting primary products in exchange for manufactures. The agriculture and mining sector $A$ performs two functions. It sends exports of primary products $X_A$ to the foreign market $F$, and it supplies domestic food $D_F$ to domestic households $H$. The exports pay for imports of capital equipment or producer goods $M_P$, which

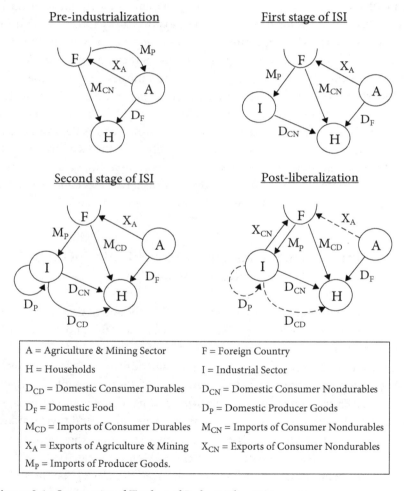

Figure 3.1. International Trade and Industrialization

are invested in the agricultural and mining sector itself, allowing it to grow or at least maintain output. The exports also pay for imports of consumer non-durables $M_{CN}$ to domestic households. These consumer nondurables are manufactured goods that were formerly produced by handicraft, such as clothing, cooking utensils, and furniture. (Some of these goods are "durable," so the commonly used label "consumer non-durables" is a bit of a misnomer.)

The second panel of Figure 3.1 shows the first stage of ISI. A domestic industrial sector $I$ now supplies households with domestically produced consumer non-durables $D_{CN}$ which substitute for imported consumer non-durables $M_{CN}$. Less foreign exchange earned from exports of primary products is spent on imports of consumer non-durables and more is spent on imports of producer goods to the industrial sector, represented by a new line from $F$ to $I$. Although imports of producer goods to the agricultural sector continue, we eliminate this line to show that most investment in production of tradeable goods is now occurring in the industrial sector.

The governments of Egypt, Syria, Tunisia, and Turkey were very active in promoting the first stage of ISI, beginning in the 1950s and 1960s. In particular, they protected domestic production of consumer non-durables by making it harder to import them. They imposed tariffs (taxes) on these imports or required import licenses. Both of these policies raised the prices of imported consumer non-durables and thereby allowed domestic suppliers to charge more. The higher prices and reduced competition encouraged domestic production.

These governments were motivated above all by the conviction that intensive growth required industrialization, and they accepted Arthur Lewis's argument (from which we quoted in the previous chapter) that "usually one begins [industrialization] by selling in a familiar and protected home market," where now the emphasis is on "protected." An economic theory that supports their actions is the *infant-industry argument*.

The infant-industry argument is deceptively simple. It states that industries in which a country can potentially produce more cheaply than foreign competitors in the long run may be stifled by foreign competition if they are not protected from imports during an initial period in which firms learn to get their costs down. This sounds reasonable, but one may ask: If these firms are going to become internationally competitive, why do they not borrow from local banks to cover their losses during the learning period and repay the loans out of future profits, like any business start-up?

Evidently a more sophisticated version of the infant-industry argument is required, one that explains why firms acting on their own will not achieve the socially optimal outcome, and how government policy can generate better results. Economists use the term "market failure" to describe a situation in which individual consumers and producers acting in their own best interests generate an outcome that is not the best for consumers and producers considered as a whole. A sophisticated infant-industry argument must establish the existence of a market failure, and it must be shown that the government can at least partially correct this failure.

There are many such versions of the infant-industry argument. The one presented here is based on Pranab Bardhan (1971). Consider a manufacturing industry in which firms are trying to adapt foreign production technology to the particular economic and social environment of their country. This is a trial-and-error process: The more any firm produces, the more it learns about what works and what does not, and the more efficient it becomes. This is another example of a "learning-by-doing" process, whose importance for economic growth we already saw in Chapter 2. An alternative way to describe a firm experiencing learning-by-doing is to say it is engaged in "joint production": It simultaneously produces goods and knowledge. This kind of knowledge, however, cannot be patented, so the firm that produced it cannot sell it to other firms. Instead, the knowledge easily leaks out to competing firms through many channels such as interfirm movement of personnel or the "watching and talking" that occurs in an industrial district. Here is the market failure: Firms do not have to pay for the knowledge produced by their competitors, so each firm has an incentive to let other firms invest first, then "free-ride" on the production of the industry as a whole.

Government can correct this market failure by granting each firm in the industry a subsidy per unit output, thereby compensating the firm for the value of the knowledge it generates for other firms as a by-product of its production process. Note that this production subsidy is not identical to a policy of protecting domestic firms from foreign competition. Protection raises the price of imports and thereby raises the price domestic firms can charge for their output, which for firms is equivalent to the effect of a production subsidy, but protection also raises prices for domestic consumers. Nevertheless, the infant-industry argument is frequently used to justify taxes or quantitative restrictions on imports, in part because of the ease of administration relative to production subsidies. All governments maintain customs services that collect trade taxes and enforce import licenses and other regulations. Developing country governments have especially limited administrative capacity, and it is easier to use an existing agency to implement protective tariffs or import licenses than to create a new agency to administer production subsidies.

Finally, it is important to remember that the infant-industry argument supports a *temporary* policy to aid import-competing manufacturing. Once the learning process is complete, government help is no longer justified. One of the rebuttals made to the infant-industry argument is that an industry powerful enough to get government help when an infant will surely be powerful enough to retain that help when it is an adult. This is another reason a production subsidy is preferable to import protection: The former is a drain on the government budget whereas the latter adds to government revenues, so the government has a greater incentive to end subsidies when they are no longer needed.

An important feature of ISI is that, if it is successful, it contains the seeds of its own destruction: Eventually there are no imports left for which to substitute. This is not a problem if the infant-industry argument is correct, because the protected firms will have learned to make their costs competitive and can now export their output, facilitating continued rapid industrial growth. In practice, exporting is difficult. First, firms know less about the preferences of foreign than domestic customers. Second, the most lucrative foreign markets are in the core industrialized countries where consumers have much higher incomes, and numerous studies have shown that high-income consumers demand higher quality goods. To become successful exporters, domestic firms must therefore learn how to cheaply produce high quality goods rather than cheaply produce low quality goods. We will return in the next section to the issue of quality as a barrier to exports.

The first stage of ISI in Egypt, Syria, Tunisia, and Turkey was successful in that these countries developed substantial industrial sectors and intensive growth began. In addition to the possibility of exporting manufactures, the success of the first stage of ISI also created an opportunity to continue rapid industrialization by a second stage of ISI. The intensive growth that accompanied the first stage of ISI generated a middle class that could afford consumer durables such as automobiles, refrigerators, and televisions. The new industrial sector needed not only capital equipment but also inputs such as plastic and steel that were not beyond domestic technological capabilities.

The third panel of Figure 3.1 illustrates the second stage of ISI. We have changed the label for the line from the foreign sector $F$ to households $H$ from $M_{CN}$ to $M_{CD}$, indicating the change in the imports for which domestic manufacturers are substituting from consumer non-durables to consumer durables. To go with this change we added a new line labeled $D_{CD}$ from the industrial sector $I$ to households $H$, indicating that domestic manufacturers are supplying domestic consumers with durables as well as non-durables. Finally, we added a loop labeled $D_P$ from the industrial sector $I$ to itself, indicating that domestic manufacturers are now supplying some producer goods—material inputs, not capital equipment.

The second stage of ISI in Egypt, Syria, Tunisia, and Turkey proved much more difficult than the first. To understand why, it is useful to refer back to Figure 2.6. Though the figure shows competition between manufacturing using power-driven equipment and handicraft production, it can also provide insight into competition between domestic manufacturing and foreign imports. The key is that the unit cost of foreign imports does not depend on the quantity imported, just as the unit cost of handicrafts does not depend on the quantity produced. We can then think of the solid horizontal line as showing the unit cost of imports and the downward-sloping curve as showing the unit cost of domestic manufacturing. Once again, there is a minimum market size necessary for domestic manufacturing to succeed. Now consider the difference between a consumer non-durable such as clothing and an input such as steel. The investment in capital equipment and structures needed to produce steel is far greater. As a result the downward-sloping curve is much higher for steel than for clothing, causing it to intersect the horizontal line at a much larger quantity. The minimum domestic market size needed for domestically produced steel to compete with imported steel is much greater than the minimum market size needed for domestically produced clothing to compete with imported clothing.

A related difficulty arises when domestic manufacturers of consumer durables such as automobiles try to compete with foreign imports. In the core industrialized countries such as Japan or the United States, the automobile industry consists of a handful of final assemblers but hundreds or thousands of firms that supply components. Bela Balassa (1980) claimed that "General Motors, for example, has ten thousand subcontractors, each producing a part or component." Just as the domestic market may be too small for one producer with a very large required investment to compete with imports, it may be too small for an industry that collectively requires a very large investment on the part of many firms to compete with imports.

The automobile industry in Turkey provides a good illustration of this difficulty. Turkey has the largest domestic market of the countries we discuss in this section; that is, its total GDP (equal to GDP per capita times population) is the largest. As of 2017, Turkey was the world's fourteenth-largest automotive producer, ahead of Italy. Yet Turkish automotive production consisted entirely of foreign-branded vehicles assembled from mostly imported parts. President Erdoğan complained of this situation in a February 2017 speech to the Turkish Union of Chambers and Commodity Exchanges (TOBB): "Assembly line manufacturing does not suit this nation. Automobile parts are only bought in from abroad, assembled here and then released to the market. . . . we will aim to manufacture a fully domestic, 'Made in Turkey' automobile under the TOBB. And as the state, we will perform our due part" (https://www.dailysabah.com/automotive/2017/08/22/15-candidates-interviewed-for-made-in-turkey-car). Turkish-assembled automobiles are internationally competitive in that they are sold in both the foreign and domestic markets, but a fully Turkish automobile is likely to require substantial government assistance.

The governments of Egypt, Syria, and Turkey were most active in promoting the second stage of ISI. However, the imports of capital equipment needed to produce consumer durables and inputs such as plastic and steel were too expensive to be paid for by dwindling exports of primary products. Beginning in the 1980s and accelerating in the 1990s and 2000s, Egypt and Turkey moved away from ISI as a comprehensive industrialization strategy and scaled back their protective tariffs and import licenses. Syria remains the most committed to ISI of the countries we discuss in this section. One thus finds "Syronics" televisions in Syrian hotels, Syronics being a state-owned manufacturer of consumer electronics.

Morocco and Tunisia joined the General Agreement on Tariffs and Trade (GATT) in 1987 and 1990, respectively. This signaled their intentions to reduce any protective tariffs and import licenses and not to rely solely on their domestic markets to promote industrialization. The GATT became the World Trade Organization (WTO) in 1995. At time of writing Turkey and all the Arab Mediterranean countries except Lebanon and Syria are members of the WTO. As their industrialization became oriented toward foreign markets, manufactures grew to dominate the goods exports of Jordan, Morocco, Tunisia, and Turkey. Figure 3.2 shows that the

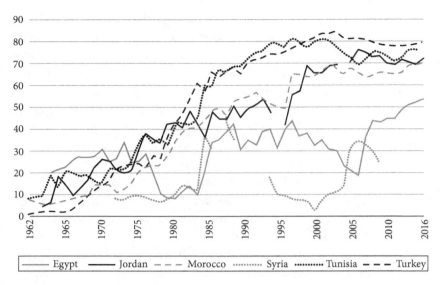

**Figure 3.2.** Arab Mediterranean and Turkey: Share of Manufactures in Merchandise Exports (Percent)
*Source of data*: World Development Indicators.

share of manufactures in the value of exports of merchandise (goods, not services) for these four countries increased from a range of 1 to 9 percent in the early 1960s to a range of 71 to 80 percent in 2016. The early boost to industrialization from policies to promote ISI in Tunisia and Turkey is evident from the facts that manufactures reached 60 percent of their merchandise exports a decade or more before reaching that level in Jordan and Morocco, and still have a greater share by five percentage points or more in the most recent data. The contrast between these four countries and Syria is dramatic, though part of the reason for the relatively small share of manufactures in Syrian merchandise exports is that Syria exports some oil as well. (Note that the data from Syria end with the beginning of the Syrian civil war in 2011.) Egypt is intermediate between Syria and the other countries in Figure 3.2; at least part of the reason is that Egypt is a substantial oil exporter.

Another way to gauge the importance of manufactures exports for the economies of the Arab Mediterranean countries and Turkey is to compare their values to the GDPs of these countries. Since the ratio of manufactures exports to GDP equals the share of manufactures in merchandise exports shown in Figure 3.2 times the ratio of merchandise exports to GDP, the ratio of manufactures exports to GDP would not provide any new information relative to Figure 3.2 if the ratio of merchandise exports to GDP were the same for all countries. In fact, the ratio of merchandise exports to GDP tends to be greater for smaller economies, because producers in larger economies have more opportunities to sell in their larger domestic markets rather than sell to the rest of the world. Table 3.1 groups together three smaller economies, Jordan, Morocco, and Tunisia, and two larger economies, Egypt and Turkey. Data are for the year 2010, before the economic disruptions associated with the Arab Spring. Syria is omitted due to lack of GDP data. The tendency for merchandise exports, and therefore manufactures exports, to be larger relative to GDP for smaller economies is clearly evident. Lebanon, which was omitted from Figure 3.2, is included at the bottom of Table 3.1. Despite being a smaller economy, its ratio of manufactures exports to GDP is in the range of the two larger economies. For Lebanon, foreign exchange earned from tourism is much greater than foreign exchange earned from exports of manufactures, as we will see in the section titled "Service Exports to High-Income Consumers: Tourism."

Table 3.1 brings out more clearly than Figure 3.2 the relative success Tunisia has had with manufactures exports. The ratio of manufactures exports to GDP for Tunisia is higher than for Jordan even though Tunisia's

**Table 3.1.** Exports of Manufactures Relative to GDP, 2010
Arab Mediterranean and Turkey

| Country | Share of Manufactures in Merchandise Exports | Merchandise Exports (US$ Billions) | Manufactures Exports (US$ Billions) | GDP (US$ Billions) | Ratio of Manufactures Exports to GDP |
|---|---|---|---|---|---|
| Jordan | 0.736 | 7.0 | 5.1 | 26.4 | 0.193 |
| Morocco | 0.663 | 17.8 | 11.8 | 93.2 | 0.127 |
| Tunisia | 0.760 | 16.4 | 12.5 | 44.1 | 0.283 |
| Egypt | 0.434 | 26.4 | 11.5 | 218.9 | 0.053 |
| Turkey | 0.792 | 113.9 | 90.2 | 771.9 | 0.117 |
| Lebanon | 0.636 | 5.0 | 3.2 | 38.4 | 0.083 |

*Note*: The data in the first and second columns are multiplied to obtain the data in the third column.
*Source of data*: World Development Indicators.

GDP is nearly twice as large, and the dollar value of manufactures exports for Tunisia is larger than for Morocco even though Morocco's GDP is more than double that of Tunisia. Table 3.1 also brings out more clearly the relative lack of success Egypt has had with manufactures exports. The ratio of Egypt's manufactures exports to its GDP is less than half that of Turkey even though Turkey's GDP is more than three times larger (measured in US dollars). The November 2016 devaluation of the Egyptian pound should have made Egyptian manufactures more competitive in world markets and could lead to a substantial increase in the ratio of manufactures exports to Egyptian GDP in the near future.

To represent the role of international trade in the current industrialization of Egypt, Jordan, Morocco, Tunisia, and Turkey, we add a fourth panel to Figure 3.1. The most important change between the third and fourth panels is the addition of a line labeled $X_{CN}$ from the industrial sector $I$ to the foreign sector $F$. This represents the manufactured exports shown in Figure 3.2, which are mostly consumer non-durables, though consumer durables and inputs such as automobile parts are also important for Tunisia and Turkey. The lines labeled $X_A$ and $D_{CD}$ and the loop labeled $D_P$ are broken, to reflect the varying importance for the different countries of primary product exports, domestic production of consumer durables, and domestic production of producer inputs.

I conclude this section with three observations. First, the transformation of the Arab Mediterranean world and Turkey from exporters of primary products to exporters of manufactures is mostly completed. Figure 3.2 shows that in the last two decades the increase in the manufactures share of goods exports has leveled off in Jordan, Morocco, Tunisia, and Turkey, though perhaps not in Egypt. Second, the governments of these countries, with the possible exception of Syria, have given up on promotion of ISI as an overall development strategy. Membership in the WTO constrains the trade policy of all the countries besides Lebanon and Syria, though as developing countries they are given more time to implement WTO agreements, and we shall see in Chapter 9 that trade policy is still used to favor politically connected firms. Third, all of these countries remain dependent on imports for their capital equipment. Continued growth of their industrial sectors therefore depends on exports that earn the foreign exchange to pay for these imports. The difference between the post-liberalization panel and the two ISI panels of Figure 3.1 is that the industrial sector itself is now the source of most of these exports.

## Manufactured Exports to High-Income Consumers

Exports from the Arab Mediterranean countries and Turkey have been directed mainly to the developed-country markets represented by $F$ in Figure 3.1. In Table 3.2 we show the destination market shares in 2010 for the total exports (not only manufactures exports) of the countries in Figure 3.2. We use 2010 so that data are still available for Syria. The destinations shown are the world's two largest developed-country markets, the European Union and the United States; the Middle East, consisting of the Arab countries, Iran, and Turkey; and the rest of the world. The European Union is the largest single market for Morocco, Tunisia, and Turkey, and also very important for Egypt and Syria. Together the EU and the United States account for more than three-quarters of Tunisia's exports, nearly two-thirds of Morocco's exports, and half of Turkey's exports; they also account for 37 and 44 percent of the exports of Egypt and Syria, respectively. Jordan is an exception to the general pattern. The United States is a much more important market than the EU for Jordan, reflecting in part the impact of the free trade agreement implemented by Jordan and the United States at the end of 2001. Jordan also borders on Saudi Arabia, and a closer look at the data shows that the GCC absorbs as large a share of Jordan's exports as the EU and United States together.

Table 3.2. Markets for Exports of Arab Mediterranean Countries and Turkey, 2010 (Percent)

| Country | European Union | United States | Middle East | Rest of World |
|---|---|---|---|---|
| Egypt | 30.5 | 6.4 | 33.9 | 29.2 |
| Jordan | 3.7 | 15.6 | 50.7 | 30.1 |
| Morocco | 59.4 | 3.6 | 7.0 | 30.0 |
| Syria | 40.2 | 3.5 | 51.1 | 5.2 |
| Tunisia | 75.9 | 2.5 | 12.7 | 8.9 |
| Turkey | 46.5 | 3.4 | 23.0 | 27.2 |

*Note*: Middle East includes all Arab countries, Iran, and Turkey. Row totals may not sum to 100 due to rounding error.

*Source of data*: International Monetary Fund Direction of Trade Statistics, May 2018.

All of the Mediterranean Arab countries except Syria have Euro-Mediterranean Association Agreements to facilitate trade with the EU. Turkey has a much older Association Agreement. In addition, Jordan and Morocco have free trade agreements with the United States. Laura Márquez-Ramos and Inmaculada Martínez-Zarzoso (2014) studied trade between the EU and Egypt, Jordan, and Tunisia during the period 1995–2008. They found that the main impact of the Euro-Mediterranean Association Agreements on exports of these Arab countries occurred when more generous interpretations of "rules of origin" (RoOs) were implemented. RoOs determine when a good is eligible for trade preferences such as duty-free imports. If, for example, a final good is assembled from inputs produced in countries that are not parties to the agreement, it may not have enough "local content" to be eligible. It was thus crucial for inputs produced in the Arab countries (such as Tunisian auto parts, discussed below) to be included in local content.

Most consumers in developed countries such as the Western European countries and the United States have much higher incomes than typical consumers in the Arab Mediterranean countries and Turkey. High-income consumers demand high-quality goods. Success in developed country markets therefore requires products of higher quality than those demanded in the domestic markets of the Arab Mediterranean countries and Turkey. Upgrading quality in turn requires Arab and Turkish firms to invest in better capital equipment and hire more quality-control staff. The resulting demand for workers with higher skills may create an issue for government policy insofar as acquiring these higher skills requires higher education. We will discuss government expenditure on higher education in Chapter 4.

High-quality manufacturing, especially for export, requires that certain standards be met, e.g., for low levels of pesticide residues in processed food or for resistance to breakage for tools. High-quality manufacturers depend on their suppliers in order to meet these standards. Tolerance for defects is also very low. If manufacturers receive defective inputs from their suppliers, they will not be able to use them in the products they export. They must be confident that they can reject sub-standard or defective shipments from their suppliers without interminable court battles. We will discuss the efficiency of Arab and Turkish (and Iranian) courts in Chapter 9.

In sum, the ability of Arab and Turkish manufacturers, and developing country manufacturers more generally, to export to developed country markets depends in important ways on the actions of their governments. An educated labor force and courts that efficiently resolve commercial disputes facilitate production of the high-quality goods that high-income consumers demand.

Given these obstacles, it is fortunate that when seeking to upgrade the quality of their products for export, developing country firms sometimes receive assistance from the foreign buyers themselves. Exports are typically purchased by other firms, be they retailers, wholesalers, or manufacturers, rather than by consumers. A foreign buyer, having found a cheap supplier, may find it more profitable to instruct that cheap supplier in how to upgrade its quality than to incur the cost of searching for a better supplier. In other words, foreign buyers can be agents of technology transfer. This is not patented, cutting-edge technology but rather older technology and managerial know-how that is common among the more developed country suppliers from which the firm purchases but less common among developing country suppliers.

The activities of foreign buyers are described by Mary Lou Egan and Ashoka Mody (1992), who surveyed US buyers operating in developing countries, including "manufacturers, retailers, importers, buyers' agents, and joint venture partners" (p. 322). They found:

> Buyers also render long-term benefits to suppliers in the form of information on production technology. This occurs principally through various forms of in-plant training. The buyer may send international experts to train local workers and supervisors . . . . Buyers may also arrange short-term worker training in a developed country plant. (p. 328)

Yung Whee Rhee, Bruce Ross-Larson, and Garry Pursell (1984) surveyed Korean exporters of manufactures. Their findings were similar to those of Egan and Mody:

> The relations between Korean firms and the foreign buyers went far beyond the negotiation and fulfillment of contracts. Almost half the firms said they had directly benefited from the technical information foreign buyers provided: through visits to their plants by engineers or other technical staff of the foreign buyers, through visits by their engineering staff to the foreign buyers . . . . (p. 61)

A recent study by David Atkin, Amit Khandelwal, and Adam Osman (2017) succeeds in quantifying the benefits to a set of small Egyptian firms from interaction with foreign buyers seeking to upgrade the quality of the firms' products for export. The authors provided small rug producers the opportunity to export handmade carpets to high-income markets. To provide this opportunity, they partnered with a US-based non-governmental organization (NGO) and an Egyptian intermediary to secure export orders from foreign buyers through trade fairs and direct marketing channels. With orders in hand, the authors surveyed a sample of several hundred small rug manufacturers, firms with one to four employees, located in Fowa, Egypt, a poor town in the Nile Delta.

A random subsample of these firms was provided with an initial opportunity to fill these orders by producing 110 square meters of rugs (approximately eleven weeks of work); the remaining firms were not given this opportunity. As in any standard buyer-seller relationship, firms were offered subsequent orders provided they were able to fulfill the initial orders to the satisfaction of the buyer and intermediary. We will refer to the firms that received the opportunity to export as *treatment firms* and to the remaining firms as *control firms*. Thus the authors conducted a controlled experiment or *randomized controlled trial* (RCT) of the impact of an export opportunity on small Egyptian rug manufacturers.

To measure the impact of their intervention the authors tracked performance measures through periodic surveys of both treatment firms and control firms. Treatment firms reported increases in output and input prices, consistent with higher quality, and a 16- to 26-percent increase in profits relative to control firms. Treatment firms received significantly higher scores along virtually every quality dimension. At the same time, physical productivity (output per hour not adjusted for rug specifications) fell by 24 percent among treatment firms. This raises the possibility that treatment firms chose to produce fewer rugs of higher quality without having learned more about how to produce high-quality rugs.

The authors provided convincing evidence for an actual improvement in technical efficiency. At the end of the experiment, they asked both treatment and control firms to manufacture an identical domestic rug using identical inputs and a common loom in a workshop that they leased. The rugs that treatment firms produced received higher scores along every quality metric and were more accurate in terms of the desired size and weight; moreover, treatment firms did not take longer to produce these rugs despite their higher levels of quality. The authors documented learning curves: Rug quality increased with cumulative export production. They also showed that treatment firms improved quality most along the particular quality dimensions that were discussed during meetings between the intermediary and the producer, as documented by correspondence and log books. This suggests that the improvements in efficiency occurred, at least in part, through knowledge transfer from buyers, a process known as "learning by exporting."

Both learning by exporting and the overall process of industrialization in the Mediterranean Arab countries and Turkey have generated intensive growth. As intensive growth brings about increased wages, the Mediterranean Arab countries and Turkey can no longer rely only on low-wage labor to make their manufactures cheap enough to penetrate foreign markets. They must "move up the ladder" to goods for which relatively low-skill workers are a smaller share of production costs. Ndiame Diop and Sofiane Ghali (2012) find that, among the Arab countries, Tunisia has made substantial progress in this regard. In the mid-1990s, Tunisia abandoned its ambition to build "made in Tunisia" cars and focused on automobile parts and components. The local content partnerships built with EU automakers rapidly led to increased participation in EU automobile production networks (primarily France, Italy and Germany) and double-digit growth in exports of engineering and electrical machinery since 1997 (Tunisia's Euro-Mediterranean Association Agreement entered into force in 1998). As of 2010, this category had overtaken textiles and clothing as Tunisia's largest export sector. Products included electrical wiring systems, electrical motors and generators, wheels and rubber tires, plastic auto components, and various mechanical auto parts. At the time Diop and Ghali were writing, Tunisia was among Europe's top ten suppliers of electrical wiring systems and the country's global market share in this segment was about 2.2 percent.

## Service Exports to High-Income Consumers: Tourism

The Mediterranean is exceptionally well situated for tourism exports: a warm area with beautiful beaches and a rich cultural history adjacent to a wealthy, colder area. It is thus not surprising that all of the Arab Mediterranean countries, and Turkey, have exceptionally high shares of international tourism receipts in their total exports of goods and services. Table 3.3 reports these shares and the rankings of these shares among all countries with at least one million population. (The population restriction excludes many tourist islands, including the Arab country Comoros, that would otherwise be very highly ranked.). We see that in 2010, just before the Arab Spring, all of the Arab Mediterranean countries and Turkey are in the top thirty countries worldwide (with population at least one million) by importance of tourism in exports.

Another way to assess the importance of tourism in the international trade of the Arab Mediterranean countries and Turkey is to compare international tourism receipts to the exports of manufactures shown in Table 3.1. Table 3.4 shows this comparison, adding Lebanon, which was not included in Table 3.1. We see that international tourism receipts are actually greater than the value of manufactures exports for the two countries, Egypt and Syria, for which Figure 3.2 shows that manufactures exports have risen least as a share of goods exports. For Jordan and Morocco, international tourism receipts are less than the value of manufactures exports, but comparable in magnitude. Only for Tunisia and Turkey are tourism exports clearly less important than exports of manufactures.

Lebanon stands out in both Table 3.3 and Table 3.4, ranked third in the world by share of tourism in total exports and with a value of tourism

**Table 3.3.** Ranking by 2010 Tourism Share of Exports

| Country | Tourism Share (Percent) | Rank |
|---------|------------------------|------|
| Lebanon | 38.7 | 3 |
| Jordan | 34.4 | 6 |
| Syria | 32.2 | 9 |
| Morocco | 30.2 | 13 |
| Egypt | 27.9 | 17 |
| Turkey | 16.7 | 29 |
| Tunisia | 15.7 | 30 |

*Notes*: Tourism share = international tourism receipts divided by total exports of goods and services.
Rank is out of all countries with population ≥ 1M.
*Source of data*: World Development Indicators.

**Table 3.4.** Tourism Receipts Relative to Exports of Manufactures, 2010 Arab Mediterranean and Turkey, US$ Billion

| Country | Tourism Receipts | Manufactures Exports |
|---|---|---|
| Egypt | 13.6 | 11.5 |
| Jordan | 4.4 | 5.1 |
| Lebanon | 8.0 | 3.2 |
| Morocco | 8.2 | 11.8 |
| Syria | 6.3 | 3.2 |
| Tunisia | 3.5 | 12.5 |
| Turkey | 26.3 | 90.2 |

*Sources*: World Development Indicators and Table 3.1.

exports two and one-half times its value of manufactured exports. Two characteristics of Lebanon help to explain its exceptional attraction for international tourists. First, Lebanon has high, cool mountains that provide welcome relief from summer heat for wealthy Arabs from the GCC countries. Second, millions of people of Lebanese descent living all over the world maintain family ties to Lebanon. Many of them visit regularly, especially in the summer. The extraordinary importance of international tourism for Lebanon means that its economy resembles that of a tourist island as much as it resembles the economies of the other Arab Mediterranean countries.

We have data on international tourism receipts until 2015. This allows us to compare post-Arab Spring to pre-Arab Spring tourism for the Arab Mediterranean countries, much as we compared post-Arab Spring to pre-Arab Spring human development in Tables 1.11 and 1.12. Instead of a table we will use a graph that shows every year of the period 2005–2015, because the graph reveals the impacts of other important events both pre- and post-Arab Spring that strongly affected tourism. We see in Figure 3.3 that the years 2005–2008 were a boom period for Arab Mediterranean tourism, with strong growth in international tourism receipts for every country except Lebanon. The Great Recession that began in 2008 caused a reduction in international tourism receipts in 2009, or at least a pause in their growth, for every country except Lebanon and Syria. Growth resumed for all countries except Tunisia from 2009 to 2010. Then, in the Arab Spring year, 2011, a sharp distinction emerged between the more and less affected countries.

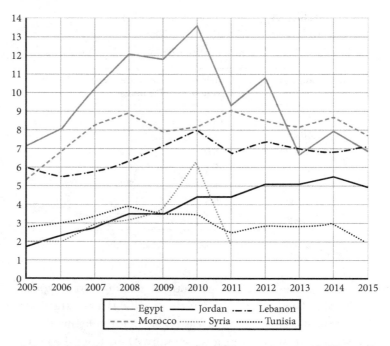

**Figure 3.3.** Arab Mediterranean: International Tourism Receipts (Billions of US$)
*Source of data*: World Development Indicators.

International tourism receipts collapsed for Syria and decreased 32 and 29 percent for Egypt and Tunisia, respectively. In contrast, receipts grew for Morocco, remained unchanged for Jordan, and decreased 15 percent for Lebanon. In 2012 international tourism receipts recovered somewhat in both Egypt and Tunisia. Data are no longer available for Syria after 2011, but in light of the civil war it is safe to assume that international tourism receipts decreased even further from their 2011 level. In 2013, violence leading up to another change in head of state caused tourism to plunge in Egypt. Attacks inspired by the "Islamic State" on tourists in Tunisia in 2015 caused an even sharper decline in international tourism receipts for Tunisia from 2014 to 2015 than had occurred from 2010 to 2011. The Islamic State also claimed responsibility in 2015 for the crash of a jet leaving Sharm el Sheikh carrying mostly Russian tourists. Turning to the countries less affected by the Arab Spring, international tourism receipts grew modestly for Jordan from 2011 to 2015, remained basically flat for Lebanon, and decreased somewhat for Morocco.

In summary, international tourism receipts grew for all of the Arab Mediterranean countries between 2005 and 2010. From 2010 to 2015, receipts collapsed in Syria, decreased to roughly their 2005 level in Egypt, and shrank to well below their 2005 level in Tunisia. For Jordan, Lebanon, and Morocco, international tourism receipts in 2015 remained substantially above their levels in 2005, but the strong growth of the 2005–2010 period has not resumed. Ironically, the greatest percentage growth in international tourist receipts among the Arab Mediterranean countries from 2005 to 2010 was in Syria. It appears that Syrian tourism "caught on" just before the beginning of Syria's civil war.

Except in Syria, the fundamental features that make the Arab Mediterranean countries so attractive for tourism have not changed, so we can expect a revival in growth of their international tourism receipts in the long run. The question then arises of what could be done to enhance the positive impact of tourism on their economies. Once inside a country, the single item that accounts for the largest share of tourist expenditure is hotels. In Cairo, one is struck by the scarcity of Egyptian-branded major hotels. Even Arab-owned chains such as the UAE-based Rotana Group and Syria-based Cham Palace and Hotels Group have not established a hotel in Cairo (though there is a Rotana Hotel in Egypt in Sharm El Sheikh). Cairo hotels appear to be an example of the "missing middle" in developing country firms noted by James Tybout (2000) and others, where medium-size firms are underrepresented compared to developed countries. In Cairo there is little or nothing between major international chains such as Hilton and Marriott and hotels in high-ceilinged colonial-era buildings that have never been upgraded. Unlike manufacture of capital equipment, hotels are not a high-technology enterprise, so the scarcity of mid- to high-range local ownership is both a puzzle and an opportunity. A likely explanation is a low supply of capable manager-entrepreneurs. Nicholas Bloom, Benn Eifert, Aprajit Mahajan, David McKenzie, and John Roberts (2013) have shown that lack of trained managers is a constraint on growth of locally-owned businesses in developing countries.

Is the market share of Arab-owned hotels in the Mediterranean Arab countries important? At a minimum, a larger market share implies a larger share of hotel profits accruing to Arabs. It is possible that a larger market share for Arab-owned hotels would also generate more demand for locally produced hotel inputs such as furnishings and linens. This would not occur because of government policy, but because internationally owned hotels may source their inputs from a common, foreign supplier in order to realize economies of scale. The scope for "import-substituting industrialization" for tourism industry inputs is an open question.

## Natural Resource Rents and OPEC

We now turn to the beginning of intensive growth for the Arab fuel-endowed countries and Iran. Recall that Lloyd Reynolds (1983) estimated the start dates of intensive growth only for countries with at least ten million population in 1980. These include Iran and the Arab fuel-endowed countries Algeria and Iraq. The date for both Iran and Iraq is 1950. This was roughly the year in which, following the example of Venezuela, the world's other oil-exporting countries renegotiated their agreements with the foreign oil companies that were extracting and marketing their oil in order to capture a greater share of the oil rents. The date for Algeria is 1880 and was discussed at the end of Chapter 2. The primary product exports of Algeria did not become dominated by oil and natural gas until the 1960s.

The existence of oil does not guarantee the existence of oil *rents*. To understand why producing oil in Iraq, the other fuel-endowed Arab countries, and Iran generated oil rents, we need to better understand the concept of rent. We must first note that "rent" is short for "economic rent," as opposed to the everyday use of the word to mean payment for use of an asset one does not own (e.g., the monthly rent paid to use an apartment). We continue with the explanation of Daniel Yergin:

> Ricardo developed the concept that was to provide the framework for the battle between nation-states and oil companies. It was the notion of "rents" as something different from normal profits. His case study involved grain, but it could also apply to oil. Let there be two landlords, said Ricardo, one with fields much more fertile than the other. They both sell their grain at the same price. But the costs of the one with the more fertile field are much less than those of the one with the less fertile fields. The latter makes perhaps a profit, but the former, the one with the more fertile fields, receives not only a profit, but also something much larger—rents. His reward—rents—are derived from the particular qualities of his land which result not from his ingenuity or hard work, but uniquely, from nature's bountiful legacy.

Oil was another of nature's legacies. Its geological presence had nothing to do with the character or doings of the peoples who happened to reside above it or of the nature of the particular political regime that held sway over the region in which it was found. This legacy too generated rents which could be defined as the difference between the market price, on one hand, and on the other the costs of production plus an allowance for additional costs—transportation, processing and distribution—and for some return on capital. (1991, p. 432)

Oil rent is thus a special case of a *natural resource rent*: the profit made by a producer with cheap access to a resource, compared to expensive access that makes the producer just indifferent between resource extraction and the most profitable alternative use of its assets, i.e., the "normal" return on capital.

Yergin provides a numerical illustration of why oil rents for the Arab fuel-endowed countries and Iran were so large:

For example, in the late 1940s oil was selling for around $2.50 a barrel. Some grizzled stripper-well operator in Texas might only make a 10 cent profit on his oil. But in the Middle East it only cost 25 cents a barrel to produce oil. Deducting 50 cents for other costs such as transportation, and allowing a profit of 10 cents on the $2.50 barrel, that would still leave a very large sum—$1.65 on every barrel of Middle Eastern oil. That sum would constitute rents. Multiply it by whatever the rising production numbers, and the money added up very rapidly. (1991, p. 432)

Yergin goes on to describe the March 1943 agreement reached between the government of Venezuela and the foreign oil companies, which greatly increased the share of oil rents going to the former, as "a landmark event in the history of the oil industry . . . . the various royalties and taxes would be raised to the point at which the government's take would about equal the companies' net profits in Venezuela. The two sides would, in effect, become equal partners, dividing the rents down the middle" (1991, p. 435). Worried that the Arab oil exporters' lower share of oil rents would give them a competitive advantage, the government of Venezuela urged the Arab governments to negotiate the same equal split. Saudi Arabia signed an agreement along these lines in December 1950, and the equal division principle rapidly spread to the other Arab oil exporters and to Iran.

Having increased their share of rents, the next goal for the Arab fuel-endowed countries and Iran was to increase the rents themselves by increasing the price of oil. They were able to use OPEC for this purpose. Venezuela initiated the establishment of OPEC in 1960. The founding members in addition to Venezuela were Iran, Iraq, Kuwait, and Saudi Arabia. By 2017 the membership also included Algeria, Angola, Ecuador, Equatorial Guinea, Gabon, Libya, Nigeria, Qatar, and UAE.

OPEC is, perhaps, the most important and successful case in history of a natural resource *cartel*. A cartel is a group of producers that band together to act as a monopoly, reducing output in order to raise prices relative to the level that would prevail under competition. Successful cartels are rare in part because of the incentives members have to produce more output than their allocation under the cartel agreement. If one member of a cartel increases its output, the price will not fall very much, and the member's profits will increase. However, if all members behave this way, the price will fall to the competitive level and the cartel is effectively destroyed.

Because the members of OPEC are countries, the members' incentives are more complicated than in a cartel of firms. Country governments are concerned with the interests of consumers as well as producers. Price increases hurt domestic consumers. Using the additional profits they receive from higher prices, either directly (if the producers are state-owned) or indirectly (through taxes), governments can compensate consumers for the price increases, but this compensation is likely to be imperfect. It is therefore likely that consumers will oppose their country's membership in OPEC, preferring greater output and lower prices of refined petroleum products such as gasoline.

Charles Mason and Stephen Polasky (2005) used these insights to construct a statistical model that predicted the probability that a country is a member of OPEC. They found that the probability increased with a country's proven oil reserves and decreased with its annual oil consumption. Table 3.5 shows the predicted probabilities for the years 1975, 1987, 1992, and 1997 for the countries that were members of OPEC in 1975 and the countries that were "shadow OPEC members," meaning they attended OPEC meetings but could not vote on policy. Mason and Polasky note that the predicted probabilities for Ecuador and Gabon are low and declining, and that Ecuador and Gabon dropped out of OPEC after 1992 and 1995, respectively. (Ecuador and Gabon rejoined OPEC in 2007 and 2016, respectively.) Even more impressive pieces of evidence supporting their model are two predictions that were fulfilled after their article was published. By

Table 3.5. Implied Probability of OPEC Membership

| Country | 1975 | 1987 | 1992 | 1997 |
|---|---|---|---|---|
| **OPEC Members** | | | | |
| Algeria | 0.8160 | 0.8675 | 0.3489 | 0.7436 |
| Ecuador | 0.1185 | 0.0177 | 0.0729 | 0.0036 |
| Gabon | 0.1456 | 0.1485 | 0.1412 | 0.0565 |
| Indonesia | 0.9946 | 0.6505 | 0.1770 | 0.0235 |
| Iran | 1.0000 | 0.9999 | 0.9999 | 1.0000 |
| Iraq | 1.0000 | 1.0000 | 0.9999 | 1.0000 |
| Kuwait | 1.0000 | 1.0000 | 0.9999 | 1.0000 |
| Libya | 1.0000 | 0.9999 | 0.8519 | 0.9999 |
| Nigeria | 0.9998 | 0.9923 | 0.6037 | 0.9810 |
| Qatar | 0.6621 | 0.4162 | 0.2142 | 0.1992 |
| Saudi Arabia | 1.0000 | 1.0000 | 1.0000 | 1.0000 |
| UAE | 1.0000 | 0.9999 | 0.9999 | 1.0000 |
| Venezuela | 0.8762 | 0.5524 | 0.9869 | 1.0000 |
| **Shadow OPEC Members** | | | | |
| Angola | 0.1175 | 0.2145 | 0.1698 | 0.4088 |
| Bahrain | 0.0709 | 0.1259 | 0.1299 | 0.0326 |
| Brunei | 0.0643 | 0.2345 | 0.1819 | 0.0659 |
| Colombia | 0.0137 | 0.0014 | 0.0337 | 0.0002 |
| Egypt | 0.2182 | 0.0706 | 0.1290 | 0.0232 |
| Malaysia | 0.0210 | 0.0244 | 0.0530 | 0.0003 |
| Mexico | 0.0209 | 0.2822 | 0.4620 | 0.0977 |
| Norway | 0.1015 | 0.0034 | 0.0513 | 0.0107 |
| Oman | 0.6439 | 0.4996 | 0.2100 | 0.3159 |
| Yemen | n/a | 0.0780 | 0.1724 | 0.1125 |
| Kazakhstan | n/a | n/a | n/a | 0.0824 |
| Russia | n/a | n/a | n/a | 0.00000001 |

Source: Mason and Polasky (2005), Table 3.

1997, Indonesia's predicted probability fell to a very low level and Angola's predicted probability rose to over 40 percent, leading Mason and Polasky to predict that Indonesia would leave OPEC and Angola would join. Sure enough, Indonesia left OPEC after 2008 and Angola joined in 2007. (Mason and Polasky also predicted that Oman would become a member of OPEC, which has not yet happened.)

OPEC burst onto the world scene when it was able to quadruple oil prices from $3 to $12 per barrel during a roughly five-month period that began with the October 1973 Arab-Israeli War. The ability of OPEC to influence oil prices since that time is controversial, but it seems likely that the accumulated wealth of the Arab fuel-endowed countries and Iran is higher than it would have been in the absence of OPEC.

Table 3.6 provides evidence for the leading role of fuel reserves in the intensive growth of the Arab fuel-endowed countries and Iran. The countries are listed in order of their 1980 fuel reserves per capita, which was the criterion we used in Chapter 1 to classify countries as fuel-endowed. We can compare this ranking with their ranking by 2010 GDP per capita, where we use 2010 because it precedes the economic disruptions that followed the Arab Spring (see Table 1.12). We see that the countries ranked first through fourth by 1980 fuel reserves per capita, Qatar, Kuwait, UAE, and Saudi Arabia, are ranked in exactly the same order by 2010 GDP per capita. Iraq and Algeria, ranked ninth and tenth by 1980 fuel reserves per capita, are ranked tenth and ninth by 2010 GDP per capita. (By 2016, the most recent year for which data are available at time of writing, Iraq had

**Table 3.6.** Arab Fuel-Endowed Countries and Iran, Ranked by 1980 Fuel Reserves per Capita

| Country | 1980 Fuel Reserves per Capita (BTU Billions) | 2010 GDP per Capita (2011 P$) | 2010 Share of Fuel in Merchandise Exports (Percent) |
|---|---|---|---|
| Qatar | 530.3 | 125,141 | 92.6 |
| Kuwait | 313.9 | 75,204 | 92.8 |
| UAE | 250.9 | 57,580 | 64.8 |
| Saudi Arabia | 113.4 | 45,421 | 87.5 |
| Libya | 46.5 | 29,630 | 97.7 |
| Bahrain | 23.9 | 40,571 | 74.3 |
| Iran | 21.6 | 17,946 | 70.8 |
| Oman | 14.6 | 45,335 | 77.8 |
| Iraq | 14.3 | 12,718 | 99.6 |
| Algeria | 9.6 | 12,871 | 97.3 |

*Note*: UAE share of fuel in merchandise exports is for the year 2008.
*Sources of data*: BP Statistical Review, World Development Indicators.

sufficiently recovered from the war that began in 2003 to pass Algeria in GDP per capita.) The only country for which the 1980 fuel reserves per capita ranking badly predicts the 2010 GDP per capita ranking is Oman, ranked eighth by fuel reserves per capita but fifth by GDP per capita.

The last column of Table 3.6 shows that, although fuel dominated the goods exports of all the Arab fuel-endowed countries and Iran in 2010, its export share was below 90 percent for four of the GCC countries and Iran. For all of these countries except Bahrain, the fuel share of goods exports was above 90 percent in the 1970s, following the big increase in the price of oil led by OPEC. In more recent years the governments of many fuel-endowed countries have adopted policies intended to diversify their economies and reduce dependence on fuel exports. These policies have achieved their best-known success in UAE, where one of the Emirates, Dubai, has become a major tourist destination, financial center, and global transportation hub. The case of Dubai suggests that, at least for the GCC countries, services are a more promising sector than goods for new sources of export earnings. (As a consequence of its development into a global transportation hub, Dubai exports many non-fuel goods after importing and repackaging them, which may be showing up in the reduced UAE fuel share of goods exports.) The need for diversification has increased with the 2015 Paris climate accord, to which most of the world's countries were party at time of writing. Efforts by countries that are parties to the accord to reduce their greenhouse gas emissions will lead to less demand for fossil fuels, especially coal and oil.

For the GCC countries, the goal of diversification is to maintain standards of living that are already high. For Algeria, Iran, and Iraq, the goal of diversification is to accelerate growth of GDP per capita, which is more ambitious and difficult. (Libya must end its civil war before it has a government capable of making policy to achieve economic goals.) Collectively, Algeria, Iran, and Iraq perfectly illustrate the "oil curse" of slow economic growth mentioned in Chapter 1. In 1970, the population-weighted average of GDP per capita for these three countries was 2011 P$12,117. By 2010, this had increased to 2011 P$15,511, implying an average annual growth rate of only 0.6 percent per year. If the population-weighted average GDP per capita of Algeria, Iran, and Iraq had instead grown at the rate of the Arab Mediterranean world during these four decades, it would have been 2011 P$38,812 in 2010. The typical person living in Algeria, Iran, and Iraq would now have a standard of living somewhat higher than the standard of living typical of the European Union, rather than a bit higher than the standard of living typical of Latin America.

Sometimes the oil curse is attributed to a negative effect that fuel endowments are said to have on incentives to obtain education, causing slower economic growth because less educated workers are less productive. (We discuss the connection between education and worker productivity in the next chapter of this book.) The argument is that fuel endowments enable even uneducated workers to earn relatively high wages in the short run, causing them not to obtain the education needed to earn even higher wages in the long run. Patrick Asea and Amartya Lahiri (1999) and Thorvaldur Gylvason (2001) both present cross-country evidence that school enrollment is negatively associated with indicators of natural resource abundance, which include fuel endowments. However, Table 1.9 from Chapter 1 shows that fuel-endowed countries do not lag other countries in educational attainment. In 2010, the mean years of schooling in the Arab fuel-endowed countries was slightly higher than in the Arab Mediterranean, and the mean years of schooling in the non-Arab fuel-endowed countries was the same as in the rest of the non-Arab world. It could be that the incentives to obtain education are lower in fuel-endowed countries, but this is offset by the greater ability of those countries to pay for students' costs of obtaining education.

A more common explanation for the oil curse is that exports of oil and natural gas reduce manufacturing production. This could happen, for example, because the oil and natural gas sector competes with the manufacturing sector for scarce investment capital and skilled labor. The negative impact of fuel exports on manufacturing production was first noted in connection with natural gas exports from the Netherlands; hence this explanation of the oil curse is known as the "Dutch disease" (Sweder van Wijnbergen, 1984). The Dutch disease explanation for slow growth in GDP per capita assumes that production of manufactures makes a greater contribution to overall economic growth than production of oil and natural gas. Perhaps manufacturing generates more useful knowledge for the rest of the economy. This part of the Dutch disease explanation remains a conjecture.

If the Dutch disease explanation for why GDP per capita grows slowly in fuel-endowed countries is correct, diversification away from dependence on fuel exports toward exports of manufactures should solve the problem. However, if this were easy then the Dutch disease would not be a disease in the first place. The Arab Mediterranean and Turkey were able to overcome the difficulties involved in shifting their exports from primary products to manufactures in part because of the cost advantage provided by low wages. Data are scarce, but wages are very likely higher in Algeria, Iran, and Iraq today than they were in the Arab Mediterranean and Turkey when their manufactured exports took off in the 1980s. Though Turkey and some of the Arab Mediterranean countries (particularly Tunisia) have been able to upgrade some of their manufactured exports to more skill-intensive, higher-wage industries, they are building on experience gained from exporting low-skill, low-wage manufactures. For Algeria, Iran, and Iraq to become internationally competitive in more skill-intensive, higher-wage manufacturing without first having become internationally competitive in low-skill, low-wage manufacturing might be unprecedented. That does not mean it is impossible: Unlike Algeria and Iraq, Iran has made significant progress in diversification, with manufactures having reached 16 percent of merchandise exports by 2010 (more recent data were not available at time of writing). Algeria, Iran, and Iraq are the three largest fuel-endowed countries that we study in terms of population (see Table 1.6), so their diversification efforts will affect many more lives than those of the GCC countries.

We conclude this section on the Arab fuel-endowed countries and Iran with a brief discussion of the two Arab sub-Saharan African countries that have begun intensive growth, Sudan and Yemen. Although their fuel reserves per capita are far below the level needed to classify Sudan or Yemen as fuel-endowed, they have proved sufficient to dominate their exports and fund sustained growth of GDP per capita. In both countries this intensive growth began around 1990. Starting near zero in 1999, the fuel share of Sudan's goods exports increased to 69 percent in 2000, and increased further to 94 percent by 2010. It seems likely that the investment needed to prepare for these fuel exports caused the beginning of intensive growth in Sudan. At time of writing it is unclear whether Sudan's intensive growth can continue to be led by fuel exports, given the loss of most of its proven oil reserves to South Sudan, which became independent from Sudan in 2011. Nevertheless, as we saw in Table 1.12, growth of GDP per capita continued at a rapid pace in Sudan from 2010 to 2016. The fuel share of Yemen's goods exports increased from 8 percent in 1991 to 95 percent in 1995, and was still 91 percent in 2010. Fuel production and exports collapsed, along with the rest of Yemen's economy, with the 2015 civil war.

## Foreign Direct Investment

Foreign investors supplied the capital and technology that initiated oil (and, later, natural gas) exports from the Arab fuel-endowed countries and Iran. In the previous section we saw that these countries began their intensive growth by gaining a greater share of the rents generated from these natural resources at the expense of foreign investors. Although this may have reduced the incentives for continued foreign investment, we shall see in this section that recent data show that interest of foreign investors in the natural resource sectors of the Arab fuel-endowed countries has remained strong. We will also examine recent data on foreign investment in manufacturing and tradeable services (which include tourism), the sectors that drive intensive growth for the Arab Mediterranean countries.

Our interest in this section is in *foreign direct investment* (FDI), as opposed to *portfolio investment*. FDI occurs when investors control the operation of the assets in which they have invested. A typical example is the establishment of a foreign subsidiary by a multinational corporation; the corporation is the investor and it controls the operation of its subsidiary. Another typical example is a *joint venture* between a multinational corporation and a business in the host country; this is counted as FDI if the multinational has a "controlling interest" in the joint venture. By convention a controlling interest is defined as ownership of at least 10 percent of the stock in a joint venture. In contrast, portfolio investment occurs when investors acquire debt of foreign companies (i.e., lend them money) or buy less than 10 percent of the stock in foreign companies.

FDI, unlike portfolio investment, is more than just money: It comes with the technological know-how of the multinational corporation. As a consequence, FDI has potential benefits and costs for domestically owned businesses that portfolio investment does not have. When foreign subsidiaries or joint ventures compete directly with companies that are entirely domestically owned, they are typically able to gain market share at the expense of the latter thanks to superior advertising and technological expertise.

A study of Venezuela's manufacturing firms by Brian Aitken and Ann Harrison (1999) showed that total factor productivity in the domestic firms competing with foreign joint ventures decreased, probably because they were less able to take advantage of economies of scale. On the other hand, when foreign subsidiaries or joint ventures purchase inputs from domestic companies, they bring the benefits of foreign buyers that we discussed above in the section titled "Manufactured Exports to High-Income Consumers." For example, Beata Javorcik reports that "after a Czech producer of aluminum alloy castings for the automotive industry signed its first contract with a multinational customer, the staff from the multinational would visit the Czech firm's premises for two days each month over an extended period to work on improving the quality control system. Subsequently, the Czech firm applied these improvements to its other production lines (not serving this particular customer) and reduced the number of defective items produced" (2004, p. 608). Using data from Lithuania, Javorcik found that total factor productivity of domestically owned manufacturing firms increased with the shares of output in their industries that were purchased by foreign joint ventures.

The data in Table 3.7, collected by the World Bank (2013a), show FDI in sectors labeled Resources and Oil Manufacturing, Non-Oil Manufacturing, Commercial Services, and Nontradable Services. Resources are dominated by oil and natural gas, though there are other important mineral resources such as phosphate in Morocco and Tunisia that contribute to the primary product exports of those countries. Oil Manufacturing refers to refining of crude oil into products such as gasoline and heating oil. Commercial Services mainly covers FDI in infrastructure, tourism, and financial services. Nontradable Services is dominated by property development (real estate). It is typically found that the *backward linkages* from foreign subsidiaries to domestically owned businesses are greater for manufacturing than for resource extraction and processing, meaning that manufacturing subsidiaries purchase a greater share of their inputs from domestic suppliers. Non-Oil Manufacturing FDI is therefore likely to have greater backward linkages than Resources and Oil Manufacturing FDI. If Non-Oil Manufacturing FDI goes to production for export, the benefits to domestic firms from strong backward linkages will not be offset by greater competition in the domestic market. Unfortunately, the FDI data do not distinguish between manufacturing for export and manufacturing for the domestic market. Hence the most we can say about our data is that the *potential* benefits net of costs

**Table 3.7.** Distribution of Greenfield FDI in MENA by Source and Sector, 2003–2012 (US$ Billion)

|  | Resources and Oil Manufacturing | Non-Oil Manufacturing | Commercial Services | Nontradable Services |
|---|---|---|---|---|
| Developed Countries | 200.1 (40) | 90.6 (18) | 102.4 (20) | 109.5 (22) |
| EU Members | 74.7 (38) | 31.0 (16) | 41.7 (21) | 48.0 (25) |
| United States | 64.8 (50) | 20.6 (16) | 24.8 (19) | 19.3 (15) |
| Other | 60.6 (34) | 39.0 (22) | 35.9 (20) | 42.2 (24) |
| MENA | 23.2 (7) | 29.8 (9) | 125.7 (40) | 139.0 (44) |
| UAE | 13.8 (8) | 9.1 (6) | 76.2 (47) | 64.5 (39) |
| Bahrain | 0.2 (0) | 0.3 (1) | 12.3 (27) | 32.0 (71) |
| Kuwait | 0.9 (2) | 2.6 (7) | 21.5 (61) | 10.3 (29) |
| Qatar | 4.1 (13) | 3.2 (10) | 7.2 (22) | 18.4 (56) |
| Saudi Arabia | 0.0 (0) | 6.2 (42) | 3.3 (22) | 5.1 (35) |
| Non-MENA Developing Countries | 59.2 (51) | 33.0 (28) | 13.0 (11) | 11.8 (10) |

*Notes:* European Union Members: France, Germany, Italy, Netherlands, Spain, United Kingdom. Percent of row sum in parentheses.
*Source of data:* World Bank (2013a).

to domestic businesses of Non-Oil Manufacturing FDI are larger than for Resources and Oil-Manufacturing FDI. FDI in Nontradable Services is very likely to have strong backward linkages to domestic construction businesses. The same will be true of much FDI in Commercial Services, which may also create competitors for domestic firms such as hotels and banks. Not enough is known about the impacts of services FDI on quality upgrading or total factor productivity of domestic suppliers to even speculate about the net benefits to domestically owned businesses.

With these considerations in mind, let us turn to Tables 3.7–3.9. These tables cover "greenfield investment" in MENA countries. Greenfield investment refers to creation of new assets, as opposed to mergers and acquisitions which involve changes in ownership of existing assets. The restriction to greenfield FDI is not an important limitation of the data, because in MENA greenfield FDI is much larger than mergers and acquisitions FDI (see World Bank 2013a, figure 2.7). The period covered by the data, 2003–2012, includes the first two years of the Arab Spring period and eight years preceding it. FDI flows into MENA over the ten years are added together to get the total values in billions of US dollars. Tables 3.7–3.9 show FDI in MENA by source and sector, destination and source, and destination and sector, respectively. The complete breakdown by source, sector, and destination is not available.

Table 3.7 shows that Resources and Oil Manufacturing is the largest sector for developed country FDI in MENA. From Table 3.8 we can compute that 76 percent of developed country FDI is in the fuel-endowed MENA countries, and 59 percent is in the GCC alone. It seems very likely, then, that developed country FDI in Resources and Oil Manufacturing is

Table 3.8. Distribution of Greenfield FDI in MENA by Destination and Source, 2003–2012 (US$ Billion)

|  | Developed Countries | MENA | Non-MENA Developing Countries |
|---|---|---|---|
| Arab Fuel-Endowed Countries | 369 (60) | 166 (27) | 80 (13) |
| GCC | 293 (66) | 89 (20) | 64 (14) |
| Bahrain | 13 (46) | 13 (46) | 2 (7) |
| Kuwait | 6 (67) | 3 (33) | 0 (0) |
| Oman | 17 (41) | 11 (27) | 13 (32) |
| Qatar | 70 (68) | 21 (20) | 12 (12) |
| Saudi Arabia | 94 (70) | 22 (16) | 18 (13) |
| UAE | 91 (71) | 18 (14) | 20 (16) |
| Algeria | 31 (48) | 25 (39) | 8 (13) |
| Iraq | 36 (53) | 29 (43) | 3 (4) |
| Libya | 9 (24) | 23 (62) | 5 (14) |
| Iran | 12 (34) | 2 (6) | 21 (60) |
| Arab Mediterranean Countries | 113 (42) | 141 (52) | 17 (6) |
| Egypt | 39 (38) | 57 (55) | 8 (8) |
| Jordan | 7 (23) | 21 (70) | 2 (7) |
| Lebanon | 3 (27) | 8 (73) | 0 (0) |
| Morocco | 33 (70) | 12 (26) | 2 (4) |
| Syria | 14 (41) | 16 (47) | 4 (12) |
| Tunisia | 17 (38) | 27 (60) | 1 (2) |

*Notes*: The World Bank (2013a) data also included US$4 billion in Djibouti from MENA, US$5 billion in Yemen from Developed Countries, and US$4 billion in Yemen from MENA. Percent of row sum in parentheses.

*Source of data*: World Bank (2013a).

overwhelmingly concentrated in the fuel-endowed MENA countries and especially in the GCC. The historical pattern, in which production of oil and natural gas for export is the largest purpose of developed country FDI in the MENA countries, has persisted. FDI by non-MENA developing countries (mostly accounted for by India and China) follows the same pattern, with Resources and Oil Manufacturing the largest sector and 86 percent in the fuel-endowed MENA countries. FDI by the MENA countries themselves, however, departs from this pattern. The largest sectors by far are Commercial Services and Nontradable Services, and 44 percent is in the Arab Mediterranean countries compared to 23 percent for the developed countries. Remarkably, the dollar value of MENA FDI in these sectors and countries is greater than developed-country FDI in these sectors and countries, despite the vastly greater total GDP and numbers of leading multinational corporations in the developed countries. (Morocco is an exception to the rule that the Arab Mediterranean countries get the largest share of their FDI from MENA, in part due to high FDI from France (not shown separately), its former colonizer.) We can compute from Table 3.7 that the GCC countries are the source of 92 percent of the FDI coming from MENA, with UAE alone accounting for 51 percent.

We see from Table 3.9 that, as expected, Resources and Oil Manufacturing absorb a greater share of FDI in the Arab fuel-endowed countries and Iran than in the Arab Mediterranean countries. The difference in these shares between the two Arab country groups is narrowed by Egypt and Syria, because these Arab Mediterranean countries are both minor oil exporters. The unexpected result in Table 3.9 is that Non-Oil Manufacturing absorbs a smaller share of FDI in the Arab Mediterranean countries than in the Arab fuel-endowed countries or Iran. The FDI shares of Non-Oil Manufacturing in Jordan, Morocco, and Tunisia, the three countries for which manufacturing dominates merchandise exports, are 19, 17, and 8 percent, respectively, about the same as or less than the 18 percent share for the Arab fuel-endowed country group. The unexpectedly low relative shares of Non-Oil Manufacturing in FDI in these countries can be attributed to the fact that, except for Morocco, most of their FDI comes from the MENA countries (especially the GCC), which lack manufacturing expertise.

It appears that the Arab Mediterranean countries are missing out on the potential benefits to domestic businesses from manufacturing FDI. Recall

**Table 3.9.** Distribution of Greenfield FDI in MENA by Destination and Sector, 2003–2012 (US$ Billion)

|  | Resources and Oil Manufacturing | Non-Oil Manufacturing | Commercial Services | Nontradable Services |
|---|---|---|---|---|
| Arab Fuel-Endowed Countries | 192.0 (31) | 109.3 (18) | 149.5 (24) | 165.2 (27) |
| GCC | 136.6 (31) | 87.1 (20) | 114.9 (26) | 106.0 (24) |
| Bahrain | 4.1 (15) | 3.7 (13) | 13.7 (49) | 6.4 (23) |
| Kuwait | 1.6 (18) | 0.2 (2) | 4.4 (52) | 2.4 (28) |
| Oman | 7.5 (18) | 16.4 (40) | 5.0 (12) | 11.9 (29) |
| Qatar | 46.5 (45) | 11.9 (12) | 14.7 (14) | 29.2 (29) |
| Saudi Arabia | 69.1 (52) | 30.1 (23) | 23.1 (17) | 11.4 (9) |
| UAE | 7.8 (6) | 24.8 (19) | 54.0 (41) | 44.9 (34) |
| Algeria | 21.1 (33) | 19.2 (30) | 12.7 (20) | 11.9 (18) |
| Iraq | 24.6 (36) | 1.3 (2) | 18.8 (28) | 23.3 (34) |
| Libya | 9.7 (25) | 1.7 (4) | 3.1 (8) | 24.0 (62) |
| Iran | 23.2 (67) | 10.0 (29) | 0.7 (2) | 1.0 (3) |
| Arab Mediterranean Countries | 61.4 (23) | 33.5 (12) | 86.3 (32) | 89.5 (33) |
| Egypt | 31.9 (31) | 12.1 (12) | 18.9 (18) | 41.6 (40) |
| Jordan | 2.3 (8) | 5.8 (19) | 15.4 (50) | 7.1 (23) |
| Lebanon | 0.4 (4) | 1.2 (11) | 5.6 (54) | 3.2 (31) |
| Morocco | 9.9 (21) | 8.1 (17) | 15.4 (33) | 13.8 (29) |
| Syria | 11.7 (35) | 2.5 (7) | 14.7 (44) | 4.5 (13) |
| Tunisia | 5.2 (12) | 3.8 (8) | 16.3 (37) | 19.3 (43) |

*Notes*: The World Bank (2013a) data also showed 43 and 57 percent of FDI in Djibouti in Commercial Services and Nontradable Services, respectively; and 62, 7, 16, and 14 percent of FDI in Yemen in Resources and Oil Manufacturing, Non-Oil Manufacturing, Commercial Services, and Nontradable Services, respectively. Yemen, like Egypt and Syria, is a minor oil exporter. Percent of row sum in parentheses.
*Source of data*: World Bank (2013a).

that the merchandise exports of Turkey, like those of Jordan, Morocco, and Tunisia, are dominated by manufacturing. Although we have no data comparable to Tables 3.7–3.9 for Turkey, the more limited data from the United Nations Conference on Trade and Development (2012) indicate that Turkey has proportionately less FDI from the GCC countries and more FDI in manufacturing. The importance of the GCC for FDI in the Arab Mediterranean countries has directed FDI into finance, infrastructure, real estate development, and tourism. These are the sectors of economic integration between the GCC and the Arab Mediterranean, rather than manufacturing.

# 4
# Human Resources

### Introduction

The Arab countries, Iran, and Turkey have had considerable success expanding access to education and improving health. These successes have brought new challenges. As educational enrollment has increased, maintaining the quality of education has become a priority. The evidence presented in the section titled "Education" does not suggest any problems with the quality of education in Iran or Turkey, but the evidence consistently points to low quality of education in Arab sub-Saharan Africa and the Arab fuel-endowed countries. It also appears that the Arab countries allocate too large a share of their educational expenditures to the tertiary (university) level. In addition the section describes how the Arab countries have struggled to find the right balance between education in Arabic and education in a colonial language. In the section titled "Health," we show that, as the burden of communicable diseases has fallen outside of sub-Saharan Africa, heart diseases have emerged as a top health problem for the Arab fuel-endowed countries, Arab Mediterranean, Iran, and Turkey. This problem is exacerbated by high rates of obesity, especially among women. In Arab sub-Saharan Africa, infectious and parasitic diseases have not yet been brought under control. We show that the incentives to develop new drugs and vaccines are greatest in rich, temperate countries, so progress in treatment of tropical diseases depends more on efforts by non-profits and international organizations.

The fall in death rates in the countries we study led to an acceleration of population growth to unsustainable levels. In the section titled "The Demographic Transition," we show that this fall in death rates has now been followed by a fall in birth rates, which will slow future population growth to a more manageable level in the Arab fuel-endowed countries and Arab Mediterranean, and to near zero in Iran and Turkey. Arab sub-Saharan Africa, like the rest of sub-Saharan Africa, is an exception to this reduction in fertility and consequent slowing of population growth. Government

92  THE ECONOMICS OF THE MIDDLE EAST

efforts to promote family planning have played some role in the reduction in fertility that has occurred in most countries, but we present evidence that this has not been the most important factor. Finally, we document that falling birth rates have begun to reduce the youth shares of country populations and thus increase the ratios of workers to dependents, with possibly beneficial economic consequences.

> **Box 4.1**
>
> **The "Difference-in-Difference" Technique of Evaluating Government Interventions.** Government plays a large or even dominant role in provision of education and health care in nearly all the Arab countries, Iran, and Turkey. Economists have become much more careful in evaluating the impacts of government interventions in these sectors. A simple comparison of before and after is inadequate because it does not take into account ongoing socioeconomic changes that could be having the same (or opposite) effect as the government intervention.
>
> To correct this problem it is now standard for economists to compare before and after both for the individuals subjected to the government intervention (the "treatment group") and for the individuals not subjected to the government intervention (the "control group"). The key is to subtract the difference between before and after outcomes for the control group from the same difference for the treatment group—a double difference or "difference-in-differences." Table 4.1, adapted from an article by Esther Duflo (2001), illustrates the difference-in-difference technique. The entries in the table show the average years of schooling for Indonesian adults. The column
>
> Table 4.1. Mean Years of Schooling for Indonesian Adults
>
> |  | Level of Program in Region of Birth | | |
> | --- | --- | --- | --- |
> |  | High | Low | Difference |
> | Aged 2 to 6 in 1974 | 8.49 | 9.76 | −1.27 |
> | Aged 12 to 17 in 1974 | 8.02 | 9.40 | −1.39 |
> | Difference | 0.47 | 0.36 | 0.12 |
>
> Source: Duflo (2001), Table 3.

labels "high" and "low" refer to a government program to construct primary schools. The difference between the number of schools constructed per 1,000 children in high and low program regions is 0.90. The row labels "aged 2 to 6 in 1974" and "aged 12 to 17 in 1974" refer to the ages of the adults at the time the school construction program was begun. Adults aged 12 to 17 were too old to benefit from the program, whereas adults aged 2 to 6 were young enough to benefit from the program. Hence the younger adults are the treatment group and the older adults are the control group. Finally, the column labeled "difference" equals the first column minus the second column, and the row labeled "difference" equals the first row minus the second. The entry in the lower right-hand corner of Table 4.1 is the difference-in-differences and must be equal whether constructed using the column or row differences. (Using the row differences yields 0.11 instead of 0.12 because of rounding error.)

The third column in Table 4.1 shows that adults in both the treatment and control groups completed *fewer* years of schooling in high than low program regions. This reflects the government intention to build more schools in regions where school enrollment was low. Using the difference in differences accounts for this fact and yields the estimate that 1 additional school per 1,000 children increased adult completed schooling by 0.13 years (0.12 divided by 0.90). The third row in Table 4.1 shows that younger adults completed more years of schooling than older adults in both high and low program regions. This reflects an ongoing trend toward increased educational attainment. Again, using the difference in differences accounts for this fact and thereby correctly identifies the effect of the program.

## Education

Education is not just a contributor to human development in its own right, but may also contribute to growth in per capita incomes. Economists see education as a form of investment in *human capital*, the skills that make an individual more productive. The analogy is to investment in physical capital. The owner of a firm can use some of her profits to invest in capital equipment, rather than buying goods for her own consumption. Similarly, an individual can use some of her time to invest in her skills (human capital) by attending school, rather than working for money she can spend on consumer goods. The analogy can be extended to view human capital as an input to production like physical capital. Just as increasing the amount of capital equipment will generate more output, increasing the amount of worker skills (human capital) will generate more output.

If education is an investment, it is natural to ask, what is the return to this investment? Economists answer this question by examining data on wage earnings for workers at all levels of schooling, and estimating by what percentage wage earnings increase for each additional year of schooling received. This percentage is called the *rate of return to education*, or return to education for short. The return to education can be calculated as an average over all years of schooling, or it can be calculated separately for primary (elementary), secondary (high school), and tertiary (college) schooling.

Claudio Montenegro and Harry Patrinos (2014) collected estimated returns to education for all available countries. In Table 4.2 we use the

**Table 4.2.** Estimated Rates of Return to Education Percent per Year of School

|  | All Schooling | Primary | Secondary | Tertiary |
|---|---|---|---|---|
| Arab sub-Saharan Africa | 6.0 | 13.7 | 4.2 | 14.4 |
| Non-Arab sub-Saharan Africa | 13.1 | 16.6 | 10.6 | 20.5 |
| Iraq | 3.4 | 7.7 | 1.2 | 3.2 |
| Non-Arab fuel-endowed countries | 7.5 | 12.7 | 4.1 | 12.2 |
| Arab Mediterranean | 8.0 | 10.9 | 5.5 | 12.9 |
| Rest of non-Arab world | 11.2 | 6.5 | 7.1 | 17.4 |
| Turkey | 10.0 | 10.4 | 6.2 | 16.6 |
| Latin America | 10.0 | 7.4 | 5.5 | 17.3 |
| Southern Europe | 7.2 | 3.6 | 5.5 | 9.5 |

*Notes*: The population-weighted averages for each country group include the countries listed in the Appendix. Some countries listed are missing estimates for one or more of the three schooling levels (primary, secondary, and tertiary). The excluded countries were missing estimates for all schooling and for the three schooling levels. For each country, estimates are used for the most recent available year, shown in parentheses in the Appendix.

*Source of data*: Montenegro and Patrinos (2014).

most recent estimates they collected to compute population-weighted average returns to education for Arab sub-Saharan Africa, the Arab Mediterranean, and the comparison country groups, as well as Turkey. Iraq was the only one of the Arab fuel-endowed countries with available estimates, and no estimates were available for Iran. We see that, averaged over all years of schooling, the returns to education for Arab sub-Saharan Africa, Iraq, and the Arab Mediterranean are consistently lower than for their comparison country groups, except for the Arab Mediterranean relative to Southern Europe. In contrast, the return to education in Turkey averaged over all years of schooling is similar to the returns in the rest of the non-Arab world and in Latin America. The lower Arab returns to all schooling appear to be driven by lower Arab returns to higher education, especially tertiary education. Returns to Arab primary education are similar to or higher than in the rest of the world. Note also that returns to education for the fuel-endowed countries, Arab and non-Arab, are lower than in the rest of the world, which is consistent with the theoretical arguments in the previous chapter that incentives to acquire education are lower in fuel-endowed countries.

Lower returns to education in Arab sub-Saharan Africa, Iraq, and the Arab Mediterranean could be evidence for lower quality of Arab education than in their counterparts in the rest of the world. According to this interpretation, Arabs gain less in wage earnings from their educations because they learn fewer useful skills in school. However, the facts that Arab returns to education are roughly equal or greater at the primary level, and show the greatest gaps with the rest of the world at the tertiary level, suggest a different interpretation: Too many Arabs are receiving a college education, and they are driving down wages for college-educated workers in Arab countries. This interpretation is consistent with high Arab unemployment for these workers documented in Chapter 6.

Todd Schoellman (2012) proposes a different way to use returns to education to compare educational quality across countries. The problem with comparing returns to education as in Table 4.2 is that these returns reflect both the quality of education and the extent to which each country rewards education of a given quality. If the workers educated in different countries all earned wages in the same country, their different returns to education would only reflect their different qualities of education. Following this reasoning, Schoellman estimates the returns to education of immigrants from different countries to the United States.

Schoellman uses data for immigrants from the 2000 US Census to estimate their returns to education. He controls for English language proficiency so that return to education will not be confused with return to English language skills. Figure 4.1 shows his results. On the horizontal axis is the logarithm of GDP per worker for the immigrant's country of origin in dollars adjusted for purchasing power, which is slightly different from GDP per capita (per person) used in previous figures. On the vertical axis is the estimated rate of return to education, *not* multiplied by 100 to obtain percent—that is, a 5 percent rate of return in Table 4.2 is equivalent to 0.05 on the vertical axis in Figure 4.1. The main message of the figure is that the quality of education in an immigrant's country of origin tends to increase with productivity in the country of origin as measured by GDP per worker. An alternative interpretation of the figure is that the skills learned in countries that are similar to the United States in productivity are more transferable to the United States than the skills learned in less productive countries. Schoellman (2012, pp. 397–398) presents some evidence against this alternative interpretation.

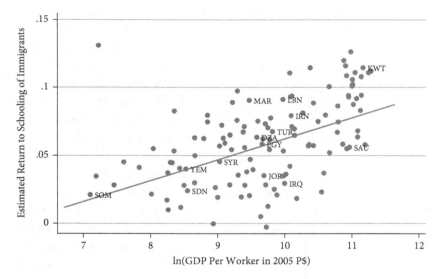

**Figure 4.1.** Quality of Education Measured by Returns to Schooling of Immigrants

*Source:* Todd Schoellman, "Education Quality and Development Accounting," *Review of Economic Studies* 79(1) (2012): 388–417, by permission of Oxford University Press.

Figure 4.1 allows us to think about the quality of Arab education in a slightly different way than Table 4.2. In Figure 4.1 we can take into account the tendency for a country's quality of education to increase with its productivity, hence its per capita income. We can then ask whether Arab educational quality is high or low, taking this tendency into account, i.e., are the Arab countries above or below the line plotted in Figure 4.1? There are twelve Arab countries plotted in the figure: Somalia (SOM), Sudan (SDN), and Yemen (YEM) from Arab sub-Saharan Africa; Algeria (DZA), Iraq (IRQ), Kuwait (KWT), and Saudi Arabia (SAU) of the Arab fuel-endowed countries; and Egypt (EGY), Jordan (JOR), Morocco (MAR), Lebanon (LBN), and Syria (SYR) from the Arab Mediterranean. Iran (IRN) and Turkey (TUR) are also plotted. We see that Somalia and Yemen are close to the line in Figure 4.1 whereas Sudan is well below the line. We can then conclude that, on average, Arab sub-Saharan African countries have low educational quality, even taking into account the tendency for low productivity countries to have low educational quality. Turning to the Arab fuel-endowed countries, we see that Iraq is well below the line and Kuwait is well above it. Algeria and Saudi Arabia are closer to the line (slightly above and somewhat below it, respectively). Since Iraq's population is so much larger than Kuwait's, we conclude that the population-weighted average educational quality for the Arab fuel-endowed countries is low, adjusting for the effect of country productivity on country educational quality. We reach the opposite conclusion for the Arab Mediterranean: Egypt and Syria are close to the line, Jordan is well below it, but Lebanon and Morocco are well above it. Finally, Iran and Turkey are both somewhat above the line in Figure 4.1.

For Arab sub-Saharan Africa and the Arab fuel-endowed countries, then, returns to education are low compared to their counterparts in the rest of the world and compared to what Figure 4.1 predicts on the basis of their productivity. The evidence thus consistently points to low quality of education in these Arab country groups. For the Arab Mediterranean, returns to education are low compared to their counterparts in the rest of the world but high compared to what Figure 4.1 predicts on the basis of their productivity. For this Arab country group, the evidence suggests that returns to education are depressed by providing tertiary education to too many students relative to what their economies demand. This may also be a problem for the other Arab country groups. Evidence for Turkey consistently indicates average educational quality. For Iran we only know that returns to education are somewhat higher than what is predicted by its productivity, indicating a quality of education that is somewhat above average.

## Box 4.2

**Ability Differences, Spillovers, and Private versus Social Returns to Education.** The returns to education shown in Table 4.2 and Figure 4.1 are *private* returns to education: They do not reflect the costs to society of providing education (taxes to pay for public schools), and they do not reflect any benefits to society from a worker's education other than his higher wages. The cost of providing tertiary education is much higher than the cost of providing secondary or primary education. George Psacharopoulos (1991) argues that for this reason the *social* returns to tertiary education are typically lower than the social returns to primary education, despite private returns to tertiary education that are typically higher, as in Table 4.2.

Even the computation of private returns to education is not without controversy. When economists call the percentage increase in wage earnings for each additional year of schooling "the (private) return to education," they implicitly assume that the innate abilities of workers with more and less schooling are the same, and therefore have no effect on their earnings differential. Suppose instead that differences in years of schooling are partly caused by differences in ability: High-ability students graduate from secondary school, say, whereas low-ability students drop out. In this case part of the higher earnings of secondary school graduates reflects their higher ability, and the return to secondary education is overestimated. Economists try to remove this "ability bias" from their estimated returns to education by examining wage differences between workers for whom the only cause of differences in educational attainment is differences in the resources to which the workers had access when students: for example, whether or not primary schools were present in their villages, as in Box 4.1.

One can also argue that earnings differentials *under*estimate the social return to education. People learn from those around them, so if I have an education I improve the learning environment for my co-workers. This positive spillover or "human capital externality" may raise the wages of my co-workers, but they do not pay me for it. James Rauch (1993) has provided evidence for the existence of such spillovers in the United States, finding that workers earn more, the higher is the average level of education in their city, controlling for their individual characteristics and other important attributes of the city.

> With all these caveats, it is unwise to place great importance on the precise numerical values of estimated returns to education such as those reported in Table 4.2. What one hopes is that these caveats do not systematically affect our comparisons of returns to education across countries.

The returns to education inform us about the outputs of the educational process. We can also investigate the inputs. We are particularly interested in whether Arab governments spend more on tertiary education relative to their counterparts in the rest of the world and thereby encourage too many students to attend college. One way to judge this is to examine the ratio of government expenditure per tertiary student to government expenditure per secondary student. University education is expected to be more expensive than high school education, but this does not have to be completely reflected in government expenditure because students or their families may bear more of the costs of college education than of high school education.

Table 4.3 shows the ratio of government expenditure per tertiary to secondary student, and for comparison also shows the ratio of government expenditure per secondary to primary student. For each country included in the population-weighted averages, the data are for the most recent year during the period 2006–2016. We see that, for both the Arab fuel-endowed countries and the Arab Mediterranean, the ratio of tertiary to secondary expenditure exceeds the ratios in the comparison country groups. In contrast, the ratio for Turkey is the same as for Latin America and slightly below the ratio for the rest of the non-Arab world. This is consistent with the estimates in Table 4.2 that show Turkey has a similar return to tertiary education as Latin America and the rest of the non-Arab world, rather than lower as in the Arab countries. For the ratio of secondary to primary expenditure, the Arab fuel-endowed countries are lower than the non-Arab fuel-endowed countries and the Arab Mediterranean is lower than the rest of the non-Arab world, though higher than Latin America or Southern Europe. For both Arab and non-Arab sub-Saharan Africa, the ratios of expenditure per tertiary student to secondary student are extraordinarily high, especially for non-Arab sub-Saharan Africa. It is hard to know what these high ratios mean, but one possibility is that there was extensive building of new universities in sub-Saharan Africa during the period 2006–2016.

Setting aside the data for sub-Saharan Africa, Table 4.3 shows that Arab governments spend relatively more than their rest-of-the-world

**Table 4.3.** Expenditure per Student: Ratios of Secondary to Primary and Tertiary to Secondary

|  | Secondary ÷ Primary | Tertiary ÷ Secondary |
|---|---|---|
| Arab sub-Saharan Africa | 0.8 | 6.2 |
| Non-Arab sub-Saharan Africa | 2.1 | 15.8 |
| Arab fuel-endowed countries | 1.0 | 1.3 |
| Non-Arab fuel-endowed countries | 1.6 | 1.0 |
| Iran | 1.9 | 0.9 |
| Arab Mediterranean | 1.5 | 2.6 |
| Rest of non-Arab world | 1.6 | 2.1 |
| Turkey | 0.8 | 1.9 |
| Latin America | 1.1 | 1.9 |
| Southern Europe | 1.2 | 1.1 |

*Notes*: Countries are included if data are available during the period 2006–2016. For each country, data are used for the most recent available year. The population-weighted averages for each country group include the countries listed in the Appendix. The excluded countries were missing data.

*Source of data*: World Development Indicators.

counterparts on tertiary education. This suggests a need for Arab students and their families to bear more of the costs of university education. Forcing them to do so, however, would be politically difficult. In Egypt, for example, free tuition is enshrined in the constitution.

In attempting to provide their students with a high quality of education, the Arab countries have struggled with the issue of language of instruction. As we noted in Chapter 1, most of the Arab countries gained political independence by the 1940s or later. Under colonialism, the language of non-religious instruction was the language of the colonial power, which was nearly always English or French. Teachers were trained in English or French and textbooks were written in English or French. After independence, the Arab governments were confronted with the issue of whether to maintain this system or to introduce instruction in Arabic. If Arabic instruction was introduced, then the question arose of whether Arabic should replace English or French entirely, or only in certain subjects or at certain grade levels.

There are reasons to think a switch to Arabic could increase or decrease the return to education. On the one hand, students might learn more effectively if Modern Standard Arabic is closer than English or French to the language they use at home. On the other hand, English or French is likely to be the main language in which business is conducted, especially given the pattern of international trade documented in Table 3.2.

Joshua Angrist and Victor Lavy (1997) studied the impact on the return to education in Morocco of the replacement of French by Arabic as the language of instruction for grades six and above, starting in the fall of 1983. (By that time Arabic was already the language of instruction for the lower grades.) They were able to carry out a difference-in-difference analysis of the type described in Box 4.1. Specifically, Angrist and Lavy compared wage earnings and test scores for men who were young enough to have been affected by the change in language of instruction (the treatment group) to men who were too old to have been affected (the control group). For the treatment group they found that the difference in the logarithm of hourly earnings between men with six or more years of schooling and men with less than six years of schooling is 0.137, implying that the additional schooling raised wages by about 15 percent. The same difference for the control group is 1.07, implying that the additional schooling nearly tripled their wages. The difference in differences is -0.933, indicating an enormous reduction in the return to Arabic language education compared to French language education. Repeating the exercise for an index of French writing ability yields a difference of 0.635 for the treatment group and 1.44 for the control group, for a difference in differences of -0.805, roughly equivalent to a decline from functional competence to only some ability or from some ability to no ability. Angrist and Lavy estimate that the decrease in French writing ability explains some but not all of the decrease in return to education resulting from the switch from French to Arabic instruction.

The dividing age between the treatment group of men and the control group of men in the Angrist and Lavy article is 21. They point out that the younger men (the treatment group) are less likely to have realized the full benefits of their educations in the workplace so that the difference in differences overestimates the reduction in the return to education resulting from the switch from French to Arabic instruction. One also needs to be cautious in applying their results to Arab countries other than Morocco. Arabic is used at home less in Morocco than in most Arab countries, and the Moroccan dialect is less similar to Modern Standard Arabic than in most Arab countries. For these reasons the beneficial effects on student learning of a change to instruction in Arabic are likely to be lower in Morocco than in most Arab countries.

At time of writing, Arabic has become the primary language of instruction in public schools in nearly all Arab countries. However, Arab public school administrators (and Arab parents) are aware of the benefits to students of knowing English or French. Rather than using English or French as the language of instruction, they introduce English or French as a foreign language to very young students. Ideally, the students will become effectively bilingual. Table 4.4 shows the grades at which foreign language instruction begins in Arab public schools and the number of hours

Table 4.4. Foreign Language Instruction in the Arab Countries

| Country (Foreign Language) | Grade in Which Foreign Language Instruction Begins | Number of Hours per Week |
|---|---|---|
| **Arab sub-Saharan Africa** | | |
| Comoros* | | |
| Djibouti* | | |
| Mauritania (French) | 2 | 6 |
| Sudan (English) | 5 | 2 |
| Yemen (English) | 7 | 3 1/3 |
| **Arab fuel-endowed countries** | | |
| Algeria (French) | 2 | 3 |
| Bahrain (English) | 3 | 4 1/6 |
| Iraq (English) | 5 | 2 2/3 |
| Kuwait (English) | 1 | 3 |
| Oman (English) | 4 | 2 2/3 |
| Qatar (English) | 1 | 3 1/3 |
| Saudi Arabia (English) | 7 | 3 |
| UAE (English) | 1 | 2 2/3 |
| **Arab Mediterranean** | | |
| Egypt (English) | 1 | 2 1/4 |
| Jordan (English) | 5 | 3 3/4 |
| Lebanon (French or English) | 1 | 5 1/4 |
| Morocco (French) | 3 | 8 |
| Syria (English or French) | 5 | 2 1/4 |
| Tunisia (French) | 3 | 8 |

*French is the primary language of instruction

Notes: In Bahrain, English is taught as a second language for 1 2/3 hours in grade 3, and 4 1/6 hours thereafter.

Source of data: http://www.ibe.unesco.org/en/document/world-data-education-seventh-edition-2010-11. Data were not available for Libya and Somalia.

of instruction per week, based on country reports to the United Nations Educational, Scientific, and Cultural Organization (UNESCO) for the 2010/11 edition of *World Data on Education* (the most recent edition at time of writing). The starting grade for foreign language instruction varies from one to seven and the number of hours per week varies from two to eight. Clearly, Arab countries differ greatly in their efforts to foster bilingualism in their public school students. Considering an early start as grade three or lower and a strong effort as at least one hour per day, the countries with the greatest commitment to bilingualism are Mauritania in Arab sub-Saharan Africa and Lebanon, Morocco, and Tunisia in the Arab Mediterranean.

At higher levels of education, sometimes in high school but mainly at the university level, public institutions in many Arab countries teach math, science, and related technical subjects in English or French. According to Reem Bassiouney (2009, table 5.2), Tunisian public high schools teach math and science in French, but Algerian and Moroccan public high schools retain Arabic as the language of instruction for these subjects. However, public universities in all three countries teach technical subjects in French. Bassiouney also reports that Egyptian public universities teach technical subjects using Arabic lectures and English textbooks.

## Health

In Chapter 1 we noted the large increases in life expectancy in the three Arab worlds that occurred from 1970 to 2010: 14.5 years in Arab sub-Saharan Africa, 19.0 years in the Arab fuel-endowed countries, and 18.5 years in the Arab Mediterranean (see Table 1.8). These increases were made possible by adoption of better medical technology, especially antibiotics and vaccines that controlled or even eradicated infectious diseases. Though life expectancy in Arab sub-Saharan Africa in 2010 was considerably higher than in the rest of sub-Saharan Africa (61.4 versus 56.7 years), it was still far lower than in the Arab fuel-endowed countries (72.9 years) and the Arab Mediterranean (72.0 years). We noted in Chapter 1 that tropical diseases were a key explanation for poor socioeconomic performance in sub-Saharan Africa. Though Arab sub-Saharan Africa has made greater progress in controlling these diseases than the rest of sub-Saharan Africa, we will show that infectious and parasitic diseases are still a much greater health problem for Arab sub-Saharan Africa than for the other two Arab worlds. For the Arab fuel-endowed countries and the Arab Mediterranean, and for Iran and Turkey, the diseases of middle and old age such as cancer and heart disease are now the leading health problems.

Table 4.5 shows the burdens of infectious and parasitic diseases, cancers, and heart diseases for the three Arab worlds, Iran, Turkey, and the comparison country groups. Disease burdens are measured in Disability Adjusted Life Years (DALY) per 100,000 population. DALY are a way to add together years of life lost and years lost to disability (inability to work or attend school). Box 4.3 gives a more detailed description of DALY. The DALY in Table 4.5 are "age-standardized." Countries with longer life expectancies will automatically tend to have more DALY per 100,000 population due to cancers and heart diseases because their populations are older, and countries with shorter life expectancies will automatically tend to have more DALY per 100,000 population due to infectious and parasitic diseases that kill children such as diarrheal diseases. Using age-standardized DALY corrects for these tendencies. The data in Table 4.5 are for 2004, the most recent year available from the World Health Organization. Because these data are older than we would like, we will use Table 4.5 to highlight certain broad trends rather than attach too much importance to specific numbers.

> **Box 4.3**
>
> **Disability Adjusted Life Years (DALY).** DALY are used by the World Health Organization (WHO) to aggregate years of healthy life lost due to all diseases and health conditions into one measure. According to the WHO (http://www.who.int/healthinfo/global_burden_disease/metrics_daly/en/), "one DALY can be thought of as one lost year of 'healthy' life. The sum of these DALY across the population, or the burden of disease, can be thought of as a measurement of the gap between current health status and an ideal health situation where the entire population lives to an advanced age, free of disease and disability."
>
> DALY for a disease or health condition are calculated as the sum of the Years of Life Lost (YLL) due to premature mortality in the population and the Years Lost due to Disability (YLD) for people living with the health condition or its consequences: DALY = YLL + YLD. For a given cause, age, and sex, YLL are calculated using the formula YLL = N × L, where N is the number of deaths and L is the standard

life expectancy, in years, at age of death. To estimate YLD for a particular cause in a particular time period, the number of incident cases in that period is multiplied by the average duration of the disease and a weight factor that reflects the severity of the disease on a scale from 0 (perfect health) to 1 (dead). The basic formula for YLD is the following: YLD = I × DW × T, where I is the number of incident cases, DW is the disability weight, and T is the average duration (time) of the case until remission or death, in years.

Table 4.5 delivers three main messages. First, infectious and parasitic diseases are a greater problem than cancers and heart diseases for sub-Saharan Africa, but the opposite is true for the rest of the world. Second, Arab sub-Saharan Africa has reduced the burden of infectious and parasitic diseases to a much greater extent than has non-Arab sub-Saharan Africa.

**Table 4.5.** Age-Standardized Burdens of Disease, 2004
DALY per 100,000 Population

|  | Infectious Diseases | Cancers | Heart Diseases |
|---|---|---|---|
| Arab sub-Saharan Africa | 8541 | 1554 | 4721 |
| Non-Arab sub-Saharan Africa | 19,002 | 1456 | 3565 |
| Arab fuel-endowed countries | 1924 | 1264 | 3569 |
| Non-Arab fuel-endowed countries | 915 | 1084 | 2851 |
| Iran | 945 | 1064 | 3375 |
| Arab Mediterranean | 1165 | 915 | 3720 |
| Rest of non-Arab world | 2280 | 1288 | 2641 |
| Turkey | 822 | 1233 | 4082 |
| Latin America | 1370 | 1280 | 1983 |
| Southern Europe | 243 | 1326 | 1133 |

*Notes:* We use the disease classifications of the World Health Organization. Infectious diseases = infectious and parasitic diseases. Cancers = malignant neoplasms. Heart diseases = cardiovascular diseases.

The population-weighted averages for each country group include the countries listed in the Appendix. The excluded countries were missing data.

*Source of data:* www.who.int/healthinfo/global_burden_disease/estimates_country/en/.

Third, heart diseases are a greater problem for all three Arab worlds, and for Iran and Turkey, than for the comparison country groups.

Table 4.6 shows age-standardized DALY per 100,000 population for nine major infectious and parasitic diseases. We see that the degree to which Arab sub-Saharan Africa has succeeded better than the rest of sub-Saharan Africa in reducing the burden of infectious disease is exaggerated in Table 4.5 by the fact that in 2004 the AIDS epidemic was near its height in non-Arab sub-Saharan Africa: the population-weighted average for DALY per 100,000 attributable to HIV/AIDS in 2004 was 7,918 for non-Arab sub-Saharan Africa versus 1,068 for Arab sub-Saharan Africa. Even if we were to ignore the contribution of HIV/AIDS, however, Arab sub-Saharan Africa would still have a substantially lower burden of infectious and parasitic diseases than non-Arab sub-Saharan Africa because of greater progress in reducing DALY attributable to tuberculosis, diarrheal diseases, and malaria. We also see from Table 4.6 that diarrheal diseases are the single largest cause of the greater burden of infectious and parasitic diseases in the Arab fuel-endowed countries than in the non-Arab fuel-endowed countries. The major cause of diarrheal diseases is unsafe water, an issue we will cover as part of the discussion of water pollution in Chapter 7 on environmental challenges.

The Arab Mediterranean, Iran, and Turkey have all had comparable success in reducing their burdens of infectious and parasitic diseases. Nevertheless, Table 4.5 shows that they have a long way to go before achieving the low infectious and parasitic disease burden of Southern Europe. At the same time, Table 4.5 shows that heart diseases are perhaps the greatest health challenge facing the Arab fuel-endowed countries, the Arab Mediterranean, Iran, and Turkey. The burden of heart diseases for the Arab Mediterranean, for example, is more than three times the burden of infectious and parasitic diseases, and more than three times the burden of heart diseases for Southern Europe. Heart diseases are very much affected by lifestyle. Below we will discuss one contributor to the high heart disease burden in the Arab world, Iran, and Turkey: obesity.

For Arab sub-Saharan Africa, infectious and parasitic diseases are still the greatest health challenge. Pharmaceuticals that were crucial to reducing the infectious and parasitical disease burden outside of sub-Saharan Africa have been less effective within sub-Saharan Africa because, in part, many of the diseases that afflict sub-Saharan Africa are different from the diseases that afflict the temperate world. Michael Kremer (2002) has pointed out

**Table 4.6.** Age-Standardized Burdens of Nine Major Infectious and Parasitic Diseases, 2004 DALY per 100,000 Population

| | Tuberculosis | STDs Excluding HIV | HIV/AIDS | Diarrheal Diseases | Childhood-Cluster Diseases | Meningitis | Hepatitis B | Malaria | Tropical-Cluster Diseases |
|---|---|---|---|---|---|---|---|---|---|
| Arab sub-Saharan Africa | 1196 | 243 | 1068 | 1873 | 1143 | 276 | 47 | 1210 | 453 |
| Non-Arab sub-Saharan Africa | 1833 | 373 | 7918 | 2809 | 899 | 527 | 44 | 2334 | 880 |
| Arab fuel-endowed countries | 148 | 167 | 38 | 900 | 88 | 136 | 61 | 11 | 28 |
| Non-Arab fuel-endowed countries | 74 | 88 | 131 | 367 | 11 | 47 | 15 | 3 | 57 |
| Iran | 84 | 88 | 82 | 442 | 11 | 52 | 17 | 2 | 47 |
| Arab Mediterranean | 109 | 125 | 32 | 424 | 56 | 111 | 74 | 21 | 20 |
| Rest of non-Arab world | 457 | 114 | 206 | 574 | 244 | 92 | 30 | 27 | 99 |
| Turkey | 108 | 54 | 5 | 345 | 29 | 117 | 29 | 0 | 2 |
| Latin America | 169 | 95 | 280 | 373 | 22 | 62 | 13 | 13 | 103 |
| Southern Europe | 11 | 23 | 84 | 30 | 7 | 16 | 12 | 0 | 0 |

*Notes:* These are the first nine infectious and parasitic diseases or disease groups listed by the World Health Organization in its source data. The population-weighted averages for each country group include the countries listed in the Appendix. The excluded countries were missing data.

*Source of data:* www.who.int/healthinfo/global_burden_disease/estimates_country/en/.

that pharmaceutical firms have much lower incentives to invent drugs to control diseases in poor tropical countries than to control diseases in rich, temperate countries. Table 4.7 shows that sub-Saharan Africa accounted for only 1 percent of the world market for pharmaceuticals in 2014 despite having 13 percent of world population. In contrast, the United States, the European Union, and Japan accounted for two-thirds of the world pharmaceutical market though their share of world population was roughly the same as the share of sub-Saharan Africa. Per capita spending on pharmaceuticals by the United States, the European Union, and Japan was 75, 46, and 64 times greater than per capita spending in sub-Saharan Africa, respectively.

Recognition that the incentives for profit-making firms to develop new drugs to control tropical diseases may be inadequate has led to major efforts by non-profits, both non-governmental organizations (NGOs) and international governmental organizations such as the World Health Organization (WHO). For example, the Bill and Melinda Gates Foundation has a program on Neglected Tropical Diseases that funds research into new drugs and delivery of existing drugs to treat or eliminate these diseases. Arab sub-Saharan Africa can be expected to benefit from these efforts. The WHO Office for the Eastern Mediterranean covers all of the Arab world, including Arab sub-Saharan Africa, except for Algeria, Comoros, and Mauritania. It funds a Special Program for Research and Training in Tropical Diseases (http://www.emro.who.int/entity/tropical-diseases-research/index.html). This program is unlikely to develop new vaccines or other drugs, but it helps to translate research results into policies and practices that will reduce disease burdens using existing scientific knowledge.

We saw in Table 4.5 that the burden of heart diseases was much greater than the burden of infectious diseases for the Arab fuel-endowed countries, the Arab Mediterranean, Iran, and Turkey. These countries are in a position to benefit greatly from development in rich, temperate countries of new drugs and surgical procedures to treat heart diseases. At the same time, as the lifestyles in these countries come to resemble more the lifestyles in rich, temperate countries, they increasingly develop similar risk factors for heart diseases. Obesity in particular has become a major problem for the Arab fuel-endowed and Mediterranean countries, Iran, and Turkey. Table 4.8 shows obesity rates for all adults and for men and women separately in 2016, the latest year for which data were available at time of writing. Focusing first on the comparison country groups, we see that in

**Table 4.7.** World Pharmaceutical Market, 2014

| Region/Country | Pharmaceutical Sales US$ Billions | Population Millions | Pharmaceutical Sales per Capita (US$) | Share of World Pharmaceutical Market (%) | Share of World Population (%) |
|---|---|---|---|---|---|
| United States | 316 | 326 | 970 | 29 | 5 |
| European Union | 309 | 523 | 592 | 28 | 7 |
| Japan | 106 | 127 | 837 | 10 | 2 |
| China | 99 | 1370 | 72 | 9 | 19 |
| Latin America and the Caribbean | 72 | 621 | 117 | 7 | 9 |
| Sub-Saharan Africa | 13 | 953 | 13 | 1 | 13 |
| Rest of the world | 182 | 3230 | 56 | 17 | 45 |
| Total | 1098 | 7150 | | | |

*Source of data*: International Federation of Pharmaceutical Manufacturers & Associations, *The Pharmaceutical Industry and Global Health: Facts and Figures 2017*, Annex 2, 2017.

non-Arab sub-Saharan Africa the obesity rate for all adults, and especially for men, is substantially below the obesity rates in the other comparison country groups. This is consistent with obesity being a greater problem in richer countries. Turning to the obesity rates for all adults in the countries we study, we see that they are always greater than in the comparison country groups. Finally, Table 4.8 shows that the gaps between the obesity rates for the countries we study and for the comparison country groups are always larger for women than for men. This is especially dramatic when we consider the Arab Mediterranean and Turkey, which have obesity rates for women that are nearly triple the rate in the rest of the non-Arab world and nearly double the rate in Southern Europe.

As we will note in Chapter 6, many of the countries we study subsidize food prices, particularly bread or flour and sugar. This probably contributes to their high rates of adult obesity. We will see in Chapter 5 that women in the countries we study work outside the home to a much lower extent than in the comparison country groups. Insofar as staying home is associated with eating and inactivity, this is one likely reason why obesity in the

**Table 4.8.** Age-Standardized Obesity Rates, 2016
Percent of Population Ages 18 and Over

|  | Both Sexes | Male | Female |
|---|---|---|---|
| Arab sub-Saharan Africa | 13.9 | 8.9 | 18.6 |
| Non-Arab sub-Saharan Africa | 8.9 | 4.4 | 13.2 |
| Arab fuel-endowed countries | 31.1 | 24.9 | 38.3 |
| Non-Arab fuel-endowed countries | 25.5 | 20.2 | 30.7 |
| Iran | 25.8 | 19.3 | 32.2 |
| Arab Mediterranean | 30.2 | 22.1 | 38.2 |
| Rest of non-Arab world | 12.1 | 10.7 | 13.4 |
| Turkey | 32.1 | 24.4 | 39.2 |
| Latin America | 24.2 | 20.1 | 27.9 |
| Southern Europe | 21.8 | 22.1 | 21.4 |

*Notes*: Obesity is defined as body mass index 30 and above, where body mass index equals weight in kilograms divided by square of height in meters. The population-weighted averages for each country group include the countries listed in the Appendix. The excluded countries were missing data.

*Source of data*: http://www.who.int/gho/ncd/risk_factors/overweight_obesity/obesity_adults/en/.

**Figure 4.2.** Egyptians Exercise at a Rooftop Gym
*Source:* Photograph by Sima Diab, "Egyptians Take to the Streets Again, Now in Workout Gear," *The New York Times*. Digital image. https://www.nytimes.com/2016/08/24/world/middleeast/egypt-exercise-fitness-revolution.html?ref=todayspaper&_r=0.

countries we study is an even greater problem for women than for men. The people of the Arab Mediterranean are becoming increasingly aware of the need to change their eating habits and lifestyles. According to the *New York Times* (August 23, 2016), "a fitness craze has taken hold" in Egypt (see Figure 4.2).

---

**Box 4.4**

---

**Health to Education to More Health: A Virtuous Circle?** There is evidence that improvements in health lead to higher educational attainment, and that higher educational attainment leads to improvements in health. Better education and better health are thus mutually reinforcing. This evidence comes from outside the countries we study, but the incentives and mechanisms that produce this virtuous circle should also function in these countries.

> Education and health tend to go together for many reasons, one being that higher income allows individuals to pay for both more schooling and better health care. Showing that health *causes* education or vice-versa is difficult. The strategy used by economists is to find a mechanism that causes health, say, but does not affect education (not even indirectly through income), and then see if the additional health caused by this mechanism predicts greater education. Seema Jayachandran and Adriana Lleras-Muney (2009) found such a mechanism in Sri Lanka. A government expansion of health services caused a sudden drop in the risk of death during childbirth, thereby increasing life expectancy for girls. The greater likelihood that girls would survive long enough to benefit from their educations increased the incentives for their parents to send them to school. Jayachandran and Lleras-Muney found that girls' literacy increased more than boys' after this government health intervention. Turning to the effect of education on health, Lleras-Muney (2005) found a mechanism in the United States that increased education but did not affect health. A number of states increased the age for which school attendance is mandatory. Years of schooling increased in these states, and adults in these states lived longer, probably because their educations helped them to better manage their health care.
>
> Note that the particular government interventions studied in these articles need not be implemented in order for the virtuous circle to work. These interventions were the best for establishing causality, but other government programs may be more effective in increasing educational attainment and health.

## The Demographic Transition

In the countries we study and in other developing countries, progress in control of infectious and parasitic diseases led to a sharp fall in mortality and consequent increase in life expectancy. The reduction in mortality initiated a *demographic transition*: a change from high birth rates (births per thousand population) and high death rates (deaths per thousand population) to low birth rates and low death rates. In the initial phase of the demographic transition, population growth is low because high birth rates are offset by high death rates. In the final phase of the demographic transition, population growth is again low because births per woman have fallen to the replacement level or lower ("replacement fertility" equals 2.1 births per woman). In the intermediate phase, however, death rates have fallen but birth rates have not, leading to accelerated population growth. This intermediate phase is also known as an *incomplete demographic transition*.

The Arab countries are currently in the midst of an incomplete demographic transition. Table 4.9 shows population growth rates in the three Arab worlds compared to their counterparts in the rest of the world from 1970 to 2016, the most recent year for which data are available at time of writing. Arab population growth rates are consistently higher. One way to interpret this finding is that the demographic transitions in the counterparts of the three Arab worlds are more advanced. In this case we should see that births per woman in the three Arab worlds are higher than in their counterparts, but are converging toward them. Table 4.10 is consistent with this expectation. We see in Table 4.10 that in 1970, fertility was uniformly high across the three Arab worlds: from 6.5 to 7.5 births per woman, consistently higher than in the comparison country groups. We also see in Table 4.10 that in each of the three Arab worlds fertility decreased more from 1970 to 2016 than in the comparison country

**Table 4.9.** Population Growth, 1970–2016
Average Annual Growth Rate (Percent)

| | |
|---|---|
| Arab sub-Saharan Africa | 3.1 |
| Non-Arab sub-Saharan Africa | 2.8 |
| Arab fuel-endowed countries | 3.1 |
| Non-Arab fuel-endowed countries | 2.1 |
| Iran | 2.3 |
| Arab Mediterranean | 2.1 |
| Rest of non-Arab world | 1.3 |
| Turkey | 1.8 |
| Latin America | 1.7 |
| Southern Europe | 0.4 |

*Notes*: For each country group the growth of total population is shown, where total population is the sum of the populations of the countries listed in the Appendix. The excluded countries were missing data.

*Source of data*: World Development Indicators.

groups. By 2016, births per woman in Arab sub-Saharan Africa had fallen below the level in non-Arab sub-Saharan Africa. Nevertheless, Arab births per woman in 2016 were above replacement fertility of 2.1 by 2.5 births in Arab sub-Saharan Africa and 0.9 birth in the Arab fuel-endowed countries and the Arab Mediterranean. In contrast, by 2016 Iran (1.7 births per woman) and Turkey (2.1 births per woman) had completed their demographic transitions, as had the rest of the world outside of sub-Saharan Africa.

As a result of the sharp reductions in fertility shown in Table 4.10, the United Nations forecasts that population growth in the countries we study will slow dramatically. Table 4.11 shows the "medium variant" of the United Nations population forecast for the period 2020–2066, which can be compared to the period 1970–2016 in Table 4.9. Population growth for Iran and Turkey is expected to be near zero. Population growth for Arab sub-Saharan Africa, the Arab fuel-endowed countries, and the Arab Mediterranean is expected to decrease by 1.3, 1.9, and 1.1 percentage points, respectively. For Arab sub-Saharan Africa, population growth is forecast to fall slightly below that in non-Arab sub-Saharan Africa, but population growth rates

**Table 4.10.** Births per Woman, 1970 and 2016

|  | 1970 | 2016 | Change 1970–2016 |
| --- | --- | --- | --- |
| Arab sub-Saharan Africa | 7.2 | 4.6 | −2.6 |
| Non-Arab sub-Saharan Africa | 6.8 | 4.9 | −1.9 |
| Arab fuel-endowed countries | 7.5 | 3.0 | −4.5 |
| Non-Arab fuel-endowed countries | 5.8 | 1.8 | −3.9 |
| Iran | 6.4 | 1.7 | −4.8 |
| Arab Mediterranean | 6.5 | 3.0 | −3.5 |
| Rest of non-Arab world | 4.6 | 2.0 | −2.6 |
| Turkey | 5.6 | 2.1 | −3.6 |
| Latin America | 5.4 | 2.0 | −3.3 |
| Southern Europe | 2.6 | 1.3 | −1.2 |

*Notes*: Due to rounding errors, some "change" column figures may appear to be inconsistent with the other figures in corresponding table rows. The population-weighted averages for each country group include the countries listed in the Appendix. The excluded countries were missing data.

*Source of data*: World Development Indicators.

for the Arab fuel-endowed countries and the Arab Mediterranean are forecast to remain substantially above those in the comparison groups of countries. Nevertheless, slower population growth in the Arab fuel-endowed countries and Arab Mediterranean will sharply change their demographic futures. Using the population growth rates in Table 4.9, the populations of the Arab fuel-endowed countries and the Arab Mediterranean will double every 22 and 33 years, respectively; whereas using the population growth rates in Table 4.11 will lengthen the doubling period to 58 and nearly 70 years, respectively.

The cause of the fall in death rates during the demographic transition is clear, but what is the cause of the fall in birth rates? There are many hypotheses. The simplest is that the fall in death rates itself, particularly the fall in infant and child mortality, causes the fall in birth rates, with some delay. According to this hypothesis, parents have in mind a certain "target family size"—a number of children they want to see live to adulthood. When mortality is high, they need to have many births to achieve this target, but when mortality is low, they need to have few births to achieve it. The delay occurs because one or more generations are required for people to adjust fully to

Table 4.11. United Nations Forecast Population Growth, 2020–2066
Average Annual Growth Rate (Percent)

| | |
|---|---|
| Arab sub-Saharan Africa | 1.8 |
| Non-Arab sub-Saharan Africa | 2.1 |
| Arab fuel-endowed countries | 1.2 |
| Non-Arab fuel-endowed countries | 0.3 |
| Iran | 0.1 |
| Arab Mediterranean | 1.0 |
| Rest of non-Arab world | 0.2 |
| Turkey | 0.3 |
| Latin America | 0.4 |
| Southern Europe | -0.3 |

*Notes*: The "medium variant" of the United Nations forecast is used. For each country group the growth of total population is shown, where total population is the sum of the populations of the countries listed in the Appendix. The excluded countries were missing data.

*Source of data*: https://esa.un.org/unpd/wpp/.

the lower infant and child mortality. A second hypothesis is that the availability of new drugs and improved health care that reduced death rates also reduced the cost and increased the quality of contraception. A third hypothesis is that socioeconomic changes that occur coincident with the fall in death rates reduce the benefits and raise the costs of having children. Urbanization means children cannot help around the family farm, and child labor laws prevent children from working for wages. Children are more likely to receive secondary or tertiary education, which imposes both monetary and time costs on parents. Typically the main responsibility for child care continues to fall on women, but the time of women becomes more expensive, both because they receive more education and because they work more outside the home.

Djavad Salehi-Isfahani (2016) evaluated the second hypothesis using a difference-in-difference study of a contraception program in rural Iran. Health clinics were constructed and family planning was promoted starting in 1989. Table 4.10 shows that between 1970 and 2016 the number of births per woman in Iran fell from 6.4 to 1.7, slightly more than the decrease of 4.5 for the population-weighted average of Arab fuel-endowed countries. Figure 4.3 shows that most of this fall occurred starting in the mid-1980s.

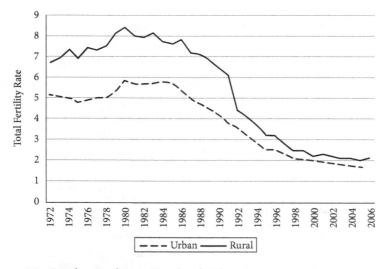

**Figure 4.3.** Fertility Decline in Rural and Urban Iran
Source: Djavad Salehi-Isfahani, "Family Planning and Female Empowerment in Iran," in *Women, Work and Welfare in the Middle East and North Africa*, ed. Nadereh Chamlou and Massoud Karshenas (London: Imperial College Press, 2016).

At that time rural fertility was about two births per woman higher than urban fertility, which is consistent with higher benefits to farmers of having children. The timing of the fall in fertility, and the near-elimination of the rural-urban difference, suggest that the contraception program might have been a major cause. However, the difference-in-difference analysis of Salehi-Isfahani does not support that conclusion. Table 4.12 shows the ratio of children aged zero to four to women aged fifteen to forty-nine, the child-woman ratio (CWR), for program (treatment) villages and non-program (control) villages in 1986 and 1996. The control villages did not have a health clinic in 1986 or 1996, and the treatment villages did not have a health clinic in 1986 but had acquired one by 1996. The CWR is a good measure of recent fertility. The difference column shows that the CWR fell by 460 children per 1,000 women in the treatment villages and 425 children per 1,000 women in the control villages, for a difference-in-differences of only 35 children per 1,000 women, less than 8 percent of the decrease in the CWR in the treatment villages.

Although we are not aware of similar studies for the Arab fuel-endowed countries or the Arab Mediterranean countries (or Turkey), Salehi-Isfahani's results for Iran suggest that improved access to contraception is only a small part of the explanation for the steep decline in fertility in these countries. Hypotheses based on target family size and coincident socioeconomic changes would therefore have to provide most of the explanation. Unfortunately, the contributions made by these factors are extraordinarily difficult to quantify.

When a country experiences a demographic transition, the age structure of its population changes dramatically. The fall in mortality rates that begins the demographic transition most strongly affects infants and children,

Table 4.12. Ratio of Children Aged 0–4 to Women Aged 15–49, Iran

|  | 1986 | 1996 | Difference over Time |
|---|---|---|---|
| Comparison villages | 1.001 | 0.576 | -0.425 |
| Program villages | 0.964 | 0.503 | -0.460 |
| Difference between villages | -0.038 | -0.073 | -0.035 |

*Source*: Salehi-Isfahani (2016), table 18.1.

causing the population share of the young to increase. The next stage in the demographic transition is a fall in birth rates, leaving a youth "bulge" from past high birth rates. As this youth bulge ages into adulthood, the population share of the young decreases. When the youth bulge reaches retirement age, the population share of working-age adults decreases. Table 4.13 shows the changes in age structure that occurred in the three Arab worlds, Iran, Turkey, and the comparison country groups from 1970 to 2016, the most recent year for which data were available at time of writing. Age structure is expressed in terms of "dependency ratios." The youth dependency ratio is the ratio of population younger than fifteen to population ages fifteen to sixty-four, and the overall dependency ratio is the ratio of population younger than fifteen or older than sixty-four to population ages fifteen to sixty-four. The term "dependency ratio" is used because the young and the old depend on working-age adults to support them.

**Table 4.13.** Youth and Overall Dependency Ratios

|  | Youth Dependency Ratio |  |  | Overall Dependency Ratio |  |  |
|---|---|---|---|---|---|---|
|  | 1970 | 2016 | Change 1970–2016 | 1970 | 2016 | Change 1970–2016 |
| Arab sub-Saharan Africa | 87.8 | 75.6 | −12.2 | 93.6 | 81.3 | −12.3 |
| Non-Arab sub-Saharan Africa | 83.6 | 80.4 | −3.2 | 89.2 | 86.0 | −3.2 |
| Arab fuel-endowed countries | 89.6 | 46.2 | −43.4 | 96.6 | 52.1 | −44.5 |
| Non-Arab fuel-endowed countries | 81.6 | 35.4 | −46.1 | 88.8 | 44.3 | −44.5 |
| Iran | 83.8 | 33.3 | −50.5 | 90.1 | 40.6 | −49.5 |
| Arab Mediterranean | 85.9 | 51.2 | −34.6 | 93.4 | 60.0 | −33.4 |
| Rest of non-Arab world | 64.8 | 34.4 | −30.4 | 74.2 | 48.8 | −25.5 |
| Turkey | 76.2 | 37.9 | −38.3 | 83.5 | 49.8 | −33.7 |
| Latin America | 79.8 | 37.5 | −42.3 | 87.2 | 49.3 | −37.9 |
| Southern Europe | 41.5 | 21.8 | −19.7 | 57.9 | 54.4 | −3.5 |

Notes: Youth dependency ratio = ratio of population younger than 15 to population ages 15–64. Overall dependency ratio = ratio of population younger than 15 or older than 64 to population ages 15–64. Both ratios are multiplied by 100. Due to rounding errors, some "change" column figures may appear to be inconsistent with the other figures in corresponding table rows. The population-weighted averages for each country group include the countries listed in the Appendix. The excluded countries were missing data.

Source of data: World Development Indicators.

In sub-Saharan Africa, the decline in the population share of the young has just started. The youth dependency ratios in 2016 show that in Arab sub-Saharan Africa there are more than three youths for every four working-age adults, and in non-Arab sub-Saharan Africa there are more than four youths for every five working-age adults. The change in the youth dependency ratios from 1970 to 2016 shows that the demographic transition has made somewhat more progress in Arab sub-Saharan Africa than in non-Arab sub-Saharan Africa. The fact that the change in overall dependency ratios is almost identical to the change in youth dependency ratios shows that the youth bulge has not yet reached retirement age.

Outside of sub-Saharan Africa fertility rates have fallen much further, as we saw in Table 4.10, and the demographic transition has made much more progress. However, progress in the Arab fuel-endowed countries and the Arab Mediterranean has been less than in Iran, Turkey, or the comparison country groups. The youth dependency ratios in 2016 show that in the Arab fuel-endowed countries and the Arab Mediterranean there is roughly one youth for every two working-age adults, whereas the ratios are closer to one to three for Iran, Turkey, and the comparison country groups other than Southern Europe. Southern Europe is at the end of the demographic transition. Its youth bulge has aged into retirement, and its overall dependency ratio is more than double its youth dependency ratio. As a result, the overall dependency ratio for Southern Europe has almost stopped falling.

The decrease in the youth and overall dependency ratios caused by the aging of the youth bulge before it reaches retirement can yield a "demographic dividend." A weak version of the demographic dividend hypothesis is that if GDP per worker (productivity) remains constant, the increase in working-age adults (hence workers) per capita mechanically increases GDP per capita, boosting economic growth. A stronger version of the demographic dividend hypothesis is that the higher ratio of working to dependent population increases growth by both raising savings rates and increasing demand for investment in housing and infrastructure. David Bloom and Jeffrey Williamson (1998) attribute to the demographic dividend as much as one-third of per capita GDP growth in East Asia (China, Japan, South Korea, Singapore, and Taiwan) during the period 1965–1990. It is still too early to make a thorough assessment of the contribution of the demographic dividend, if any, to economic growth in the Arab world, Iran, or Turkey.

# 5
# Gender Gaps

## Introduction

The sharp fall in fertility documented in the previous chapter has made it possible for women in the Arab world, Iran, and Turkey to transform their lives by closing the "gender gaps"—in education, labor force participation, and health—between themselves and men. In the section titled "Education," we will see that, except in the sub-Saharan African Arab countries, school enrollment of girls has caught up to that of boys, and in some countries women outnumber men at the university level. In the section titled "Labor Force Participation," however, we will see that the gap between labor force participation of women and men has barely closed in most of the countries we study, and in all of them labor force participation of women remains far below the levels in the comparison groups of countries. Given the positive effect of education on health noted in Box 4.4, it seems likely that the increased education of women in the Arab countries, Iran, and Turkey is contributing to raising healthier and better educated children, but much less to economic growth directly.

The most extreme manifestation of gender inequality is lower female survival rates. These give rise to the phenomenon of "missing women" in many developing countries, where the ratio of women to men in the population is substantially below the level that would be expected in the absence of discrimination. We will see in the section of this chapter titled "Health" that this phenomenon is present in the Arab world, Iran, and Turkey, though it is not as prominent as in some countries, notably China and India. We will also cover two issues that are specific to the health of girls and women: female genital mutilation and domestic violence. We will see that female genital mutilation is associated much more strongly with geography than culture or language, and some Arab countries are in the affected geographic area. The data on domestic violence are more scarce, so that it is difficult to compare most of the countries we study to the rest of the world. Data are available for four Arab Mediterranean countries and Turkey, however. For all of these countries except Egypt, domestic violence is at or below the level for Latin America though well above the level for Southern Europe. Domestic violence in Egypt is much higher and close to the level for non-Arab sub-Saharan Africa.

## Education

We first examine the gender gap in education. From the list of possible education indicators, we choose the ratio of female to male school enrollment, which the World Bank calls the "gender parity index." This ratio is available separately at the primary, secondary, and tertiary levels of education. In the absence of educational discrimination against girls, we expect the ratio of female to male enrollment to be very close to one at the primary and secondary levels of schooling. It is less clear what ratio to expect at the tertiary level. At the current time women tend to attend college more than men in most countries, yielding a ratio above one, but there is no specific ratio above one that indicates discrimination is absent. By comparing past to present school enrollment ratios we can also see how educational discrimination has changed over time. This is preferable to comparing measures of educational attainment between women and men, such as years of schooling or literacy. Lower educational attainment of women than men reflects a mix of past discrimination and current discrimination without allowing us to distinguish between the two. Though we concentrate on school enrollment, we should keep in mind that equal treatment regarding enrollment does not guarantee that girls and women are being treated equally in other aspects of their educational experiences.

Table 5.1 shows the ratios of female to male enrollment for all three levels of schooling for the most recent year for which data are available at time of writing, usually 2016, and the oldest year for which data are available, usually 1971. We see immediately that in the past, educational discrimination against girls at the primary and secondary levels was stronger in the three Arab worlds, Iran, and Turkey than in the comparison groups of countries. In Arab sub-Saharan Africa, roughly two girls attended primary school for every five boys in 1971, compared to roughly three girls for every five boys in non-Arab sub-Saharan Africa. In Turkey, two girls attended secondary school for every five boys in 1971, compared to more than four girls for every five boys in Latin America and Southern Europe. We also see from Table 5.1 that the three Arab worlds, Iran, and Turkey increased their

**Table 5.1.** Gender Parity in Primary, Secondary, and Tertiary Education Ratio of Female to Male School Enrollment

|  | Primary 1971 | Primary 2016 | Change 1971–2016 | Secondary 1971 | Secondary 2016 | Change 1971–2016 | Tertiary 1971 | Tertiary 2016 | Change 1971–2016 |
|---|---|---|---|---|---|---|---|---|---|
| Arab sub-Saharan Africa | 0.41 | 1.02 | 0.60 | 0.36 | 0.93 | 0.58 |  | 0.79 |  |
| Non-Arab sub-Saharan Africa | 0.62 | 0.96 | 0.34 | 0.44 | 0.86 | 0.42 |  | 0.67 |  |
| Arab fuel-endowed countries | 0.62 | 0.97 | 0.35 | 0.43 | 1.02 | 0.59 | 0.31 | 1.53 | 1.21 |
| Non-Arab fuel-endowed countries | 0.74 | 1.03 | 0.29 | 0.71 | 1.02 | 0.31 | 0.37 | 0.95 | 0.57 |
| Iran | 0.6 | 1.1 | 0.5 | 0.5 | 1.0 | 0.5 | 0.4 | 0.9 | 0.5 |
| Arab Mediterranean | 0.63 | 0.98 | 0.36 | 0.47 | 0.97 | 0.50 | 0.32 | 1.07 | 0.75 |
| Rest of non-Arab world | 0.78 | 1.04 | 0.26 | 0.65 | 1.01 | 0.36 | 0.48 | 1.11 | 0.63 |
| Turkey | 0.7 | 1.0 | 0.3 | 0.4 | 1.0 | 0.6 | 0.2 | 0.9 | 0.7 |
| Latin America | 0.96 | 0.99 | 0.03 | 0.88 | 1.05 | 0.17 | 0.49 | 1.21 | 0.72 |
| Southern Europe | 1.00 | 1.00 | 0.00 | 0.81 | 0.98 | 0.17 | 0.54 | 1.25 | 0.71 |

*Notes:* 1971 = earliest year in period 1971–1976; 2016 = latest year in period 2011–2016. 1971 omitted for tertiary education in sub-Saharan Africa because data are missing for all Arab sub-Saharan African countries. Due to rounding errors, some "change" column figures may appear to be inconsistent with the other figures in corresponding table rows. The population-weighted averages for each country group include the countries listed in the Appendix. The excluded countries were missing data.

*Source of data*: World Development Indicators.

enrollment of girls relative to boys at the primary and secondary levels from 1971 to 2016 more than did the comparison groups of countries. As a result, by 2016 enrollment discrimination against girls was nearly gone at the primary and secondary levels in the countries we study. In Iran and Turkey enrollment ratios are at or above one. For the Arab fuel-endowed countries, enrollment ratios are above one at the secondary level and just below one at the primary level, and for the Arab Mediterranean enrollment ratios are just below one at both the primary and secondary levels. Only at the secondary level in Arab sub-Saharan Africa is the enrollment ratio substantially below one, though still higher than in the rest of sub-Saharan Africa.

Assessing the state of educational discrimination at the tertiary level in the three Arab worlds, Iran, and Turkey is more complex. For Arab sub-Saharan Africa we cannot compare past to current discrimination due to lack of data. In 2016 in Arab sub-Saharan Africa there were roughly four women enrolled in college for every five men, compared to two women for every three men in non-Arab sub-Saharan Africa. Table 5.1 shows that the Arab fuel-endowed countries, the Arab Mediterranean, and Turkey all had lower ratios of female to male enrollment at the tertiary level in 1971 than the comparison groups of countries. By 2016 there were roughly three women enrolled in college for every two men in the Arab fuel-endowed countries, the highest ratio in Table 5.1. In the Arab Mediterranean in 2016 the ratio of female to male enrollment was substantially above one at the tertiary level, but not as high as in the comparison groups of countries. The ratios in Iran and Turkey in 2016 were both substantially below one. A tentative assessment is that enrollment discrimination against women remains at the tertiary level in Arab sub-Saharan Africa, Iran, and Turkey, but is clearly gone in the Arab fuel-endowed countries and nearly or completely gone in the Arab Mediterranean.

To summarize, in the early 1970s educational discrimination against girls and women at all three levels of schooling was clearly stronger in the countries we study than in the rest of the world, but over the next four and a half decades that discrimination was largely eliminated. A small indication of discrimination remains at the primary level for the Arab fuel-endowed countries and the Arab Mediterranean. At the secondary level there is again a small indication of discrimination for the Arab Mediterranean, and more substantial discrimination in Arab sub-Saharan Africa, though less than in the rest of sub-Saharan Africa. The record at the tertiary level is the most varied. Given the powerful trends shown in Table 5.1, one can predict the disappearance of the remaining vestiges of enrollment discrimination in the Arab fuel-endowed countries, Arab Mediterranean, Iran, and Turkey in the near future. Elimination of enrollment discrimination in Arab sub-Saharan Africa (and the rest of sub-Saharan Africa) may take more time.

## Labor Force Participation

Labor force participation is defined as work producing goods and services that are counted in GDP or GNI by the National Income and Product Accounts. Not counted is work on home-produced services such as cooking, cleaning, or care of one's own children. It follows that, when we discuss the shares of women and men that participate in the labor force, it is reasonably accurate to think of these as the shares of women and men that work outside the home.

Table 5.2 shows the percentages of men and women, age fifteen and above, who participate in the labor force. We will call the difference between these percentages the gender gap in labor force participation. We examine both the current gender gaps in the countries we study and how these gender gaps have been changing over time. The most recent year for which data are available at time of writing is 2016, and the oldest year is 1990 (still older data are available, but for only a few of the countries we study).

We see from Table 5.2 that in both 1990 and 2016 the gender gaps in labor force participation in all three Arab worlds and in Iran and Turkey exceed the gender gaps in the comparison country groups. The gender gaps for Arab sub-Saharan Africa and the Arab Mediterranean exceed the gender gaps in their comparison country groups by especially large margins. Between 1990 and 2016 the labor force participation gender gaps decreased for all three Arab worlds, Iran, and Turkey, but the gender gaps in the comparison country groups usually decreased more. The contrast with education gender gaps is striking: As we saw in Table 5.1, these always decreased more over time in the countries we study than in the comparison country groups.

Closer examination of Table 5.2 shows that the reason the gender gaps in the countries we study are larger than in the comparison country groups is lower female labor force participation rather than higher male labor force participation. The point is best illustrated by sub-Saharan Africa. In 2016, male labor force participation in Arab sub-Saharan Africa was 3.9 percentage

**Table 5.2.** Labor Force Participation, Age 15+, Male and Female

| | 1990 | | | 2016 | | | Change 1990–2016 | | |
|---|---|---|---|---|---|---|---|---|---|
| | Male | Female | Difference | Male | Female | Difference | Male | Female | Difference |
| Arab sub-Saharan Africa | 75.5 | 21.8 | 53.7 | 70.2 | 18.1 | 52.1 | -5.3 | -3.7 | -1.5 |
| Non-Arab sub-Saharan Africa | 77.0 | 62.8 | 14.2 | 74.1 | 65.4 | 8.8 | -2.8 | 2.6 | -5.4 |
| Arab fuel-endowed countries | 77.9 | 13.6 | 64.2 | 76.0 | 22.5 | 53.6 | -1.8 | 8.9 | -10.7 |
| Non-Arab fuel-endowed countries | 80.9 | 20.5 | 60.4 | 73.0 | 28.3 | 44.7 | -7.9 | 7.8 | -15.7 |
| Iran | 81.8 | 9.8 | 72.0 | 71.5 | 17.1 | 54.4 | -10.3 | 7.3 | -17.6 |
| Arab Mediterranean | 75.5 | 21.8 | 53.7 | 72.6 | 21.4 | 51.3 | -2.9 | -0.4 | -2.5 |
| Rest of non-Arab world | 80.8 | 51.2 | 29.5 | 75.8 | 47.8 | 28.0 | -4.9 | -3.4 | -1.5 |
| Turkey | 80.8 | 34.0 | 46.8 | 72.2 | 32.5 | 39.7 | -8.6 | -1.5 | -7.1 |
| Latin America | 81.3 | 39.2 | 42.1 | 77.8 | 51.4 | 26.4 | -3.5 | 12.2 | -15.7 |
| Southern Europe | 67.7 | 36.0 | 31.7 | 61.4 | 45.8 | 15.5 | -6.3 | 9.9 | -16.2 |

*Notes:* The underlying data are International Labour Organization estimates based mainly on nationally representative labor force surveys. Due to rounding errors, some "change" or "difference" column figures may appear to be inconsistent with the other figures in corresponding table rows. The population-weighted averages for each country group include the countries listed in the Appendix. The excluded countries were missing data.

*Source of data:* World Development Indicators.

points *lower* than in non-Arab sub-Saharan Africa, but female labor force participation was 47.3 percentage points lower, yielding an Arab gender gap that was 43.4 percentage points (47.3 − 3.9) higher than the non-Arab gender gap. In general, male participation rates are relatively similar across countries. In 2016 in Table 5.2, male labor force participation rates are all in a range from 70 to 78 percent, except for Southern Europe.

There are two reasons for both male and female labor force participation to fall from 1990 to 2016. First, the demographic transition we discussed in the previous chapter is gradually increasing the share of the population above retirement age, thereby reducing the shares of men and women age fifteen and above that are working. Second, school enrollment at the secondary and tertiary levels has been increasing. This means more men and women age fifteen and above are in school instead of in the labor force. We see in Table 5.2 that male labor force participation between 1990 and 2016 has decreased worldwide, but female labor force participation has decreased less or even increased despite the greater increases in female school enrollment. Apparently a worldwide trend for women to work more outside the home has dominated the impacts on labor force participation of retirement and school enrollment, and indeed many women going to high school and college do so with the intention of entering the labor force and earning more than they would have with only primary education.

As we saw in Table 5.1, female school enrollment has been increasing relative to male school enrollment more in the countries we study than in the rest of the world, especially at the secondary level. This would tend to reduce female, relative to male, labor force participation, and probably caused the decreases in labor force participation gender gaps in the countries we study to be smaller relative to the comparison country groups than they otherwise would have been. Moreover, increases in female labor force participation from 1990 to 2016 have been large in the Arab fuel-endowed countries and Iran, so at least some of the countries we study have been affected by the worldwide trend for women to work more outside the home. Nevertheless, the fact remains that female labor force participation rates in the three Arab worlds, Iran, and Turkey are all below the rates in the comparison country groups.

One possible explanation for the persistently low female labor force participation rates in the countries we study is that all of them are predominantly Muslim. This explanation seems plausible in light of historic practices of secluding women in their homes that are associated with Islam, notably the *harem* and *purdah*. One way to check this hypothesis is to compare female labor force participation in the countries we study to other Muslim-majority countries, and to compare both the countries we study and other Muslim-majority countries to non-Muslim majority countries. If female labor force participation in other Muslim-majority countries is also very low compared to non-Muslim majority countries, it would be evidence that Islam is the main reason for low female labor force participation in the countries we study.

Table 5.3 shows 2016 population-weighted averages of labor force participation rates for all the countries we study, all other Muslim-majority countries, and all non-Muslim majority countries. The data are the same as in the 2016 columns of Table 5.2, but for different country groupings. The largest countries in the group of other Muslim-majority countries are Bangladesh, Indonesia, and Pakistan. We see that women participate in the labor force in other Muslim-majority countries at nearly double the rate as in the countries we study, though still at a rate roughly ten percentage points lower than in the non-Muslim majority countries. The other Muslim-majority countries also have a male labor force participation rate that is substantially higher than in the countries we study, so their gender gap in labor force participation is a bit closer to that in the countries we study than in the non-Muslim majority countries.

The evidence in Table 5.3 supports the view that Islam explains part but not all of the low female labor force participation in the countries we study. This evidence is consistent with research by Jen'nan Read (2004) on

**Table 5.3.** Labor Force Participation, Age 15+, Male and Female, 2016

|  | Male | Female | Difference |
| --- | --- | --- | --- |
| Arab countries, Iran, and Turkey | 72.9 | 22.1 | 50.8 |
| Other Muslim-majority countries | 80.5 | 42.0 | 38.4 |
| Non-Muslim majority countries | 74.9 | 51.8 | 23.2 |

*Notes*: The underlying data are International Labour Organization estimates based mainly on nationally representative labor force surveys. Due to rounding errors, some "difference" column figures may appear to be inconsistent with the other figures in corresponding table rows. The population-weighted averages for each country group include the countries listed in the Appendix. The excluded countries were missing data.

*Source of data for labor force participation*: World Development Indicators.

*Source of data for Muslim-majority status in 2010*: http://www.pewforum.org/2015/04/02/religious-projection-table/2010/number/all/.

Arab-American women, more of whom are Christian than Muslim. Read finds that the labor force participation rate of Arab-American women is unusually low for both Christians and Muslims—that is, Muslim religious identification is not associated with lower work outside the home, keeping all other characteristics of the women equal. In contrast, marriage to a husband of Arab descent is associated with significantly lower labor force participation, which may indicate that the woman has more traditional values or that she is subject to greater pressure to stay at home.

If low female relative to male labor force participation can be explained only in part by the fact that the countries we study are predominantly Muslim, then we need to search for other explanations. Tables 4.10, 5.1, and 5.2 show that women in the countries we study are having fewer children and have greatly increased their levels of education, yet have mostly not increased the extent to which they work outside their homes. It may be that these women are obtaining education less to make themselves valuable in the workplace and more to make themselves valuable as wives and as mothers of fewer but better-educated and healthier children. The question is whether this is their choice or whether it is being forced upon them, either by workplace discrimination or by social pressure.

We will examine this question for the Arab countries, which have been more thoroughly studied in this regard, though we can guess that much of the discussion will apply to Iran and Turkey as well. Arab countries have laws prohibiting discrimination against women in the workplace that look more or less like laws in other countries (UN Development Fund for Women 2004, p. 227), so discrimination would have to be established *de facto* rather than *de jure*, requiring careful studies that to our knowledge have not been done. Now that Saudi Arabia has finally allowed women to drive, women in all Arab countries are legally as free to commute to work as are men. Our sense is that the presence of women in the workplace is not objectionable in most of Arab society, but also that the expectation that married women should be financially supported by their husbands and should stay home to care for their children remains very strong.

A study of female employment in manufacturing firms in eight Arab countries—Algeria, Egypt, Jordan, Lebanon, Morocco, Oman, Syria, and Yemen—provides indirect evidence for the existence of *de facto* discrimination. Ali Fakih and Pascal Ghazalian (2015) find that an increase in foreign ownership is associated with an increase in the proportion of female workers in total firm employment. They explain, "multinational enterprises, particularly those headquartered in countries with higher records of national gender equality than those prevailing in MENA countries, are arguably more resistant to the implications of social gender inequality in MENA countries. Then, they would transfer this relative immunity into the business culture and hiring practices of their affiliated firms in MENA countries, resulting in higher female employment rates" (p. 44).

Nadereh Chamlou, Silvia Muzi, and Hanane Ahmed (2016) report survey results from three Arab capital cities: Amman, Jordan; Cairo, Egypt; and Sana'a, Yemen. Their findings support the hypothesis that pressure to stay home is felt more strongly by married than single women. Specifically, they find that being married has a much stronger effect on women staying home than does the presence of children under age six, which is the opposite of the typical result from studies of developed countries. Married women are, on average and other things being equal, from 13 percent to 24 percent less likely to participate in the labor market than are single women across the three cities. Chamlou, Muzi, and Ahmed also collected data on attitudes of men and women regarding women working outside the home. These results are shown in Figure 5.1. We see that in all three cities more than 60 percent of men and more than 75 percent of women state that women working outside the home is acceptable. We also see that men are much more likely than women to say that women working outside the home is acceptable "under no circumstances." This might reflect the pressure men feel to be the sole breadwinner, or a more general male desire to control women.

Using data from a survey of urban Moroccan women, Ragui Assaad and Sami Zouari (2003) find that married women who work outside the home are much more likely to work in the public than the private sector. By way of explanation, they state, "Although Moroccan law in theory provides for paid and unpaid maternity leaves in all sectors, these are often only respected in the public sector. Mothers in that sector can also benefit from child care services and can generally work significantly shorter hours than in the private sector" (p. 12). Many Arab countries, and Iran, began attempts to shrink the public sector in the 1980s. Data assembled by the World Bank (2004, p. 100) show that Iran and Jordan sharply reduced their public sector shares of female employment from 1986 to 2000 and from 1987 to 1996, respectively. Algeria (1987–1990), Egypt (1988–1998), Morocco (1991–1999), and Tunisia (1997–2001) all slightly reduced their public sector shares of female employment, whereas Syria (1984–1991) shows a slight increase. The

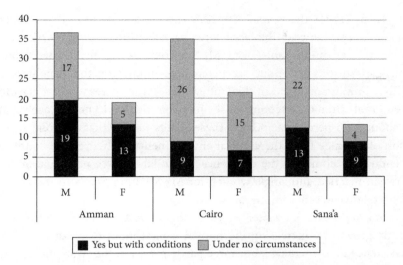

**Figure 5.1.** Non-Acceptance of the Idea of Women Working Outside the Home (Percent)

*Notes:* M = male; F = female; respondents ages fifteen to sixty-four.

*Source:* Nadereh Chamlou, Silvia Muzi, and Hanane Ahmed, "The Determinants of Female Labor Force Participation in the MENA Region," in *Women, Work and Welfare in the Middle East and North Africa*, ed. Nadereh Chamlou and Massoud Karshenas (London: Imperial College Press, 2016).

results of Assaad and Zouari suggest that these policies may have worked against closing the gender gap in labor force participation.

Lisa Anderson, former president of the American University of Cairo, believes that there is a boom in telecommuting by professional Arab women who want to reconcile their careers with their roles as wives and mothers. This hypothesis is consistent with recent research by Lisa Dettling (2017) for the United States. She finds that the introduction of high-speed home Internet led to an increase in labor market participation by married women, especially college-educated women with children, but had no effect on men or single women. Research is needed to reveal how common this practice might be in Arab countries, and whether the resulting increase in female labor market participation is being captured by labor force participation statistics.

The gap in labor force participation between married and single women has been found to erode among MENA immigrants to the United States more than among other immigrants. Calculations by the World Bank

(2013c, p. 71) for the years 2000–2009 show a gap of more than 30 percentage points between the labor force participation rates of married and single women immigrants from MENA countries to the United States. This gap shrinks to about six percentage points for the daughters of MENA immigrants born in the United States. The corresponding gaps for immigrants from other countries shrink from roughly 13 percentage points to about eight percentage points. These results suggest that only one generation of distance from the cultural environments of their origin countries is enough to eliminate the difference in the labor force participation gap between married and single women for MENA immigrants to the United States relative to other immigrants.

From the previous chapter we recall that education contributes to economic growth by increasing the human capital input to production. The persistence of low female labor force participation in the Arab world, Iran, and Turkey means that these countries are missing most of the potential contribution to marketed output from higher female educational attainment. It should be mentioned, however, that there is strong evidence that more educated mothers raise more educated and healthier children (see, e.g., the 2006 survey by Michael Grossman). More educated Arab, Iranian, and Turkish women who do not work outside the home are not contributing their human capital to current marketed production, but they are probably increasing the human capital of the next generation.

## Health

The ultimate gender gap is in survival. Measurement of this gender gap, however, is difficult. Let us suppose, counterfactually, that males and females are born in equal numbers, and that males and females have equal chances of survival thereafter, given equal health care. We could then measure the gender gap in survival by the ratio of males to females in the population—the sex ratio, for short. The farther is the sex ratio above one, the larger is the gender gap in survival.

In reality, more boys are born than girls. The sex ratio at birth varies between countries due to environmental and genetic factors, but is always above one. In the United States the sex ratio at birth is approximately 1.05. After birth, girls are more likely to survive than boys and women are more likely to survive than men, given equal health care. The older is a population, the less important is the sex ratio at birth and the more important is the tendency for females to survive more than males, so we expect an older population to have a lower sex ratio than a younger population. To measure the gender gap in survival, then, we cannot simply compare the actual sex ratio to one, but must compare it to the expected sex ratio based on the age structure of the population.

Stephan Klasen and Claudia Wink (2003) computed expected sex ratios around the year 2000 for countries and regions in which actual sex ratios were unusually high, or had been unusually high in earlier years. Their results are shown in Table 5.4. The gender gaps in survival can then be measured by the differences between the actual sex ratios and the expected sex ratios. However, Klasen and Wink followed a more popular way to express the gender gap, which had been developed by the Nobel Prize-winning economist Amartya Sen (1992). Sen coined the term "missing women" for the difference between the expected number of women in a population and the actual number of women. Klasen and Wink therefore used their results to estimate the number of missing women for the countries and regions for which they computed expected sex ratios. To obtain the expected number of women column in Table 5.4, they multiplied the actual number of women by the actual sex ratio and divided by the expected sex ratio. The percentage of missing women is then calculated as 100(expected women − actual women) ÷ (actual women). It can be shown that if the expected sex ratio were one, the ratio of missing to actual women would exactly equal the difference between the actual sex ratio and the expected sex ratio.

The last column of Table 5.4 shows that the percentages of missing women are highest in Afghanistan, China, India, and Pakistan. The data for Afghanistan are considered unreliable, so most attention has been focused on China, India, and Pakistan, with percentages of missing women equal to 6.7, 7.9, and 7.8, respectively. Among the countries we study for which separate data are available, the percentage of missing women ranges from a high of 4.5 for Egypt to a low of 1.2 for Algeria. (Many Arab countries for which we do not have separate data are grouped into West Asia along with non-Arab countries.)

Two causes for the gender gap in survival that manifests itself in missing women have been well documented, though not for the countries we study. One is neglect of girls relative to boys, especially in infancy and early childhood. Most studies find that neglect of health care for girls contributes more to reducing their survival than neglect of their nutrition. An

**Table 5.4.** Number and Percent of Women Who Are "Missing," Circa 2000

| | Year | Actual Number of Women | Actual Sex Ratio | Expected Sex Ratio at Birth | Expected Sex Ratio | Expected Number of Women | Missing Women | Percent Missing |
|---|---|---|---|---|---|---|---|---|
| China | 2000 | 612.3 | 1.067 | 1.050 | 1.001 | 653.2 | 40.9 | 6.7 |
| Taiwan | 1999 | 10.8 | 1.049 | 1.052 | 1.002 | 11.3 | 0.5 | 4.7 |
| South Korea | 1995 | 22.2 | 1.008 | 1.047 | 1.000 | 22.4 | 0.2 | 0.7 |
| India | 2001 | 495.7 | 1.072 | 1.039 | 0.993 | 534.8 | 39.1 | 7.9 |
| Pakistan | 1998 | 62.7 | 1.081 | 1.042 | 1.003 | 67.6 | 4.9 | 7.8 |
| Bangladesh. | 2001 | 63.4 | 1.038 | 1.040 | 0.996 | 66.1 | 2.7 | 4.2 |
| Nepal | 2001 | 11.6 | 0.997 | 1.037 | 0.992 | 11.7 | 0.1 | 0.5 |
| Sri Lanka | 1991 | 8.6 | 1.005 | 1.052 | 1.006 | 8.6 | 0.0 | 0.0 |
| West Asia of which: | 2000 | 92.0 | 1.043 | 1.042 | 1.002 | 95.8 | 3.8 | 4.2 |
| Turkey | 1990 | 27.9 | 1.027 | 1.047 | 1.003 | 28.5 | 0.7 | 2.4 |
| Syria | 1994 | 6.7 | 1.047 | 1.048 | 1.016 | 6.9 | 0.2 | 3.1 |
| Afghanistan | 2000 | 11.1 | 1.054 | 1.024 | 0.964 | 12.1 | 1.0 | 9.3 |
| Iran | 1996 | 29.5 | 1.033 | 1.039 | 0.996 | 30.6 | 1.1 | 3.7 |
| Egypt | 1996 | 29.0 | 1.048 | 1.044 | 1.003 | 30.3 | 1.3 | 4.5 |
| Algeria | 1998 | 14.5 | 1.018 | 1.043 | 1.005 | 14.7 | 0.2 | 1.2 |
| Tunisia | 1994 | 4.3 | 1.021 | 1.043 | 1.000 | 4.4 | 0.1 | 2.1 |
| Sub-Saharan Africa | 2000 | 307.0 | 0.987 | 1.017 | 0.970 | 312.5 | 5.5 | 1.8 |

*Source:* Klasen and Wink (2003), Table 3.

especially interesting early study of the Punjab region of India by Monica Das Gupta (1987) finds that this neglect is more severe for later-born girls, and among them even worse for girls with older sisters. A second cause of missing women is sex-selective abortions: Parents find out the sex of the unborn child, typically using ultrasound technology, and abort the birth if the child is a girl. The importance of sex-selective abortions is inferred from increased sex ratios at birth. A remarkable study of China by Avraham Ebenstein (2010) shows that after China adopted its One Child Policy, sons were over 60 percent of births to mothers with one daughter, and over 70 percent of births to mothers with two daughters. The implication is that parents whose first child was not a boy were willing to pay the penalties to have another child, but wanted to make sure it was a boy by aborting girls if necessary. Supporting this interpretation was the fact that the average time lag between first and second births was greater if the second birth was a boy, implying that one or more "failed" pregnancies intervened before the desired result was obtained.

For the Arab countries with separate data, and for Iran, Turkey, and West Asia more generally, Klasen and Wink found that the percentage of missing women fell slightly or substantially between the 1980s and 1990s. Good recent estimates are lacking, partly because China and India have dominated recent research. However, there are solid reasons to believe that the downward trend in the countries we study should have continued at least until the Arab Spring. First, the increased income and improved health noted in Chapter 1 mean that Arab, Iranian, and Turkish parents are less likely to feel they have to choose between providing health care and nutrition for their sons versus their daughters. Second, abortions are typically very hard to obtain in the countries we study. According to the United Nations (http://www.un.org/en/development/desa/population/publications/pdf/policy/AbortionPoliciesReproductiveHealth.pdf), as of 2013 only Bahrain, Tunisia, and Turkey legally permitted abortions on request. Sex-selective abortions are therefore unlikely to become common enough to offset the fall in missing women due to improved survival after birth.

An important health issue that affects women but not men is female genital mutilation (FGM), also called female genital cutting and female circumcision. As can be seen from Figure 5.2, available data from large-scale representative surveys show that the practice of FGM is highly concentrated in a swath of countries from the Atlantic coast to the Horn of Africa, plus Egypt and (to a far lesser extent) Iraq. In terms of the total

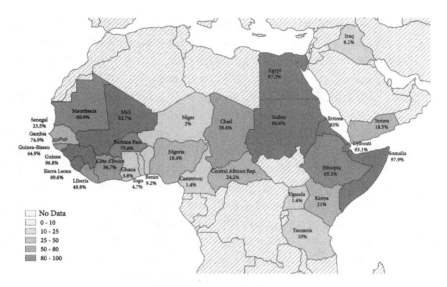

**Figure 5.2.** Percentage of Girls and Women Aged 15–49 Who Have Undergone Female Genital Mutilation

*Notes:* Data are available for twenty-nine countries where FGM is concentrated. Data are for the most recent survey year, none of which is older than 2004. This map is for illustrative purposes and does not imply the expression of any opinion on the part of the author concerning the legal status or name of any country or territory or concerning the delimitation of frontiers or boundaries.

*Source:* UNICEF Global Databases (data.unicef.org).

number of girls and women affected, FGM in the Arab world is dominated by Egypt (FGM is virtually absent in Iran and Turkey). Egypt outlawed the practice in 2008, and in 2016 the Egyptian Parliament increased the penalties to include lengthy prison terms. Recent surveys show that the prevalence of FGM in Egypt has decreased from the high level shown in Figure 5.2, but the same surveys also show considerable resistance to elimination of the practice.

Unfortunately, FGM is not the only women's health issue involving physical violence. Women are also victims of domestic violence, sometimes called intimate partner violence. The United Nations (2015, p. 143) defines violence as "acts aimed at physically hurting the victim and include, but are not limited to, pushing, grabbing, twisting the arm, pulling the hair, slapping, kicking, biting or hitting with the fist or object, trying to strangle or suffocate, burning or scalding on purpose, or attacking with some sort of weapon, gun or knife." The UN finds that intimate partner violence accounts for the majority of women's experience of violence.

To judge the prevalence of intimate partner violence across countries, the UN collected national surveys in which women were asked whether they had been victims of intimate partner violence in the last twelve months. The results of these surveys must be compared cautiously because they are not standardized across countries; for example the age ranges of women covered are not all the same. In Table 5.5 we report results for the latest year surveyed for all countries we study. Unfortunately, only five Arab countries and Turkey have data available. Four of the five Arab countries are from the Arab Mediterranean. We can compare these countries and Turkey to the population-weighted averages for the corresponding country groups, and get a reasonably complete picture of the prevalence of intimate partner violence against women in our Mediterranean countries. One of the five Arab countries, Comoros, is from Arab sub-Saharan Africa. Comoros has the smallest population of the Arab sub-Saharan African countries and is not very representative. Nevertheless, we report the population-weighted average for non-Arab sub-Saharan Africa, less to compare with Comoros

**Table 5.5** Percent of Women Subjected to Intimate Partner Violence, Last Twelve Months

| | |
|---|---|
| Comoros | 4.2 |
| Non-Arab sub-Saharan Africa | 20.5 |
| Arab Mediterranean | 14.2 |
| Egypt, Arab Rep. | 18.2 |
| Jordan | 11.2 |
| Morocco | 6.4 |
| Tunisia | 7.2 |
| Rest of non-Arab world | 14.0 |
| Turkey | 8.0 |
| Latin America | 11.0 |
| Southern Europe | 3.5 |

*Notes*: The most recent available survey was used for each country. The population-weighted averages for each country group were computed using 2016 populations and include the countries listed in the Appendix. The excluded countries were missing data.

*Source of data*: United Nations (2015).

than to compare with the other country groups. There are not enough data to report a population-weighted average for the non-Arab fuel-endowed countries.

Table 5.5 shows that, among the comparison country groups, the share of women surveyed who were subjected to intimate partner violence in the last twelve months is highest in non-Arab sub-Saharan Africa and lowest in Southern Europe, with the rest of the non-Arab world and Latin America about midway in between. We also see in Table 5.5 that in Jordan, Morocco, Tunisia, and Turkey, the share of women subjected to intimate partner violence is at or below the level for Latin America, well below the level for the rest of the non-Arab world, and well above the level for Southern Europe. For Egypt, however, this share of women is closer to the level for non-Arab sub-Saharan Africa, and as a result the population-weighted average for the Arab Mediterranean is roughly equal to that for the rest of the non-Arab world. Egypt thus stands out from the other countries in the Arab Mediterranean for prevalence of intimate partner violence against women as well as for prevalence of FGM. Comparable survey data in the future should tell us if the problem of intimate partner violence against women in the Arab Mediterranean countries and Turkey is improving, both absolutely and relative to the comparison country groups.

# 6

# Income Inequality, Poverty, Migration, and Unemployment

## Introduction

The measure of standard of living that we use most often in this book, GDP per capita in 2011 P$, is an average over the entire country population. An average can conceal a great deal of inequality and thus misrepresent the income of the typical individual. The Gini index is the most widely used measure of income inequality. We describe the Gini index in the section titled "Income Inequality as Measured by the Gini Index," and show that measured by the Gini index all three Arab worlds have low income inequality relative to their comparison country groups. Income inequality in Iran and Turkey is about average. Low income inequality causes the Arab countries to have lower poverty than would be expected on the basis of their GDPs per capita, as seen in the section titled "Poverty Headcounts."

We present evidence that low income inequality does not completely explain low Arab poverty. Another explanation is remittances from migrants. In the section titled "Migration and Remittances," we show that Egypt, Jordan, Lebanon, Morocco, Tunisia, and Yemen are among the world's top recipients of remittances as a share of GDP. Most remittances to Egypt, Jordan, and Yemen come from migrants living in the GCC countries; most remittances to Morocco and Tunisia come from migrants living in Europe. Though remittances from migrants help reduce poverty in their countries of origin, not all migrants from these countries are from poor families. Many return to start businesses.

In this section we also show that the GCC countries are among the top ten countries in the world by share of migrants in total population. Despite the importance of the GCC countries as hosts of Arab migrants, most of the migrants they host are from South Asia. The GCC migrant labor force works predominantly in the private sector, and GCC citizens work predominantly in the public sector.

We conclude the section by noting that some migrants leave their countries to find safety rather than economic opportunity. Syria, Somalia, Sudan, and Iraq are four of the top ten sources of refugees in the world, and Turkey, Lebanon, and Jordan have become the first, fourth, and ninth largest hosts of refugees in the world. There is evidence that refugees are straining social services in these host countries.

The section titled "Public and Private Sector Expenditure to Reduce Poverty" presents evidence that government anti-poverty programs in the MENA countries are not well-targeted at the poor, and that there is too much expenditure on food subsidies. Private, religious charity may be more effective, but its impact is hard to quantify. The fact remains that relatively low poverty rates are an economic strength of the countries we study. In contrast, an economic weakness of the countries we study is high unemployment rates, discussed in the section titled "Unemployment and Self-Employment." High unemployment is important because unemployment may not only indicate economic inefficiency but also cause exceptional unhappiness, as measured by responses to survey questions (Bruno Frey and Alois Stutzer 2002). Reliable unemployment data for the countries we study are scarce, but the data we have indicate that unemployment is especially high among more educated workers.

## Income Inequality as Measured by the Gini Index

The components of the Human Development Index are all population averages: average years of life expectancy, average years of attained and expected education, and average income. All of these averages conceal considerable inequality and thus may not accurately represent the experience of the typical individual. For example, in a country with eight years of attained education on average, half of the adults could have zero education and half could have completed tertiary education (sixteen years).

The potential for the average to misrepresent the experience of the typical individual is greatest for income. The reason is that the range of possible outcomes is much greater for income, which is measured in dollars, than for life expectancy and education, which are measured in years. A person cannot live much longer than one hundred years or acquire much more than twenty years of education, but someone who succeeds in business, say, can have an annual income of tens of millions of dollars. When computing an average, therefore, a very rich person can offset many more poor people than a long-lived or highly educated person can offset short-lived or low-educated people.

The more unequal is the distribution of income, the more misleading is the average. We therefore want to measure income inequality in the countries we study. This raises two difficulties. The first concerns data. We need to gather data at the household rather than individual level because we do not want to compare incomes of individuals at different stages of their lives—students or retirees to working adults, say. Moreover, we need to survey a sample of households that is representative of the entire country. By contrast, to estimate average income (GNI per capita) we only need estimates of two quantities: total income and total population. Because the data collection requirements are so great, countries report estimates of their income distributions much less frequently than estimates of their GNIs per capita, and for many countries there exist no reliable estimates of income distribution at all. The second difficulty is that we need to summarize the level of inequality implied by any given income distribution. The most popular summary measure of income inequality is the *Gini index*. The Gini index ranges from zero, for perfect equality (every household has the same income), to one hundred, for perfect inequality (one household has all the income). The values of the Gini index actually observed for countries range between 20 and 70. Box 6.1 explains the Gini index in much greater detail.

---

**Box 6.1**

---

**The Lorenz Curve and the Gini Index.** The Gini index for a country can be computed using the *Lorenz curve* for that country. A Lorenz curve plots the percentage of a country's income received by the poorest $x$ percent of households against $x$, as shown in Figure 6.1. In practice the Lorenz curve is typically fitted to data giving income shares by decile, that is, the points on the Lorenz curve that are actually observed are the percentage of income received by the poorest ten percent of households, the percentage of income received by the poorest twenty percent of households, and so on. For example, if the poorest ten percent of households received two percent of a country's income and the poorest twenty percent of households received six percent of a country's income, we would plot the points (10,2) and (20,6) in Figure 6.1. Note that the points $O$ (0,0) and $H$ (100,100) will always be included in the plot because zero percent of households receive zero percent of income and 100 percent of households receive 100 percent of income. Connecting all such points would yield the downward-bending Lorenz curve *L*. Complete equality would occur only if *x* percent of households received *x* percent of income, yielding the 45-degree line *E* in Figure 6.1. The opposite of complete equality is complete inequality, where one household has 100 percent of the country's income. With complete inequality, the poorest *x* percent of households receive zero percent of a country's income if *x* is less than 100. Plotting these points yields the box edge *OGH* in Figure 6.1.

Intuitively, it seems that if the Lorenz curve is higher (closer to the line of complete equality), the income distribution must be more equal than if the Lorenz curve is lower (closer to the box edge of complete inequality). We do in fact say that income distribution α is more equal than income distribution β if the Lorenz curve for α lies above that for β for at least one point and never lies below it, i.e., if distribution α *Lorenz-dominates* distribution β. It can be shown (see, e.g., Gary Fields and John Fei 1978) that if distribution α Lorenz-dominates distribution β for the same level of income, it means α can be obtained from β by transferring positive amounts of income from the relatively rich

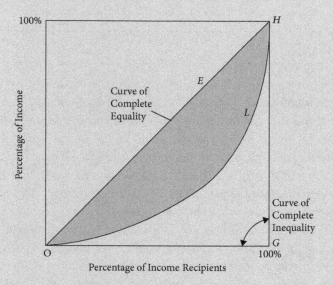

Figure 6.1. The Lorenz Curve

to the relatively poor. This feature makes measurement of income inequality using Lorenz curves very attractive. Unfortunately, it does not allow us to compare inequality of income distributions whose Lorenz curves cross. The Gini index provides one way to deal with this problem. To compute the Gini index, divide the area between the line of complete equality and the Lorenz curve (the shaded area in Figure 6.1) by the total area under the line of complete equality (the triangle OGH in Figure 6.1), and multiply by one hundred. Since the ratio of the areas varies between zero and one, the Gini index varies between zero and one hundred. It is clear that if one income distribution Lorenz-dominates another, its Gini index will be smaller, but the Gini index also allows us to rank inequality for income distributions whose Lorenz curves cross: The smaller is the Gini index, the more equal are the income distributions.

To compare income inequality across countries we use the most recent Gini indices computed by the World Bank and reported in the World Development Indicators. The World Bank cautions that, "Because the underlying household surveys differ in methods . . . , data are not strictly comparable across countries," though "World Bank staff have made an effort to ensure that the data are as comparable as possible." In Table 6.1 we focus on the population-weighted average Gini indices for each of the three Arab worlds and the comparison country groups, which reduces the importance of any unusual features in the survey data for any one country. We also break Iran out of the fuel-endowed comparison country group and Turkey out of the rest of the world comparison country group. Most countries have data for the year 2010 or later. The exceptions among the Arab countries are Morocco (2006), Sudan (2009), and Syria (2004). Income inequality in a country usually changes slowly, so it is reasonable to hope that even these older Gini indices are close to what we would observe today. We use the most recent available (2016) populations to construct the population-weighted averages so that Table 6.1 can give us information about income inequalities in the Arab and non-Arab country groups that is as up-to-date as possible.

The most important information conveyed by Table 6.1 is that income inequality in each of the three Arab worlds is lower than in the relevant comparison country groups, usually by substantial margins. We also see that the country groups with the highest inequality are Latin America and

**Table 6.1.** Gini Indices for Household Income Inequality

| | |
|---|---|
| Arab sub-Saharan Africa | 35.9 |
| Non-Arab sub-Saharan Africa | 43.8 |
| Arab fuel-endowed countries | 28.5 |
| Non-Arab fuel-endowed countries | 40.5 |
| Iran | 38.8 |
| Arab Mediterranean | 34.4 |
| Rest of non-Arab world | 38.2 |
| Turkey | 41.9 |
| Latin America | 47.4 |
| Southern Europe | 35.4 |

*Notes*: Gini indices for country groups are population-weighted averages using 2016 population. The most recent Gini index available was used for each country. The population-weighted averages for each country group include the countries listed in the Appendix. The excluded countries were missing data.

*Source of data*: World Development Indicators.

non-Arab sub-Saharan Africa. Ironically, the same lack of abundant land suitable for cash crop production that delayed the start of intensive growth in the Arab world (and Iran) may have contributed to lower Arab income inequality today. Recall from Chapter 2 that Engerman and Sokoloff (2002) argued that climate and soil conditions in Latin America led to agricultural practices that generated a relatively unequal distribution of income. William Easterly (2001) found that tropical commodity exporting more generally is associated with high income inequality, which is consistent with the high Gini index for non-Arab sub-Saharan Africa. Easterly also found that oil exporting is associated with high income inequality, which does not show up for the Arab fuel-endowed countries in Table 6.1. We should note that only Algeria and Iraq are included in the population-weighted average for the Arab fuel-endowed countries. Data are not available for Libya and the GCC countries. In any case, Gini indices for the GCC countries might be especially difficult to compare with other countries because income inequality in the GCC countries could be dominated by inequality between GCC citizens and migrants. Table 6.6 in the section titled "Migration and Remittances" shows that the migrant shares of population in the GCC countries are among the highest in the world.

## Poverty Headcounts

Relatively low income inequality in the Arab countries means that their per capita incomes are less misleading about the living standards of their typical households. This has important consequences for poverty. In this section we will consider "absolute poverty," which refers to people living below a poverty line defined in dollars. In contrast, "relative poverty" refers to people living below a poverty line defined as a percentage of a standard. For example, the poverty line for each country in the European Union is 60 percent of the median household income in the country. If every household in a country becomes richer, absolute poverty must decline. Relative poverty, however, could remain the same, increase, or decrease, depending on how much the incomes of the households that set the standard change relative to the incomes of poorer households. Many national poverty lines are relative poverty lines, because governments want to know how many of their citizens are poor relative to the standards of their countries. For the same reason, national poverty lines are not useful for comparing poverty across countries.

There is a direct connection between income inequality and absolute poverty. Consider two countries with the same average level of income. In the country where income is more unequally distributed, there will be more households living below any absolute poverty line. We should therefore expect the Arab countries, for which income is relatively equally distributed, to have lower absolute poverty than other countries with the same levels of average income.

We will consider two absolute poverty lines constructed by the World Bank. Both are measured in 2011 purchasing power parity dollars. The first poverty line is P$1.90 per day, or P$694 per year. This is the World Bank's line for "extreme" poverty, derived from the work of Martin Ravallion, Shaohua Chen, and Prem Sangraula (2009). It is based on the poverty lines for fifteen of the world's poorest countries, which in turn are based on the estimates made by those countries' governments of the income necessary for their citizens to meet their "basic needs" for food, health care, shelter, etc. The second World Bank absolute poverty line is P$3.20 per day, or P$1,168 per year. Use of this poverty line greatly increases the number of people considered poor, increasing that number by a factor of three or more for many countries. It holds countries to a much higher standard for reducing poverty.

146 THE ECONOMICS OF THE MIDDLE EAST

Figures 6.2 and 6.3 plot the shares of the population below the P$1.90 and P$3.20 poverty lines, respectively, against the logarithm of GDP per capita for the most recent year available. These shares are known as the *poverty headcount ratios*. The years covered by the figures range from 2003 to 2015, with most countries having data more recent than 2010. We use GDP per capita for the year in which the poverty headcount ratios are observed. We do not show countries with ln(GDP per capita) greater than 10 (approximately 2011 P$22,000), because all of those countries have poverty headcount ratios close to zero or do not even report them. As a result Figures 6.2 and 6.3 exclude the GCC countries and Turkey. Also missing from Figures 6.2 and 6.3 are Libya, Somalia, and Syria, because they lack data.

The figures confirm the prediction, based on the Gini indices we reported in Table 6.1, that the Arab countries tend to have fewer people in poverty than would be expected based on their average incomes. The downward-sloping lines in the figures show the average relationships between ln(GDP per capita) and the poverty headcount ratios, i.e., the rates at which poverty

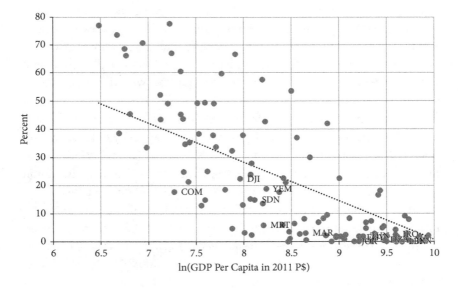

**Figure 6.2.** Poverty Headcount Ratio (P$1.90) by GDP Per Capita

Notes: Poverty headcount ratio = percent of population below poverty line. List of included country-year observations available on request.

*Source of data*: World Development Indicators.

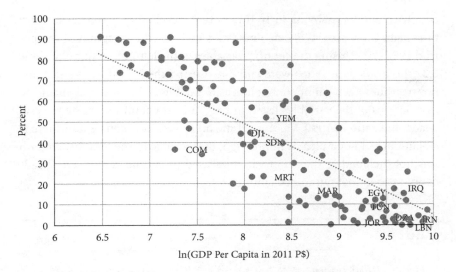

**Figure 6.3.** Poverty Headcount Ratio (P$3.20) by GDP Per Capita

*Notes:* Poverty headcount ratio = percent of population below poverty line. List of included country-year observations available on request.

*Source of data:* World Development Indicators.

is predicted to fall as countries become richer. When using the lower poverty line of P$1.90 in Figure 6.2, all of the Arab countries are below the downward-sloping line and therefore have less poverty than would be expected given their GDPs per capita. When using the higher poverty line of P$3.20 in Figure 6.3, all of the Arab countries except Iraq and Yemen have less poverty than would be expected. Yemen's poverty headcount ratio using the higher poverty line increased from 38.8 percent in 2005 to 52.2 percent in 2014, the year used in Figure 6.3. This was probably the result of the economic disruption in Yemen following the Arab Spring. Iran is also labeled in Figures 6.2 and 6.3 and is just below the downward-sloping lines in both figures, indicating that it has slightly less poverty than would be expected given its GDP per capita.

Low poverty headcount ratios in the countries we study are not a new phenomenon, but date back at least to the 1980s. A study by Richard Adams and John Page (2003) of poverty in Algeria, Egypt, Iran, Jordan, Morocco, Tunisia, and Yemen during the period 1980–2000 concludes that low poverty headcount ratios in these countries cannot be completely explained by their low income inequalities. Adams and Page gather data for these countries and as many as forty-three other developing countries and try to explain their poverty headcount ratios in 1990, the midpoint of the period 1980–2000, using the country variables in the leftmost column of Table 6.2. The headcount ratios were computed using the World Bank's extreme poverty line. Each numbered column in Table 6.2 shows the signs of the associations of the variables listed in the leftmost column with the poverty headcount ratio in 1990, holding all the other variables constant. If there is a blank instead of a plus or minus sign, the variable in the leftmost column was not included in the set of variables used to explain the poverty headcount ratio in that numbered column.

---

**Box 6.2**

**How to Read Tables 6.2, 8.2, 9.3, and 9.5.** These tables show simplified results from *multiple regression analysis*. Multiple regression analysis is

Table 6.2. Poverty Headcount Ratio, 1990

| Country Variable | (1) | (2) | (3) | (4) | (5) | (6) | (7) | (8) |
|---|---|---|---|---|---|---|---|---|
| GDP per capita, 1990 (1995 US$) | −** | −** | −** | −** | −** | −** | −** | −** |
| Gini index | +** | +** | +** | +** | +** | + | +** | +** |
| MENA indicator (1 if MENA country) | −** | | −** | | −** | | −** | |
| Remittances received ÷ GDP, 1990 | | −** | − | − | | | | |
| (MENA indicator) × (Remittances/GDP) | | | | −** | | | | |
| Government share of employment | | | | | | −** | − | − |
| (MENA indicator) × (Government share) | | | | | | | | −** |

*Notes:* Columns (1) – (4) cover fifty countries, columns (5) – (8) cover thirty-two countries. All variables in logarithms. Plus (minus) sign indicates positive (negative) elasticity of poverty headcount ratio with respect to variable in left column. **Different from zero with 95-percent confidence.

*Source:* Adams and Page (2003, tables 2 and 3).

a statistical technique that enables us to estimate linear relationships (slopes) between a *dependent variable* and multiple *explanatory variables*. What makes multiple regression analysis so useful is that it allows us to estimate the association of each explanatory variable with the dependent variable *holding all other explanatory variables constant* or "controlling" for the other explanatory variables. It is important to keep in mind that multiple regression analysis only reveals correlations between the explanatory variables and the dependent variable. As with any correlation, causality is not necessarily implied.

Multiple regression analysis not only estimates the slopes of the relationships between the dependent variable and the explanatory variables; it provides *standard errors* for these estimates. We say a slope is precisely estimated if it is large relative to its standard error, and imprecisely estimated otherwise. If a slope is precisely estimated we are confident that a relationship between the dependent variable and explanatory variable really exists, whereas when a slope is imprecisely estimated we believe the apparent relationship may be an artifact of statistical noise.

In Tables 6.2, 8.2, 9.3, and 9.5, we show the signs of the estimated slopes (positive or negative) rather than their numerical values. That is because we are more concerned with the directions than the strengths of the relationships between the explanatory variables and the dependent variable. We also provide indicators of how precisely estimated the slopes are. One, two, and three stars indicate we can be 90, 95, and 99 percent confident, respectively, that the slope is not zero, i.e., that there is really a relationship between the dependent and explanatory variable. No stars indicates that the slope is not statistically different from zero.

Beginning with column (1), we first see that GDP per capita is negatively associated with poverty, which is consistent with the downward-sloping line in Figure 6.2. The next row of column (1) shows that the Gini index is positively associated with poverty. This is consistent with the argument of the previous section: More income inequality (a higher Gini index) implies more poverty, holding average income (GDP per capita) constant. The last row of column (1) shows that if a country is in the MENA region (as are Algeria, Egypt, Iran, Jordan, Morocco, Tunisia, and Yemen) poverty is lower, holding constant (controlling for) both GDP per capita and the Gini index.

If lower income inequality does not completely explain lower poverty in the seven MENA countries, what else does? The last row of column (2) shows that the ratio of remittances received by a country to the GDP of that country is negatively associated with poverty. Remittances are funds sent by citizens of a country working abroad back to their country of origin, usually to their families. Their negative association with poverty indicates that some families receiving these funds would otherwise fall below the poverty line. Column (3) reintroduces the MENA indicator variable that was omitted from column (2). This indicator is still negatively associated with poverty, though the magnitude of the association (not shown) falls a bit compared to column (1). The association of remittances with poverty continues to be negative, but is no longer estimated precisely enough for us to be confident it is not zero. In column (4) the MENA indicator variable is replaced by the ratio of remittances to country GDP multiplied by the MENA indicator. This variable equals the ratio of remittances to country GDP for the MENA countries and zero for the non-MENA countries. It has a negative association with poverty, whereas remittances not multiplied by the MENA indicator have an association with poverty in the non-MENA countries that is too weak for us to be confident it is not zero. The main message of columns (3) and (4) is that on average remittances reduce poverty in the seven MENA countries, but do not complete the explanation of the lower poverty in these countries.

Columns (5)–(8) in Table 6.2 essentially repeat the exercise of columns (1)–(4), replacing the ratio of remittances to country GDP with the public sector share of country employment. This variable is available for only five MENA countries (Iran and Yemen are dropped) and only twenty-seven other developing countries. Despite the smaller sample of countries, the results of the exercise are essentially the same, making the change from remittances to government employment. That is, the main message of columns (7) and (8) in Table 6.2 is that on average public sector employment reduces poverty in the five MENA countries, but does not complete the explanation of the lower poverty in these countries.

We discuss the unusually high share of public sector employment in the MENA countries in the section titled "Unemployment and Self-Employment." To understand the unusually high ratio of remittances to GDP for these countries requires that we learn more about their patterns of migration, because remittances are sent by migrants.

## Migration and Remittances

In order to judge what ratio of remittances to GDP is unusually high, we can rank all countries by this ratio. We do this for the year 2010, just before the economic disruptions following the Arab spring, so that the rankings of countries that were strongly affected (particularly Yemen) are not inflated by reductions in their GDPs (in the denominators of their ratios). Excluding countries with populations less than 1 million leaves 140 countries with data available. We find that 42 countries or 30 percent of the total have a ratio of at least 0.05. As shown in Table 6.3, 6 of the countries we study are in this top 30 percent: Egypt, Jordan, Lebanon, Morocco, Tunisia, and Yemen. All of these except Lebanon are included in the seven MENA countries covered by Adams and Page. (The two MENA countries covered by Adams and Page that are not in the top 30 percent, Algeria and Iran, have ratios well below 0.01.) There is a large gap between the countries in Table 6.3 and the next Arab country in the ranking, Sudan, which has a ratio of 0.02. (If countries with less than one million population were not excluded, Comoros would rank very high, in between Lebanon and Jordan.)

Table 6.4 shows the source regions for the remittances received by the countries listed in Table 6.3. A clear division emerges between the countries that are relatively close to the Gulf region and the countries that are

**Table 6.3.** 2010 Ratio of Remittances Received to GDP

| Country | Remittances ÷ GDP | Rank |
|---------|-------------------|------|
| Lebanon | 0.18 | 8 |
| Jordan | 0.14 | 15 |
| Morocco | 0.07 | 32 |
| Egypt | 0.06 | 33 |
| Yemen | 0.05 | 38 |
| Tunisia | 0.05 | 41 |

*Note*: Rank is out of all countries with population ≥ 1M.

*Source of data*: World Development Indicators.

relatively close to Europe. The GCC countries are the dominant source of remittances to Egypt, Jordan, and Yemen. In 2016, Saudi Arabia alone accounts for 39 percent of the remittances to both Egypt and Jordan, and 62 percent of the remittances to Yemen. The EU countries are the dominant source of remittances to Morocco and Tunisia. France alone accounts for 31 percent of the remittances to Morocco and 59 percent of the remittances to Tunisia in 2016. Lebanon's sources of remittances are less concentrated, with about one-quarter each coming from the GCC, the EU, and the United States and Canada.

By definition, remittances are sent by migrants. The last three columns of Table 6.4 show the 2013 shares of migrants from the six high-remittance Arab countries living in the GCC, EU, and US and Canada. These shares are very close to, and in some cases identical to, the shares of remittances received from those regions. This fact suggests that migrants working in different countries send similar amounts of money back to their countries of origin. However, we should not place too much weight on this conclusion because the migration data were used to help construct the remittance data.

The GCC countries are not only large sources of people-to-people transfers to the poorer Arab countries through remittances, they are also large sources of government-to-government transfers through Official Development Assistance (foreign aid). Saudi Arabia has usually been the largest single source. The Organization for Economic Cooperation and Development (OECD) provides data for Official Development Assistance (ODA) donated by Kuwait, Saudi Arabia, and UAE. In 2015, Saudi Arabia donated roughly US$6.5 billion in ODA to other Arab countries (we lack data for 2016). This is very generous by international standards, yet it is only slightly more than half as much as the US$12.7 billion of remittances sent from Saudi Arabia to other Arab countries in 2016, US$6.4 billion to Egypt alone. ODA from Kuwait and UAE to other Arab countries in 2016 was US$0.9 billion and US$3.8 billion, respectively. By comparison, remittances sent from Kuwait and UAE to other Arab countries in 2016 were US$3.2 billion and $US3.5 billion, respectively.

Following the study of Adams and Page, we have emphasized the negative association of migration with poverty through remittances. Migration may also have a direct negative effect on measured poverty if the poor migrate and as a result are not counted by surveys in their countries of origin. It is important to note, however, that not all migrants from the countries in Table 6.3 are poor, and not all families of migrants would be poor in the absence of remittances from the regions in Table 6.4. This only needs to be

**Table 6.4.** 2016 Sources of Remittances Received and 2013 Shares of Migrants Hosted (Percent)

| Country | Share of Remittances Received from: | | | Share of Migrants Hosted by: | | |
|---|---|---|---|---|---|---|
| | GCC | EU | US + Canada | GCC | EU | US + Canada |
| Egypt | 73 | 1 | 7 | 69 | 7 | 6 |
| Jordan | 72 | 5 | 10 | 68 | 5 | 11 |
| Yemen | 90 | 2 | 4 | 88 | 2 | 4 |
| Lebanon | 26 | 27 | 27 | 25 | 27 | 26 |
| Morocco | 1 | 88 | 4 | 1 | 88 | 4 |
| Tunisia | 3 | 87 | 3 | 3 | 87 | 3 |

*Sources of data*: http://www.knomad.org/data/remittances, Bilateral remittance matrix; http://www.knomad.org/data/migration/emigration, Bilateral migration matrix.

true for some cases. Migrants from Jordan and Lebanon in particular tend to be highly skilled and from households in the upper part of the income distribution. Figure 6.4, from a study by Jackline Wahba (2014) using survey data from 2010, shows the percentages of Jordanian migrants that held various occupations in their host countries. More than half—56 percent—were managers or professionals. The concentration of Jordanian migrants in managerial and professional jobs is not surprising given that, according to Wahba (p. 174), 62 percent of them had a university degree.

The effects of migrants on their countries of origin are not limited to remittances. When migrants return to their countries of origin they bring back business contacts and skills. These are especially valuable because the countries in which the migrants worked, the GCC countries and EU countries in the case of Arab migrants, are richer and more technologically advanced than their countries of origin. Table 6.5, from a different study by Wahba (2007) using survey data from 1988 and 1998, shows a strong impact of migration on the tendency of returning Egyptian migrants to go into business. The share of migrants who were employers increased from 8.2 percent before migration to 18.2 percent after migration, and the share who were self-employed increased from 7.5 to 10.1 percent. This occurred despite the fact that these Egyptian return migrants were much less educated and held much less skilled occupations overseas than the migrants in Wahba's study of Jordan: Only 25 percent of them held a university degree and only 21 percent of them worked in technical, scientific, or managerial occupations overseas.

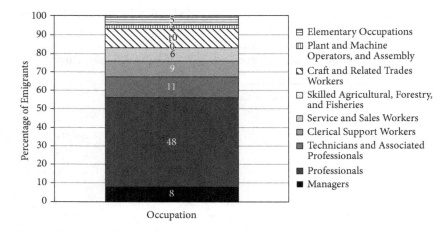

**Figure 6.4.** 2009 Occupation Shares for Migrants from Jordan
*Source:* Jackline Wahba, "Immigration, Emigration, and the Labor Market in Jordan," figure 6.2a, in *The Jordanian Labour Market in the New Millennium*, ed. Ragui Assaad (Oxford: Oxford University Press, 2014).

**Table 6.5.** Employment Status and Sector of Employment of Return Migrants, Egypt (Percent)

|  | Before Migration | After Return |
|---|---|---|
| *Employment Status* | | |
| Wage worker | 62.0 | 63.1 |
| Employer | 8.2 | 18.2 |
| Self-employed | 7.5 | 10.1 |
| Unpaid family worker | 5.9 | 3.1 |
| Unemployed | 6.6 | 2.8 |
| Out of the labor force | 9.8 | 2.7 |
| Unknown | n. a. | 4.8 |
| *Sector of Employment* | | |
| Public | 53.2 | 39.5 |
| Private | 46.8 | 60.5 |

*Note:* Migrants are males ages 15–65. n. a. = not applicable.
*Source:* Wahba (2007), Table 8.4.

## Box 6.3

**Rafiq Hariri, a Lebanese Migrant Who Became a Billionaire.** In Lebanon, migrating abroad to make one's fortune and eventually returning has been a way of life for generations. A famous example of such a migrant is Rafiq Hariri. Hariri, the son of a vegetable vendor, migrated to Saudi Arabia in 1965. He founded the construction firm Saudi Oger in 1978 and, with the aid of contracts from the Saudi royal family, built it into a multibillion-dollar conglomerate that diversified into related areas such as real estate development. After returning to Lebanon in the early 1980s Hariri went into politics, becoming prime minister from 1992 to 1998 and again from 2000 to 2004. He was listed by Forbes as the 108th richest person in the world in 2004, with an estimated net worth of roughly $4 billion. Hariri was assassinated on Valentine's Day in 2005. He was buried next to the mosque on Beirut's Martyrs' Square shown in Figure 6.5, the construction of which he had financed.

**Figure 6.5.** Mosque Financed by Rafiq Hariri, Martyrs' Square, Beirut, Lebanon
*Source:* https://www.explorra.com/destinations/beirut_12096#photo-1.

Table 6.4 shows that the GCC countries are the dominant hosts of migrants from poorer nearby Arab countries. We can also look at this migration from the perspective of the GCC countries themselves. All of the GCC countries are ranked among the top ten countries in the world by 2010 share of migrants in total population, excluding countries with populations less than one million. Table 6.6 shows that UAE, Qatar, Kuwait, and Bahrain respectively occupy positions one through four in this ranking, with more than 80 percent of the populations of UAE and Qatar having migrated from other countries. If we included non-GCC Arab countries, Jordan would be ranked sixth in this table, but this is due to the presence of Palestinian refugees (see discussion of refugees later in this section) rather than economic migrants.

Table 6.7 shows that migrants in the GCC countries come mainly from South Asia. India is the single largest source of South Asian migrants, with Bangladesh and Pakistan not far behind. For each GCC country the share of migrants from the Arab world is second to the share from South Asia, with Southeast Asia as the third most important source of GCC migrant labor. The last column in Table 6.7 shows that the Arab share of migrants has fallen in every GCC country since 1975, especially in Kuwait and Saudi Arabia. Andrzej Kapiszewski (2006) describes the many factors, both economic and political, that have caused the Arab share to fall and the South and Southeast Asian shares to rise since 1975.

Many scholars have questioned whether remittances from South and Southeast Asian migrants in the GCC countries have been effective in

**Table 6.6.** 2010 Share of Migrants in Total Population, GCC Countries (Percent)

| Country | Migrant Share | Rank |
|---|---|---|
| UAE | 87.8 | 1 |
| Qatar | 82.5 | 2 |
| Kuwait | 61.2 | 3 |
| Bahrain | 52.2 | 4 |
| Saudi Arabia | 30.0 | 8 |
| Oman | 27.7 | 9 |

*Note*: Rank is out of all countries with population ≥ 1M.
*Source of data*: World Development Indicators.

Table 6.7. Sources of Migrants to GCC Countries (Percent)

| Country | 2013 Share of Migrants from: Arab World | S. Asia | SE Asia | 1975 Share of Migrants from: Arab World |
|---|---|---|---|---|
| Bahrain | 19 | 63 | 10 | 22 |
| Kuwait | 31 | 53 | 9 | 80 |
| Oman | 7 | 83 | 5 | 16 |
| Qatar | 17 | 65 | 12 | 33 |
| Saudi Arabia | 33 | 45 | 19 | 91 |
| UAE | 13 | 65 | 13 | 26 |

*Notes:* Arab world includes West Bank and Gaza. South Asia consists of Afghanistan, Bangladesh, Bhutan, India, Iran, Maldives, Nepal, Pakistan, and Sri Lanka. Southeast Asia consists of Brunei Darussalam, Cambodia, Indonesia, Laos, Malaysia, Myanmar, Philippines, Singapore, Thailand, Timor-Leste, and Vietnam. These definitions of South Asia and Southeast Asia are from the United Nations Geoscheme for Asia.

*Sources of data:* http://www.knomad.org/data/migration/emigration, Bilateral migration matrix (2013 data); Kapiszewski (2006) (1975 data).

alleviating poverty in their countries of origin. For example, a study of Bangladeshi migrants to the GCC by Md. Mizanur Rahman (2015) suggests that their remittances are mostly going to pay middlemen who recruited them and money-lenders from whom they borrowed the costs of migration. Rahman calculates an average cost of migration to the GCC for a Bangladeshi worker in 2009 of US$2,750, and estimates that a migrant household takes roughly two and one-quarter years to recover the financial cost of migration. His estimate does not include payments that migrant households must make to money-lenders, who charge up to 7–10 percent interest per month. Rahman finds that almost two-thirds of migrants surveyed had outstanding loans to pay back, even though most of them had been working in the GCC countries for at least three years.

The large migrant population shares in the GCC have led to dominance of private sector employment by migrants, whereas citizens are employed largely or even almost entirely in the public sector. Figure 6.6 contrasts the distributions of employed citizens and migrants ("expats," or expatriates) between the public and private sectors in the UAE in 2009. For both male and female UAE citizens, employment is overwhelmingly in the public sector, with less than 10 percent of male or female employment in the private sector. Migrant employment, on the other hand, is mainly in the

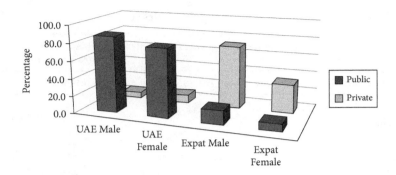

**Figure 6.6.** Distribution of Employed by Nationality and Sector in UAE, 2009

Source: George S. Naufal, "The Economics of Migration in the Gulf Cooperation Council Countries," figure 27.15, in *Handbook of the Economics of International Migration*, ed. Barry R. Chiswick and Paul W. Miller (Amsterdam: Elsevier, 2015).

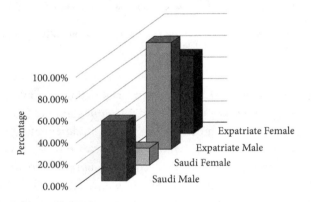

**Figure 6.7.** Private Sector Employment Share in Saudi Arabia, Average 2005–2011

Source: George S. Naufal, "The Economics of Migration in the Gulf Cooperation Council Countries," figure 27.5, in *Handbook of the Economics of International Migration*, ed. Barry R. Chiswick and Paul W. Miller (Amsterdam: Elsevier, 2015).

private sector, especially for males. Figure 6.7 shows the shares of employed citizens and migrants in the private sector in Saudi Arabia for the period 2005–2011. For both males and females the migrant shares are much higher than the citizen shares, though about half of employed male Saudi Arabia citizens work in the private sector, a much higher share than in UAE. Additional data collected by George Naufal (2015) suggest that the shares of citizen employment in the private sectors in the other GCC countries may be closer to the UAE than the Saudi Arabia levels.

As we noted in Chapter 3, the GCC governments are trying to reduce the dependence of their countries on fuel exports. A key part of their strategies is establishment and growth of internationally competitive private sector firms in non-oil manufacturing and especially services. The hope is that these firms will provide managerial, professional, and technical jobs for GCC citizens. It is still too early to tell whether this strategy will be successful, or whether these positions will be filled predominantly by highly educated migrants such as those in the study by Wahba (2014). In other words, the GCC countries face a two-part challenge: first, establishment of internationally competitive businesses outside the fuel sector, and second, staffing those businesses with GCC citizens.

We conclude this section on migration by shifting the discussion from migrants seeking economic opportunities to refugees fleeing war. We will count refugees using the "total population of concern" reported by the United Nations High Commissioner for Refugees (UNHCR). Total population of concern includes "refugee[s] and people in refugee-like situations" and "asylum-seekers." Asylum-seekers are almost always a very small proportion of the total population of concern.

Table 6.8 shows that Arab countries are four of the top ten sources of refugees in the world. Five and one-half million refugees have fled Syria, more than any other country, Arab or non-Arab. There is a large gap between the countries listed in Table 6.8 and the other countries we study; the next largest source of refugees among the countries we study is Iran, with 162,001 refugees.

Table 6.8. Mid-2016 Number of Refugees, by Country of Origin

| Country | Number of Refugees | Rank | Largest Host Countries (percent) |
|---------|--------------------|------|----------------------------------|
| Syria   | 5,564,195          | 1    | Turkey (49), Lebanon (19), Jordan (12) |
| Somalia | 1,159,982          | 3    | Kenya (34), Yemen (22), Ethiopia (22) |
| Sudan   | 684,619            | 5    | Chad (45), South Sudan (35), Ethiopia (6) |
| Iraq    | 571,855            | 7    | Germany (23), Turkey (22), Jordan (10) |

*Notes*: Number of Refugees = "total refugee and people in refugee-like situations" + "asylum-seekers"; internally displaced persons (IDPs) are not included. Rank is out of all countries; the categories "stateless" and "various/unknown" are not included. Percent is the share of the refugees from the country in the leftmost column residing in the host country.

*Source of data*: United Nations High Commissioner for Refugees (UNHCR) Population Statistics Database.

Like Syria, Libya and Yemen are in the midst of civil wars, yet they have not become large sources of refugees. Relatively few people fleeing their homes in Libya and Yemen have crossed borders into other countries and become international migrants. Instead they have sought safety inside their countries of origin, becoming "internally displaced persons" (IDPs). The UNHCR counts 286,000 IDPs in Libya and 2.1 million IDPs in Yemen as of mid-2016. The countries listed in Table 6.8 have mid-2016 numbers of internally displaced persons comparable to their numbers of refugees, or much larger: 6.6 million IDPs in Syria, 1.1 million IDPs in Somalia, 3.2 million IDPs in Sudan, and 4.4 million IDPs in Iraq.

Neighboring countries are usually the easiest countries for refugees to reach. This is why the largest hosts of Syrian refugees are Turkey, Lebanon, and Jordan, as shown in Table 6.8. Similarly, the largest hosts of Somali refugees are Kenya, Yemen, and Ethiopia, and the largest hosts of Sudanese refugees are Chad, South Sudan, and Ethiopia. Iraqi refugees are a partial exception: Germany is the largest host country, ahead of Turkey and Jordan. Roughly half of Iraqi refugees in Germany have applied for asylum.

In addition to the human development tragedy of the refugees themselves, large refugee populations may retard human development in host countries. The three largest hosts of Syrian refugees, Turkey, Lebanon, and Jordan, have become the first, fourth, and ninth largest hosts of refugees in the world, as shown in Table 6.9. We also see from Table 6.9 that Lebanon, Jordan, and Turkey respectively host the first, third, and fifth highest numbers of refugees per capita. (Jordan and Lebanon also host roughly two million and one-half million Palestinian refugees, respectively, according to the United Nations Relief and Works Agency (https://www.unrwa.org/resources/about-unrwa/unrwa-figures-2017).)

Shanta Devarajan and Lili Mottaghi (2017) find some evidence that the influx of Syrian refugees has worsened education and health outcomes in Lebanon and Jordan. In 2017, Lebanon enrolled 51 percent of its Syrian refugee students in public formal education. The country opened 313 second-shift schools that operate solely to serve Syrian students. As can be seen in Figure 6.8, the increase in refugee students was coupled with a slight decrease in Lebanese enrollment in public schools at the onset of the refugee crisis, due to a loss of confidence in the quality of public education. However, after three years of enrollment fee subsidies to Lebanese students, this loss was recouped. In Jordan and Lebanon, previously

Table 6.9. Mid-2016 Number of Refugees, by Country of Residence

| Country | Number of Refugees | Rank | Largest Source (percent) | Refugees ÷ Population | Rank |
|---------|--------------------|------|--------------------------|------------------------|------|
| Turkey  | 3,006,245 | 1 | Syria (91) | 0.038 | 5 |
| Lebanon | 1,054,191 | 4 | Syria (98) | 0.176 | 1 |
| Iran    | 978,274   | 6 | Afghanistan (97) | 0.012 | 23 |
| Jordan  | 721,390   | 9 | Syria (91) | 0.076 | 3 |

*Notes*: Number of Refugees = "total refugee and people in refugee-like situations" + "asylum-seekers"; internally displaced persons (IDPs) and Palestinians registered with United Nations Relief and Works Agency (UNRWA) are not included. Rank for number of refugees is out of all countries; rank for ratio of refugees to total country population is out of all countries with population ≥ 1M. Percent is share of refugees resident in host country from largest source country.

*Sources of data*: United Nations High Commissioner for Refugees (UNHCR) Population Statistics Database (number of refugees); World Development Indicators (total country population).

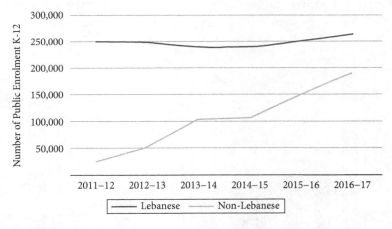

Figure 6.8. Enrollment Trends in Public Schools in Lebanon, 2011–2017

*Source*: Shanta Devarajan and Lili Mottaghi, "Meeting the Development Challenge for Refugees in Middle East and North Africa," figure 2.2, *Middle East and North Africa Economic Monitor* (October) (Washington, DC: World Bank, 2017).

well-controlled communicable diseases including measles and tuberculosis have re-emerged. Waiting times for health services have increased in both countries. In Jordan these delays became so long in 2016 that referrals to non-Ministry of Health hospitals increased more than 50 percent over the previous year.

## Public and Private Sector Expenditure to Reduce Poverty

Governments in the Arab countries have a wide variety of programs intended to reduce poverty. These include cash transfers; in-kind transfers of goods such as food and school supplies; workfare, meaning short-term employment in labor-intensive public works; price subsidies, mainly for food and fuel; and fee waivers for services such as health care, schooling, utilities, or transportation. Joana Silva, Victoria Levin, and Matteo Morgandi (2013) undertook a study of the effectiveness of these programs for the World Bank. Their study covered most of the Arab countries in MENA excluding the GCC countries, but did not cover Iran. They refer to anti-poverty programs as social safety net programs (SSNs), and divide them into price subsidies and all others (non-subsidy SSNs).

Figure 6.9 shows the coverage of the poorest quintile (20 percent) of individuals by non-subsidy SSNs in various Arab countries, the

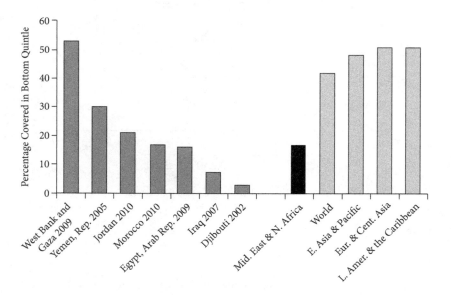

**Figure 6.9.** Coverage of Bottom Quintile by Non-Subsidy Social Safety Net Programs

*Note:* Regional averages are population-weighted.

*Source:* Joana Silva, Victoria Levin, and Matteo Morgandi, *Inclusion and Resilience: The Way Forward for Safety Nets in the Middle East and North Africa*, figure O.17 (Washington, DC: World Bank, 2013).

population-weighted average of coverage for these countries (labeled MENA), and coverage for comparison regions. All the individuals in a household are considered to be covered if at least one member of the household receives benefits. West Bank and Gaza, which is outside the scope of this book, is a clear outlier; this can be explained by the fact that its non-subsidy SSNs are mainly funded internationally. This outlier has little effect on the population-weighted average for MENA because the population of West Bank and Gaza is small. We see from Figure 6.9 that non-subsidy SSNs cover less than 20 percent of the poorest households in MENA, compared to 40–50 percent in the other regions. This evidence and other evidence in the World Bank study make it unlikely that non-subsidy SSNs can help to explain relatively low poverty headcounts in the MENA countries.

The MENA countries covered in the World Bank study spend about 1.1 percent of their GDPs on food subsidies, and another 4.5 percent on fuel subsidies. We do not consider fuel subsidies to be a social safety net program because, as the study by Silva et al. shows (2013, figure 3.16, p. 136), rich households in the MENA countries benefit more from fuel subsidies than poor households. One reason for this outcome is that poor households do not usually own cars. We therefore postpone discussion of the exceptionally high MENA expenditures on fuel subsidies to Chapter 8. Food subsidies do indeed reduce poverty substantially in some MENA countries, notably Egypt and Iraq. Nevertheless, there is nearly universal agreement among economists that food subsidies should be replaced by direct cash transfers to the poor. That is, instead of enabling poor households to save $x$ dollars by purchasing certain food items for less than their market prices, the government should simply give poor households $x$ dollars.

There are at least three reasons to replace food subsidies with cash transfers. First, the poor can spend the funds on what they need most rather than being forced, in effect, to spend the funds on food. A review of nineteen studies by David Evans and Anna Popova (2017) concludes that poor households spend their cash transfers wisely, in that they actually reduce their expenditures on alcohol and tobacco despite having more money. Second, cash transfers can be much more accurately targeted to poor households than can food subsidies. It is hard to prevent non-poor households from gaining access to subsidized food. Third, MENA food subsidies primarily reduce the prices of bread or flour and sugar, which may contribute to the obesity problem discussed in Chapter 4.

Although governments in Arab countries spend relatively little on social safety net programs other than food subsidies, this does not necessarily mean that safety nets are weak, because they may be funded by the private sector. In any Muslim-majority country there is the potential for *zakat* or almsgiving to raise households above the poverty line. *Zakat* is a religious obligation for Muslims. According to Zafar Iqbal and Mervyn Lewis (2014), the generally accepted amount of *zakat* is a one-fortieth (2.5 percent) assessment on assets held for a full year (after a small initial exclusion), the purpose of which is to transfer income from the wealthy to the needy. *Zakat* is typically assessed and delivered privately, though it is collected by the government in a few Arab countries.

The data on *zakat* are too sparse to allow a systematic assessment of its impact on poverty in the Arab world. More studies are needed like the one carried out in Sana'a, the capital of Yemen, by the World Bank in 2010. As described by Silva, Levin, and Morgandi (2013), the World Bank survey found that *zakat* was received by over 35 percent of households ranked in the poorest quintile of the income distribution. Among receivers in the poorest 10 percent of the income distribution, *zakat* boosted incomes by about 25 percent. Receivers were usually related to or lived near the donors. Eighty-two percent of donors said that the person to whom they gave *zakat* was related to them or their households, and 60 percent of donors said the person to whom they gave *zakat* last year had already received *zakat* from them for more than three years. This reflects a weakness of any informal safety net: Those unconnected to wealthy households through social networks are left out.

---

**Box 6.4**

---

**Zakat and Islamic Banks.** According to Iqbal and Lewis (2014), banks and financial institutions operating under Islamic principles have established separate *zakat* accounts for collecting the funds and distributing them exclusively to the poor, either directly or through other religious institutions. *Zakat* is assessed on the initial capital of the bank, on its reserves, and on its profits. Responsibility for collecting and distributing *zakat* funds provided by the bank is vested in the *Shari'ah* Supervisory Board.

Islamic banks differ from conventional banks in other ways besides collection and distribution of *zakat*. Islamic banks do not invest in certain activities that are seen as inconsistent with Islamic principles, such as businesses that sell alcohol or pork. In this respect Islamic banks are like "socially responsible" investment funds (Arno Riedl and Paul Smeets 2017).

Islamic banking assets account for a large share of total domestic banking sector assets in many of the countries we study. By law, all banks in Iran and Sudan follow Islamic principles, so the market share of Islamic banking in those two countries is 100 percent. The Islamic Financial Services Board (https://www.ifsb.org) judges Islamic banking to be "systemically important" when its market share exceeds 15 percent. As of 2016, among the countries we study Islamic banking has surpassed this threshold in Saudi Arabia (51.1 percent), Kuwait (39.0 percent), Yemen (31–32 percent), Qatar (26.6 percent), UAE (19.6 percent), Djibouti (16.2 percent), and Jordan (15.2 percent).

Most studies of Islamic banking have focused on the commercial activities of the banks rather than their charitable activities. For economists the most striking feature of Islamic banks is that they are not supposed to charge interest on loans. Instead, an Islamic bank is supposed to act as a partner or major stockholder for the borrower, sharing in the profit or loss of the borrower rather than receiving a guaranteed rate of interest. In practice, Islamic banks often make contracts with clients in which they charge fees or mark up the value of an asset so that they receive a return that is equivalent to interest. As an example of such a contract, consider a client who approaches an Islamic bank wanting to buy a new car. The price quoted by the car dealer is US$20,000. The bank agrees to purchase the car on behalf of the client, and stipulates that the client must pay the bank US$22,000 in one year in order to take ownership of the car. This contract is similar to a conventional loan with a 10 percent interest rate. It is not exactly the same, however, because the bank clearly owns the car during the year-long duration of the contract, whereas under a conventional loan the car is collateral that the bank can claim if the client does not repay the loan.

Tarik Yousef (2004) collected data from Islamic banks and divided their contracts into profit-and-loss-sharing contracts and markup contracts. He found that on average the amount of funds committed to markup contracts is much greater than the amount of funds committed to profit-and-loss-sharing contracts. Other evidence presented

> by Yousef suggests that, relative to the rest of the world, Islamic banking has not shifted the mix of finance in Muslim-majority countries away from contracts that are like interest-bearing debt toward contracts that are like profit-and-loss-sharing equity. Research by Thorsten Beck, Asli Demirgüç-Kunt, and Ouarda Merrouche (2013) that uses more recent data comes to the same conclusions.

Benefits to the poor from Muslim charitable activities are not limited to cash. Like religious organizations in non-Muslim majority countries, Muslim religious organizations provide social services. They run hospitals and schools that typically charge less than private schools and hospitals that are not faith-based. As with *zakat*, data are scarce. A study by Jane Harrigan and Hamed El-Said (2009) of the activities of the Islamic Society Charity Center in Jordan in 2005 found that this organization ran 17 hospitals and clinics that served roughly 486,000 patients, and 51 kindergartens, primary and high schools with about 15,000 students.

## Unemployment and Self-Employment

Unemployment is usually studied in the context of business cycles. Unemployment rates rise during recessions and fall during recoveries. For example, the unemployment rate in the United States reached 10 percent in the depths of the Great Recession in 2009 and fell below 4 percent in 2018 after a long recovery. However, it is also recognized that some countries have sustained higher or lower *average* rates of unemployment, that is, averaging out the booms and busts of the business cycle. The best-studied example is the difference between the United States and Western Europe. The US unemployment rate has averaged about 6 percent since the end of World War II, whereas unemployment rates in some Western European countries like Ireland and Spain have averaged over 12 percent for the last several decades.

The causes of sustained differences in unemployment rates across countries are not well understood. For developing countries there is an additional complication of uncertainty as to how unemployment should be measured. The reason is that in most developing countries a large fraction of the labor force consists of *own-account* workers. These are self-employed individuals without paid employees. Most of them are involved in low-skill activities such as street vending, scavenging (recycling trash), and subsistence agriculture. Sometimes these workers are described as "underemployed." Uncertainty about how to classify such workers led the World Bank to write, "unemployment is not a very telling indicator in countries where a large fraction of the labor force is not salaried" (2012, p. 35). Yet at the same time the World Bank confidently asserts, "Unemployment in MENA is persistently higher than in other regions" (2013b, p. 43). For example, the World Bank reports that unemployment rates in Morocco averaged over 20 percent during the 1990s and early 2000s (2004, figures 3.21 and 3.22). However, the recent research by Ying Feng, David Lagakos, and James Rauch (2018) on which we draw below finds that Moroccan unemployment rates were stable at about 11.5 percent from 1994 to 2004. The discrepancy may be caused by the fact that roughly one-quarter of Moroccan workers were self-employed in low-skill occupations during this period (Feng et al. 2018).

This confusion suggests that we must be exceptionally clear about what we mean by "unemployment," and exceptionally careful to measure unemployment consistently across countries. Feng, Lagakos, and Rauch use 199 nationally representative household surveys covering 84 countries conducted in recent years, mostly between 2000 and 2010. An individual is defined as unemployed if he or she answers "no" to the survey question "Are you currently working?" and "yes" to the survey question "Are you searching for work?" Importantly, work includes wage employment, self-employment, and unpaid work in a family farm or business, but excludes home activities like cooking, cleaning, and care of one's own children. Search for work only counts if it is recent, typically within the last week. Feng et al. compute unemployment rates in each survey as (number of adults not working but searching for work) ÷ (number working + those not working but searching), then average over all surveys for each country to obtain average unemployment rates.

Feng et al. find that average unemployment rates are substantially lower in poor countries than in rich countries. In the poorest quarter of countries unemployment averages about 2.5 percent, and in the richest quarter of countries unemployment averages about 8 percent. To understand this surprising result, Feng et al. examine unemployment rates separately for workers with less than a high school education and workers with a high school education or more. They find that unemployment rates for the more educated have almost no trend in GDP per capita, but unemployment rates for the less educated increase steeply with GDP per capita. These two facts together imply that the *ratio* of unemployment for the less to more educated increases with GDP per capita.

To explain their results, Feng et al. return to the aforementioned importance of self-employment in low-skill occupations in poor countries. The self-employed do not have to search for jobs, so their unemployment rate is zero. In contrast, working for a business owned by someone else involves unemployment while searching for an employer with a suitable opening, and more unemployment if one is laid off and has to search for a new job. In order to tolerate occasional unemployment, workers must earn substantially more working for wages than they would earn through self-employment. Most more-educated workers earn substantially more even in poor countries, but not most less-educated workers. By contrast, in rich countries employers are much more productive, and nearly all low- as well as high-educated workers can earn wages much greater than their incomes from occupations like street vending and scavenging. Feng et al. compare the share of adults aged twenty-five to fifty-four that is self-employed in low-skill occupations in the poorest countries in their data (Malawi and Mali) to the same share for the richest countries in their data (Canada and Switzerland). For adults with low education this share is about 60 percentage points less in the richest than in the poorest countries, but only 15 percentage points less for adults with high education. Overall unemployment therefore goes up with GDP per capita, because workers are changing from a situation of zero unemployment to a situation of positive unemployment, and the ratio of unemployment of low- to high-educated workers also goes up, because a much greater percentage of low-educated workers is making this change.

Figure 6.10 shows the increase in average unemployment rates with GDP per capita found by Feng et al. (In order to compress the vertical dimension of the graph, the vertical axis in Figure 6.10 uses a base 2 logarithmic scale, in which the unemployment rate doubles with every tick mark.) Only four of the countries we study are included in their data. The years of each country's surveys and its average unemployment rate are: Iran (IRN), 2006 and 2011, 10.5 percent; Iraq (IRQ), 1997 and 2012, 11.3 percent; Morocco (MAR), 1994 and 2004, 11.5 percent; and Turkey (TUR), 1990 and 2000, 8.1 percent. We see from Figure 6.10 that all of these average unemployment rates are greater than those predicted by the GDPs per capita of the four countries. The results of Feng et al. are therefore consistent with the

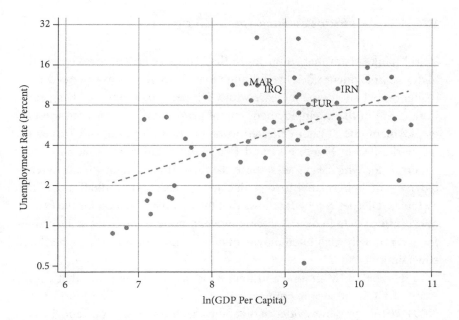

**Figure 6.10. Unemployment Rates by GDP Per Capita**

*Notes:* GDP per capita is in 2011 P$. Unemployment rates cover adults aged twenty-five to fifty-four.

*Source:* Ying Feng, David Lagakos, and James E. Rauch, National Bureau of Economic Research Working Paper No. 25171, figure 1 (October 2018).

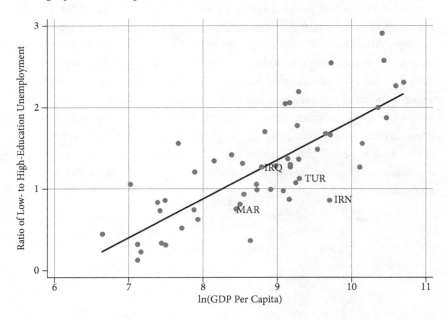

**Figure 6.11. Ratios of Unemployment Rates by GDP Per Capita**

*Notes:* GDP per capita is in 2011 P$. Unemployment rates cover adults aged twenty-five to fifty-four. Low education = less than high school, high education = high school or greater.

*Source:* Ying Feng, David Lagakos, and James E. Rauch, National Bureau of Economic Research Working Paper No. 25171, figure 3 (October 2018).

World Bank's claim that countries in the MENA region have exceptionally high unemployment rates, even though that claim may be exaggerated.

Figure 6.11 shows the increase with GDP per capita found by Feng et al. in the ratio of the unemployment rate of low-educated workers to the unemployment rate of high-educated workers. Iran, Morocco, and Turkey lie below the line in Figure 6.11 and Iraq is on it, indicating that all of our countries for which Feng et al. have data have the same or greater unemployment of high- relative to low-educated workers than would be predicted by their GDPs per capita. It follows that the first place to look for the causes of exceptionally high overall unemployment in these countries is the causes for exceptionally high unemployment of workers with at least a high school education.

In the section "Migration and Remittances," we saw evidence that a high share of GCC citizens is employed in the public sector. The World Bank (2004, 2013b) presents evidence that other Arab countries, Iran, and Turkey also have high shares of workers employed in the public sector, though lower than in the GCC countries. As mentioned in the section "Poverty Headcounts," Adams and Page (2003) found that government employment contributed to lower poverty in MENA countries. The World Bank (2004, 2013b) has argued that educated workers in particular *expect* to receive public sector jobs. Governments outside the GCC are not rich enough to deliver on these expectations as soon as students graduate, so graduates have to wait for positions to become available. They could take private sector jobs in the meantime, but this may hinder their search for public sector openings. Instead, they turn down private sector jobs that are not as good as the public sector jobs they expect and live with their parents while continuing to search, hence showing up as unemployed in surveys. This is a plausible story, but must be considered a conjecture until there is better evidence.

# 7
# Environmental Challenges

## Introduction

Except for Lebanon and Turkey, part or all of the land areas of the countries we study lie in a desert climate zone, receiving less than 200 millimeters (7.87 inches) of rainfall per year. This creates two special environmental challenges, water scarcity and desert dust. We will investigate how these challenges affect the countries we study using a framework set out by the World Bank (1993) in a landmark 1992 World Development Report titled *Development and the Environment*. In this report the World Bank classified environmental problems into three types. The first type of problem improves as GDP per capita increases, the second type gets worse but then improves as GDP per capita increases, and the third type steadily worsens as GDP per capita increases.

The main examples of the first type of environmental problem are lack of access to safe water and lack of access to adequate sanitation. These problems arise in part because population growth generates human waste that fouls rivers and springs, making the water unsuitable for drinking or washing. Increased GDP per capita gives countries the resources to treat water and provide sanitation facilities, causing these problems to improve.

The main example of the second type of environmental problem is air pollution. Industrial processes, motor vehicle use, and electric power generation rise with GDP per capita and emit air pollutants, causing air pollution to become worse as GDP per capita increases. At the same time households become richer and demand government action to regulate the sources of air pollution. In 1992 the World Bank found that the first effect was stronger when GDP per capita was low and the second effect was stronger when GDP per capita was high, so that air pollution became worse as GDP per capita increased below some threshold and improved as GDP per capita increased above that threshold.

The main examples of the third type of environmental problem are municipal wastes and greenhouse gas emissions. As GDP per capita increases and households consume more, they generate more waste, mainly packaging and food waste. Burying wastes in municipal landfills puts this problem "out of sight, out of mind," preventing the emergence of public demands to address the problem. Increased GDP per capita causes greater emissions of greenhouse gases for the same reason it causes greater emissions of air pollutants that have more immediate and local health consequences. The negative environmental impact of greenhouse gas emissions, global warming, is poorly understood by the public, occurs mainly in the future, and is felt worldwide rather than only locally. For all these reasons increasing GDP per capita has not generated demand to reduce greenhouse gas emissions until recently.

In the next section of this chapter, titled "Water Scarcity and Lack of Access to Basic Drinking Water and Sanitation Services," we find that most of the countries we study have exacerbated their problems of water scarcity by charging water utility customers less than the cost of supplying them with the water they use. Nevertheless, on average they have been able to provide access to safe drinking water at the same rate or better than predicted by their GDPs per capita. They have been even more successful at solving the problem of lack of access to sanitation, where water scarcity is a much less severe handicap. As a result the countries we study tend to be less burdened by water-borne diseases than the comparison country groups.

The section titled "Air Pollution" shows that the countries we study have been much less successful at solving the problem of air pollution, measured by atmospheric concentration of fine particulate matter. The cause appears to be desert dust. For this reason the countries we study tend to be more burdened by respiratory and cardiovascular diseases caused by air pollution than are the comparison country groups.

We find in the section titled "Municipal Waste and Greenhouse Gas Emissions" that most countries we study generate about the same or less municipal wastes per capita than predicted by their GDPs per capita. Nevertheless, as their GDPs per capita grow, so do their problems with municipal waste disposal, and in Lebanon the problem has turned into a crisis. We also find that the GCC countries and Iran generate more carbon dioxide emissions, the main component of greenhouse gases, than predicted by their GDPs per capita. However, their emissions are not great enough to significantly affect the world total, which is what ultimately drives global warming.

The section titled "The Consequences of Global Warming for the Arab Countries, Iran, and Turkey" focuses on two main consequences of global warming, rising sea levels and heat waves. Forecasts of damages from rising sea levels by 2100 are especially high for Algeria, Egypt, and Morocco. In just the next two decades the numbers of heat wave days are predicted to triple or more in most of the countries we study. Similar consequences of global warming are faced by countries throughout the world, and only a worldwide solution is possible.

## Water Scarcity and Lack of Access to Basic Drinking Water and Sanitation Services

Most of the Arab countries and Iran are attempting to provide their populations with at least basic drinking water services in an environment of pervasive water scarcity. Table 7.1 shows the world ranks of the countries

Table 7.1. World Rank by Freshwater Withdrawal as Percent of Total Renewable Water Resources

| Arab Sub-Saharan Africa | | Arab Fuel-Endowed Countries | | Arab Mediterranean | |
|---|---|---|---|---|---|
| Comoros | 161 | Algeria | 21 | Egypt | 8 |
| Djibouti | 93 | Bahrain | 6 | Jordan | 9 |
| Mauritania | 72 | Iraq | 17 | Lebanon | 46 |
| Somalia | 48 | Kuwait | 1 | Morocco | 28 |
| Sudan | 18 | Libya | 4 | Syria | 14 |
| Yemen | 7 | Oman | 13 | Tunisia | 19 |
| | | Qatar | 5 | | |
| | | Saudi Arabia | 3 | | |
| | | UAE | 2 | | |
| Non-Arab countries | | Iran | 20 | Turkey | 51 |

*Notes*: World ranks for countries are based on data for the years shown below. These were the most recent years available.
Arab sub-Saharan Africa: Comoros (1999), Djibouti (2000), Mauritania (2005), Somalia (2003), Sudan (2011), and Yemen (2005).
Arab fuel-endowed countries: Algeria (2012), Bahrain (2003), Iraq (2000), Kuwait (2002), Libya (2012), Oman (2003), Qatar (2005), Saudi Arabia (2006), and UAE (2005).
Non-Arab fuel-endowed countries: Iran (2004).
Arab Mediterranean: Egypt (2010), Jordan (2015), Lebanon (2005), Morocco (2010), Syria (2005), and Tunisia (2011).
Rest of non-Arab world: Turkey (2008).
*Source of data*: Food and Agriculture Organization of the United Nations, AQUASTAT database.

we study by a standard measure of water scarcity, freshwater withdrawal as a percentage of total renewable water resources (the sum of renewable surface and groundwater). The countries we study include the top nine most water scarce countries in the world, and sixteen of the top twenty-one. The most water-scarce country group is the Arab fuel-endowed countries, but even in Arab sub-Saharan Africa the two countries that account for most of the population, Sudan and Yemen, are ranked number eighteen and seven, respectively.

Water scarcity raises the costs of supplying water reliably to households. Water must be transported over longer distances. Reservoirs must be built to store water for dry periods. The World Bank notes, "About 85 percent of total surface freshwater resources in the Middle East and North Africa are stored in reservoirs, compared to a global average of ten percent" (2017, pp. 57–58). The countries we study have increasingly turned to desalination, that is, removal of salt from seawater to turn it into freshwater. Desalination is the largest single source of water for four of the GCC countries, Bahrain, Kuwait, Qatar, and UAE (World Bank 2017, figure 2.8). As technological progress continues to lower the cost of desalination, making it competitive with other sources of freshwater, we can expect the importance of desalinized water as a source of freshwater to continue to increase for the countries we study that border on a source of seawater.

Given their high costs of supplying water, one would expect the water utilities in the countries we study to charge consumers more than water utilities in the comparison country groups. Table 7.2 shows that the opposite is usually true. Water tariffs (prices charged by water utilities) are lower in Arab sub-Saharan Africa than in non-Arab sub-Saharan Africa, and lower in the Arab Mediterranean than in any of its comparison country groups. Water tariffs in the Arab fuel-endowed countries are higher than in the non-Arab fuel-endowed countries, but still lower than in the rest of the non-Arab world. Water utilities in Iran charge only $0.21 per cubic meter of water (approximately 264 gallons), roughly one-tenth of what water utilities charge in Turkey. Turkey is exceptional among the countries we study, but not because its water tariffs are extraordinarily high: Water tariffs in Turkey are in between those for Latin America and Southern Europe. Low water tariffs in the Arab countries and Iran fit a pattern of government subsidization of basic consumer goods and services, including food subsidies (discussed in the previous chapter) and energy subsidies (covered in the next chapter); Turkey is a consistent exception to this pattern. Artificially

**Table 7.2.** Water Tariffs per Cubic Meter (Current US$)

| | |
|---|---|
| Arab sub-Saharan Africa | 0.35 |
| Non-Arab sub-Saharan Africa | 1.47 |
| Arab fuel-endowed countries | 1.01 |
| Non-Arab fuel-endowed countries | 0.42 |
| Iran | 0.21 |
| Arab Mediterranean | 0.57 |
| Rest of non-Arab world | 1.48 |
| Turkey | 2.14 |
| Latin America | 1.49 |
| Southern Europe | 3.75 |

*Notes*: Data are for the most recent year available, usually 2016 or 2017. One cubic meter = 1,000 liters = approximately 264 gallons. Tariffs are utility rates based on consumption of six cubic meters per month. When there are data for more than one utility in a country, the tariff for that country equals the average weighted by population served by each utility. The population-weighted averages for each country group include the countries listed in the Appendix. The excluded countries were missing data.

*Source of data*: International Benchmarking Network for Water and Sanitation Utilities, https://tariffs.ib-net.org.

cheap water leads to greater freshwater withdrawal and thus exacerbates the water scarcity documented in Table 7.1.

The flip side of artificially low water tariffs is that there is much scope to encourage water conservation in the Arab countries and Iran by raising water tariffs to reflect the true costs of water supply. In the majority of these countries most water is used by agriculture, so that modest conservation by farmers can make sufficient water available to satisfy growing urban demand. According to the World Bank, if agricultural water use could be reduced by 20 percent by 2030, most of the MENA countries would be able to meet their projected increases in municipal water demand without having to augment water supplies (2017, p. 57). We must also bear in mind that the countries we study have a long history of managing water scarcity. The World Bank explains, "Middle East and North Africa is home to some of the best hydraulic engineers in the world, the region manages sophisticated irrigation and drainage systems, and has spearheaded advances in desalination technology" (2007b, p. xxiv).

With this background in place, we are ready to examine the ability of the Arab countries, Iran, and Turkey to supply households with at least basic drinking water services. Basic drinking water services are defined by the World Bank as "drinking water from an improved source, provided collection time is not more than 30 minutes for a round trip. Improved water sources include piped water, boreholes or tubewells, protected dug wells, protected springs, and packaged or delivered water." In Figure 7.1 we plot the share of the population that lacks access to basic drinking water services against the logarithm of GDP per capita. The figure confirms that lack of access to relatively safe water is an environmental problem that improves with GDP per capita. Indeed, above GDP per capita of roughly 2011 P$22,000 (ln(GDP per capita) greater than 10), nearly all countries have virtually universal access to at least basic drinking water services. We therefore omit

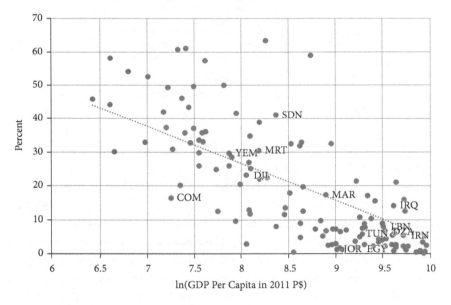

**Figure 7.1.** Population Lacking Access to Basic Drinking Water Services by GDP Per Capita, 2015

*Notes:* Data are provided as "population using at least basic drinking water services." We subtract this from one hundred to obtain "population lacking access to basic drinking water services." List of included countries available on request.

*Source of data:* World Development Indicators.

these countries, which include Turkey and the GCC, from Figure 7.1. We see that most Arab countries and Iran are near or below the line in Figure 7.1, indicating that they are doing as well or better than expected, on the basis of their GDPs per capita, at providing water services. The exceptions are Mauritania (MRT), Sudan (SDN), and Iraq (IRQ). As discussed in the next chapter, Iraq's difficulties with drinking water supply are symptomatic of a broader problem with infrastructure services caused by the destruction of past wars.

Besides lack of access to safe water, the other environmental problem we will consider that improves with GDP per capita is lack of access to basic sanitation services. Basic sanitation services are defined by the World Bank as including toilets that flush/pour flush to piped sewer systems, septic tanks or pit latrines; ventilated improved pit latrines; and composting toilets or pit latrines with slabs. In Figure 7.2 we plot the share of the population that lacks access to basic sanitation services against the logarithm of GDP per capita.

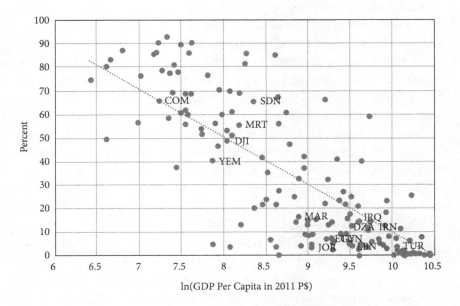

**Figure 7.2.** Population Lacking Access to Basic Sanitation Services by GDP Per Capita, 2015

*Notes:* Data are provided as "population using at least basic sanitation services." We subtract this from one hundred to obtain "population lacking access to basic sanitation services." List of included countries available on request.

*Source of data:* World Development Indicators.

The figure confirms that lack of access to basic sanitation is an environmental problem that improves with GDP per capita. All countries with GDP per capita above roughly 2011 P$36,300 (ln(GDP per capita) greater than 10.5), which include the GCC, have essentially solved the problem of lack of access to sanitation and we omit them from Figure 7.2. Comparing Figure 7.2 with Figure 7.1 shows that the Arab countries and Iran have had even greater success with providing access to sanitation than drinking water, indicating that water scarcity may have had some negative impact on drinking water provision. In particular, Iraq (IRQ), Morocco (MAR), and Yemen (YEM) are below the levels of lack of access predicted by their GDPs per capita in Figure 7.2, whereas they are at or above those levels in Figure 7.1.

Lack of access to basic drinking water and sanitation are important environmental problems because they have serious health consequences. In computing the disability-adjusted life years (DALY) caused by exposure to unsafe water and sanitation, the World Health Organization (WHO) focuses on diarrheal diseases. It combines data on DALY caused by diarrheal diseases, which we saw in Table 4.6, with the data on exposure to unsafe water and sanitation used in Figures 7.1 and 7.2 to compute a "population attributable fraction," the fraction of DALY caused by diarrheal diseases that can be attributed to unsafe water and sanitation. WHO does not do this calculation for high-income countries because very few DALY are caused by diarrheal diseases in these countries and there is very little exposure to unsafe water and sanitation.

Table 7.3 shows DALY attributable to unsafe water and sanitation (through their causation of diarrheal diseases) for the three Arab worlds, Iran, Turkey, and the comparison country groups. The GCC countries are excluded from the Arab fuel-endowed countries because WHO does not provide data for them due to their high incomes. Data are for the year 2012 and, unlike the data in Table 4.6, are not adjusted for the age structure of the population because WHO did not make the adjustments. We see that the burdens of disease attributable to unsafe water and sanitation are far greater in sub-Saharan Africa than elsewhere, and somewhat less in Arab sub-Saharan Africa than in non-Arab sub-Saharan Africa. The burdens of disease attributable to unsafe water and sanitation in Iran are lower than in the non-GCC Arab fuel-endowed countries. It is interesting that the number of DALY per 100,000 population attributable to unsafe sanitation in Iran is close to the number for Turkey, whereas for unsafe water the number

**Table 7.3.** Burdens of Disease Attributable to Unsafe Water and Sanitation, 2012 (DALY per 100,000 Population)

|  | Unsafe Water | Unsafe Sanitation |
|---|---|---|
| Arab sub-Saharan Africa | 1726 | 938 |
| Non-Arab sub-Saharan Africa | 2108 | 1165 |
| Arab fuel-endowed countries | 180 | 23 |
| Non-Arab fuel-endowed countries | 73 | 9 |
| Iran | 74 | 6 |
| Arab Mediterranean | 125 | 12 |
| Rest of non-Arab world | 320 | 181 |
| Turkey | 41 | 7 |
| Latin America | 67 | 21 |

*Notes*: The population-weighted averages for each country group include the countries listed in the Appendix. The excluded countries were missing data.
*Source of data*: Global Health Observatory, World Health Organization.

is much higher. This probably results from the greater problem of water scarcity in Iran than in Turkey. Similarly, the number of DALY per 100,000 population attributable to unsafe sanitation in the Arab Mediterranean is much lower than the number for Latin America and less than one-tenth the number in the rest of the non-Arab world, whereas for unsafe water the number is nearly double that for Latin America and more than one-third the number for the rest of the non-Arab world.

Outside of sub-Saharan Africa, the Arab countries, Iran, and Turkey have had great success in solving the environmental problem of lack of access to basic sanitation. Water scarcity has made it more difficult for the Arab countries and Iran to solve the problem of lack of access to basic drinking water, yet most of these countries are doing as well or better than predicted by their GDPs per capita. By raising the tariffs charged by their water utilities to reflect their costs of supplying water, these countries could not only encourage water conservation but also finance improvements in water treatment that will reduce the incidence of diarrheal diseases.

## Air Pollution

The air pollutant of greatest concern for the countries we study is fine particulate matter. We will measure this by micrograms per cubic meter of $PM_{2.5}$: suspended particles less than 2.5 microns in aerodynamic diameter. Since air pollution varies within a country from day to day and from place to place, the World Bank calculates an average over the year, weighted by population, of the measurements taken from different sites around a given country. Exposure to $PM_{2.5}$ has greater health consequences than exposure to larger particulate matter. Fine particulates reach the lungs rather than being filtered out by the upper respiratory system, and enter the bloodstream from the lungs. This causes respiratory disorders such as asthma and pneumonia, and cardiovascular diseases including strokes.

In *Development and the Environment*, the World Bank cited particulate matter air pollution as an example of an environmental problem that initially worsens as GDP per capita increases, then improves. Particulates typically form in the atmosphere as a result of chemical reactions undergone by pollutants emitted from power plants, industrial processes, and motor vehicles. These sources of pollutants grow with GDP per capita, causing increased atmospheric concentration of particulate matter. However, increased GDP per capita is also associated with a reduction in infectious diseases, as we saw in Chapter 4, and consequently a larger role for the kinds of diseases caused by particulates in determining overall health. This leads to greater public demand for government action to reduce air pollution. Richer countries are also better at enforcing regulations on sources of particulate matter such as automobile exhaust. These factors eventually reduce atmospheric concentration of particulate matter despite continued growth of power generation, industry, and motor vehicle use.

The same reasons for particulate air pollution to increase or decrease with GDP per capita are present in the countries we study. In many of them, however, another source of $PM_{2.5}$ is even more important: desert dust. This source is unrelated to GDP per capita. The relationship between atmospheric concentration of $PM_{2.5}$ and GDP per capita for the countries we study may therefore be very different than in the rest of the world.

Figure 7.3 plots exposure to $PM_{2.5}$ against GDP per capita for 2015, the same year used in Figures 7.1 and 7.2. If the environmental problem of $PM_{2.5}$ exposure initially worsened as GDP per capita increased, then improved, we would see a hump-shaped curve in Figure 7.3. In fact, a downward-sloping

ENVIRONMENTAL CHALLENGES    181

line describes the relationship between PM$_{2.5}$ exposure and (the logarithm of) GDP per capita better than does a hump-shaped curve. Evidently the world has changed since 1992, when *Development and the Environment* was published. We also see that nearly all the countries we study lie above the downward-sloping line in Figure 7.3, many far above. Although the data do not allow us to separate desert dust particulates from other sources of particulate pollution, we can guess that dust from the Arabian, Sahara, and Somali deserts is responsible for the exceptionally high levels of PM$_{2.5}$ exposure in, respectively: Bahrain (BHR), Iraq (IRQ), Kuwait (KWT), Oman (OMN), Qatar (QAT), Saudi Arabia (SAU), UAE (ARE), and Yemen (YEM); Egypt (EGY), Mauritania (MRT), and Sudan (SDN); and Djibouti (DJI). The populations of Algeria (DZA), Morocco (MAR), and Tunisia (TUN) are concentrated near their coasts, and are hence much less exposed to Sahara desert dust despite having large Sahara desert land areas.

In sum, in the world as a whole particulate air pollution tends to be worst in the poorest countries, but among the countries we study it tends to be worst in the richest countries. The reason is that the GCC countries suffer

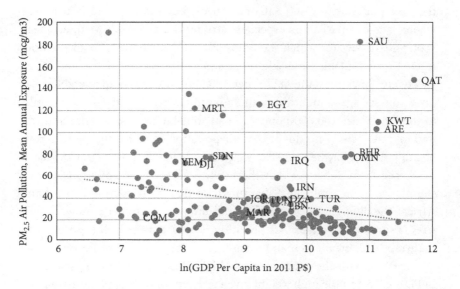

**Figure 7.3.** Particulate Air Pollution by GDP Per Capita, 2015

*Notes*: PM$_{2.5}$ = suspended particles less than 2.5 microns in aerodynamic diameter; mcg/m3 = micrograms per cubic meter of air. List of included countries available on request.
*Source of data*: World Development Indicators.

greatly from desert dust pollution, as well as having high particulate emissions from oil and natural gas extraction.

As is the case with particulate matter from other sources, harmful effects on health of desert dust are well documented, especially for $PM_{2.5}$. Xuelei Zhang and co-authors (2016) do a comprehensive survey of recent studies. The evidence is strong enough that use of the WHO estimates of DALY caused by ambient (outdoor) air pollution is warranted for our region, even though the strength of the connection between the most injurious component of air pollution, $PM_{2.5}$, and various diseases was developed for sources of fine particulates other than desert dust. WHO assigns to outdoor air pollution fractions of the burdens of the following diseases: acute respiratory infections in young children, cerebrovascular diseases in adults (related to strokes), ischemic heart diseases in adults, chronic obstructive pulmonary disease in adults (bronchitis and emphysema), and lung cancer in adults.

Table 7.4 reports age-standardized DALY per 100,000 population in 2012 attributable to outdoor air pollution for the three Arab worlds, Iran, Turkey, and the comparison groups of countries. Comparing Table 7.3 to Table 7.4 shows that unsafe water and sanitation are a much larger health problem than air pollution for sub-Saharan Africa, but the opposite is true elsewhere. The comparison is especially striking for the Arab Mediterranean, Iran, and Turkey, for which the ratios of DALY attributable to air pollution to DALY attributable to unsafe water and sanitation are 11, 15, and 26, respectively. Since only the DALY per 100,000 population attributable to air pollution are age-standardized, these numbers are not strictly comparable to the DALY per 100,000 population attributable to unsafe water and sanitation, but there is no doubt that air pollution is by far the more serious health problem for the countries we study outside of sub-Saharan Africa.

We see from Table 7.4 that the health effects of air pollution are only slightly worse in Arab sub-Saharan Africa than in non-Arab sub-Saharan Africa. The difference between the Arab and non-Arab fuel-endowed countries is somewhat greater. Air pollution is a far greater health problem for the Arab Mediterranean than for Latin America or Southern Europe, which is consistent with the extraordinarily high $PM_{2.5}$ exposure in Egypt shown in Figure 7.3 and the high weight given to Egypt in the population-weighted average for the Arab Mediterranean in Table 7.4. Particulate pollution in Cairo does not only cause the poor visibility shown in Figure 7.4; it also causes poor health. The DALY per 100,000 population attributable to air

**Table 7.4.** Age-Standardized Burdens of Diseases Attributable to Outdoor Air Pollution, 2012 (DALY per 100,000 Population)

| | |
|---|---|
| Arab sub-Saharan Africa | 1394 |
| Non-Arab sub-Saharan Africa | 1321 |
| Arab fuel-endowed countries | 1304 |
| Non-Arab fuel-endowed countries | 1038 |
| Iran | 1239 |
| Arab Mediterranean | 1533 |
| Rest of non-Arab world | 1233 |
| Turkey | 1239 |
| Latin America | 445 |
| Southern Europe | 246 |

*Notes*: The population-weighted averages for each country group include the countries listed in the Appendix. The excluded countries were missing data.

*Source of data*: Global Health Observatory, World Health Organization

pollution in the Arab Mediterranean are not so much greater than in the rest of the non-Arab world, however. Closer inspection of the data reveals that the DALY per 100,000 population attributable to air pollution in China and India are similar to the level in Egypt, and these two countries have very large weights in the population-weighted average for the rest of the non-Arab world.

The ability of countries to reduce air pollution will be greater when the sources of pollution are human activity rather than the natural environment. In this regard it is interesting to compare Iran and Turkey. Their levels of DALY per 100,000 population attributable to air pollution are the same, and quite high, though not as high as in the Arab fuel-endowed countries or Arab Mediterranean. However, Iran is more vulnerable to desert dust than is Turkey, so the scope for policy to reduce air pollution ($PM_{2.5}$ exposure in particular) and its health effects should be greater in Turkey than in Iran.

Since desert dust cannot be reduced by government policies, citizens of the countries we study that are especially vulnerable to desert dust must find other ways to protect their health. One possibility is to use

**Figure 7.4.** View from Window of Sixteenth-Century Al-Ghuriya Minaret to Twin Minarets of Fifteenth-Century Al-Mu'ayyad Shaykh Mosque, 400 Meters (1,300 feet) Away
*Source:* Photograph by Doris Bittar.

particulate-filtering facemasks. In China the use of particulate-filtering facemasks has become popular during periods of peak air pollution, according to research by Junjie Zhang and Quan Mu (2018). They note, "field experiments are required to measure the actual effect of facemasks on protecting health. There is only one known experiment that studied the daily use [of] facemasks against the ambient air pollution. This experiment in Beijing found that wearing a typical anti-PM facemask reduced personal exposure to particulate matter by 96.6 percent. As a result, in this experiment, facemasks were found to diminish the adverse effects of air pollution on blood pressure and heart rate variability" (pp. 3–4). The encouraging results of this experiment suggest that a similar experiment be carried out in one or more of the countries we study. The GCC countries are natural candidates, since Figure 7.3 shows they have a serious $PM_{2.5}$ pollution problem, and they can afford to conduct such experiments.

## Municipal Waste and Greenhouse Gas Emissions

As we stated in the introduction to this chapter, municipal waste and greenhouse gas emissions are environmental problems that grow steadily worse as GDP per capita increases. Figure 7.5 confirms that municipal waste per capita increases with GDP per capita. For each country we use data for the most recent available year. This is typically 2015, but can be as far back as 2000. Many countries lack data. We see that the countries we study that have data available produce roughly the same or lower amounts of municipal waste than predicted by their GDPs per capita, with the exception of Qatar (QAT).

Government-sponsored recycling is gradually spreading to the richer countries we study, such as UAE. In poorer countries recycling is mainly handled informally, by scavengers. This is a significant source of the own-account self-employment discussed in Chapter 6. Recycling slows but does not stop the accumulation of waste in landfills. One might think that countries with sparsely populated deserts, like most of the countries we study, could easily find space to safely bury their municipal waste. In practice,

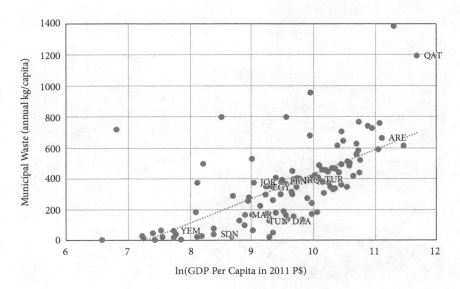

Figure 7.5. Municipal Waste by GDP Per Capita

*Notes*: kg = kilogram = 2.2 pounds. List of included country-year observations available on request.
*Source of data*: United Nations Statistics Division, Environment Statistics Database.

however, trucking waste from the densely populated areas that produce it to sparsely populated areas is too expensive, so landfills are typically located in or near cities. This is true both inside and outside the region we study. San Diego, California is sixty miles from a sparsely populated desert, but its municipal landfill is well within its city limits.

Since 2015 the environmental problem of municipal waste has exploded into a full-scale health crisis in Lebanon. Lebanon is one of the most densely populated countries in the world, and the second-most densely populated country we study, after Bahrain. Space for landfills is scarce. Moreover, the government of Lebanon is very weak. The combination of a weak government and scarce landfill space has created effects that are both disastrous and comical, as discussed in Box 7.1.

### Box 7.1

**Municipal Waste in Lebanon.** In 2015 the main garbage dump for Beirut, Lebanon, already beyond its capacity, was closed. Mountains of trash piled up in the streets, and an infamous "river" of garbage

Figure 7.6. "River of Trash" in Suburb of Beirut, Lebanon, 2016
*Source:* Associated Press, http://www.apimages.com/metadata/Index/Pictures-Of-The-Week-Photo-Gallery/488d4307c0c6402990656788c19f1a6e/1/0.

> formed in one suburb (see Figure 7.6). In 2016 the government hauled the trash off the streets to temporary dumps along the Mediterranean, one of which is near the international airport. As reported by Nabih Bulos (2017) this attracted birds, which became a flight hazard for the planes using the airport. The government then hired hunters to shoot the birds! This put Lebanon in violation of the Agreement on the Conservation of African-Eurasian Migratory Waterbirds, which the government signed in 2002.
>
> At time of writing the environmental damage and health effects caused by municipal waste in Lebanon do not appear to be contained. Garbage is fouling the Mediterranean, and Lebanese increasingly resort to burning trash in the open air. Is Lebanon the proverbial "canary in the coal mine" for the countries we study, and for the rest of the world?

At present there are no data available that allow us to compare the health problems caused by municipal wastes in the countries we study to other countries, or even to quantify the health effects of municipal waste in any one country. There are many alternatives to burying waste in landfills that may do less environmental damage, but no one solution has clearly emerged as the best. Figure 7.5 suggests that the problem of municipal waste will grow progressively worse worldwide as GDPs per capita increase, so we can expect the search for solutions to intensify, and hope that one or more solutions will prove viable in the countries we study.

We now turn to the other environmental problem found to grow worse as GDP per capita increases, greenhouse gas emissions, which scientists believe are causing global warming. Thus the environmental problem caused by greenhouse gas emissions is not local, like the other environmental problems we have discussed in this chapter, but global. Carbon dioxide emissions are roughly three-quarters of world greenhouse gas emissions. Carbon dioxide emissions are mainly caused by burning fossil fuels, especially coal but also oil and natural gas. Carbon dioxide emissions can therefore be reduced by switching from fossil fuels to renewable sources of energy such as solar and wind power. This switch will eventually reduce the value of fuel exports from the Arab fuel-endowed countries and Iran, hence the need discussed in Chapter 3 for them to diversify their exports. Nevertheless, all of these countries have signed the Paris climate accord pledging to reduce their emissions of greenhouse gases, because they recognize the severe consequences they will suffer from global warming, discussed in the next section of this chapter.

Panel (a) of Figure 7.7 confirms that carbon dioxide ($CO_2$) emissions increase with GDP per capita. In fact, carbon dioxide emissions increase with GDP per capita at an accelerating rate—the curve in Panel (a) of Figure 7.7 gets steeper as GDP per capita increases. We see that the GCC countries, especially Bahrain (BHR), Kuwait (KWT), and Saudi Arabia (SAU), lie above the curve. The GCC countries are so prominent in the upper right of Panel (a) of Figure 7.7 that one wonders whether they are driving the accelerating relationship between carbon dioxide emissions and GDP per capita. For this reason we remove all six of them from the data completely in Panel (b) of Figure 7.7, and also truncate the horizontal and vertical axes at 11 and 20, respectively, so the remaining data can be seen more clearly. The curve in Panel (b) is only slightly flatter than in Panel (a). Of the countries we study, Iran (IRN) stands out most above the curve in Panel (b).

Carbon dioxide emissions increase with GDP per capita because the main sources of carbon dioxide emissions increase with GDP per capita: electric power generation, industrial processes, and motor vehicle use. By this same logic, however, emissions of fine particulate matter should increase with GDP per capita, yet we saw in Figure 7.3 that atmospheric concentrations of fine particulates are falling with GDP per capita. The reason is that richer countries decrease their particulate emissions per dollar of GDP enough to more than offset their higher GDPs per capita. It is possible to achieve the same results for carbon dioxide emissions, despite the tendency shown in Figure 7.7 for the positive relationship between emissions and GDP per capita to strengthen as GDP per capita increases. Carbon dioxide emissions equal GDP times carbon dioxide emissions divided by GDP. We will call carbon dioxide emissions divided by GDP the carbon dioxide *intensity* of GDP. If the carbon dioxide intensity of GDP decreases faster than GDP increases, carbon dioxide emissions decrease. The European Union has been steadily reducing its carbon dioxide emissions since at least 1990 by reducing the carbon dioxide intensity of its GDP.

Table 7.5 shows the carbon dioxide intensity of GDP for the three Arab worlds, Iran, Turkey, and the comparison country groups in 2014. Carbon dioxide intensity is highest for the fuel-endowed countries, and even higher for the non-Arab fuel-endowed countries, especially Iran, than for the Arab fuel-endowed countries. This is why Iran was above the curve in Panel (b) of Figure 7.7 and why the GCC countries were above the curve in Panel (a). The high carbon dioxide intensity of the fuel-endowed countries occurs for at

(a)

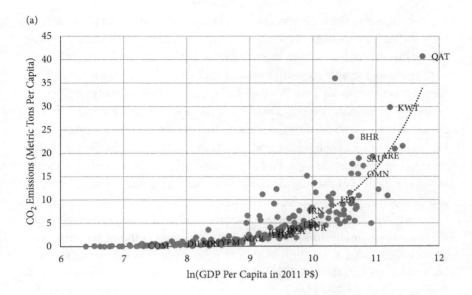

(b)

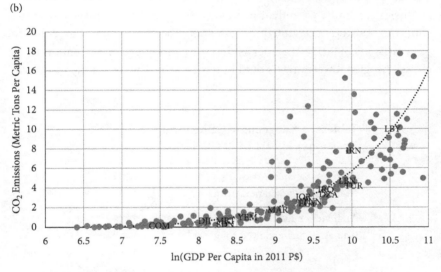

**Figure 7.7.** (a) $CO_2$ Emissions by GDP Per Capita, 2010
(b) $CO_2$ Emissions by GDP Per Capita, No GCC Countries, 2010

Notes: 1 metric ton = 1,000 kilograms; 1 kilogram = 2.2 pounds. 2010 is most recent year for which data are available for most countries. List of included countries available on request.
Source of data: World Development Indicators.

least two reasons. First, the process of fuel extraction itself is very intensive in carbon dioxide emissions. Second, as we will discuss in the next chapter, the fuel-endowed countries keep their prices of petroleum products artificially low, causing excessive consumption and thus excessive emissions of carbon dioxide. We also see in Table 7.5 that the carbon dioxide intensity of GDP for Arab sub-Saharan Africa is essentially the same as in non-Arab sub-Saharan Africa. For the Arab Mediterranean and Turkey, carbon dioxide intensity of GDP is less than in the rest of the non-Arab world but more than in Latin America or Southern Europe. Part of the reason that carbon dioxide intensity is high in the rest of the non-Arab world is that China has one of the world's most carbon dioxide-intensive economies.

Clearly the Arab fuel-endowed countries and Iran have scope to sharply decrease their emissions of carbon dioxide by reducing the carbon intensity of their GDPs. Yet their contribution to greenhouse gas emissions is small on a global scale. Table 7.6 shows that the Arab fuel-endowed countries and Iran account for more than half of the greenhouse gas emissions from the countries we study, yet only 4 percent of the world total. All together the countries we study accounted for less than 7 percent of world greenhouse gas emissions in 2012. This means that the consequence of greenhouse gas emissions, global warming, is out of their control. The rest of the world will

**Table 7.5.** Kilograms of Carbon Dioxide Emissions per 2011 P$ of GDP, 2014

| | |
|---|---|
| Arab sub-Saharan Africa | 0.155 |
| Non-Arab sub-Saharan Africa | 0.154 |
| Arab fuel-endowed countries | 0.346 |
| Non-Arab fuel-endowed countries | 0.446 |
| Iran | 0.489 |
| Arab Mediterranean | 0.239 |
| Rest of non-Arab world | 0.342 |
| Turkey | 0.200 |
| Latin America | 0.192 |
| Southern Europe | 0.167 |

*Notes*: 1 kilogram = 2.2 pounds. The population-weighted averages for each country group include the countries listed in the Appendix. The excluded countries were missing data.
*Source of data*: World Development Indicators.

Table 7.6. Percentage of Three Arab Worlds, Iran, and Turkey in World Greenhouse Gas Emissions, 2012

| | |
|---|---|
| Arab sub-Saharan Africa | 1.1 |
| Arab fuel-endowed countries | 2.7 |
| Iran | 1.3 |
| Arab Mediterranean | 1.0 |
| Turkey | 0.8 |
| Total | 6.9 |

*Notes*: Data are for latest available year. The percentage for each country group equals the sum of the percentages for every country in the group. The countries in each group are listed below.

Arab sub-Saharan Africa: Comoros (2012), Djibouti (2012), Mauritania (2012), Somalia (2012), Sudan (2012), and Yemen (2012).

Arab fuel-endowed countries: Algeria (2012), Bahrain (2012), Iraq (2012), Kuwait (2011), Libya (2012), Oman (2012), Qatar (2012), Saudi Arabia (2011), and UAE (2012).

Iran (2007).

Arab Mediterranean: Egypt (2012), Jordan (2012), Lebanon (2008), Morocco (2012), Syria (2012), and Tunisia (2012).

Turkey (2012).

*Source of data*: World Development Indicators.

determine climate change, and the Arab countries, Iran, and Turkey must cope with it as best they can.

## The Consequences of Global Warming for the Arab Countries, Iran, and Turkey

Almost by definition, the consequences of global warming will be felt worldwide. Yet it is difficult to compare the forecast impacts across regions because the climate models used often differ between regions and because each forecast is subject to considerable uncertainty. In this section we will therefore not use comparison country groups to help gauge the severity of climate change impacts on the countries we study, but we should still keep in mind that consequences similar to those we discuss will be occurring almost everywhere in the world. We will also focus on impacts of climate change that are predicted with greater certainty.

One of the most important consequences of climate change is sea-level rise. This is caused primarily by two factors related to global warming: the added water from melting ice sheets and glaciers, and the expansion of seawater as it warms. Several of the countries we study are highly exposed to inundation related to rising sea levels because of their low-lying topographies. One study cited by the World Bank (2014, p. 148) found that with one meter (thirty-nine inches) of sea-level rise, Qatar could lose 2.7 percent of its total land area and Egypt would lose 13.1 percent of its agricultural area. In terms of the percentage of urban area lost to one meter of sea-level rise, Egypt (5.52 percent), Libya (5.39 percent), UAE (4.8 percent), and Tunisia (4.5 percent) were all found to be highly vulnerable.

Projections of sea-level rise by the year 2100 for the countries we study, under the intermediate climate change scenario of global warming of 2.6°C (4.7°F) relative to 1990, are close to one-half meter (twenty inches) rather than one meter. Table 7.7, based on World Bank (2014, p. 149), reports these projections and the associated costs for the countries we study that lie on the coast of Africa. The reported costs assume these countries have not invested in adaptations to sea-level rise such as sea walls. The estimated economic damages do not include possible negative impacts on beach tourism.

Table 7.7 shows that nearly two million people in each of Egypt and Morocco will suffer from flooding. Damage costs in the year 2100 are

**Table 7.7.** Projected Sea Level Rise and Associated Costs, 2100
2.6°C (4.7°F) Warming Scenario, No Adaptation

|          | Sea-Level Change Relative to 1995 (Meters (Inches)) | People Flooded (Thousands) | Land Lost to Submergence (sq. km. (sq. mi.)) | Damage Costs ($ Millions) |
|----------|---|---|---|---|
| Djibouti | 0.42 (17) | 86   | 0.3 (0.1)   | 232  |
| Algeria  | 0.46 (18) | 435  | 7.1 (2.7)   | 6547 |
| Libya    | 0.50 (20) | 39   | 16.1 (6.2)  | 1757 |
| Egypt    | 0.54 (21) | 1970 | 19.4 (7.5)  | 6519 |
| Morocco  | 0.44 (17) | 1820 | 14.5 (5.6)  | 5524 |
| Tunisia  | 0.49 (19) | 264  | 73.3 (28.3) | 3460 |

*Notes:* Damage costs include the costs of forced migration, land loss, salinization, sea floods, and river floods.
*Source:* World Bank (2014, table 4.7).

projected to exceed $6.5 billion each in Algeria and Egypt, and $5.5 billion in Morocco. Tunisia is expected to lose the most land due to submergence, over seventy-three square kilometers (twenty-eight square miles).

A sometimes overlooked consequence of global warming is the heat itself. The countries we study are already very hot in the summer, and climate change is making them even hotter. Jos Lelieveld et al. (2014, table 1) project that temperatures in cities in the Eastern Mediterranean and Middle East will typically rise by about 0.45°C (0.8°F) per decade through 2099. Lelieveld et al. argue that, because populations adapt to the average temperature, the most dangerous health consequences come from heat waves. They point to the example of a heat wave that hit large parts of Europe in the summer of 2003. Average summer temperatures were about 3°C (5.4°F) higher than the long-term mean, and in major cities the daily maximum temperature exceeded 35°C (95°F) for more than a week, causing about 70,000 excess deaths in parts of southern, western and central Europe.

Table 7.8 shows projected heat wave days per year for 2010–2039, the current decade and two decades into the future, using the same climate

**Table 7.8.** Projected Heat Wave Days per Year, 2010–2039

| | | Heat Wave Days | | |
| | Period of Observations | Observed | Model 1961–1990 | Model 2010–2039 |
|---|---|---|---|---|
| Baghdad, Iraq | 1950–2000 | 10 | 11.5 | 42.5 |
| Kuwait | | | 7.5 | 31.5 |
| Riyadh, Saudi Arabia | 1970–2004 | 8 | 12 | 59 |
| Tripoli, Libya | 1956–1990 | 12 | 8 | 10 |
| Abadan, Iran | 1951–2000 | 10 | 9 | 33 |
| Tehran, Iran | 1956–1999 | 7 | 12 | 43 |
| Amman, Jordan | 1959–2004 | 7 | 8 | 23 |
| Beirut, Lebanon | 1951–2010 | 6 | 11 | 38 |
| Cairo, Egypt | | | 7.5 | 23 |
| Damascus, Syria | 1965–1993 | 19 | 9 | 29 |
| Ankara, Turkey | 1951–2003 | 12 | 10.5 | 34 |
| Istanbul, Turkey | 1951–2010 | 7 | 6.5 | 21 |

*Source*: Lelieveld et al. (2014, table 2).

change scenario as in Table 7.7. Major cities in the eastern part of the region we study are covered, but there is no coverage of Arab sub-Saharan Africa, Algeria, Morocco, or Tunisia. Abadan, a city in the south of Iran, is meant to stand for the GCC countries Bahrain, Qatar, and UAE, for which data are too scarce to make forecasts. Heat wave days for a city are defined as a spell of at least six consecutive days with maximum temperatures in the top 10 percent of what was observed for the city during the period 1961–1990. The accuracy of the model used by Lelieveld et al. can be gauged by comparing its predictions for the period 1961–1990 with the heat wave days actually observed for the periods given in the "period of observations" column in Table 7.8. For example, an average of ten heat wave days per year were observed during the period 1950–2000 in Baghdad, Iraq. The model predicts an average of 11.5 heat wave days per year during the period 1961–1990, a bit higher than the average during the period of observations, but close enough to give us confidence in the model's forecast for the future. For the period 2010–2039, the model predicts an average of 42.5 heat wave days per year, a quadrupling relative to the period of observations.

Relative to the periods of observations, Table 7.8 shows that the model used by Lelieveld et al. over-predicts heat wave days in some cities, such as Beirut, Lebanon and Tehran, Iran, and under-predicts heat wave days in others, such as Damascus, Syria and Tripoli, Libya, but is usually close. For most cities the average number of heat wave days per year forecast for the period 2010–2039 is at least triple the average number for the period of observations. Lelieveld et al. caution that their model may have a "warm bias," causing a systematic over-prediction of the number of heat wave days for the period 2010–2039 in Table 7.8. Nevertheless, it appears that in the region we study air-conditioning in the summer will increasingly become necessary not only for comfort but for survival. The same will be true in much of the rest of the world, and one can only hope that technological progress and rising incomes will make air-conditioning affordable for the vast majority of the affected population.

# 8

# Government Spending

## Urban Infrastructure, Energy Subsidies, and the Military

### Introduction

The demands made on governments are great, and governments are usually straining to raise the funds needed to satisfy those demands. The next section of this chapter notes that urban infrastructure is an area where demands for government investment are growing especially strongly in the countries we study. At the same time governments in the region are trying to develop new sources of finance to replace tariffs and printing money. These new sources, such as income taxes, are administratively more difficult to collect. The section titled "Urban Primacy" shows that this strain on public finance can be exacerbated by excessive urban primacy, meaning the tendency for the largest city in a country to garner more than its share of government investment in urban infrastructure. We present evidence that excessive urban primacy among the countries we study is a severe problem only for Egypt, where the enormity of Cairo appears to have retarded the urbanization of the entire rest of the country.

The sections titled "Energy Subsidies" and "Military Spending" cover two types of expenditure that claim exceptional shares of government resources in most of the countries we study. The section titled "Energy Subsidies" shows that the fuel-endowed countries heavily subsidize petroleum products to prevent high export prices from being reflected in the prices paid by their consumers. The Arab Mediterranean countries usually subsidize electricity more than petroleum products, and both the Arab Mediterranean and the Arab sub-Saharan African countries tend to subsidize energy more than the comparison country groups. Consumers in most of the countries we study (Turkey is an important exception) have come to expect cheap energy, so governments have found it difficult to reduce energy subsidies. This section concludes with a description of an innovative subsidy reduction strategy in Iran. The section titled "Military Spending" shows that military expenditure, like energy subsidies, tends to be higher in the countries we study than in the comparison country groups. This is especially true for the Arab fuel-endowed countries. Their military spending rose still further after the Arab Spring.

The sections titled "Slums" and "Infrastructure Quality" provide evidence for whether governments in the countries we study have been able to meet the demands of households and businesses for urban infrastructure, despite the drains on their resources from energy subsidies and military spending. The "Slums" section covers the shares of urban populations living in slums, which are defined in part by the shares of households that lack infrastructure services such as piped-in water and sewer lines. Urban slum population shares are relatively high in Arab sub-Saharan Africa and in the Arab fuel-endowed countries and Iran, but not in the Arab Mediterranean and Turkey. The "Infrastructure Quality" section covers infrastructure quality as experienced by businesses. Electric power is unreliable and water insufficiencies are common in Arab sub-Saharan Africa even compared to the high levels in non-Arab sub-Saharan Africa. The opposite is true for the Arab Mediterranean relative to its comparison country groups. Infrastructure quality experienced by businesses in Turkey is similar to the level in Latin America. Data for the Arab fuel-endowed countries are too scarce for us to judge their infrastructure quality.

## Urbanization and Strain on Public Finance

The Arab countries, Iran, and Turkey are rapidly urbanizing, as are other developing countries. Table 8.1 shows the share of population living in urban areas in 1970 and 2016 in the countries we study and in the comparison country groups. We should approach this table with caution because national statistical offices may define "urban area" in different ways. Nevertheless, there is remarkable similarity in both levels and changes of urban population shares between Arab and non-Arab sub-Saharan Africa, and between the Arab and non-Arab fuel-endowed countries. Urban population shares increased by 20 percentage points in both Arab and non-Arab sub-Saharan Africa, more than doubling relative to their 1970 levels. Urban population shares increased by 27 to 29 percentage points in both the Arab and non-Arab fuel-endowed countries, rising to over three-quarters of their populations.

**Table 8.1.** Urban Share of Population (Percent)

|  | 1970 | 2016 | Change 1970–2016 |
|---|---|---|---|
| Arab sub-Saharan Africa | 16.8 | 37.1 | 20.2 |
| Non-Arab sub-Saharan Africa | 18.1 | 38.4 | 20.3 |
| Arab fuel-endowed countries | 48.0 | 76.7 | 28.7 |
| Non-Arab fuel-endowed countries | 50.6 | 77.5 | 26.9 |
| Iran | 41.2 | 73.9 | 32.7 |
| Arab Mediterranean | 41.1 | 53.5 | 12.4 |
| Arab Mediterranean excluding Egypt | 40.7 | 65.7 | 25.0 |
| Rest of non-Arab world | 37.7 | 56.1 | 18.4 |
| Turkey | 38.2 | 73.9 | 35.7 |
| Latin America | 57.4 | 80.4 | 22.9 |
| Southern Europe | 62.8 | 73.4 | 10.6 |

*Notes*: Due to rounding errors, some "change" column figures may appear to be inconsistent with the other figures in corresponding table rows. The population-weighted averages for each country group include the countries listed in the Appendix. The excluded countries were missing data.
*Source of data*: World Development Indicators.

There is more diversity in the levels and changes of urban population shares for the Arab Mediterranean, Turkey, and their comparison country groups. Turkey (and Iran) urbanized exceptionally fast from 1970 to 2016. The Arab Mediterranean appears to have urbanized slowly relative to the rest of the non-Arab world or to Latin America, though not relative to Southern Europe. However, the population-weighted averages for the Arab Mediterranean are strongly influenced by the very unusual data for Egypt, which show almost no increase (from 41.5 to 43.2 percent) in urban population share from 1970 to 2016. Excluding Egypt, the Arab Mediterranean has urbanized faster than the rest of the non-Arab world or Latin America, though not as fast as Turkey. In the next section we will suggest an explanation for the unusually slow urbanization of Egypt.

Urbanization creates massive demand for piped-in water, sewer lines, centrally generated electricity, gas lines, paved roads, and mass transit. All of these fall under the heading of *urban infrastructure*. Providing urban infrastructure is almost universally considered the responsibility of government. This does not necessarily mean the government provides the services directly or through state-owned entities. Sometimes infrastructure services such as electric power are supplied by privately owned companies operating under government supervision. In practice, however, the public sector is by far the most common supplier of urban infrastructure. Vernon Henderson (2002) finds a strong relationship between a country's urban population growth and its share of public investment in GDP. We should note that even if the urban share of population is not increasing, as in Egypt, the exceptionally rapid population growth in the three Arab worlds, Iran, and Turkey seen in Table 4.9 would cause high urban population growth.

At the same time that rapid urbanization in developing countries has increased the need for public investment, other changes have reduced sources of revenue upon which developing country governments have traditionally relied to help finance their investments. One of these sources is tariffs. In Chapter 3 we noted that the Arab Mediterranean countries and Turkey had lowered tariffs as part of a move away from an import-substituting industrialization strategy toward an export-oriented industrialization strategy. Panel (a) of Figure 8.1, based on a study by Joshua Aizenman and Yothin Jinjarak (2009), shows that developing countries in general sharply reduced tariff rates from the 1980s to the 1990s. A second traditional source of revenue is *seigniorage*, used here as a synonym for *inflation tax*. Seigniorage or inflation tax is defined as implicit taxation of citizens by lowering the value of the money they hold in currency and bank accounts. The government implicitly collects seigniorage by increasing the supply of money and causing the level of prices to increase (inflation). Panel (b) of Figure 8.1 shows that inflation fell in most developing regions, including MENA, from the 1980s to the 1990s.

Developing countries have reduced tariffs and inflation because they were believed to be economically harmful, but they have struggled with replacement of these traditional sources of revenue by sources typically used in developed countries, such as income taxes and value-added taxes. Income taxes and value-added taxes are believed to be less economically harmful, but are administratively more difficult to collect. A value-added tax or VAT is a tax collected on the value that is added at each stage of production and distribution. It is not collected only from retailers, like a sales tax, but also from wholesalers and manufacturers. Panel (c) of Figure 8.1 shows percentage changes in GDP shares from 1980–1984 to 1995–1999 for tariff and seigniorage revenue, income tax and VAT revenue, and total tax revenue. Both developing and developed (high-income) countries reduced their GDP shares of tariff and seigniorage revenue and increased their GDP

GOVERNMENT SPENDING 199

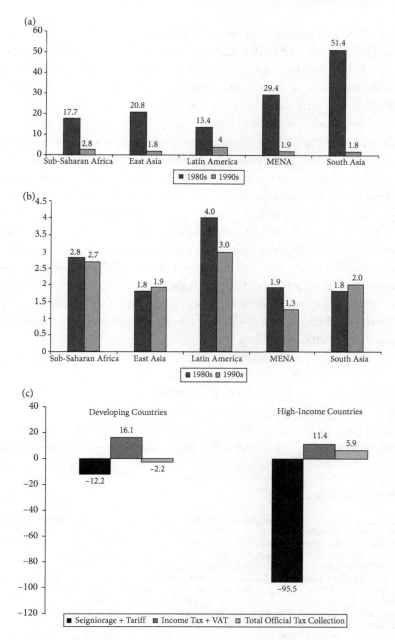

**Figure 8.1** (a) Weighted Average Tariff Rates
(b) Logarithm of CPI Inflation Rate
(c) Percentage Change in Tax/GDP, 1980–1984 to 1995–1999

*(continued)*

shares of income tax and VAT revenue. However, the net effect for the developing countries was to decrease the total tax share of GDP, whereas it increased for the high-income countries. The high-income countries achieved this increase despite reducing the tariff and seigniorage share of GDP almost to zero, because tariffs and seigniorage were not such a large share of government revenue to begin with.

The combination of high demand for government spending due to urbanization and loss of traditional revenue sources places a severe strain on public finance in developing countries. This strain is exacerbated by three factors: a tendency for the largest city to absorb more than its share of spending, payments to lower energy prices for consumers, and military spending. In the next three sections of this chapter we will discuss these three factors in detail and measure their severity for the countries we study relative to other countries. In the last two sections of this chapter we will see how well the governments of the countries we study have been able to provide urban infrastructure despite the strains on their finances, as measured by the shares of their urban populations living in slums and by access to and reliability of electric power and water.

## Urban Primacy

As cities grow larger, the problems of congestion increase. Rents rise, poorer urban residents are pushed to the city edges, and their travel times to work

---

Figure 8.1 (Continued)

*Notes:* Import values are used as weights in weighted average tariff rates. CPI = Consumer Price Index. Developing countries list: Sub-Saharan Africa: Cameroon, Gabon, Guinea, Lesotho, Mauritius, Namibia, South Africa, Zambia, Zimbabwe; East Asia: Indonesia, Korea, Malaysia, Myanmar, Thailand; Eastern Europe: Azerbaijan, Belarus, Bulgaria, Croatia, Czech Republic, Estonia, Hungary, Latvia, Lithuania, Poland, Romania, Russian Federation, Turkey; Latin America: Argentina, Bolivia, Brazil, Chile, Colombia, Costa Rica, Mexico, Nicaragua, Paraguay, Peru, Trinidad and Tobago, Uruguay, Venezuela; Middle East and North Africa: Iran, Morocco, Tunisia; South Asia: India, Nepal, Pakistan, Sri Lanka. High-income countries list: Australia, Canada, Cyprus, Denmark, Iceland, Israel, Japan, Malta, Norway, Slovenia, Sweden, Switzerland, United Kingdom. Weighted average tariff rates and logarithm of CPI inflation rate include six countries from the sub-Saharan Africa group, five countries from the East Asia group, twelve countries from the Latin America group, two countries from the MENA group, and two countries from the South Asia group. Percentage change in tax/GDP includes thirty-one countries from the developing countries list and nine countries from the high-income countries list.

*Source:* Adapted from Aizenman and Jinjarak (2009, figure 1).

lengthen. Automobiles spend more time on the roads, increasing air pollution. Urban waste must be trucked farther away, raising costs, or burned, increasing air pollution still further. These problems of congestion tend to limit how large any one city can grow. Businesses and residents will choose to locate in other cities where rents are lower and the quality of life is higher.

It is the job of government to build roads, collect and dispose of waste, and provide other infrastructure services needed to ease congestion and facilitate city growth. However, sometimes the government favors one city at the expense of other cities. This is especially likely if the city is the national capital. Most obviously, government officials who live and work in the national capital want a higher quality of life for themselves. Moreover, the government does not want foreign investors who visit the national capital to be discouraged by difficulty of getting to meetings or an impression that the country's infrastructure is inadequate.

Government investment in a favored city tends to attract still more businesses and residents, creating more congestion that requires yet more investment. The favored city grows to gigantic size while the other cities in the country are starved of government investment in needed infrastructure and their qualities of life suffer. Thus, when one city is much larger than all the others, it is often a symptom of government favoritism.

The urban primacy hypothesis states that the greater is the share of the largest (primate) city in a country's urban population, the lower will be the quality of life in the non-primate cities. Moreover, it is so expensive to make the largest city livable that urban primacy increases overall public investment.

In his study mentioned above, Henderson (2002) found evidence that the public investment share of GDP increases with the share of the largest city in a country's urban population, controlling for growth of the urban population and the logarithm of GDP per capita. He also examined the association of urban primacy with the percentage of households with access to potable water, the percentage of households with regular waste collection, and the child (under age five) mortality rate. Although the child mortality rate was examined separately, we expect it to go up if the shares of households with safe water or regular waste collection go down because safe water and regular waste collection reduce the risk of diarrhea, which is one of the leading killers of children under age five.

Henderson worked with UN-Habitat data covering almost three hundred cities around the world in 1996. However, the number of cities (and countries) with data for any particular quality of life measure is much smaller, as is shown in the last two rows of Table 8.2. Each column in Table 8.2 headed by a quality of life measure shows the signs of the associations of the variables listed in the leftmost column with that quality of life measure, holding all the other variables constant. The first row of Table 8.2 shows that, as expected, richer cities (cities with higher logarithms of average income) have greater shares of households with access to potable water and regular waste collection and lower child mortality. The second row shows that larger cities (greater logarithm of metro area population) are also associated with greater shares of households with access to potable water and regular waste collection and lower child mortality, though the association with regular waste collection is not statistically different from zero. This probably occurs because larger cities are more likely to be provided with piped-in water and, possibly, better hospitals. The third row of Table 8.2 shows that faster city growth (higher metro area annual population growth rate) is associated with smaller shares of households with access to potable water and regular waste collection and greater child mortality, though again the association with regular waste collection is not statistically different

Table 8.2. Urban Quality of Life, Urban Characteristics, and National Urban Primacy, 1996

| Metro Area Variable | Percent of Households with | | Child Mortality Rate (Under Age Five) |
| --- | --- | --- | --- |
| | Access to Potable Water | Regular Waste Collection | |
| Logarithm of average income | +** | +** | −** |
| Logarithm of population | +* | + | −** |
| Annual population growth rate | −* | − | +** |
| National urban primacy | −* | −** | +** |
| Number of cities | 67 | 57 | 56 |
| Number of countries | 29 | 28 | 27 |

*Notes*: National urban primacy is a country rather than metro area variable. Plus (or minus) sign indicates positive (or negative) association of column variable with row variable. **Different from zero with 95-percent confidence. *Different from zero with 90-percent confidence.

*Source*: Henderson (2002, table 3).

from zero. Apparently, if city growth is too fast, governments cannot keep pace in terms of provision of infrastructure services. The fourth row of Table 8.2 addresses the urban primacy hypothesis. We see that in countries with greater shares of population in the largest city (national urban primacy), smaller shares of households have access to potable water and regular waste collection and child mortality is higher.

We can expect that in the Arab world, Iran, and Turkey, large primate cities have the same negative effects as elsewhere on quality of life in other cities. We must then ask, is urban primacy especially great, hence an especially large problem, in the countries we study? We cannot answer this question by simply comparing the urban population shares of these countries' largest cities with the averages for other countries, because urban primacy is strongly affected by the size of a country's population. A very small country may be able to support only one city, which will therefore account for 100 percent of its urban population. At the other extreme, there is a limit to how large cities can grow even with government favoritism, so even the largest city can only account for a small share of the urban population of a very large country. We thus need to control for population size when judging urban primacy.

Figure 8.2 plots urban primacy (the share of urban population in the largest city) against the logarithm of total country population for the year 2016. We see that, as expected, urban primacy decreases with country population size. Three of the countries we study show urban primacy far above the levels predicted by their populations: Djibouti (DJI), Egypt (EGY), and Kuwait (KWT). Urban primacy for Sudan (SDN) is also exceptionally high. The total 2016 population of Djibouti is only 942,000, so its largest city would be of modest size even if it accounted for 100 percent of its urban population. Kuwait is one of the world's richest countries, so we need not be very worried about its government's ability to pay for urban infrastructure. This leaves Cairo, Egypt as the primate city of greatest concern for the countries we study, with Khartoum, Sudan next in line. The World Bank estimate of the 2016 metro area population of Cairo is roughly 19 million, making it one of the largest cities in the world. Note that Istanbul, with 2016 metro area population estimated by the World Bank at roughly 14 million, is also among the world's largest cities, yet according to Figure 8.2 its urban population share is in line with what we would predict on the basis of the total population of Turkey.

Here we have a possible explanation for the slow urbanization of Egypt noted in the previous section of this chapter. Cairo is reaching the limits of

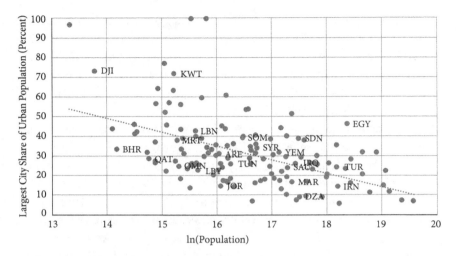

**Figure 8.2.** Urban Primacy by Population, 2016
*Note:* List of included countries available on request.
*Source of data:* World Development Indicators.

how large it can grow, and at the same time it is starving Egypt's other cities of the public investment they need to satisfy the demand for urban location that can no longer be satisfied by Cairo. The Cairo metro (rail mass transit) illustrates the dilemma posed by excessive urban primacy. It is needed very badly, because Cairo's giant size has made automobile traffic impossible. At the same time it has proven too expensive for the government to build, with three of six planned lines not yet started after more than thirty years of constructing the system. Sudan appears to be headed in the same direction of excessive urban primacy, but the government can still prevent Khartoum from becoming as great a problem as Cairo if it gives priority to other cities.

## Energy Subsidies

Governments in many countries intervene in energy markets to reduce prices for consumers. Directly or indirectly, governments wind up paying the differences between consumer prices and the costs of gasoline, diesel, kerosene, natural gas, and electricity. These differences are called *subsidies*. The International Monetary Fund (2013) estimated the amounts of these subsidies in 2011. The first two columns of Table 8.3 show expenditure on petroleum product subsidies and electricity subsidies, respectively, as a percentage of GDP. The next two columns of Table 8.3 show these same subsidy expenditures as percentages of government revenue, which makes the strain these subsidies place on public finances more clear. We see from Table 8.3 that petroleum subsidies tend to be higher in fuel-endowed countries, both Arab and non-Arab, as a percentage of GDP or government revenue. Moreover, petroleum subsidies for the Arab country groups are consistently higher than for the non-Arab country groups as a percentage of GDP, though not always as a percentage of government revenue. On the other hand, expenditure on electricity subsidies is lower in Arab sub-Saharan Africa and in the Arab fuel-endowed countries than in the comparison country groups, both as a share of GDP and as a share of government revenue. The opposite is true for the Arab Mediterranean relative to its comparison country groups. Expenditure on energy subsidies is not an issue for Turkey.

To better understand the findings in Table 8.3, we need to know how energy subsidies are computed. First consider internationally traded products, which include gasoline, diesel, kerosene, and (usually) natural gas. If the country exports the product, the subsidy equals the export price minus the consumer price, minus the cost of transporting the product to the port. Box 8.1 explains why this is the correct calculation to use. If the country imports the product, the subsidy equals the import price minus the consumer price, plus the cost of transportation to consumers. Now consider products that are not internationally traded, which usually include electricity. The subsidy equals the cost of production minus the consumer price.

Governments pay for energy subsidies in various ways. Suppose, for example, a government requires a state-owned power company to charge consumers less than the cost of production for electricity. The state-owned power company then loses an amount of money equal to this subsidy, and the government must cover its losses to keep it in operation. Similarly, the government may require a state-owned oil refinery or natural gas company to charge consumers less than the export price minus the cost of transportation to the port. State-owned firm profits are reduced by the amount of this subsidy. These lost profits are lost government revenue. If the energy product is imported, the government may directly pay the importer-distributor the difference between the import price plus cost of transportation to consumers and the consumer price.

**Table 8.3.** Energy Subsidies, as Percent of GDP and as Percent of Government Revenues, 2011

|  | Subsidy Percent of GDP | | Subsidy Percent of Government Revenues | |
| --- | --- | --- | --- | --- |
|  | Petroleum | Electricity | Petroleum | Electricity |
| Arab sub-Saharan Africa | 2.5 | 1.2 | 11.2 | 5.0 |
| Djibouti | 0.0 | 0.5 | 0.0 | 1.3 |
| Mauritania | 0.0 | 0.9 | 0.0 | 3.1 |
| Sudan | 1.4 |  | 7.3 |  |
| Yemen | 4.7 | 1.3 | 19.0 | 5.4 |
| Non-Arab sub-Saharan Africa | 0.4 | 1.7 | 1.4 | 7.1 |
| Arab fuel-endowed countries | 6.2 | 1.6 | 11.4 | 3.3 |
| Algeria | 4.3 | 1.1 | 10.8 | 2.7 |
| Bahrain | 5.4 | 2.6 | 19.0 | 9.1 |
| Iraq | 9.9 | 1.4 | 12.7 | 1.8 |
| Kuwait | 3.1 | 2.9 | 4.6 | 4.3 |
| Libya | 6.4 | 1.9 | 16.6 | 4.8 |
| Oman | 3.0 | 0.8 | 7.3 | 1.8 |
| Qatar | 1.2 | 1.2 | 3.2 | 3.1 |
| Saudi Arabia | 7.5 | 2.5 | 14.0 | 4.7 |
| UAE | 0.5 | 1.9 | 1.4 | 5.3 |
| Non-Arab fuel-endowed countries | 4.4 | 2.9 | 15.7 | 11.2 |
| Iran | 4.2 | 3.6 | 17.0 | 14.5 |
| Arab Mediterranean | 4.4 | 2.5 | 19.7 | 10.7 |
| Arab Mediterranean excluding Egypt | 0.8 | 3.2 | 3.0 | 11.9 |
| Egypt | 6.7 | 2.3 | 30.6 | 10.4 |
| Jordan | 2.2 | 3.8 | 8.1 | 14.4 |
| Lebanon | 0.1 | 4.5 | 0.3 | 19.0 |
| Morocco | 0.7 |  | 2.4 |  |
| Tunisia | 0.8 | 2.2 | 2.4 | 7.0 |
| Rest of non-Arab world | 0.5 | 0.6 | 2.7 | 2.9 |
| Turkey | 0.0 |  | 0.0 |  |
| Latin America | 0.2 | 0.2 | 0.6 | 0.4 |
| Southern Europe | 0.0 |  | 0.0 |  |

*Notes*: The population-weighted averages for each country group for petroleum subsidies include the countries listed in the Appendix. The excluded countries were missing data. For electricity subsidies, many more countries were missing data, which is reflected in the blank spaces in the electricity columns.

*Source of data*: International Monetary Fund (2013).

## Box 8.1

**The Price of Fuel and Opportunity Cost.** We learned in Chapter 3 that the Arab fuel-endowed countries and Iran are able to export their oil and natural gas at prices well above the costs of production, thereby earning natural resource rents. One way to view the subsidies provided by the governments of these countries is that they enable consumers to buy refined oil products (e.g., gasoline) and natural gas at the cost of production. Without the subsidies, domestic consumers would pay the export prices, minus the costs of transporting the products to the port. The reason is that if the prices were lower, traders would buy the products and sell them at the port, making guaranteed profits.

Economists believe that consumers *should* pay the export prices, minus any costs of transporting the products to the port. The reason is that the export prices, rather than the production costs, are the correct *opportunity costs* of the products. If a consumer pumps a gallon of gasoline into her car rather than that gallon of gasoline being exported, the goods and services that could have been imported in exchange for that gallon of gasoline are lost. The true cost to society of consuming the gallon of gasoline is the cost of these lost imports, not the (lower) cost of resources used to produce the gallon of gasoline. (This does not count the cost of pollution caused by burning the gasoline.)

By reducing prices below export prices (minus any transportation costs), government subsidies cause over-consumption of fuel: Consumers buy too much gasoline, diesel, kerosene, and natural gas and too little of everything else. Aside from this inefficiency (and increased pollution), subsidies encourage smuggling and corruption. Traders buy subsidized products intended for consumers and export them to get the higher prices, and bribe officials to look the other way. Sometimes the officials are themselves the traders. In short, fuel subsidies not only strain government finances in many Arab countries and Iran; they impose serious costs on their societies.

These examples can help explain why the fuel-endowed countries tend to spend the most on petroleum subsidies. Insofar as the fuel-endowed countries tend to export petroleum products, their cost of subsidies does not show up as government expenditure, but instead takes the form of lost revenue that may not even be calculated. Moreover, people living in these countries may feel entitled to purchase products refined from their abundant oil at the cost of production rather than being charged what foreigners pay. We can see evidence for these hypotheses by comparing petroleum to electricity subsidies for individual countries in Table 8.3. With the exception of UAE, all of the fuel-endowed countries including Iran have higher petroleum than electricity subsidy expenditure. With the exception of Egypt, all of the Arab Mediterranean countries have lower petroleum than electricity subsidy expenditure. The contrast between countries within Arab sub-Saharan Africa provides additional evidence. Djibouti and Mauritania have lower petroleum than electricity subsidy expenditure, whereas the opposite is true for Yemen. Though not classified as fuel-endowed, Yemen has enough oil to have intensive growth led by fuel exports, as noted in Chapter 3.

Table 8.3 is useful for comparing fuel-endowed countries to other countries and Arab countries to non-Arab countries, but for any given country these tables exaggerate the strain placed on public finances by energy subsidies because these subsidies were unusually high in 2011. Table 8.4, based on a more recent study by the International Monetary Fund (2017) of only Arab countries, shows that for most countries energy subsidies in 2016 were a much lower share of GDP than in 2013. (We cannot make a direct comparison to the 2011 figures in Table 8.3 because the figures in Table 8.4 add together petroleum, natural gas, and electricity subsidies.) The main reason for this decrease in spending on energy subsidies was the fall in the price of oil from its historic highs during the period 2011–2014. This reduced the export and import prices of petroleum products, thereby reducing the amount of subsidies needed to lower consumer prices to their target levels.

In recent years many governments, Arab and non-Arab, have attempted to reduce their energy subsidies. Their efforts have been hampered by the "endowment effect": Consumers tend to value the same thing more when they have it than when they do not have it. Because of the endowment effect, consumers are more upset when a subsidy is taken away than they are pleased when they receive the same subsidy. To combat the endowment effect, the government of Iran adopted an innovative strategy

**Table 8.4.** Energy Subsidy Changes as Percent of GDP, 2013–2016

|  | 2013 | 2016 | Change 2013–2016 |
|---|---|---|---|
| Djibouti | 0.4 | 0.4 | 0.0 |
| Mauritania | 0.7 | 1.0 | 0.3 |
| Sudan | 2.7 | 0.0 | −2.7 |
| Algeria | 8.5 | 5.3 | −3.2 |
| Bahrain | 6.9 | 3.8 | −3.1 |
| Iraq | 7.7 | 2.2 | −5.5 |
| Kuwait | 7.3 | 6.8 | −0.5 |
| Oman | 7.4 | 3.0 | −4.4 |
| Qatar | 5.1 | 3.8 | −1.3 |
| Saudi Arabia | 9.4 | 4.4 | −5.0 |
| UAE | 2.0 | 0.7 | −1.3 |
| Egypt | 10.0 | 4.1 | −5.9 |
| Jordan | 3.3 | 1.6 | −1.8 |
| Lebanon | 5.9 | 6.7 | 0.8 |
| Morocco | 1.0 | 0.2 | −0.9 |
| Tunisia | 4.6 | 2.8 | −1.8 |

*Notes:* Subsidies include regular gasoline, diesel, kerosene, natural gas, and electricity. Due to rounding errors, some "change" column figures may appear to be inconsistent with the other figures in corresponding table rows.
*Source:* International Monetary Fund (2017).

when it attempted to reduce energy subsidies starting in December 2010. Before raising consumer prices, the government deposited cash transfers into new bank accounts for households, which were to be financed by the revenue from the price increases. These transfers were equal across households, so for poor households they were actually greater than the amount of money the households had saved due to lower prices. The strategy was successful in that energy subsidies were reduced and many Iranians were lifted out of poverty. According to a study by Ali Enami, Nora Lustig, and Alireza Taqdiri (2016, p. 7), the cash transfer program reduced the share of Iranians living below a P$4 per day poverty line (measured in 2005 purchasing power parity dollars) from 22 to 10 percent. However, the government was unable to implement a second round of price increases and cash transfers that was planned for the second half of 2012.

Considering countries that are not fuel-endowed, Table 8.4 shows that, of the Arab countries in 2016, Egypt spent the second most (after Lebanon) on energy subsidies as a share of GDP. It was thus not surprising when, in November 2016, the Egyptian government negotiated an agreement with the International Monetary Fund to phase in fuel price increases over three years. If fuel import prices stay near their current relatively low levels, prices for Egyptian consumers will not have to rise so dramatically, which increases the probability that the agreement will be implemented successfully.

Governments want to reduce energy subsidies not only to save money, but to increase efficiency. As with the food subsidies discussed in Chapter 6, it is more efficient to give people cash and let them decide how to spend it than to subsidize consumption of a particular good. Just as food subsidies had the side effect of encouraging too much consumption of fattening food, leading to obesity, the energy subsidies lead to overconsumption of energy, generating additional pollution as discussed in Chapter 7.

## Military Spending

Military spending by governments leaves fewer resources to address the urban infrastructure needs that we have discussed in this chapter. Even before the Arab Spring, the region we are studying was plagued by a high level of external and internal warfare, so it would not be surprising if military spending tended to be greater than in the rest of the world. Table 8.5 shows military spending as a share of GDP in 2010, before the Arab Spring, and in 2015, after the Arab Spring. (It would also be useful to examine the amounts of military spending relative to overall government expenditure, as we did with energy subsidies, but these data are missing for too many countries.) Military spending includes expenditures on personnel, operation and maintenance, purchasing (e.g., of weapons), research and development, and aid to foreign militaries. Estimates of military spending are provided to the World Bank by the Stockholm International Peace Research Institute (SIPRI), rather than by the governments themselves. Governments may not be fully transparent about their military spending. In cases where SIPRI is not able to discover the true amounts of military spending, the figures reported in Table 8.5 will be inaccurate.

**Table 8.5.** 2010 and 2015 Military Expenditure Shares of GDP (Percent)

|  | 2010 | 2015 |
|---|---|---|
| Arab sub-Saharan Africa | 4.7 | 1.8 |
| Mauritania |  | 2.8 |
| Somalia |  | 0 |
| Sudan |  | 2.4 |
| Yemen, Rep. | 4.7 |  |
| Non-Arab sub-Saharan Africa | 1.3 | 1.3 |
| Arab fuel-endowed countries | 4.8 | 8.1 |
| Algeria | 3.5 | 6.3 |
| Bahrain | 3.3 | 4.6 |
| Iraq | 2.7 | 5.3 |
| Kuwait | 3.8 | 4.8 |
| Oman | 8.3 | 14.4 |
| Qatar | 1.5 |  |
| Saudi Arabia | 8.6 | 13.4 |
| UAE | 6.0 |  |
| Non-Arab fuel-endowed countries | 2.2 | 2.6 |
| Iran, Islamic Rep. | 2.8 | 2.7 |
| Arab Mediterranean | 2.6 | 2.4 |
| Egypt, Arab Rep. | 2.1 | 1.7 |
| Jordan | 5.9 | 4.3 |
| Lebanon | 4.1 | 4.5 |
| Morocco | 3.4 | 3.2 |
| Tunisia | 1.3 | 2.3 |
| Rest of non-Arab world | 2.2 | 2.1 |
| Turkey | 2.3 | 1.8 |
| Latin America | 1.5 | 1.4 |
| Southern Europe | 1.7 | 1.5 |

*Notes*: The population-weighted averages for each country group in 2010 and 2015 include the countries listed in the Appendix. The excluded countries were missing data.
*Source of data*: World Development Indicators.

Beginning at the top of Table 8.5, we see that for non-Arab sub-Saharan Africa the population-weighted average of military spending as a share of GDP is 1.3 percent in both 2010 and 2015. The population-weighted average for Arab sub-Saharan Africa includes only Yemen in 2010 and only Mauritania, Somalia, and Sudan in 2015. Instead of using the population-weighted average, we can compare the military spending shares of GDP for the individual Arab sub-Saharan African countries directly with the population-weighted average for non-Arab sub-Saharan Africa. The share for Yemen in 2010 is between three and four times as great as the share for non-Arab sub-Saharan Africa in 2010, and the shares for Mauritania and Sudan in 2015 are roughly double the share for non-Arab sub-Saharan Africa in 2015. Somalia lacks a central government with authority over the entire country that can allocate expenditure to its military. Excluding Somalia, Arab sub-Saharan African expenditure on the military as a share of GDP is far higher than in the rest of sub-Saharan Africa.

Turning to the fuel-endowed countries, we see that in 2010 the population-weighted average of military spending as a share of GDP for the Arab fuel-endowed countries was more than double the share for the non-Arab fuel-endowed countries. The military expenditure shares for the GCC countries tended to be especially high. Saudi Arabia, the largest of the GCC countries, had the highest military expenditure share of any fuel-endowed country in 2010. Iran's military spending share of GDP was comparable to the shares of Algeria and Iraq, the two Arab non-GCC fuel-endowed countries with available data.

For the Arab fuel-endowed countries the population-weighted average of military spending as a share of GDP rose dramatically from 2010 to 2015, increasing from more than double to more than triple the share for the non-Arab fuel-endowed countries. Looking at individual countries, we see that the largest increases in military spending shares of GDP were in nations that bordered on countries that descended into civil war after the Arab Spring. A country may increase its military spending in response to a civil war on its border to prevent the war from spreading into its territory, to contain warfare that has already spread into its territory, or to intervene in the civil war on behalf of one side. From 2010 to 2015 Oman and Saudi Arabia increased their military spending shares of GDP by more than 6 and nearly 5 percentage points, respectively; both border on Yemen. Both Algeria and Iraq nearly doubled their military spending shares of GDP; Algeria borders on Libya and Iraq borders on Syria. Though the GCC countries might be rich enough to "afford" their extraordinary military spending, the strain on public finance for Algeria and Iraq must be severe. Indeed, below we will find some evidence for impacts of this strain for Iraq (we will not have any data for Algeria).

The population-weighted average of military spending as a share of GDP was only slightly higher for the Arab Mediterranean in 2010 and 2015 than for the rest of the non-Arab world that is not sub-Saharan or fuel-endowed. Comparing the Arab Mediterranean to Latin America or Southern Europe, however, we see that the population-weighted average of military spending is about 1 percent of GDP higher for the Arab Mediterranean. The military spending share of GDP for Turkey is in between the Arab Mediterranean share and the Latin American and Southern European shares in both 2010 and 2015. Tunisia is the only Arab Mediterranean country with a large increase in its military spending share of GDP from 2010 to 2015. This was likely to have been caused by attempts to contain the spread of violence from the civil war in neighboring Libya. Jordan, Lebanon, and Turkey all border on Syria, yet despite the civil war in Syria military spending as a share of GDP declined substantially in Jordan and decreased somewhat in Turkey, while increasing slightly in Lebanon. It is possible that these countries were able to conceal from SIPRI some military spending related to the Syrian civil war.

To summarize, military spending as a share of GDP is higher for all three Arab worlds than for their comparison country groups. The differences are especially large for Arab sub-Saharan Africa and the Arab fuel-endowed countries. The military spending shares of GDP for Iran and Turkey are lower than for the Arab fuel-endowed countries and Arab Mediterranean, respectively. The strain on public finance caused by high levels of military spending is probably greatest for Arab sub-Saharan Africa and the non-GCC Arab fuel-endowed countries.

## Slums

When urban population growth outstrips the ability of the government to provide infrastructure services, neighborhoods form without access to piped-in water, sewer lines, centrally-generated electricity, gas lines, paved roads, or trash collection. Such neighborhoods are commonly called *slums*. Figure 8.3 shows a slum in Cairo. However, for the practical reason that

**Figure 8.3.** A Slum in Cairo
*Source:* https://progrss.com/wp-content/uploads/2016/06/7-1-6.jpg.

governments regularly conduct household surveys, the United Nations Human Settlements Programme (UN-Habitat) computes the percentage of the urban population living in slums as the percentage living in slum households rather than slum areas. To compute the percentages shown in Table 8.6 below, UN-Habitat defines a household as living in a slum if it lacks one or more of the following: improved water, improved sanitation, durable housing, or sufficient living area. (See Box 8.2 for more details. Improved water and improved sanitation are essentially the same as access to basic drinking water and sanitation used in Figures 7.1 and 7.2, respectively.) Note that a household may satisfy this definition even if it has access to infrastructure services such as piped-in water and sewer lines, because it lacks a durable home or sufficient living space.

Neighborhoods that lack infrastructure services are usually "informal settlements." An informal settlement is a neighborhood settled illegally, that is, without government permission. Typically households living in informal settlements do not hold legal titles to their homes. Informal settlements often form on the outskirts of built-up urban areas, on previously agricultural land. The government does not provide infrastructure services to

> **Box 8.2**
>
> The UN-Habitat Slum Criteria. In table 1.2 of the revised version of chapter 1 of its *Global Report on Human Settlements*, UN-Habitat provides details on its slum criteria: (1) improved water, (2) improved sanitation, (3) durable housing, and (4) sufficient living area (2010, p. 16). (1) A household has an improved drinking water supply if it uses water from: pipes into its dwelling, plot or yard; a public tap or stand pipe; a tube well or borehole; a protected dug well; a protected spring; or rain water collection. (2) A household has access to improved sanitation if it uses: a flush or pour flush to a piped sewer system, septic tank or pit latrine; a pit latrine with a slab; a composting toilet; or a ventilated improved pit latrine. This excreta disposal system is considered improved if it is private or shared by a reasonable number of households. (3) A house is considered durable if it is a permanent structure built in a non-hazardous location. Hazardous sites include: geologically unstable areas such as landslide/earthquake and flood areas; garbage dumpsites; high industrial pollution areas; and unprotected high-risk zones such as railroads, airports, and energy transmission lines. Permanency of a housing structure is determined by quality of construction (materials used for wall, floor and roof) and compliance with local building codes, standards, and bylaws. (4) A house has sufficient living area for household members if not more than three members share the same room.

informal settlements. However, the residents of informal settlements may acquire infrastructure services illegally. Nezar AlSayyad describes how this sometimes happens: "Many residents have been able to obtain utilities by making illegal connections to electric and water lines. And because the new subdivisions had been plotted between existing irrigation channels, these channels were gradually turned into sewers, while existing dirt roads were turned into city streets" (2011, p. 264). By gaining access to such illegal services and by building a sufficiently durable and large home, a household living in an informal settlement could be considered not to live in a slum by the data collector.

Table 8.6 shows UN-Habitat estimates of the shares of urban populations living in slums in 1990, 2005, and 2014. 1990 and 2014 are the earliest and latest years available, respectively, and for many countries 2005 is their first year in these data. UN-Habitat did not collect data for countries with relatively high incomes and omitted Europe entirely. As a result Southern Europe is no longer available as a comparison country group, and the rest of the non-Arab world is missing all of its higher-income countries.

There are almost no urban slum population share data for Arab sub-Saharan Africa in 1990, but by 2005 three countries have data and by 2014 data are available for all six Arab sub-Saharan African countries. We see from Table 8.6 that in both 2005 and 2014, all Arab sub-Saharan African countries have shares of their urban populations living in slums greater than the population-weighted average for non-Arab sub-Saharan Africa. Moreover, the urban slum population share shrinks substantially in non-Arab sub-Saharan Africa from 2005 to 2014, but only shrinks in one Arab sub-Saharan African country, Yemen.

Two Arab Mediterranean countries, Egypt and Morocco, and Turkey have data for the share of urban population living in slums in 1990. From Table 8.6 we see that Egypt's share was similar to that for the rest of the non-Arab world, Morocco's share was similar to that for Latin America, and Turkey's share was the lowest. After 1990 the urban slum population shares for Egypt and Morocco fell remarkably fast, so that by 2005 they were at levels similar to Turkey. Between 2005 and 2014, the reduction in urban slum population shares slowed or reversed in the Arab Mediterranean countries and Turkey relative to the rest of the non-Arab world and Latin America. Nevertheless, except for Lebanon all of the Arab Mediterranean countries and Turkey had lower urban slum population shares in 2014 than did the rest of the non-Arab world and Latin America.

Data for the fuel-endowed countries are especially scarce, partly because some of them were considered too rich for UN-Habitat to collect data on their slum populations. Table 8.6 shows that Iran decreased its share of urban population living in slums sharply from 1990 to 2005, yet its share in 2005 was considerably higher than the urban slum population shares in the Arab Mediterranean, Turkey, or Latin America. The urban slum population share for Saudi Arabia is surprisingly high given its wealth, higher in 2014 than in the Arab Mediterranean or Turkey and similar to the level in Latin America.

The data for Iraq, Lebanon, and Syria deserve special attention. Table 8.6 shows that between 1990 and 2005 the Iraq share of urban population living

**Table 8.6.** Urban Population Living in Slums (Percent)

|  | 1990 | 2005 | 2014 | Change 1990–2005 | Change 2005–2014 |
|---|---|---|---|---|---|
| Arab sub-Saharan Africa | 65.4 | 69.3 | 77.9 | | |
| Comoros | 65.4 | 68.9 | 69.6 | 3.5 | 0.7 |
| Djibouti | | | 65.6 | | |
| Mauritania | | | 79.9 | | |
| Somalia | | 73.5 | 73.6 | | 0.1 |
| Sudan | | | 91.6 | | |
| Yemen | | 67.2 | 60.8 | | −6.4 |
| Non-Arab sub-Saharan Africa | 72.1 | 64.5 | 56.6 | | −7.8 |
| Arab fuel-endowed countries | 17.5 | 36.5 | 33.5 | | −2.9 |
| Algeria | 11.8 | | | | |
| Iraq | 16.9 | 52.8 | 47.2 | 35.9 | −5.6 |
| Libya | 35.2 | | | | |
| Oman | 60.5 | | | | |
| Saudi Arabia | | 18.0 | 18.0 | | 0.0 |
| Non-Arab fuel-endowed countries | 51.9 | 30.7 | | | |
| Iran | 51.9 | 30.3 | | −21.6 | |
| Arab Mediterranean | 46.3 | 16.3 | 12.1 | | |
| Egypt | 50.2 | 17.1 | 10.6 | −33.1 | −6.5 |
| Jordan | | 15.8 | 12.9 | | −2.9 |
| Lebanon | | 53.1 | 53.1 | | 0.0 |
| Morocco | 37.4 | 13.1 | 13.1 | −24.3 | 0.0 |
| Syria | | 10.5 | 19.3 | | 8.8 |
| Tunisia | | | 8.0 | | |
| Rest of non-Arab world | 48.8 | 34.8 | 26.8 | −14.0 | −8.0 |
| Turkey | 23.4 | 15.5 | 11.9 | −7.9 | −3.6 |
| Latin America | 35.6 | 25.0 | 20.0 | −10.6 | −5.0 |

*Notes*: Some changes for population-weighted averages are not reported because of changes in included countries. If we use the same countries to compute the population-weighted averages in 2005 as in 1990, the 1990–2005 changes for rest of non-Arab world and Latin America will be -14.1 and -10.3, respectively. Due to rounding errors, some "change" column figures may appear to be inconsistent with the other figures in corresponding table rows. The population-weighted averages for the Arab country groups in each year include the countries for which data are shown in the table. The population-weighted averages for the non-Arab country groups in each year include the countries listed in the Appendix. The excluded countries were missing data.

*Source of data*: United Nations Human Settlements Programme (UN-Habitat), Global Urban Indicators Database (2014).

in slums jumped from 16.9 to 52.8 percent. Since UN-Habitat continued to estimate the Iraq urban slum population share at 16.9 percent in 2000, we can conclude that the high level in 2005 reflects the impact of the Iraq War that began in 2003. At 53.1 percent, the Lebanon share of urban population living in slums is far above the average for the Arab Mediterranean. In addition to the low capacity of the Lebanese government noted in Box 7.1, this reflects the impact of the Lebanese civil war that lasted from 1975 to 1990 and the presence of Palestinian refugees mentioned in Chapter 6. The increase in the Syrian share of urban population living in slums from 10.5 percent in 2005 to 19.3 percent in 2014 shows the impact of the civil war that began in 2011. Given the UNHCR estimate of 7.6 million internally displaced Syrians by the end of 2014 (http://www.unhcr.org/sy/wp-content/uploads/sites/3/2016/11/End-of-Year-Report-2014_En.pdf), it seems likely that even the 19.3-percent figure is too low, and could reflect an inability of data collectors to survey outside of areas under government control.

Though one cause of slums is war and displacement, the main cause is inability of government infrastructure provision to keep up with urban population growth, as we noted at the beginning of this section. We thus expect to see a larger share of urban population living in slums when governments are short of money due to competing demands for funds from sources such as energy subsidies and military expenditure, discussed in the sections titled "Energy Subsidies" and "Military Spending," respectively. Table 8.3 showed that petroleum subsidies were exceptionally large relative to government revenues in the Arab sub-Saharan African countries, the fuel-endowed countries, and the Arab Mediterranean countries. The same was true for electricity subsidies in Iran and the Arab Mediterranean countries. Table 8.5 showed that the Arab fuel-endowed countries spent an extraordinary share of their GDPs on their militaries, and that military spending as a share of GDP was also high relative to the comparison country groups for Arab sub-Saharan Africa, Iran, and the Arab Mediterranean. Turkey, on the other hand, spent nothing on petroleum subsidies and a typical share of GDP on its military. These strains on public finance are showing up clearly in the shares of urban populations living in slums in Arab sub-Saharan Africa, Saudi Arabia, and Iran, and the lack of public finance strain is consistent with the low urban slum population share in Turkey. The low urban slum population shares in the Arab Mediterranean, however, are a surprise. One possible explanation is that foreign direct investment from the GCC countries in Arab Mediterranean infrastructure and real estate, noted in Chapter 3, substituted for government funding. It seems unlikely that GCC investors funded housing developments for families that would otherwise have lived in slums, but it could be that by paying for infrastructure for high-end property development they freed up government funds to provide infrastructure to low-income households.

## Infrastructure Quality

Electricity is a key infrastructure service that is not covered by UN-Habitat—that is, access to electricity is not one of the slum criteria listed in Box 8.2, so households without access to electricity are not for that reason alone classified as living in slums. In the Arab fuel-endowed countries, the Arab Mediterranean, Iran, and Turkey, urban access to electricity is nearly universal. In Arab sub-Saharan Africa, the population-weighted average (which includes all six countries) for the share of urban population with access to electricity is 77.3 percent, compared to 73.6 percent for non-Arab sub-Saharan Africa.

Access to electricity, however, is not the same as reliable electric power. Power outages are a common occurrence in most developing countries. The World Bank Enterprise Surveys ask businesses about their experiences with electric power outages and other aspects of infrastructure quality. These surveys cover private-sector, registered businesses with five or more employees in the cities or regions of major economic activity in most developing countries. The answers to these surveys are an important measure of electric power reliability, and infrastructure quality in general, because provision of infrastructure services is crucial for business productivity as well as household quality of life.

In Table 8.7 we show the percentages of businesses responding to the World Bank Enterprise Surveys that experienced power outages during the previous fiscal year, and the percentage of annual sales these businesses lost due to power outages. We also report the percentage of businesses that experienced insufficient water supplies during the previous fiscal year, to get a broader view of infrastructure quality. Businesses in rich countries were not surveyed, so as in Table 8.6 the Southern Europe comparison country group is not available and the rest of the non-Arab world is missing all of its higher-income countries. Businesses in Iran were also not surveyed.

**Table 8.7.** Quality of Infrastructure, as Experienced by Businesses

|  | Firms Experiencing Electrical Outages (Percent) | Average Losses Due to Electrical Outages (Percent of Annual Sales) | Firms Experiencing Water Insufficiencies (Percent) |
|---|---|---|---|
| Arab sub-Saharan Africa | 93.4 | 8.4 | 29.3 |
| Djibouti | 80.2 | 4.6 | 45.3 |
| Mauritania | 90.7 | 2.4 | 23.1 |
| Sudan | 93.7 | 1.2 | 12.4 |
| Yemen | 93.8 | 19.7 | 54.0 |
| Non-Arab sub-Saharan Africa | 79.0 | 9.7 | 22.9 |
| Iraq | 77.3 | 8.8 | 18.5 |
| Non-Arab fuel-endowed countries | 64.6 | 8.0 | 24.2 |
| Arab Mediterranean | 36.0 | 3.3 | 5.2 |
| Egypt | 38.0 | 4.3 | 4.5 |
| Jordan | 9.9 | 2.3 | 19.2 |
| Lebanon | 97.1 | 7.0 | 24.7 |
| Morocco | 35.0 | 0.8 | 1.3 |
| Tunisia | 11.6 | 2.0 | 1.0 |
| Rest of non-Arab world | 44.6 | 4.0 | 5.8 |
| Turkey | 41.5 | 3.8 | 10.5 |
| Latin America | 47.4 | 3.1 | 9.9 |

*Notes:* Data are for latest available year. Businesses were asked about experience during the previous fiscal year. The population-weighted averages for each country group include the countries listed in the Appendix. The excluded countries were missing data.
*Source of data:* http://www.enterprisesurveys.org/data/exploretopics/infrastructure.

We see from Table 8.7 that businesses in Arab sub-Saharan Africa were more likely to experience electrical outages and water insufficiencies than in non-Arab sub-Saharan Africa (though we noted above that urban access to electricity is slightly higher). This is consistent with the relatively low supply of infrastructure services in Arab sub-Saharan Africa indicated by the relatively high share of urban population living in slums shown in Table 8.6. We only have data for one Arab fuel-endowed country, Iraq, and its poor provision of electric power (but not water) relative to the non-Arab fuel-endowed countries is another indication of the war damage that was reflected in its high urban slum population share in Table 8.6. Infrastructure quality in the Arab Mediterranean is high relative to its comparison country groups, consistent with its relatively low share of urban population living in slums. (Lebanon is an exception, as it was with slums.) Provision of infrastructure services in Turkey is not as good as in the Arab Mediterranean but is roughly similar to the quality level in Latin America.

Arab or non-Arab, Tables 8.6 and 8.7 show that sub-Saharan Africa faces an enormous demand for urban infrastructure investment, one that will take many decades to fulfill. Iraq faces a similar challenge. The needs of the other Arab fuel-endowed countries and Iran are less clear due to lack of data. Most Arab Mediterranean countries and Turkey are within striking distance of developed country levels of urban infrastructure coverage and reliability. The Arab Mediterranean countries should find it much easier to reach that goal if they reduce their energy subsidies.

# 9
# Political Economy

## Introduction

The responsibilities of governments have been the subject of many parts of this book. In Chapter 4 we saw that governments are expected to provide universal, high-quality education, control or eradicate infectious diseases, and be the main provider of other health care services or at least the provider of last resort. In Chapter 5 we saw that governments are expected to reduce discrimination against girls and women. Government antipoverty programs were discussed in Chapter 6. As described in Chapter 7, governments are expected to provide safe drinking water and sanitation services, control air pollution, and dispose of municipal wastes. Chapter 8 described expectations that governments will provide infrastructure such as roads, electric power, and urban mass transportation. As also discussed in Chapter 8, governments must collect the taxes needed to pay for all of the services they are expected to provide. In this chapter we will describe expectations for governments to provide efficient legal and regulatory services that facilitate the operation of private-sector businesses.

Staffing all of the bureaucracies needed to deliver these services with qualified, competent employees is difficult for any country, and even more difficult for developing countries that must draw on relatively small pools of educated workers to fill higher-level positions. Moreover, all of these bureaucracies must be monitored to control corruption. Though there are strategies to control corruption, such as recruiting for higher-level positions using civil service exams rather than through political appointment (James Rauch and Peter Evans 2000), simply having more resources is a great advantage. Richer countries can pay government employees more, reducing their incentives to steal. They can also afford better auditors and monitoring systems to detect corruption.

In the next section of this chapter we show that perceived corruption decreases with GDP per capita, and that most of the countries we study are perceived to be more corrupt than predicted by their GDPs per capita. This is especially true of the fuel-endowed countries, and we find evidence that the greater perceived corruption of fuel-endowed countries is explained by their greater bureaucratic inefficiency. In the section titled "Bureaucratic Performance with Regard to Starting a Business and Enforcing Contracts," we explore in more detail bureaucratic efficiency with regard to starting a business and enforcing contracts. From 2005 to 2018 we find a general tendency, shared by the countries we study, for bureaucracies to process business startups using fewer procedures with less delay and lower cost. Evidence suggests this will generate more startups, but only of small firms. There is less change from 2005 to 2018 in the efficiency with which governments enforce contracts. The Arab country groups differ little from their counterparts in efficiency of contract enforcement. Iran and Turkey do better, but their courts are still slow and costly compared to the most efficient countries.

The section titled "Politically Connected Firms in Egypt and Tunisia" covers higher-level corruption in the form of government favors to large businesses connected to government officials, their relatives and friends, and other politically powerful individuals. Much information regarding political connections was revealed following the fall of heads of state in Egypt and Tunisia during the Arab Spring. Evidence shows that politically connected firms were more profitable in Egypt when their patrons were in power, and suggests that regulations were used to hold back their competitors. In Tunisia, politically connected firms were much better able to avoid paying tariffs on goods they imported than were unconnected firms. We do not have data to compare the economic damage done by politically connected firms in Egypt and Tunisia to other countries, but we do know that politically connected firms are common around the world.

## Corruption, GDP Per Capita, and Bureaucratic Inefficiency

We would like to know how well the countries we study are able to control corruption, given their GDPs per capita. We measure corruption at the country level using the "Corruption Perceptions Index" (CPI) published by Transparency International (TI). TI defines corruption as "the abuse of entrusted power for private gain." This is a very broad definition that encompasses not only demanding bribes and theft of public funds, but also manipulating government policies to benefit businesses owned by relatives and friends of government officials, as described in the "Politically Connected Firms in Egypt and Tunisia" section. By its very nature corruption is difficult to measure, and it is even more difficult to collect data on corruption that are comparable across countries. For these reasons TI relies on "perceptions" of corruption. These are often ratings by consulting firms that advise foreign investors regarding what they can expect in dealing with host country governments. TI uses ratings of corruption in the public sector from at least three sources for each country to form its CPI, which ranges from 0 (most corrupt) to 100 (least corrupt).

In Figure 9.1 we plot the CPI against the logarithm of GDP per capita for 2015. We use 2015 because too many countries are missing GDP per capita data in later years. The figure shows that higher GDP per capita is associated with less perceived corruption, as expected. We have emphasized the causation from GDP per capita to corruption, but the relationship shown in Figure 9.1 may also reflect a tendency for less corrupt countries to achieve higher GDPs per capita. Most of the countries we study are below

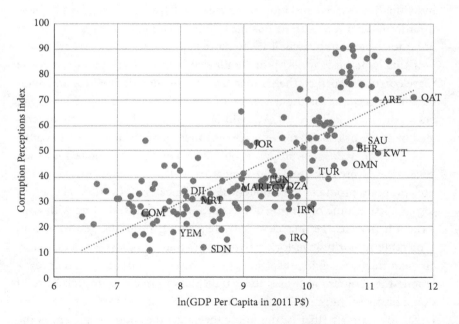

**Figure 9.1.** Corruption Perceptions Index by GDP Per Capita, 2015

*Notes:* List of included countries available on request.

*Sources of data:* "Corruption Perceptions Index 2015," www.transparency.org/cpi2015; World Development Indicators.

the line in Figure 9.1, indicating that they are perceived to be more corrupt than predicted by their GDPs per capita. Countries that especially stand out below the line, from left to right, are Sudan (SDN), Iraq (IRQ), Iran (IRN), Oman (OMN), and Kuwait (KWT). All of these except Sudan are fuel-endowed countries, and the intensive growth of Sudan has been driven by fuel exports, as we noted in Chapter 3.

Could Figure 9.1 be another illustration of the "oil curse" mentioned in Chapter 1 and discussed extensively in Chapter 3? In this version of the oil curse, fuel-endowed countries feel less pressure to make their legal and regulatory frameworks efficient, because this efficiency is less needed for oil and natural gas extraction than for manufacturing. Instead the fuel-endowed countries use their revenues from oil and natural gas exports to create government jobs in bloated bureaucracies. This helps to reduce poverty, as noted in Chapter 6, but also creates bureaucratic "tollbooths." A tollbooth is a kiosk along a highway at which a traveler must stop and pay a fee ("toll") for use of the road. A bureaucratic tollbooth is a procedure, such as obtaining approval from a government department, by which a firm (or individual) is delayed and must pay a fee—perhaps legal, perhaps a bribe—in order to continue with its business. Multiplication of such tollbooths in order to create employment leads to more opportunities for corruption.

If this hypothesis for why fuel-endowed countries are perceived to be more corrupt is correct, then a measure of bureaucratic inefficiency might be able to account for the tendency of the fuel-endowed countries to fall below the line in Figure 9.1. We will use the *Doing Business* ranking created by the World Bank to compare bureaucratic inefficiency across countries. The *Doing Business* program collects data on the efficiency with which governments provide legal and regulatory services to the private sector. This program produces the *Doing Business* indicators (www.doingbusiness.org), which at time of writing cover starting a business, dealing with construction permits, getting electricity, registering property, getting credit, protecting minority investors, paying taxes, trading across borders, enforcing contracts, resolving insolvency (bankruptcy), and labor market regulation. The program also uses these indicators to make an overall "ease of doing business" ranking. In 2015 countries were ranked from 1 to 189. The larger the number (that is, the lower the rank) the more inefficient is the country's bureaucracy in handling the needs of businesses.

In Figure 9.2 we show the impact of controlling for bureaucratic inefficiency on the relationship between perceived corruption and GDP per

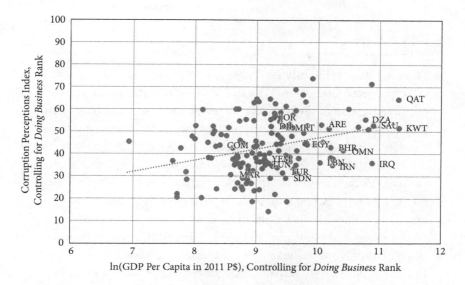

**Figure 9.2.** Corruption Perceptions Index by GDP Per Capita, 2015, Controlling for *Doing Business* Rank

*Notes:* The horizontal axis variable is the residual from a regression of ln(GDP per capita in 2011 P$) on a constant and ln(*Doing Business* rank). The vertical axis variable is the residual from a regression of CPI on a constant and ln(*Doing Business* rank). Both variables have been re-centered around the sample means. List of included countries available on request.

*Sources of data:* "Corruption Perceptions Index 2015," www.transparency.org/cpi2015; World Bank, *Doing Business* (2016); World Development Indicators.

capita that we saw in Figure 9.1. Technically, we add the logarithm of the *Doing Business* ranking as an explanatory variable to a multiple regression of the CPI on the logarithm of GDP per capita (see Box 9.1), and plot the relationship between the CPI and the logarithm of GDP per capita after controlling for this variable. We see that the line in Figure 9.2 is much flatter than the line in Figure 9.1. This happens because country bureaucracies tend to become more efficient as their GDPs per capita increase, and this accounts for much of the tendency for perceived corruption to decrease as GDP per capita increases. We also see that three of the countries we study that were below the line in Figure 9.1 are above or on the line in Figure 9.2: Algeria (DZA), Saudi Arabia (SAU), and Qatar (QAT). All of these are fuel-endowed countries. In general the countries we study are still perceived to be more corrupt than would be predicted by their GDPs per capita, but this tendency is much less pronounced in Figure 9.2 than in Figure 9.1.

> **Box 9.1**
>
> **More on the Tollbooth Hypothesis and Perceived Corruption in Fuel-Endowed Countries.** We can take a more statistical approach to our investigation of the tollbooth hypothesis for greater perceived corruption in fuel-endowed countries by using the technique of multiple regression analysis described in Box 6.2. The slope of the line in Figure 9.1 equals the coefficient of a regression of the CPI on the logarithm of GDP per capita. We can add to this regression a variable that equals one if a country is fuel-endowed, Arab or non-Arab, and zero otherwise; and a variable that equals one if a country is one of the other countries we study, and zero otherwise. We find that the coefficient on the first variable is negative and statistically significant and the coefficient on the second variable is negative but not statistically significant. These results show that both fuel-endowed countries and the non-fuel-endowed countries we study are perceived to be more corrupt on average than predicted by their GDPs per capita, but only for the fuel-endowed countries are we confident that this average effect is not just an artifact of statistical noise. We then add the logarithm of the *Doing Business* rank as an explanatory variable in this multiple regression for the CPI, and find it has a negative and statistically significant coefficient: Lower rank is associated with greater perceived corruption. Moreover, the coefficient on the variable for fuel-endowed country changes from -13.0 to -2.5 and is no longer statistically significant, which is evidence that bureaucratic inefficiency accounted for most or all of the greater perceived corruption of fuel-endowed countries, controlling for their GDPs per capita. We must add that this evidence is supportive of the tollbooth hypothesis for greater perceived corruption in fuel-endowed countries, but not decisive—for example, it may be possible to find a different variable to add to the multiple regression for the CPI that would also cause the coefficient on the variable for fuel-endowed country to lose statistical significance.

In the next section we explore in depth measurement of bureaucratic efficiency in handling business startups and enforcing contracts. We will focus on the ability of the countries we study to improve their bureaucratic efficiency in these areas over time. We also discuss the impacts of increasing bureaucratic efficiency in these areas on the kinds of new businesses that entrepreneurs start and on productivity of existing firms, rather than the impact of bureaucratic efficiency on perceived corruption.

## Bureaucratic Performance with Regard to Starting a Business and Enforcing Contracts

In this section we discuss in detail the *Doing Business* data collection for starting a business and enforcing contracts, and contrast the performance of the countries we study with the performance of the comparison country groups. We focus on starting a business because the impact of bureaucratic inefficiency in this area is especially well understood. We focus on enforcing contracts for reasons given below.

The data for starting a business were first collected in 1999 under the direction of Simeon Djankov, Rafael La Porta, Florencio Lopez-di-Silanes, and Andrei Shleifer (2002). Their investigators focused on the requirements to legally open a firm with between five and fifty employees in a country's largest city. The firm did not engage in foreign trade, generate environmental hazards, or have any other characteristic that would bring additional government regulations into consideration. Investigators counted the number of required bureaucratic procedures, such as registering for taxes or obtaining proof of no criminal record, the number of days required to complete all procedures, and the cost of official expenses and fees. The cost of bribes was never counted, even if these were typical in a given country.

Figures 9.3(a) and 9.3(b), reproduced from Djankov et al. (2002), illustrate the data collection for New Zealand and France, respectively. Each figure shows the number of procedures, number of business days, and cost as a percentage of GDP per capita required to open a new business. It is clear that in 1999 it was much easier to open a new business in New Zealand than in France. New Zealand required three procedures that took three days versus fifteen procedures and fifty-three days in France. The cost was 0.5 percent of GDP per capita in New Zealand versus 14.3 percent of GDP per capita in France.

In Table 9.1 we report *Doing Business* data for 2005 and 2018 on starting a business in the countries we study and the comparison country groups. The collection of data has changed slightly since the initial study by Djankov et al. The hypothetical firm that is navigating the bureaucratic process is

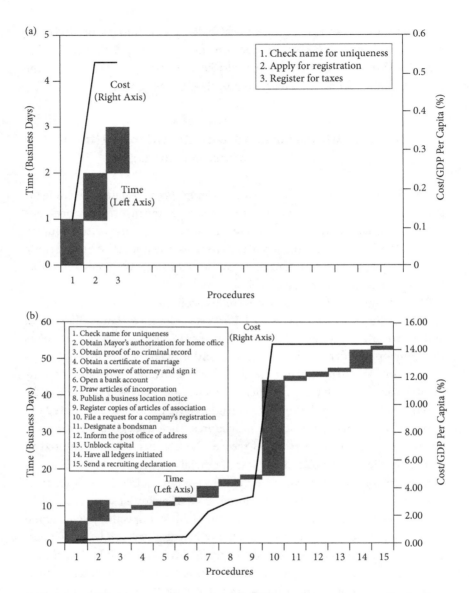

**Figure 9.3** (a) Bureaucratic Requirements to Start a Business in New Zealand

(b) Bureaucratic Requirements to Start a Business in France

(a) *Source*: Simeon Djankov, Rafael La Porta, Florencio Lopez-di-Silanes, and Andrei Shleifer, "The Regulation of Entry," *Quarterly Journal of Economics* 117, no. 1 (2002): 1–37; figure 1.

(b) *Source*: Simeon Djankov, Rafael La Porta, Florencio Lopez-di-Silanes, and Andrei Shleifer, "The Regulation of Entry," *Quarterly Journal of Economics* 117, no. 1 (2002): 1–37; figure 2.

**Table 9.1.** Procedures, Time, and Cost of Starting a Business

| | Procedures (Number) | | | Time (Days) | | | Cost (Percent of GNI Per Capita) | | |
|---|---|---|---|---|---|---|---|---|---|
| | 2005 | 2018 | Change 2005–2018 | 2005 | 2018 | Change 2005–2018 | 2005 | 2018 | Change 2005–2018 |
| Arab sub-Saharan Africa | 11.4 | 8.1 | −3.3 | 50.3 | 35.7 | −14.6 | 169.1 | 44.9 | −124.2 |
| Non-Arab sub-Saharan Africa | 11.3 | 8.0 | −3.4 | 47.2 | 23.3 | −23.9 | 204.3 | 36.8 | −167.5 |
| Arab fuel-endowed countries | 13.4 | 9.4 | −4.0 | 40.4 | 20.2 | −20.2 | 31.4 | 19.0 | −12.3 |
| Non-Arab fuel-endowed countries | 11.4 | 11.1 | −0.3 | 60.6 | 72.1 | 11.5 | 15.4 | 95.8 | 80.4 |
| Iran | 10 | 8 | −2 | 31 | 14.5 | −16.5 | 7.3 | 1.4 | −5.9 |
| Arab Mediterranean | 11.1 | 7.1 | −4.0 | 32.0 | 12.8 | −19.1 | 51.1 | 9.5 | −41.7 |
| Rest of non-Arab world | 11.1 | 8.6 | −2.4 | 68.5 | 22.6 | −45.9 | 33.6 | 9.6 | −24.0 |
| Turkey | 7 | 7 | 0 | 7 | 6.5 | −0.5 | 26 | 12.8 | −13.2 |
| Latin America | 13.1 | 9.6 | −3.5 | 87.3 | 47.7 | −39.6 | 29.6 | 13.3 | −16.4 |
| Southern Europe | 10.0 | 6.2 | −3.8 | 65.3 | 9.2 | −56.1 | 20.1 | 8.6 | −11.5 |

*Notes:* See Chapter 1 for distinction between GNI and GDP. Due to rounding errors, some "change" column figures may appear to be inconsistent with the other figures in corresponding table rows. The population-weighted averages for each country group include the countries listed in the Appendix. The excluded countries were missing data.

*Source of data:* http://www.doingbusiness.org/en/data (accessed 2018).

now described as owned either by five married men or five married women; the data in Table 9.1 were collected using the former description. The cost of official expenses and fees is expressed as a percentage of GNI per capita instead of GDP per capita.

Of the country groups shown in Table 9.1, Southern Europe has the most efficient bureaucracy for starting a business in 2018: the smallest number of procedures, shortest time, and lowest cost as a percentage of GNI per capita. Yet it is far off the pace set by New Zealand, which is ranked number one for ease of starting a business in 2018 and has improved even relative to the data shown in Figure 9.3(a). In general bureaucracies have become more efficient at handling business startups since 2005. Every country group except the non-Arab fuel-endowed countries shows a decrease in number of procedures, time, and cost; the exception is caused entirely by Venezuela. In 2018 Arab sub-Saharan Africa is somewhat less efficient than non-Arab sub-Saharan Africa. The Arab Mediterranean is more efficient than the rest of the non-Arab world or Latin America. Turkey has roughly the same number of procedures as the Arab Mediterranean and requires less time to complete its procedures but at a higher cost relative to GNI per capita. Iran is more efficient than the Arab fuel-endowed countries.

We also see from Table 9.1 that the Arab fuel-endowed countries require a greater number of procedures to start a business than Arab sub-Saharan Africa or the Arab Mediterranean. Djankov et al. (2002) found that the logarithm of the number of procedures was positively correlated with perceived corruption after controlling for GDP per capita. The same is true in our data, so this is an aspect of bureaucratic inefficiency that helps to account for the greater perceived corruption of the fuel-endowed countries.

How important is it for government bureaucracies to handle business startups efficiently? Lee Branstetter, Francisco Lima, Lowell Taylor, and Ana Venâncio (2014) used the "difference-in-difference" technique we described in Chapter 4 to evaluate the impact on business startups of an increase in bureaucratic efficiency in Portugal. In 2005 Portugal began the "On the Spot Firm" program, which established "one-stop shops" that offered prospective entrepreneurs significantly reduced administrative fees and simplified incorporation procedures. According to *Doing Business* indicators, by 2009 Portugal had reduced the number of procedures required to start a business from eleven to six, had shortened the time needed to complete those procedures from seventy-eight to five and a half days, and had decreased the administrative cost from 13.5 to 6.5 percent of GNI per capita. Crucially, the one-stop shops were not opened in all counties in Portugal at the same time, so Branstetter et al. could compare the difference in business startups before and after the program in "treatment" counties where the shops had opened to "control" counties where the shops had not yet opened.

Using this difference-in-difference technique, Branstetter et al. found that the introduction of the one-stop shop was associated with an additional 2.1 new firms per 100,000 county inhabitants, a 17-percent increase in the number of new firms. They also found that the program was associated with an increase in startup employment in new firms of seven workers per 100,000 inhabitants, a 22-percent increase. On average, therefore, each additional new firm employed about three workers at time of startup. In fact, Branstetter et al. did not find a statistically significant increase in the number of new firms with initial employment of more than five workers. They found statistically significant increases in the number of new firms in only three industries: agriculture, construction, and retail.

The results of Branstetter et al. show that improved bureaucratic efficiency in handling business startups leads to founding of more small firms, but not to founding of large firms in the most economically dynamic sectors such as manufacturing and business services. Although their results pertain to Portugal, they are likely to apply to the countries we study as well. Entrepreneurs who are able to start large businesses are likely to hire expediters or pay bribes rather than be discouraged by red tape and fees that may be small relative to their planned initial investments.

We now turn from business startups to existing firms. The aspect of the legal and regulatory environment for existing firms on which we focus is the efficiency of the government in enforcing contracts. We choose this focus for two reasons. First, as we discussed in Chapter 3, efficient contract enforcement is helpful to high-quality production, because firms can credibly threaten suppliers of substandard inputs with legal action. Second, a major determinant of contract enforcement efficiency is the speed with which courts process cases, and it can be argued that other legal and regulatory reforms depend on court speed to be effective. A good example is a bankruptcy reform in Brazil in 2005 that allowed creditors to recover more of what was owed to them by insolvent firms. Jacopo Ponticelli and Leonardo Alencar (2016) showed that this reform generated more lending in municipalities where the case backlog for courts was shorter, because lenders thought that if the firms that borrowed from them went bankrupt, they would be able to recover their money in a reasonable amount of time.

To measure the efficiency of contract enforcement, *Doing Business* collected data from local lawyers and judges regarding a hypothetical dispute concerning a lawful transaction between two businesses (Seller and Buyer), located in a country's largest business city. Buyer purchases custom-made goods worth 200 percent of the country's GNI per capita from Seller. After Seller delivers the goods to Buyer, Buyer refuses to pay for the goods on the grounds that the delivered goods were not of adequate quality. *Doing Business* considers the opposite of the situation discussed in Chapter 3: The goods *are* of adequate quality, and Seller (the plaintiff) sues Buyer (the defendant) to recover the amount under the sales agreement (that is, 200 percent of the economy's income per capita). Buyer opposes Seller's claim, and the claim is disputed on the merits. The court cannot decide the case on the basis of documentary evidence or legal title alone. Because the goods were custom-made, Seller cannot find a different buyer.

*Doing Business* chooses to complicate the hypothetical dispute by assuming that Seller attaches Buyer's movable assets (for example, office equipment and vehicles) before obtaining a judgment, because Seller fears that Buyer may become insolvent or try to hide its assets. An expert opinion is given on the quality of the delivered goods. The judgment is 100 percent in favor of Seller: The judge decides that the goods are of adequate quality and that Buyer must pay the agreed price. Buyer does not appeal the judgment. Seller decides to start enforcing the judgment as soon as the time allocated by law for appeal expires. Seller takes all required steps for prompt enforcement of the judgment. The money is successfully collected through a public sale of Buyer's movable assets. It is assumed that Buyer does not have any money in its bank account, making it impossible for the judgment to be enforced through a seizure of the Buyer's accounts.

*Doing Business* records time in calendar days, counted from the moment the plaintiff decides to file the lawsuit in court until payment. This includes both the days when actions take place and the waiting periods between. Three types of costs are recorded: court costs, enforcement costs, and average attorney fees. Table 9.2 shows the time required for contract enforcement and the costs as a percentage of Seller's claim for the countries we study and the comparison country groups, for the years 2005 and 2018. We see that Southern Europe has the lowest cost of any country group, but the longest time to enforce the hypothetical contract. Iran stands out for speed and low cost. Nevertheless, time and cost for Iran in 2018 are substantially higher than for the country ranked number one for efficiency of contract

**Table 9.2.** Time and Cost of Enforcing Contracts

|  | Time (Days) | | | Cost (Percent of Claim) | | |
|---|---|---|---|---|---|---|
|  | 2005 | 2018 | Change 2005–2018 | 2005 | 2018 | Change 2005–2018 |
| Arab sub-Saharan Africa | 673.4 | 719.8 | 46.4 | 22.6 | 23.9 | 1.4 |
| Non-Arab sub-Saharan Africa | 660.3 | 576.8 | −83.5 | 54.9 | 41.5 | −13.4 |
| Arab fuel-endowed countries | 589.4 | 567.5 | −21.8 | 25.8 | 24.1 | −1.7 |
| Non-Arab fuel-endowed countries | 513.3 | 558.3 | 45.0 | 23.9 | 23.9 | 0.0 |
| Iran | 520 | 505 | −15 | 17 | 17 | 0 |
| Arab Mediterranean | 839.6 | 837.1 | −2.5 | 26.7 | 26.7 | 0.0 |
| Rest of non-Arab world | 755.0 | 784.0 | 29.0 | 28.7 | 27.5 | −1.2 |
| Turkey | 420 | 580 | 160 | 27.3 | 24.9 | −2.4 |
| Latin America | 703.4 | 698.1 | −5.3 | 26.2 | 28.3 | 2.1 |
| Southern Europe | 959.3 | 891.3 | −68.0 | 23.0 | 19.8 | −3.2 |

*Notes:* Due to rounding errors, some "change" column figures may appear to be inconsistent with the other figures in corresponding table rows. The population-weighted averages for each country group include the countries listed in the Appendix. The excluded countries were missing data.
*Source of data:* http://www.doingbusiness.org/en/data (accessed 2018).

enforcement, South Korea: 505 days versus 290, 17 percent of the Seller's claim versus 12.7 percent.

Comparing Table 9.2 to Table 9.1 shows that, unlike with starting a business, countries are not all moving in the direction of greater efficiency of contract enforcement, and efficiency improvements are typically smaller. Evidently improving court efficiency is more difficult than removing bureaucratic obstacles to business startups. In 2018, Arab fuel-endowed countries are about the same as non-Arab fuel-endowed countries in time and cost of contract enforcement, Arab sub-Saharan Africa is slower but less expensive than non-Arab sub-Saharan Africa, and same is true for the Arab Mediterranean compared to the rest of the non-Arab world and Latin America. Turkey is faster and less expensive than the Arab Mediterranean.

More research is still needed to judge the economic impacts of the Arab countries' middling performance on contract enforcement, or the better performance of Iran and Turkey. Despite excruciatingly slow courts,

Southern Europe has reached a very high level of human development, though still below the level of Northwestern Europe. In Chapter 2 we described how, during the era of extensive growth, trade diasporas were able to conduct business in the absence of any government with the authority to enforce contracts. Even in today's economic environment, firms are reluctant to risk losing business by developing reputations for not fulfilling contracts, whether or not the other parties to the contracts can sue them successfully. The limits to economic productivity caused by reliance on reputations rather than formal legal contract enforcement are much better understood in theory than in practice (James Rauch 2005). Given the difficulty of improving court efficiency shown by Table 9.2, governments in the countries we study must carefully consider the priority they assign to improving contract enforcement relative to the other challenges they face.

## Politically Connected Firms in Egypt and Tunisia

Politically connected firms are private-sector firms that provide direct monetary benefits to government officials, their relatives, or their friends. Government officials, their relatives or friends might partly or wholly own the firms, or the firms might employ them as top executives. We can consider special treatment given to politically connected firms by the government to be a form of corruption.

In order to establish the existence of a connection between the government and a firm, one must be able to identify the owners and other key figures in the firm. This is much easier if the firm is publicly traded on a stock exchange. A publicly traded firm will have shareholders, a board of directors that represents the shareholders, and top executives who are hired by the board of directors. The firm is typically required to report the names of the board members, the names and positions of the top executives, and the names of any shareholders who own more than a certain percentage (five percent, in the United States) of the firm's stock. These names can be checked against the names of the head of state, his or her ministers, elected officials such as members of parliament, and their relatives and friends. If there is a match between a firm name and a government name, we say the firm is politically connected.

In her study of politically connected firms, Mara Faccio (2006) assembled a database that included more than twenty thousand publicly traded firms in forty-seven countries. Her work is the best known attempt to compare the prevalence of politically connected firms across countries. Unfortunately, none of the countries we study is included in her database. We will nevertheless briefly review her method and results because they provide important background for the studies of politically connected firms in Egypt and Tunisia that we will describe below.

Faccio identifies a company as being connected with a politician if at least one of its large shareholders or one of its top officers (CEO, president, vice-president, chairman, or secretary) is a member of parliament, a minister or head of state, or is closely related to a top politician or party. She defines a large shareholder as anyone controlling at least 10 percent of the voting shares in the firm. (Note that this is the same percentage we used to define "controlling interest" in our discussion of FDI in Chapter 3.) Close relationships include relatives of ministers or heads of state and friendships reported in *The Economist*, *Forbes*, and *Fortune*.

Faccio finds that connected firms account for 2.7 percent of all corporations in her database and 7.7 percent of their total stock market value. Considering the largest fifty firms in each country, she finds that 6.9 percent of them have political connections. This result is consistent with the studies of Egypt and Tunisia described below, in which politically connected firms are found to be larger than unconnected firms. Faccio also identifies countries for which connected firms are especially prevalent. In Indonesia, Italy, Malaysia, Russia, and Thailand, over 10 percent of listed corporations are politically connected. In Ireland, Malaysia, Russia, Thailand, and the United Kingdom, connected corporations account for more than 20 percent of total stock market value. Faccio observes a positive correlation between the share of firms in a country that is politically connected and an index of perceived corruption similar to the CPI we used in the section titled "Corruption, GDP Per Capita, and Bureaucratic Inefficiency." At the same time, she finds a positive correlation between an indicator for democracy and the share of politically connected firms. This points to a weakness in her study, which is that political connections are more likely to be found where information is more freely available, all else equal. Moreover, her method of identifying politically connected firms does not seem to work for Latin America. Seven of the forty-seven countries in Faccio's study are from Latin America (Argentina, Brazil, Chile, Colombia, Mexico, Peru, and Venezuela). In five of those seven countries, Faccio finds zero politically connected firms.

The difficulty of identifying politically connected firms shows why, of all the countries we study, Egypt and Tunisia are the best for examining this phenomenon. Egypt and Tunisia are the only two countries for which, as a result of the Arab Spring, heads of state were changed but civil war did not follow. Thus a great deal of information about the former governments and their connections to private-sector firms was exposed, but the data were not lost in the chaos of a civil war. In Tunisia, information revealed after the change in head of state allowed political connections to be identified for firms that were not publicly traded on a stock exchange. This is important, since if government officials and their relatives or friends do not want their connections to firms to become known, they may choose not to list their firms on a stock exchange but instead keep them privately held. Below we will describe in more detail the post-Arab Spring information that was used to identify politically connected firms in Egypt and Tunisia.

We will gain insight from the studies covered here into the specific ways in which ties to the government benefited politically connected firms in Egypt and Tunisia, and how government favors to these firms might have affected the rest of their economies. However, we will not be able to place these studies into our usual comparative context because studies of politically connected firms in other countries have focused on different economic mechanisms or outcomes, such as bank loans in Pakistan (Khwaja and Mian 2005) or worker deaths in China (Fisman and Wang 2015).

We begin with a study of politically connected firms in Egypt by Daron Acemoglu, Tarek Hassan, and Ahmed Tahoun (2018). Like Faccio, they only study firms listed on a stock exchange, in this case the Egyptian Exchange. They identify politically connected firms listed on the Egyptian Exchange and then examine how their stock prices react to news about who was likely to hold power in Egypt during the revolutionary years 2011–2013. If the stock prices of connected firms change more than the stock prices of unconnected firms, it is evidence that investors believe their profitability is affected more than the profitability of unconnected firms by which government is in power.

At the beginning of 2011 the Egyptian head of state was President Hosni Mubarak, who had held power since 1981. Mubarak led the National Democratic Party (NDP). Acemoglu, Hassan, and Tahoun obtained a list of six thousand prominent NDP members that was posted online by activists after protests drove Mubarak from power. This is the list of names against which Acemoglu et al. check names from stock exchange listings to determine political connections of firms to the NDP government. Specifically, there were 177 firms listed on the Egyptian Exchange at the beginning of 2011. These firms were required to publish quarterly reports disclosing the names of their board members and principal shareholders, defined as individuals or entities that own more than 5 percent of the firm's stock. Acemoglu et al. classify a firm as connected to the NDP if the name of at least one of the firm's major shareholders or board members appears on the list of prominent NDP members. They find 19 name matches covering 22 firms, or 12.4 percent of the 177 listed firms. Comparing this result to the prevalence of politically connected firms found by Faccio, Egypt would be in the group of countries where connected firms are most prevalent, in between Thailand (15.1 percent) and Italy (10.3 percent). However, the list of names used by Acemoglu et al. to check for political connections is much more comprehensive than the lists assembled by Faccio, so the prevalence of connected firms in Egypt may be exaggerated relative to her findings.

After the fall of the Mubarak government, two organized groups were the main competitors for power: the military and the Muslim Brotherhood. The Egyptian military owns stock in Egyptian firms through certain state-owned holding companies. (A holding company is a firm that exists for the sole purpose of controlling other firms by owning their stocks.) Acemoglu et al. classify a listed firm as connected to the Egyptian military if any of twelve military-controlled holding companies is one of its principal shareholders. They find thirty-three military-connected firms, none of which is also a NDP-connected firm. The Muslim Brotherhood was founded in Egypt in 1928 with the goal of increasing the influence of Islamic principles in the governance of Egypt. Acemoglu et al. were able to identify only one firm listed on the Egyptian Exchange as connected to the Muslim Brotherhood. Instead, they use a list of firms classified as operating according to Islamic principles, such as the Islamic banks described in Box 6.4, and call them "Islamic-connected." Acemoglu et al. argue that these firms are likely to benefit relative to their competitors under a Muslim Brotherhood-led government. They identify thirteen Islamic-connected firms on the Egyptian Exchange, five of which are also NDP-connected firms.

To summarize, of the 177 firms listed on the Egyptian stock exchange at the beginning of 2011, 22 were NDP-connected, 33 were military-connected, 13 were Islamic-connected (of which 5 were also NDP-connected), and 114 were unconnected. The average stock-market value of

NDP-connected firms was roughly five times as large as the average stock-market value of unconnected firms.

Acemoglu et al. examine the period beginning with the first large protest against the Mubarak regime on January 25, 2011. Mubarak resigned the presidency on February 11. The Egyptian Exchange, which had closed shortly after the large protests began, reopened on March 30, 2011. Over these 65 days Acemoglu et al. estimate that NDP-connected firms lost 13.1 percent of their stock market value relative to unconnected firms. They find that changes in the stock prices of military-connected and Islamic-connected firms relative to unconnected firms are not statistically different from zero. Clearly investors believed that NDP-connected firms would be less profitable without the NDP in power.

Table 9.3 shows the signs and statistical significance of the changes in stock prices of NDP-, military-, and Islamic-connected firms relative to unconnected firms during various revolutionary period events that followed the reopening of the Egyptian Exchange. The results in this table are from multiple regressions using indicators for these political connections and various control variables (not shown) to explain the percentage changes in stock prices.

The first event covers July 31–September 8, 2011, during which time the military cleared protesters from Tahrir Square. Column (1) in Table 9.3 corresponds to this period. We see from column (1) that stock prices for military-connected firms rose relative to unconnected firms, suggesting

**Table 9.3.** Percentage Changes in Stock Prices During Egypt's Revolutionary Period

| Political Connection | (1) | (2) | (3) | (4) | (5) | (6) | (7) |
|---|---|---|---|---|---|---|---|
| NDP | + | − | − | +** | − | −** | − |
| Military | +* | −** | + | +* | − | + | − |
| Islamic | − | + | + | +* | +* | − | −** |

*Notes:* Results are for the cumulative returns to owning stocks in politically connected firms relative to unconnected firms during the event periods. For stocks that paid dividends during the event periods, the cumulative returns may differ slightly from the percentage changes in stock prices. Column (1) = military crackdown, (2) = protesters retake Tahrir Square, (3) = first round of presidential election, (4) = second round of presidential election, (5) = generals fired, (6) = constitution passes, (7) = Morsi deposed by military. **Different from zero with 95-percent confidence. *Different from zero with 90-percent confidence.

*Source:* Acemoglu, Hassan, and Tahoun (2018, table 3).

that investors saw the military's assertion of control as good for the profitability of military-connected firms. Column (2) corresponds to the period November 17–20, 2011, when protesters reoccupied Tahrir Square. This event was the opposite of the event covered in column (1), and the associated direction of change in the stock prices of military-connected firms was the opposite of column (1). Column (3) corresponds to the announcement on May 28, 2012 of the results of the first round of the presidential election, which selected two candidates to run in the second round. On June 24, 2012 it was announced that Mohammed Mursi, who was closely associated with the Muslim Brotherhood, had narrowly won the second round. We see in column (4) that this event was associated with increases in the stock prices of all three types of politically connected firms relative to unconnected firms. Acemoglu et al. speculate that this reflected investors' beliefs that the three powerful groups had made a deal that would benefit all of them.

A struggle with the military dominated the first two months of Mursi's presidency. This struggle culminated with Mursi's firing of the Commander-in-Chief of the armed forces and the four highest-ranking generals on August 12, 2012. Column (5) of Table 9.3 shows that stock prices for Islamic-connected firms rose relative to unconnected firms during this event. On December 23, a new constitution promoting Islamic principles of governance but also granting expanded powers to the military passed in a referendum. We see in column (6) that this event was associated with a decrease in the stock prices of NDP-connected firms relative to unconnected firms. Perhaps investors believed that passage of the new constitution would decisively exclude the NDP from power. Finally, Egypt's revolutionary period ended when the military removed Mursi from power on July 4, 2013. During the period of this event and the mass mobilization that preceded it, column (7) shows that stock prices of Islamic-connected firms fell relative to unconnected firms.

Table 9.3 is mostly consistent with the view that stock prices of politically connected firms rise and fall with the power of the groups to which they are connected. However, this table does not tell us what actions the government takes to benefit firms that are connected to it, or how government actions to benefit politically connected firms affect the rest of the economy. These are the subjects of the study of politically connected firms in Egypt that we discuss next, by Ishac Diwan, Philip Keefer, and Marc Schiffbauer (2018).

Like Acemoglu et al., Diwan, Keefer, and Schiffbauer identify politically connected firms by matching a list of names to board members and major shareholders of firms listed on the Egyptian Exchange. Instead of using the list of names of prominent NDP members that was posted online by activists, Diwan et al. made their own list of businessmen (all were men). They either had high political positions in the NDP or in government, such that they could directly influence government policy in their favor, or they were long-term friends of the Mubarak family. Diwan et al. also considered firms that were ever listed on the Egyptian Exchange rather than restricting the possible firms to those listed in 2011. They identify 385 politically connected firms, about two-thirds of which were owned by businessmen who were either ministers in the government or led a policy committee in the NDP after 2001. The remaining one-third of the connected firms were controlled either by long-term friends of President Mubarak dating from the times they served together in the military, or by co-founders of a large investment bank partly-owned by a Cyprus-registered company that in turn was owned by the Mubarak family.

After the fall of the Mubarak government, trials of leading businessmen revealed many examples of government favors to politically connected firms. A minister of housing on the list of names compiled by Diwan et al. was found to have arranged for state-owned land to be transferred to a business partner at a substantially below-market price. A close friend of President Mubarak, also on the list compiled by Diwan et al., acquired a state-owned retail chain at a low price, while arranging for various barriers to international trade to protect the chain from competition from imported clothing. Another businessman on the list of Diwan et al. led the NDP policy committee and owned of one of the largest steel companies in Egypt. He arranged for changes to the competition law that effectively exempted his firm from liability under the law; the Egyptian Competition Authority dismissed a case against the firm in 2009.

Diwan et al. examine two areas of government policy, trade and energy, for more systematic evidence of favors to politically connected firms. Regarding trade, they show that in Egypt the reduction in tariffs we discussed in Chapters 3 and 8 was accompanied by an increase in non-tariff measures (NTMs) that allowed for greater government discretion in providing protection from import competition. Most NTMs in Egypt are license or registration requirements for importers, packaging requirements, regulations on production or distribution processes, and product-quality requirements. By selective application or enforcement of NTMs, the government could hinder imports that competed with politically connected firms while letting

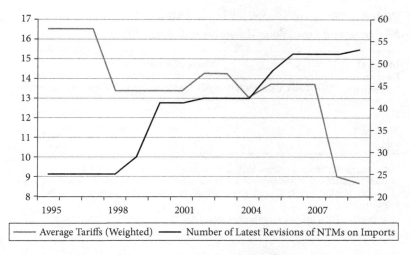

**Figure 9.4** Average Tariff Rates and Number of Non-Tariff Measures in Egypt
*Source:* Diwan, Keefer, and Schiffbauer (2018), Figure 2.

other imports enter Egypt without impediments. Figure 9.4 shows that, as average Egyptian tariffs fell from 16.5 percent in 1995 to 8.7 percent in 2009 (left scale), the number of NTMs introduced or revised rose from 25 to 53 (right scale), giving Egypt one of the highest numbers of NTMs in the world. Diwan et al. find that 81 percent of politically connected manufacturing and mining firms sold products covered by at least two NTMs and 69 percent sold products covered by at least three NTMs. The comparable figures are 27 and 4 percent, respectively, for all unconnected manufacturing and mining firms, and 50 and 16 percent, respectively, for large unconnected manufacturing and mining firms. (Large is defined as more than two hundred employees. Most connected firms are large by this definition, so large unconnected firms are more comparable to connected firms than all unconnected firms.)

We saw in the previous chapter (Table 8.3) that Egyptian spending on energy subsidies is among the highest in the world as a share of GDP. A firm has the potential to benefit more from these subsidies, the more energy it uses. A firm in a high energy-intensive industry like cement or steel can benefit more from energy subsidies than a firm in a low energy-intensive industry like furniture manufacturing. Table 9.4 shows that 49 percent of politically connected Egyptian manufacturing and mining firms operated in high energy-intensive industries, compared to 8 percent of all unconnected

**Table 9.4.** Shares of Manufacturing and Mining Firms in High, Moderate, and Low Energy-Intensive Industries (Percent)

| Industry Energy-Intensity | Politically Connected | All Unconnected | Large Unconnected |
|---|---|---|---|
| High | 49 | 8 | 30 |
| Moderate | 28 | 63 | 52 |
| Low | 23 | 29 | 16 |

*Notes:* Large unconnected firms have at least two hundred employees. Using the United Nations classification of industry energy intensity, high, moderate, and low energy-intensive industries account for 22, 37, and 42 percent of all mining and manufacturing industries, respectively.

*Source:* Diwan, Keefer, and Schiffbauer (2018, table 7).

**Table 9.5.** Ln(Profits/Assets) of 253 Egyptian Manufacturing Firms, 2003–2011

| Firm Variable | (1) | (2) | (3) | (4) | (5) |
|---|---|---|---|---|---|
| Political connection | +** | +** | — | +* | + |
| NTMs | | + | + | | |
| (Political connection) × (NTMs) | | | +* | | |
| High energy intensity | | | | + | — |
| (Political connection) × (High energy intensity) | | | | | +** |

*Notes:* The results in this table are from multiple regressions of profitability on the explanatory variables listed in the firm variable column and other control variables that are not shown. Political connection is an indicator for whether a firm is politically connected. Of the 253 firms, 48 are connected. NTMs are the number of NTMs in the industry in which the firm operates. High energy intensity is an indicator for whether the firm operates in a high energy intensity industry. **Different from zero with 95-percent confidence. *Different from zero with 90-percent confidence.

*Source:* Diwan, Keefer, and Schiffbauer (2018, table 9).

manufacturing and mining firms and 30 percent of large unconnected manufacturing and mining firms. Diwan et al. note that Egyptian firms needed government licenses to legally open new factories in industries that were heavy users of energy, and that those licenses had to be renewed annually. Politically connected firms were both more likely to get the licenses and less likely to be threatened with non-renewal after having invested in the new factories.

Table 9.5 examines the profitability of Egyptian manufacturing firms that have data available for the period 2003–2011. Profitability is measured by the logarithm of the ratio of firm profits to firm assets. Column (1) shows that politically connected firms are more profitable than unconnected firms. Column (2) adds the number of NTMs in the industry in which the firm operates as an explanatory variable. We see that the association of this variable with profitability is positive, but not statistically different from zero. In column (3) of Table 9.5, the product of the first two variables, the indicator for political connection and the number of NTMs in the firm's industry, is added as an explanatory variable. This variable equals the number of NTMs in the firm's industry for politically connected firms and zero for unconnected firms. It has a positive association with firm profitability, whereas the association of political connection with firm profitability is now not statistically different from zero. Column (3) shows that NTMs do not raise profitability for all firms in industries they cover, but only for politically connected firms. This is evidence that the NTMs are selectively used by the government to protect connected firms from foreign competition. Moreover, column (3) shows that connected firms are not more profitable than unconnected firms if they are not in industries covered by NTMs.

Columns (4) and (5) of Table 9.5 repeat the exercise of columns (2) and (3) using an indicator for whether a firm is in a high energy-intensity industry instead of the number of NTMs in the firm's industry. We see in column (4) that the association of high energy-intensity with profitability is not statistically different from zero. The explanatory variable added in column (5) equals one if a firm is politically connected and in a high energy-intensive industry and zero otherwise. Its positive association with firm profitability shows that operating in a high energy-intensive industry only raises profitability for connected firms. This might be because subsidized energy was only provided to these firms. Column (5) also shows that connected firms are not more profitable than unconnected firms if they are not in industries that especially benefit from energy subsidies. (High energy-intensive industries might overlap with industries with more NTMs.)

If, as Table 9.5 suggests, politically connected firms were given competitive advantages by the Egyptian government, we would expect their presence in an industry to be detrimental to unconnected firms in that industry.

Diwan et al. find evidence that entry of politically connected firms into an industry slowed employment growth in that industry relative to other industries in Egypt during the period 1996–2006. This indicates that the increased employment generated by entry of politically connected firms was more than offset by reduced employment by unconnected firms. Diwan et al. also find that employment in industries entered by connected firms shifted toward small firms, with fewer than ten employees. These firms may not have been in competition with connected firms, and may even have supplied them with inputs.

The evidence collected by Diwan et al. can be interpreted using the "tollbooth" hypothesis discussed in the "Corruption, GDP Per Capita, and Bureaucratic Inefficiency" section. According to the World Bank's *Doing Business* indicators (2007a), Egypt was the top reformer of laws and regulations blocking private sector development in 2006–2007. These reductions in bureaucratic delays may have primarily stimulated entry of small firms, as shown by Branstetter et al. (2014) in their study discussed in the previous section, which is consistent with the relative growth of small firms found by Diwan et al. At the same time the Egyptian government was removing these tollbooths for small firms, it was establishing new tollbooths in the form of NTMs and other discretionary regulations that disadvantaged large firms that could compete with politically connected firms. The old tollbooths helped low-level officials extract bribes, whereas the new tollbooths enabled more powerful officials to collect far more money through ownership of firms that the tollbooths made more profitable by stifling their competition.

Yet another way for politically connected firms to benefit from their ties to the government is by evading taxes. Bob Rijkers, Leila Baghdadi, and Gael Raballand (2017) investigate evasion of import taxes (tariffs) by politically connected firms in Tunisia in the period before the Arab Spring uprising that deposed the head of state, Zine El Abidine Ben Ali. Like Egypt and other developing countries, Tunisia reduced tariff rates and dependence on tariff revenue in the 1990s. Nevertheless, tariff rates for some imported goods remained high, and tariffs continue to be a significant source of government tax revenue for many developing countries, accounting for 9 percent of revenue for Tunisia (Rijkers et al. 2017, p. 460).

After the Ben Ali government fell at the start of 2011, assets of Ben Ali and his extended family were confiscated. The confiscation process affected 114 individuals, including Ben Ali himself, his blood relatives, and his in-laws. Rijkers, Baghdadi, and Raballand obtained from the Tunisian authorities a list of 662 firms that were owned by the Ben Ali clan and confiscated. This is their list of politically connected firms. Unlike the authors of the studies of politically connected firms in Egypt, Rijkers et al. do not rely on stock market data to identify connected firms.

By matching the list of Ben Ali firms with firms listed as importers by Tunisian customs, Rijkers et al. are able to identify 206 of the Ben Ali firms as importers. They also identify 27,943 other private-sector importing firms, which they divide into 7,074 "offshore" firms and 20,869 "onshore" firms. Offshore firms are exempted from having to pay tariffs on imported inputs used in the production of exported output and consequently have less incentive to evade tariffs. Onshore firms are private (as opposed to public-sector) importers that are not Ben Ali or offshore firms. Although Ben Ali importers were less than 1 percent of all importing firms, they accounted for 2.3 percent of imports, which is consistent with findings above that politically connected firms are larger than other private-sector firms.

Tariffs are typically collected as a percentage of the value of imports. One way to evade tariffs is to report a lower value of imports than the true value, so that tariffs are calculated as a percentage of a smaller number. The higher is the tariff percentage, the greater is the incentive to under-report import value. This kind of tariff evasion can be detected by comparing the value of imports with the value of exports reported by the exporting country. If there are no errors, and no costs of transportation included in the import values, the reported import values should exactly match the reported export values. To the extent that import values include transportation costs, reported import values should on average exceed reported export values by a small amount. If, on the other hand, reported export values exceed reported import values, it is evidence of tariff evasion. The evidence is especially strong if reported export values exceed reported import values more for high-tariff goods than for low-tariff goods.

In order to compare tariff evasion by Ben Ali firms to tariff evasion by other Tunisian firms, Rijkers et al. examine export and import values for 1,386 goods imported into Tunisia from its top sixteen trading partner countries for every year in the period 2002–2009. For each good-country-year, Rijkers et al. compute whether a Ben Ali firm or another type of Tunisian firm handled more than 50 percent of the imports. In this way they classify each good-country-year as shown in Table 9.6. There are 49,347 good-country-year observations. Ben Ali firms account for 760

**Table 9.6.** Evidence for Tariff Evasion in Tunisia, 2002–2009

| Imported Goods | Log Export Value Reported by Partner – Log Import Value Reported in Tunisia | | | |
|---|---|---|---|---|
| | Overall Mean | Ben Ali Mean | Offshore Mean | Onshore Mean |
| All | −0.001 | 0.356 | 0.071 | −0.036 |
| High tariff | 0.099 | 0.797 | 0.090 | 0.094 |
| Low tariff | −0.104 | −0.108 | 0.033 | −0.136 |
| Number of observations | 49,347 | 760 | 16,068 | 29,692 |

*Notes:* High-tariff and low-tariff goods are divided at the median tariff rate of 36 percent. The 49,347 total observations are divided into 24,896 for high-tariff goods and 24,451 for low-tariff goods. Not shown are 2,106 observations for which public-sector firms are the dominant importers and 721 observations for which the dominant importer is mixed (no firm type accounts for more than 50 percent of import value).

*Source:* Rijkers, Baghdadi, and Raballand (2017, table 2).

observations, offshore firms account for 16,068 observations, and onshore firms account for 29,692 observations, with the remaining observations handled by public-sector firms or having no dominant importer.

Each entry in Table 9.6 shows the average of the difference between the logarithm of the reported export value and the logarithm of the reported import value, which (for small differences) roughly equals the percentage difference between the two values. We see that for all good-country-year observations the average difference is a negligible -0.1 percent. However, the average difference for observations for high-tariff goods is roughly 10 percent whereas the average difference for observations for low-tariff goods is roughly -10 percent, which is strong evidence that on average Tunisian importers are evading tariffs on high-tariff goods by under-reporting their import values. Turning to the last column of Table 9.6, we see that the average differences for onshore firms, which account for most observations, are fairly similar to the average differences for all firms. The second column shows that for Ben Ali importers the average difference for low-tariff goods is also similar to the average difference for all importers. For high-tariff goods, however, Ben Ali firms report import values that are much more than 10 percent below the reported export values. This is clear evidence that Ben Ali importers evaded tariffs to a much greater extent than other Tunisian importers. Finally, the third column of Table 9.6 shows that the percentage difference between export and import values for offshore importers is more similar for high-tariff goods and low-tariff goods than for all importers. This is consistent with the lower incentive offshore firms have to evade tariffs.

Customs officials told Rijkers et al. that fraudulent behavior by Ben Ali firms was less likely to be reported in part because of career concerns and fear of retaliation from the extended Ben Ali family. This made it easier for Ben Ali importers than for other private-sector importers to evade tariffs.

Let us end this section about politically connected firms on a note of caution. Because we lack a comparative context for our discussion of politically connected firms in Egypt and Tunisia, it is natural to contrast the favoritism practiced by the Mubarak and Ben Ali regimes with a hypothetical ideal in which regulations and taxes are applied in a non-discretionary, equal manner across firms. However, this may not be a realistic alternative. During the Mubarak regime (1981–2010) and Ben Ali regime (1987–2010), the average annual growth of GDP per capita in Egypt and Tunisia was 2.7 and 2.9 percent, respectively. The comparable figures for percent growth of the population-weighted average GDP per capita of the rest of the world (excluding sub-Saharan Africa and fuel-endowed countries) were 2.2 for 1981–2010 and 2.3 for 1987–2010. There are many factors that influence economic growth, but we cannot rule out the possibility that one cause of slower growth in the rest of the world was that stifling of competition on behalf of politically connected firms was even worse than in Egypt and Tunisia.

This observation brings us back to the point at the beginning of this chapter that it is very difficult to monitor and professionally run government bureaucracies. Business-government collaboration is unavoidable or even desirable, but must be monitored, internally by career civil servants or externally by the press and public. The incentives for large firms to use the powers of government to gain favors and suppress competition are strong. Developing the capacity to regulate and tax fairly despite these pressures is a challenge for governments in the Arab countries, Iran, Turkey, and the rest of the world.

# 10
# Conclusion

## Some Modest Proposals for Policy

We should now have a better understanding of the achievements and shortcomings of the Arab countries, Iran, and Turkey in socioeconomic development, and of the forces behind those achievements and shortcomings. In this brief concluding chapter we build on this understanding to propose policies we hope will augment some of the achievements and mitigate some of the shortcomings.

We will resist the temptation to lay out a set of policies that we claim would, say, raise the growth rate of GDP per capita in the region we study up to the level enjoyed by China over the past four decades. There is simply not enough evidence for the ability of specific policies to change long-run economic growth rates to make such claims with any confidence. Instead we will collect and organize ideas for policy, mostly mentioned in earlier chapters, that will have more modest but more certain benefits. The mechanisms by which the policies we recommend would bring about the benefits claimed are much more direct than the mechanisms by which policies claimed to increase long-run economic growth are supposed to work. In formulating our modest proposals for policy, we will try to bring new knowledge and new technologies to bear.

At the outset of this book (in the section titled "The Human Development Index" in Chapter 1) we noted that prices in most of the countries we study are lower than what would be predicted by their GDPs per capita. We saw in later chapters that government subsidies in the Arab countries and Iran (but not Turkey) keep the prices of many necessities low, specifically energy, food, and water. Like the vast majority of economists, we recommend reducing or eliminating these subsidies, but we suggest a new approach to implementing these reductions.

Helping consumers by lowering prices of specific goods and services is inefficient, because consumers are better off if given the money they save through lower prices directly, to buy what they need most, rather than being in effect forced to spend it on the subsidized goods and services. The side effects of energy, food, and water subsidies may be even more harmful than their inefficiency. Energy subsidies cause over-consumption of fuel, increasing emissions of carbon dioxide and concentrations of airborne particulate matter. Carbon dioxide emissions contribute to global warming that will make summers in the region we study unbearable. Airborne particulate matter contributes to the exceptionally high rates of heart disease that afflict much of the region. Food subsidies cause over-consumption of food, particularly bread or flour and sugar, which are the food items most heavily subsidized in the countries we study. Excessive consumption of bread and sugar contributes to the exceptionally high rates of obesity in the region. Obesity in turn contributes to heart disease. Water subsidies cause water to be wasted in the most water-scarce region in the world.

Since the benefits from elimination of energy, food, and water subsidies are so obvious, why are the subsidies still there? As we discussed in the section titled "Energy Subsidies" in Chapter 8, because of the endowment effect consumers are more upset when a subsidy is taken away than they are pleased when they receive the same subsidy. Raising prices by eliminating government subsidies is a reliable way to bring people into the streets against the government, as experience in both Jordan and Tunisia in 2018 demonstrates. We also described in that same section of Chapter 8 how Iran has experimented with countering the endowment effect by returning the money saved by reducing subsidies directly to the public through cash transfers. The problem is that, precisely because governments are afraid to reduce subsidies, they wait until they are forced to do so by desperate needs for revenue, at which point they cannot afford to give all the money saved back to the public.

A possible solution is to give only some of the money saved by reducing subsidies back to the public, by targeting those least able to afford the price increases—the poor. We noted in the section titled "Public and Private Sector Expenditure to Reduce Poverty" in Chapter 6 that MENA governments have not been good at targeting the lowest quintiles of their populations with social safety net programs. One problem with cash transfers to the poor is that they may not have bank accounts. However, the poor typically have mobile phones. The most recent data show that mobile cellular subscriptions per person are near (or have even exceeded) one in all of the countries we study except for Comoros, Djibouti, and Somalia. A number of countries outside our region (including countries in sub-Saharan Africa) have been successful in targeting cash transfers to the poor using "mobile money," a technology that allows people to receive, store, and spend money using a mobile phone. To the best of our knowledge, no government has yet used mobile money as a way to return savings from subsidy reductions to the public. Governments in the countries we study have an opportunity to lead the way. Energy subsidies are the best place to start. They are the most expensive and have the worst side effects. Moreover, most of the subsidies go to richer consumers, who drive their own cars and run air-conditioners, so governments can compensate the poor and still keep most of the savings. This would be less true in the case of food subsidies.

Higher energy prices resulting from reduced energy subsidies will cause less burning of fossil fuels by power plants and vehicles, thereby decreasing concentrations of airborne particulate matter. As we noted in the section titled "Air Pollution" in Chapter 7, this will not address another source of airborne particulates that plagues many Arab countries and Iran: desert dust. We suggested that the Arab countries and Iran could learn from the experience of China in protecting the public from particulate air pollution during the most polluted days by making particulate-filtering facemasks available. We also noted that field tests are required to measure the actual effect of facemasks on protecting health. The results of tests in China itself are not adequate, because desert dust is not a primary cause of their particulate air pollution. We recommend testing particulate-filtering facemasks in the GCC countries, since they are among the countries most vulnerable to desert dust pollution and they can afford to conduct the tests in a scientifically rigorous manner. If the tests are successful, distribution of particulate-filtering face masks during high particulate air pollution days in the Arab countries and Iran could contribute to reducing their exceptionally high rates of heart disease.

In the section titled "Education" in Chapter 4, we found that returns to tertiary (university) education in the Arab countries were exceptionally low, and that government spending on tertiary education relative to secondary (high school) education in most Arab countries was exceptionally high. Combined with more tentative evidence in the section titled "Unemployment and Self-Employment" in Chapter 6 that unemployment in the region we study is concentrated among highly educated workers, the education data suggest that Arab countries are pushing too many students through their universities with too little value added for employers. This is similar to the problem of over-consumption of energy, food, and water caused by government subsidies. Raising university tuition for those who can afford it seems an appropriate response, but tuition increases for public universities are likely to be at least as unpopular in Arab countries as they are in the United States. One possible approach is to package tuition increases with educational reforms that can deliver higher quality at all levels. As our knowledge increases regarding strategies that work or do not work to deliver higher educational quality in developing countries (Paul Glewwe and Karthik Muralidharan 2016), such a policy package can become more convincing.

From policies affecting education, health, and the environment we turn to policies directed at productivity and urbanization. Recent research has established that the practices that constitute good management can be measured, and that application of these practices in developing countries can improve firm productivity (Bloom et al. 2013). In the section titled "Service Exports to High-Income Consumers: Tourism" in Chapter 3, we suggested that the positive impact of tourism on the Arab Mediterranean economies could be enhanced by development of more locally owned and branded mid- to high-range hotels, which might lead to more demand for locally produced hotel inputs such as furnishings and linens. Better training in hotel management could in turn generate the entrepreneurs and managers who would found and run these hotels. Hotel management can be taught successfully at an undergraduate level, and hence does not require an expensive commitment to new business schools. Universities in the Arab Mediterranean countries could partner with leading American or European universities to create programs or upgrade existing programs in hotel administration. Given the speculative nature of the benefits from this intervention, it is wise to keep its costs low.

In the section titled "Urban Primacy" in Chapter 8 we discussed the problem of excessive urban primacy, where the share of a country's urban population located in its largest city is too great. We presented evidence that, among the countries we study, this problem exists most clearly in Egypt, and is developing in Sudan. We suggested that the slow urbanization of Egypt noted in the section titled "Urbanization and Strain on Public Finance" in Chapter 8 could be explained, in part, by Cairo having starved Egypt's other cities of the government investment needed in their infrastructure. For Egypt to get its urbanization on track, and for Sudan to avoid the same fate as Egypt, their governments need to give priority for urban infrastructure investment to cities other than Cairo and Khartoum, respectively. This raises the question: which other cities? Recent economics research (e.g., Pablo Fajgelbaum and Cecile Gaubert 2018) has improved our ability to target cities whose growth would generate the greatest economic benefits. This research could help the governments of Egypt and Sudan determine their priority locations for investment in urban infrastructure. Egypt's grand "new capital" project, intended to relocate central government bureaucracies to a new city midway between Cairo and Suez, may relieve traffic congestion in Cairo but will exacerbate underprovision of infrastructure to Egypt's other cities.

The last of our modest proposals for policy is the most speculative, but it is relevant for all of the countries we study in this book. In the section titled "Labor Force Participation" in Chapter 5, we showed that female labor force participation (FLFP) is exceptionally low in all of the countries we study. We presented evidence that one cause of low FLFP is social pressure on married women to stay home. This evidence was assembled for the Arab countries, but the same cause of low FLFP is very likely to be important in Iran and Turkey as well. One might think that social pressure is the cause of low FLFP that is least susceptible to outside influence, but a new study by Leonardo Bursztyn, Alessandra González, and David Yanagizawa-Drott (2018) raises the possibility that subtle government intervention could reduce this pressure.

Bursztyn et al. investigated whether social pressure on married women to stay home might result in part from husbands' beliefs that disapproval of women working outside the home is greater than it really is. Using surveys, these authors found that the majority of married men in Saudi Arabia support FLFP outside the home, consistent with the surveys we reported for Egypt, Jordan, and Yemen in the "Labor Force Participation" section of Chapter 5. Next, the authors found that Saudi men substantially underestimated the level of support for women's work outside the home by other married men, even those from their same social setting, such as neighbors. In other words, many Saudi men incorrectly believe that, although they support FLFP outside the home, their neighbors do not. The authors then showed that correcting these beliefs increased the willingness of the men surveyed to turn down gift cards in favor of opportunities to sign up their wives for a job-matching service. Finally, the authors found that, three to five months after correcting the men's beliefs, their wives were more likely to have applied and interviewed for jobs outside their homes.

Further study is, of course, necessary to find out whether the misperception by married men that support for FLFP outside the home is lower than its actual level is widespread among countries in our region. If so, the study by Bursztyn et al. suggests that correcting these perceptions could lead to a measurable increase in FLFP. In addition to the economic benefits from greater use of women's talents, this would allow women greater freedom of choice. Insofar as staying home is associated with eating and inactivity, it is also possible that increased work outside the home will reduce the exceptionally high female relative to male obesity among the countries we study documented in the section titled "Health" in Chapter 4.

Returning to the subject of health reminds us of the virtuous circle from health to education to more health. Longer lives give people more time to benefit from their educations, hence greater incentives to acquire more schooling, and better education helps people improve care for their health. Because of this virtuous circle, many of the policies proposed here would have mutually reinforcing effects on the socioeconomic development of the region.

# Appendix

This appendix contains lists of included countries that were too long to place in the notes to the tables in the text. When the list includes a year in parentheses next to the country name, it means that data were available for different years for different countries.

## Table 1.8

Arab sub-Saharan Africa: Comoros, Djibouti, Mauritania, Somalia, Sudan, and Yemen

Non-Arab sub-Saharan Africa: Angola, Benin, Botswana, Burkina Faso, Burundi, Cameroon, Central African Republic, Chad, Congo (Dem. Rep.), Congo (Rep.), Cote d'Ivoire, Equatorial Guinea, Eritrea, Ethiopia, Gabon, Gambia, Ghana, Guinea, Guinea-Bissau, Kenya, Lesotho, Liberia, Madagascar, Malawi, Mali, Mozambique, Namibia, Niger, Nigeria, Rwanda, Sao Tome and Principe, Senegal, Sierra Leone, South Africa, Swaziland, Tanzania, Togo, Uganda, Zambia, and Zimbabwe

Arab fuel-endowed countries: Algeria, Bahrain, Iraq, Kuwait, Libya, Oman, Qatar, Saudi Arabia, and UAE

Non-Arab fuel-endowed countries: Brunei Darussalam, Iran, Norway, Trinidad and Tobago, and Venezuela

Arab Mediterranean: Egypt, Jordan, Lebanon, Morocco, Syria, and Tunisia

Rest of non-Arab world: Afghanistan, Albania, Antigua and Barbuda, Argentina, Armenia, Australia, Austria, Azerbaijan, Bahamas, Bangladesh, Barbados, Belarus, Belgium, Belize, Bhutan, Bolivia, Bosnia and Herzegovina, Brazil, Bulgaria, Cambodia, Canada, Chile, China, Colombia, Costa Rica, Croatia, Cuba, Cyprus, Czech Republic, Denmark, Dominican Republic, Ecuador, El Salvador, Estonia, Fiji, Finland, France, Georgia, Germany, Greece, Grenada, Guatemala, Guyana, Haiti, Honduras, Hungary, Iceland, India, Indonesia, Ireland, Israel, Italy, Jamaica, Japan, Kazakhstan, Kiribati, Korea (Rep.), Kyrgyz Republic, Lao PDR, Latvia, Lithuania, Luxembourg, Macedonia (FYR), Malaysia, Maldives, Malta, Mauritius, Mexico, Micronesia, Moldova, Mongolia, Montenegro, Myanmar, Nepal, Netherlands, New Zealand, Nicaragua, Pakistan, Panama, Papua New Guinea, Paraguay, Peru, Philippines, Poland, Portugal, Romania, Russian Federation, Samoa, Singapore, Slovak Republic, Slovenia, Solomon Islands, Spain, Sri Lanka, St. Lucia, St. Vincent and the Grenadines, Suriname, Sweden, Switzerland, Tajikistan, Thailand, Timor-Leste, Tonga, Turkey, Turkmenistan, Ukraine, United Kingdom, United States, Uruguay, Uzbekistan, Vanuatu, and Vietnam

Latin America: Argentina, Bolivia, Brazil, Chile, Colombia, Costa Rica, Cuba, Dominican Republic, Ecuador, El Salvador, Guatemala, Honduras, Mexico, Nicaragua, Panama, Paraguay, Peru, and Uruguay

Southern Europe: Greece, Italy, Malta, Portugal, and Spain

## Table 1.9

Arab sub-Saharan Africa: Mauritania, Sudan, and Yemen

Non-Arab sub-Saharan Africa: Benin, Botswana, Burundi, Cameroon, Central African Republic, Congo (Dem. Rep.), Congo (Rep.), Cote d'Ivoire, Gabon, Gambia, Ghana, Kenya, Lesotho, Liberia, Malawi, Mali, Mozambique, Namibia, Niger, Rwanda, Senegal, Sierra Leone, South Africa, Swaziland, Tanzania, Togo, Uganda, Zambia, and Zimbabwe

Arab fuel-endowed countries: Algeria, Bahrain, Iraq, Kuwait, Libya, Qatar, Saudi Arabia, and UAE

Non-Arab fuel-endowed countries: Brunei Darussalam, Iran, Norway, Trinidad and Tobago, and Venezuela

Arab Mediterranean: Egypt, Jordan, Morocco, Syria, and Tunisia

Rest of Non-Arab world: Afghanistan, Albania, Argentina, Armenia, Australia, Austria, Bangladesh, Barbados, Belgium, Belize, Bolivia, Brazil, Bulgaria, Cambodia, Canada, Chile, China, Colombia, Costa Rica, Croatia, Cuba, Cyprus, Czech Republic, Denmark, Dominican Republic, Ecuador, El Salvador, Estonia, Fiji, Finland, France, Germany, Greece, Guatemala, Guyana, Haiti, Honduras, Hungary, Iceland, India, Indonesia, Ireland, Israel, Italy, Jamaica, Japan, Kazakhstan, Korea (Rep.), Kyrgyz Republic, Lao PDR, Latvia, Lithuania, Luxembourg, Malaysia, Maldives, Malta, Mauritius, Mexico, Moldova, Mongolia, Myanmar, Nepal, Netherlands, New Zealand, Nicaragua, Pakistan, Panama, Papua New Guinea, Paraguay, Peru, Philippines, Poland, Portugal, Romania, Russian Federation, Singapore, Slovak Republic, Slovenia, Spain, Sri Lanka, Sweden, Switzerland, Tajikistan, Thailand, Tonga, Turkey, Ukraine, United Kingdom, United States, Uruguay, and Vietnam

Latin America: Argentina, Bolivia, Brazil, Chile, Colombia, Costa Rica, Cuba, Dominican Republic, Ecuador, El Salvador, Guatemala, Honduras, Mexico, Nicaragua, Panama, Paraguay, Peru, and Uruguay

Southern Europe: Greece, Italy, Malta, Portugal, and Spain

## Table 1.10

Arab sub-Saharan Africa: Mauritania and Sudan

Non-Arab sub-Saharan Africa: Benin, Botswana, Burkina Faso, Burundi, Cameroon, Central African Republic, Chad, Congo (Dem. Rep.), Congo (Rep.), Cote d'Ivoire, Gabon, Gambia, Ghana, Guinea-Bissau, Kenya, Lesotho, Liberia, Madagascar, Malawi, Mali, Nigeria, Rwanda, Senegal, Sierra Leone, South Africa, Swaziland, Togo, Zambia, and Zimbabwe

Arab fuel-endowed countries: Algeria, Iraq, Oman, and Saudi Arabia

Non-Arab fuel-endowed countries: Iran, Norway, Trinidad and Tobago, and Venezuela

Arab Mediterranean: Egypt, Morocco, and Tunisia

Rest of Non-Arab world: Argentina, Australia, Austria, Bahamas, Bangladesh, Belgium, Belize, Bolivia, Brazil, Canada, Chile, China, Colombia, Costa Rica, Denmark, Dominican Republic, Ecuador, El Salvador, Fiji, Finland, France, Georgia, Germany,

Greece, Guatemala, Guyana, Honduras, Iceland, India, Indonesia, Ireland, Israel, Italy, Jamaica, Japan, Kiribati, Korea (Rep.), Luxembourg, Malaysia, Malta, Mexico, Myanmar, Nepal, Netherlands, Nicaragua, Pakistan, Panama, Papua New Guinea, Paraguay, Peru, Philippines, Portugal, Seychelles, Singapore, Spain, Sri Lanka, St. Vincent and the Grenadines, Sweden, Thailand, Turkey, United Kingdom, United States, and Uruguay
Latin America: Argentina, Bolivia, Brazil, Chile, Colombia, Costa Rica, Dominican Republic, Ecuador, El Salvador, Guatemala, Honduras, Mexico, Nicaragua, Panama, Paraguay, Peru, and Uruguay
Southern Europe: Greece, Italy, Malta, Portugal, and Spain

## Table 4.2

Arab sub-Saharan Africa: Comoros (2004), Djibouti (1996), Mauritania (2000), and Yemen (2005)
Non-Arab sub-Saharan Africa: Burkina Faso (2009), Burundi (1998), Cameroon (2007), Chad (2003), Congo (Dem. Rep.) (2005), Cote d'Ivoire (2008), Ethiopia (2005), Gabon (2005), Gambia (1998), Ghana (2012), Guinea (1994), Kenya (2005), Madagascar (2010), Malawi (2010), Mali (1994), Mozambique (2008), Namibia (1993), Niger (2011), Nigeria (2003), Rwanda (2010), Sao Tome and Principe (2010), Senegal (2011), Sierra Leone (2011), South Africa (2011), Swaziland (2000), Tanzania (2011), Togo (2011), Uganda (2010), and Zambia (2010)
Arab fuel-endowed countries: Iraq (2006)
Non-Arab fuel-endowed countries: Norway (2012) and Venezuela (2006)
Arab Mediterranean: Jordan (2002), Lebanon (2011), Morocco (1998), Syria (2004), and Tunisia (2001)
Rest of non-Arab world: Afghanistan (2007), Albania (2005), Argentina (2012), Armenia (1999), Australia (2010), Austria (2012), Azerbaijan (1995), Bangladesh (2005), Belarus (1998), Belgium (2011), Belize (1999), Bolivia (2012), Bosnia and Herzegovina (2001), Brazil (2012), Bulgaria (2012), Cambodia (2008), Canada (2001), Chile (2011), China (2002), Colombia (2012), Costa Rica (2009), Croatia (2012), Czech Republic (2012), Denmark (2012), Dominican Republic (2011), Ecuador (2012), El Salvador (2009), Estonia (2012), Finland (2012), France (2012), Georgia (2010), Germany (2012), Greece (2012), Guatemala (2011), Guyana (1992), Haiti (2001), Honduras (2011), Hungary (2012), Iceland (2012), India (2009), Indonesia (2010), Ireland (2009), Italy (2012), Jamaica (2002), Japan (2007), Korea (Rep.) (2010), Kyrgyz Republic (1997), Lao PDR (2008), Latvia (2012), Lithuania (2012), Luxembourg (2012), Macedonia (FYR) (2005), Malaysia (2010), Maldives (2004), Malta (2012), Mauritius (2012), Mexico (2012), Moldova (2005), Mongolia (2011), Nepal (2010), Netherlands (2012), Nicaragua (2009), Pakistan (2010), Palau (2000), Panama (2012), Papua New Guinea (2010), Paraguay (2011), Peru (2012), Philippines (2011), Poland (2012), Portugal (2012), Romania (2012), Russian Federation (2009), Serbia (2008), Singapore (1998), Slovak Republic (2012), Slovenia (2012), Solomon Islands (2005), Spain (2012), Sri Lanka (2009), Suriname (1999), Sweden (2012), Switzerland (2012), Tajikistan (2003), Thailand (2011), Timor-Leste

(2007), Turkey (2010), Turkmenistan (1998), Ukraine (2005), United Kingdom (2012), United States (2010), and Uruguay (2012)
Latin America: Argentina (2012), Bolivia (2012), Brazil (2012), Chile (2011), Colombia (2012), Costa Rica (2009), Dominican Republic (2011), Ecuador (2012), El Salvador (2009), Guatemala (2011), Honduras (2011), Mexico (2012), Nicaragua (2009), Panama (2012), Paraguay (2011), Peru (2012), and Uruguay (2012)
Southern Europe: Greece (2012), Italy (2012), Malta (2012), Portugal (2012), and Spain (2012)

## Table 4.3

For the ratio of expenditure per secondary student to expenditure per primary student:

Arab sub-Saharan Africa: Comoros (2014), Djibouti (2008), Mauritania (2016), and Yemen (2011)
Non-Arab sub-Saharan Africa: Benin (2015), Botswana (2009), Burkina Faso (2015), Burundi (2013), Cameroon (2012), Central African Republic (2009), Chad (2012), Congo (Dem. Rep.) (2013), Cote d'Ivoire (2015), Ethiopia (2012), Gambia (2010), Ghana (2014), Guinea (2014), Kenya (2006), Lesotho (2008), Madagascar (2012), Malawi (2016), Mali (2015), Mozambique (2013), Namibia (2008), Niger (2015), Rwanda (2016), Sao Tome and Principe (2014), Senegal (2015), Sierra Leone (2016), South Africa (2012), South Sudan (2016), Swaziland (2014), Togo (2011), and Zimbabwe (2013)
Arab fuel-endowed countries: Bahrain (2015), Kuwait (2014), Oman (2016), Qatar (2009), and Saudi Arabia (2007)
Non-Arab fuel-endowed countries: Brunei Darussalam (2016), Iran (2015), Norway (2014), and Venezuela (2015)
Arab Mediterranean: Jordan (2011), Morocco (2012), Syria (2012), and Tunisia (2008)
Rest of non-Arab world: Afghanistan (2015), Albania (2015), Andorra (2016), Antigua and Barbuda (2009), Argentina (2015), Armenia (2013), Austria (2014), Bangladesh (2016), Barbados (2016), Belgium (2014), Belize (2015), Bhutan (2014), Bolivia (2014), Brazil (2014), Bulgaria (2013), Chile (2015), Colombia (2016), Costa Rica (2016), Cuba (2010), Cyprus (2014), Czech Republic (2014), Denmark (2014), Dominica (2015), Dominican Republic (2016), Ecuador (2016), El Salvador (2016), Estonia (2014), Fiji (2011), Finland (2014), France (2014), Georgia (2008), Germany (2014), Grenada (2016), Guatemala (2016), Guyana (2012), Honduras (2013), Hungary (2014), Iceland (2013), India (2013), Indonesia (2015), Ireland (2014), Israel (2014), Italy (2014), Jamaica (2016), Japan (2014), Kazakhstan (2016), Korea (Rep.) (2015), Lao PDR (2014), Latvia (2014), Liechtenstein (2011), Lithuania (2014), Luxembourg (2014), Malaysia (2016), Malta (2014), Mauritius (2016), Mexico (2014), Moldova (2016), Monaco (2011), Mongolia (2016), Nepal (2015), New Zealand (2015), Nicaragua (2010), Pakistan (2016), Panama (2011), Paraguay (2012), Peru (2016), Philippines (2008), Poland (2014), Portugal (2014), Romania (2012), Samoa (2016), San Marino (2011), Serbia (2015), Seychelles (2011), Singapore (2010), Slovak Republic (2015), Slovenia (2014), Spain (2014), Sri Lanka (2016), St. Kitts and Nevis (2015), St. Lucia (2016), St. Vincent and the Grenadines (2016), Sweden (2014), Switzerland (2014), Thailand (2013), Timor-Leste (2014),

Turkey (2014), Ukraine (2014), United Kingdom (2015), United States (2014), Uruguay (2006), and Vanuatu (2015)
Latin America: Argentina (2015), Bolivia (2014), Brazil (2014), Chile (2015), Colombia (2016), Costa Rica (2016), Cuba (2010), Dominican Republic (2016), Ecuador (2016), El Salvador (2016), Guatemala (2016), Honduras (2013), Mexico (2014), Nicaragua (2010), Panama (2011), Paraguay (2012), Peru (2016), and Uruguay (2006)
Southern Europe: Andorra (2016), Italy (2014), Malta (2014), Portugal (2014), San Marino (2011), and Spain (2014)

For the ratio of expenditure per tertiary student to expenditure per secondary student:

Arab sub-Saharan Africa: Comoros (2014) and Mauritania (2016)
Non-Arab sub-Saharan Africa: Benin (2015), Botswana (2009), Burkina Faso (2015), Burundi (2013), Cameroon (2012), Central African Republic (2009), Chad (2011), Congo (Dem. Rep.) (2013), Cote d'Ivoire (2015), Ethiopia (2012), Gambia (2010), Ghana (2014), Guinea (2014), Lesotho (2006), Madagascar (2012), Malawi (2011), Mali (2015), Mozambique (2013), Namibia (2006), Niger (2012), Rwanda (2016), Sao Tome and Principe (2014), Senegal (2015), Swaziland (2014), Tanzania (2010), Togo (2011), and Zimbabwe (2013)
Arab fuel-endowed countries: Bahrain (2013) and Oman (2016)
Non-Arab fuel-endowed countries: Brunei Darussalam (2016), Iran (2015), Norway (2014), and Venezuela (2009)
Arab Mediterranean: Lebanon (2013), Morocco (2009), Syria (2009), and Tunisia (2015)
Rest of non-Arab world: Afghanistan (2014), Albania (2015), Andorra (2016), Antigua and Barbuda (2009), Argentina (2015), Armenia (2014), Austria (2014), Bangladesh (2016), Barbados (2010), Belgium (2011), Belize (2015), Bhutan (2014), Brazil (2014), Bulgaria (2013), Chile (2015), Colombia (2016), Costa Rica (2016), Cuba (2007), Cyprus (2014), Czech Republic (2014), Denmark (2014), Ecuador (2015), El Salvador (2016), Estonia (2014), Finland (2014), France (2014), Georgia (2008), Germany (2014), Grenada (2016), Guatemala (2015), Guyana (2012), Honduras (2013), Hungary (2014), Iceland (2013), India (2013), Indonesia (2015), Ireland (2014), Israel (2014), Italy (2014), Jamaica (2015), Japan (2014), Kazakhstan (2016), Korea (Rep.) (2015), Lao PDR (2014), Latvia (2014), Liechtenstein (2007), Lithuania (2014), Luxembourg (2012), Malaysia (2016), Malta (2014), Mauritius (2015), Mexico (2014), Moldova (2016), Mongolia (2016), Nepal (2015), New Zealand (2015), Pakistan (2016), Panama (2011), Paraguay (2010), Peru (2006), Philippines (2008), Poland (2014), Portugal (2014), Romania (2014), San Marino (2011), Serbia (2015), Seychelles (2011), Singapore (2010), Slovak Republic (2014), Slovenia (2014), Spain (2014), Sri Lanka (2016), St. Kitts and Nevis (2015), St. Lucia (2011), Sweden (2014), Switzerland (2014), Thailand (2013), Turkey (2014), Ukraine (2014), United Kingdom (2015), United States (2014), and Uruguay (2006)
Latin America: Argentina (2015), Brazil (2014), Chile (2015), Colombia (2016), Costa Rica (2016), Cuba (2007), Ecuador (2015), El Salvador (2016), Guatemala (2015), Honduras (2013), Mexico (2014), Panama (2011), Paraguay (2010), Peru (2006), and Uruguay (2006)
Southern Europe: Andorra (2016), Italy (2014), Malta (2014), Portugal (2014), San Marino (2011), and Spain (2014)

262  APPENDIX

## Tables 4.5, 4.6, and 4.11

Arab sub-Saharan Africa: Comoros, Djibouti, Mauritania, Somalia, Sudan, and Yemen
Non-Arab sub-Saharan Africa: Angola, Benin, Botswana, Burkina Faso, Burundi, Cameroon, Central African Republic, Chad, Congo (Dem. Rep.), Congo (Rep.), Cote d'Ivoire, Equatorial Guinea, Eritrea, Ethiopia, Gabon, Gambia, Ghana, Guinea, Guinea-Bissau, Kenya, Lesotho, Liberia, Madagascar, Malawi, Mali, Mozambique, Namibia, Niger, Nigeria, Rwanda, Sao Tome and Principe, Senegal, Sierra Leone, South Africa, Swaziland, Tanzania, Togo, Uganda, Zambia, and Zimbabwe
Arab fuel-endowed countries: Algeria, Bahrain, Iraq, Kuwait, Libya, Oman, Qatar, Saudi Arabia, and UAE
Non-Arab fuel-endowed countries: Brunei Darussalam, Iran, Norway, Trinidad and Tobago, and Venezuela
Arab Mediterranean: Egypt, Jordan, Lebanon, Morocco, Syria, and Tunisia
Rest of non-Arab world: Afghanistan, Albania, Andorra, Antigua and Barbuda, Argentina, Armenia, Australia, Austria, Azerbaijan, Bahamas, Bangladesh, Barbados, Belarus, Belgium, Belize, Bhutan, Bolivia, Bosnia and Herzegovina, Brazil, Bulgaria, Cambodia, Canada, Chile, China, Colombia, Costa Rica, Croatia, Cuba, Cyprus, Czech Republic, Denmark, Dominica, Dominican Republic, Ecuador, El Salvador, Estonia, Fiji, Finland, France, Georgia, Germany, Greece, Grenada, Guatemala, Guyana, Haiti, Honduras, Hungary, Iceland, India, Indonesia, Ireland, Israel, Italy, Jamaica, Japan, Kazakhstan, Kiribati, Korea (Rep.), Kyrgyz Republic, Lao PDR, Latvia, Lithuania, Luxembourg, Macedonia (FYR), Malaysia, Maldives, Malta, Marshall Islands, Mauritius, Mexico, Micronesia, Moldova, Monaco, Mongolia, Myanmar, Nepal, Netherlands, New Zealand, Nicaragua, Pakistan, Palau, Panama, Papua New Guinea, Paraguay, Peru, Philippines, Poland, Portugal, Romania, Russian Federation, Samoa, San Marino, Seychelles, Singapore, Slovak Republic, Slovenia, Solomon Islands, Spain, Sri Lanka, St. Kitts and Nevis, St. Lucia, St. Vincent and the Grenadines, Suriname, Sweden, Switzerland, Tajikistan, Thailand, Tonga, Turkey, Turkmenistan, Ukraine, United Kingdom, United States, Uruguay, Uzbekistan, Vanuatu, and Vietnam
Latin America: Argentina, Bolivia, Brazil, Chile, Colombia, Costa Rica, Cuba, Dominican Republic, Ecuador, El Salvador, Guatemala, Honduras, Mexico, Nicaragua, Panama, Paraguay, Peru, and Uruguay
Southern Europe: Andorra, Greece, Italy, Malta, Portugal, San Marino, and Spain

## Table 4.8

Arab sub-Saharan Africa: Comoros, Djibouti, Mauritania, Somalia, and Yemen
Non-Arab sub-Saharan Africa: Angola, Benin, Botswana, Burkina Faso, Burundi, Cameroon, Central African Republic, Chad, Congo (Dem. Rep.), Congo (Rep.), Cote d'Ivoire, Equatorial Guinea, Ethiopia, Gabon, Gambia, Ghana, Guinea, Guinea-Bissau, Kenya, Lesotho, Liberia, Madagascar, Malawi, Mali, Mozambique, Namibia, Niger, Nigeria, Rwanda, Sao Tome and Principe, Senegal, Sierra Leone, South Africa, Swaziland, Tanzania, Togo, Uganda, Zambia, and Zimbabwe

Arab fuel-endowed countries: Algeria, Bahrain, Iraq, Kuwait, Libya, Oman, Qatar, Saudi Arabia, and UAE

Non-Arab fuel-endowed countries: Brunei Darussalam, Iran, Norway, Trinidad and Tobago, and Venezuela

Arab Mediterranean: Egypt, Jordan, Lebanon, Morocco, Syria, and Tunisia

Rest of non-Arab world: Afghanistan, Albania, Andorra, Antigua and Barbuda, Argentina, Armenia, Australia, Austria, Azerbaijan, Bahamas, Bangladesh, Barbados, Belarus, Belgium, Belize, Bhutan, Bolivia, Bosnia and Herzegovina, Brazil, Bulgaria, Cambodia, Canada, Chile, China, Colombia, Costa Rica, Croatia, Cuba, Cyprus, Czech Republic, Denmark, Dominica, Dominican Republic, Ecuador, El Salvador, Estonia, Fiji, Finland, France, Georgia, Germany, Greece, Grenada, Guatemala, Guyana, Haiti, Honduras, Hungary, Iceland, India, Indonesia, Ireland, Israel, Italy, Jamaica, Japan, Kazakhstan, Kiribati, Korea (Rep.), Kyrgyz Republic, Lao PDR, Latvia, Lithuania, Luxembourg, Macedonia (FYR), Malaysia, Maldives, Malta, Marshall Islands, Mauritius, Mexico, Micronesia, Moldova, Mongolia, Montenegro, Myanmar, Nepal, Netherlands, New Zealand, Nicaragua, Pakistan, Palau, Panama, Papua New Guinea, Paraguay, Peru, Philippines, Poland, Portugal, Romania, Russian Federation, Samoa, Serbia, Seychelles, Singapore, Slovak Republic, Slovenia, Solomon Islands, Spain, Sri Lanka, St. Kitts and Nevis, St. Lucia, St. Vincent and the Grenadines, Suriname, Sweden, Switzerland, Tajikistan, Thailand, Tonga, Turkey, Turkmenistan, Ukraine, United Kingdom, United States, Uruguay, Uzbekistan, Vanuatu, and Vietnam

Latin America: Argentina, Bolivia, Brazil, Chile, Colombia, Costa Rica, Cuba, Dominican Republic, Ecuador, El Salvador, Guatemala, Honduras, Mexico, Nicaragua, Panama, Paraguay, Peru, and Uruguay

Southern Europe: Andorra, Greece, Italy, Malta, Portugal, and Spain

## Tables 4.9 and 8.1

Arab sub-Saharan Africa: Comoros, Djibouti, Mauritania, Somalia, Sudan, and Yemen

Non-Arab sub-Saharan Africa: Angola, Benin, Botswana, Burkina Faso, Burundi, Cameroon, Central African Republic, Chad, Congo (Dem. Rep.), Congo (Rep.), Cote d'Ivoire, Equatorial Guinea, Ethiopia, Gabon, Gambia, Ghana, Guinea, Guinea-Bissau, Kenya, Lesotho, Liberia, Madagascar, Malawi, Mali, Mozambique, Namibia, Niger, Nigeria, Rwanda, Sao Tome and Principe, Senegal, Sierra Leone, South Africa, South Sudan, Swaziland, Tanzania, Togo, Uganda, Zambia, and Zimbabwe

Arab fuel-endowed countries: Algeria, Bahrain, Iraq, Kuwait, Libya, Oman, Qatar, Saudi Arabia, and UAE

Non-Arab fuel-endowed countries: Brunei Darussalam, Iran, Norway, Trinidad and Tobago, and Venezuela

Arab Mediterranean: Egypt, Jordan, Lebanon, Morocco, Syria, and Tunisia

Rest of non-Arab world: Afghanistan, Albania, Andorra, Antigua and Barbuda, Argentina, Armenia, Australia, Austria, Azerbaijan, Bahamas, Bangladesh, Barbados, Belarus, Belgium, Belize, Bhutan, Bolivia, Bosnia and Herzegovina, Brazil, Bulgaria, Cambodia, Canada, Chile, China, Colombia, Costa Rica, Croatia, Cuba, Cyprus, Czech Republic, Denmark, Dominica, Dominican Republic, Ecuador,

264 APPENDIX

El Salvador, Estonia, Fiji, Finland, France, Georgia, Germany, Greece, Grenada, Guatemala, Guyana, Haiti, Honduras, Hungary, Iceland, India, Indonesia, Ireland, Israel, Italy, Jamaica, Japan, Kazakhstan, Kiribati, Korea (Rep.), Kyrgyz Republic, Lao PDR, Latvia, Liechtenstein, Lithuania, Luxembourg, Macedonia (FYR), Malaysia, Maldives, Malta, Marshall Islands, Mauritius, Mexico, Micronesia, Moldova, Monaco, Mongolia, Montenegro, Myanmar, Nepal, Netherlands, New Zealand, Nicaragua, Pakistan, Palau, Panama, Papua New Guinea, Paraguay, Peru, Philippines, Poland, Portugal, Romania, Russian Federation, Samoa, San Marino, Seychelles, Singapore, Slovak Republic, Slovenia, Solomon Islands, Spain, Sri Lanka, St. Kitts and Nevis, St. Lucia, St. Vincent and the Grenadines, Suriname, Sweden, Switzerland, Tajikistan, Thailand, Timor-Leste, Tonga, Turkey, Turkmenistan, Ukraine, United Kingdom, United States, Uruguay, Uzbekistan, Vanuatu, and Vietnam

Latin America: Argentina, Bolivia, Brazil, Chile, Colombia, Costa Rica, Cuba, Dominican Republic, Ecuador, El Salvador, Guatemala, Honduras, Mexico, Nicaragua, Panama, Paraguay, Peru, and Uruguay

Southern Europe: Andorra, Greece, Italy, Malta, Portugal, San Marino, and Spain

## Table 4.10

Arab sub-Saharan Africa: Comoros, Djibouti, Mauritania, Somalia, Sudan, and Yemen

Non-Arab sub-Saharan Africa: Angola, Benin, Botswana, Burkina Faso, Burundi, Cameroon, Central African Republic, Chad, Congo (Dem. Rep.), Congo (Rep.), Cote d'Ivoire, Equatorial Guinea, Ethiopia, Gabon, Gambia, Ghana, Guinea, Guinea-Bissau, Kenya, Lesotho, Liberia, Madagascar, Malawi, Mali, Mozambique, Namibia, Niger, Nigeria, Rwanda, Sao Tome and Principe, Senegal, Sierra Leone, South Africa, South Sudan, Swaziland, Tanzania, Togo, Uganda, Zambia, and Zimbabwe

Arab fuel-endowed countries: Algeria, Bahrain, Iraq, Kuwait, Libya, Oman, Qatar, Saudi Arabia, and UAE

Non-Arab fuel-endowed countries: Brunei Darussalam, Iran, Norway, Trinidad and Tobago, and Venezuela

Arab Mediterranean: Egypt, Jordan, Lebanon, Morocco, Syria, and Tunisia

Rest of non-Arab world: Afghanistan, Albania, Antigua and Barbuda, Argentina, Armenia, Australia, Austria, Azerbaijan, Bahamas, Bangladesh, Barbados, Belarus, Belgium, Belize, Bhutan, Bolivia, Bosnia and Herzegovina, Brazil, Bulgaria, Cambodia, Canada, Chile, China, Colombia, Costa Rica, Croatia, Cuba, Cyprus, Czech Republic, Denmark, Dominican Republic, Ecuador, El Salvador, Estonia, Fiji, Finland, France, Georgia, Germany, Greece, Grenada, Guatemala, Guyana, Haiti, Honduras, Hungary, Iceland, India, Indonesia, Ireland, Israel, Italy, Jamaica, Japan, Kazakhstan, Kiribati, Korea (Rep.), Kyrgyz Republic, Lao PDR, Latvia, Lithuania, Luxembourg, Macedonia (FYR), Malaysia, Maldives, Malta, Mauritius, Mexico, Micronesia, Moldova, Mongolia, Montenegro, Myanmar, Nepal, Netherlands, New Zealand, Nicaragua, Pakistan, Panama, Papua New Guinea, Paraguay, Peru, Philippines, Poland, Portugal, Romania, Russian Federation, Samoa, Singapore,

Slovak Republic, Slovenia, Solomon Islands, Spain, Sri Lanka, St. Lucia, St. Vincent and the Grenadines, Suriname, Sweden, Switzerland, Tajikistan, Thailand, Timor-Leste, Tonga, Turkey, Turkmenistan, Ukraine, United Kingdom, United States, Uruguay, Uzbekistan, Vanuatu, and Vietnam

Latin America: Argentina, Bolivia, Brazil, Chile, Colombia, Costa Rica, Cuba, Dominican Republic, Ecuador, El Salvador, Guatemala, Honduras, Mexico, Nicaragua, Panama, Paraguay, Peru, and Uruguay

Southern Europe: Greece, Italy, Malta, Portugal, and Spain

## Table 4.13

Arab sub-Saharan Africa: Comoros, Djibouti, Mauritania, Somalia, Sudan, and Yemen

Non-Arab sub-Saharan Africa: Angola, Benin, Botswana, Burkina Faso, Burundi, Cameroon, Central African Republic, Chad, Congo (Dem. Rep.), Congo (Rep.), Cote d'Ivoire, Equatorial Guinea, Ethiopia, Gabon, Gambia, Ghana, Guinea, Guinea-Bissau, Kenya, Lesotho, Liberia, Madagascar, Malawi, Mali, Mozambique, Namibia, Niger, Nigeria, Rwanda, Sao Tome and Principe, Senegal, Sierra Leone, South Africa, South Sudan, Swaziland, Tanzania, Togo, Uganda, Zambia, and Zimbabwe

Arab fuel-endowed countries: Algeria, Bahrain, Iraq, Kuwait, Libya, Oman, Qatar, Saudi Arabia, and UAE

Non-Arab fuel-endowed countries: Brunei Darussalam, Iran, Norway, Trinidad and Tobago, and Venezuela

Arab Mediterranean: Egypt, Jordan, Lebanon, Morocco, Syria, and Tunisia

Rest of non-Arab world: Afghanistan, Albania, Antigua and Barbuda, Argentina, Armenia, Australia, Austria, Azerbaijan, Bahamas, Bangladesh, Barbados, Belarus, Belgium, Belize, Bhutan, Bolivia, Bosnia and Herzegovina, Brazil, Bulgaria, Cambodia, Canada, Chile, China, Colombia, Costa Rica, Croatia, Cuba, Cyprus, Czech Republic, Denmark, Dominican Republic, Ecuador, El Salvador, Estonia, Fiji, Finland, France, Georgia, Germany, Greece, Grenada, Guatemala, Guyana, Haiti, Honduras, Hungary, Iceland, India, Indonesia, Ireland, Israel, Italy, Jamaica, Japan, Kazakhstan, Kiribati, Korea (Rep.), Kyrgyz Republic, Lao PDR, Latvia, Lithuania, Luxembourg, Macedonia (FYR), Malaysia, Maldives, Malta, Mauritius, Mexico, Micronesia, Moldova, Mongolia, Montenegro, Myanmar, Nepal, Netherlands, New Zealand, Nicaragua, Pakistan, Panama, Papua New Guinea, Paraguay, Peru, Philippines, Poland, Portugal, Romania, Russian Federation, Samoa, Seychelles, Singapore, Slovak Republic, Slovenia, Solomon Islands, Spain, Sri Lanka, St. Lucia, St. Vincent and the Grenadines, Suriname, Sweden, Switzerland, Tajikistan, Thailand, Timor-Leste, Tonga, Turkey, Turkmenistan, Ukraine, United Kingdom, United States, Uruguay, Uzbekistan, Vanuatu, and Vietnam

Latin America: Argentina, Bolivia, Brazil, Chile, Colombia, Costa Rica, Cuba, Dominican Republic, Ecuador, El Salvador, Guatemala, Honduras, Mexico, Nicaragua, Panama, Paraguay, Peru, and Uruguay

Southern Europe: Greece, Italy, Malta, Portugal, and Spain

## Table 5.1

For primary education:
Arab sub-Saharan Africa: Comoros (1971/2014), Djibouti (1971/2016), and Mauritania (1971/2016)
Non-Arab sub-Saharan Africa: Angola (1971/2011), Benin (1971/2015), Botswana (1971/2014), Burkina Faso (1971/2016), Burundi (1971/2016), Cameroon (1971/2016), Central African Republic (1971/2016), Chad (1971/2016), Congo (Dem. Rep.) (1971/2015), Congo (Rep.) (1971/2012), Cote d'Ivoire (1971/2016), Equatorial Guinea (1971/2015), Ethiopia (1971/2015), Gabon (1971/2011), Gambia (1971/2016), Ghana (1971/2016), Guinea (1971/2014), Kenya (1971/2016), Lesotho (1972/2016), Liberia (1971/2015), Madagascar (1971/2016), Malawi (1972/2016), Mali (1971/2016), Mozambique (1973/2015), Niger (1971/2016), Nigeria (1971/2013), Rwanda (1971/2016), Sao Tome and Principe (1971/2016), Senegal (1971/2016), Sierra Leone (1971/2016), Swaziland (1971/2015), Tanzania (1971/2015), Togo (1971/2016), Uganda (1971/2016), Zambia (1971/2013), and Zimbabwe (1971/2013)
Arab fuel-endowed countries: Algeria (1971/2016), Bahrain (1971/2016), Kuwait (1971/2016), Oman (1971/2016), Qatar (1971/2016), and UAE (1971/2016)
Non-Arab fuel-endowed countries: Brunei Darussalam (1971/2016), Iran (1971/2015), Norway (1971/2016), and Venezuela (1971/2016)
Arab Mediterranean: Egypt (1971/2016), Lebanon (1971/2016), Morocco (1971/2016), Syria (1971/2013), and Tunisia (1971/2016)
Rest of non-Arab world: Afghanistan (1971/2015), Albania (1976/2016), Antigua and Barbuda (1971/2015), Argentina (1971/2015), Australia (1971/2016), Austria (1971/2016), Bahamas (1976/2016), Bangladesh (1971/2016), Barbados (1971/2016), Belgium (1971/2015), Belize (1971/2016), Bhutan (1971/2016), Bolivia (1971/2016), Bulgaria (1971/2016), Cambodia (1971/2016), Canada (1971/2016), Chile (1971/2016), China (1974/2016), Colombia (1971/2016), Costa Rica (1971/2016), Cuba (1971/2015), Cyprus (1971/2015), Czech Republic (1971/2015), Denmark (1971/2016), Dominica (1971/2016), Dominican Republic (1971/2016), Ecuador (1971/2016), El Salvador (1971/2016), Fiji (1971/2015), Finland (1972/2016), France (1971/2015), Greece (1971/2015), Grenada (1971/2016), Guatemala (1971/2016), Guyana (1971/2012), Honduras (1971/2016), Hungary (1971/2016), Iceland (1971/2015), India (1971/2016), Indonesia (1971/2016), Ireland (1971/2016), Israel (1973/2016), Italy (1971/2015), Japan (1971/2015), Kiribati (1971/2016), Korea (Rep.) (1971/2015), Lao PDR (1971/2016), Luxembourg (1971/2015), Malaysia (1975/2016), Malta (1971/2016), Mauritius (1971/2016), Mexico (1971/2016), Micronesia (1971/2015), Mongolia (1975/2016), Myanmar (1971/2014), Nepal (1972/2016), Netherlands (1971/2016), New Zealand (1971/2016), Pakistan (1971/2016), Panama (1971/2015), Papua New Guinea (1971/2012), Paraguay (1971/2012), Peru (1973/2016), Philippines (1976/2015), Poland (1972/2016), Portugal (1971/2016), Romania (1971/2016), Samoa (1971/2016), Seychelles (1971/2016), Solomon Islands (1971/2016), Spain (1971/2016), Sri Lanka (1971/2016), St. Vincent and the Grenadines (1971/2016), Suriname (1971/2016), Sweden (1971/2015), Switzerland (1973/2016), Thailand (1971/2015), Tonga (1971/2014), Turkey (1971/2015), United Kingdom (1971/2015), Uruguay (1971/2015), Vanuatu (1971/2015), and Vietnam (1976/2016)

Latin America: Argentina (1971/2015), Bolivia (1971/2016), Chile (1971/2016), Colombia (1971/2016), Costa Rica (1971/2016), Cuba (1971/2015), Dominican Republic (1971/2016), Ecuador (1971/2016), El Salvador (1971/2016), Guatemala (1971/2016), Honduras (1971/2016), Mexico (1971/2016), Panama (1971/2015), Paraguay (1971/2012), Peru (1973/2016), and Uruguay (1971/2015)
Southern Europe: Greece (1971/2015), Italy (1971/2015), Malta (1971/2016), Portugal (1971/2016), and Spain (1971/2016)

For secondary education:
Arab sub-Saharan Africa: Comoros (1971/2014) and Djibouti (1971/2016)
Non-Arab sub-Saharan Africa: Angola (1971/2011), Benin (1971/2015), Burkina Faso (1971/2016), Burundi (1971/2016), Cameroon (1971/2016), Central African Republic (1971/2016), Chad (1971/2016), Congo (Dem. Rep.) (1971/2015), Congo (Rep.) (1971/2012), Cote d'Ivoire (1971/2016), Ethiopia (1971/2015), Ghana (1971/2016), Guinea (1971/2014), Lesotho (1971/2016), Liberia (1971/2015), Madagascar (1971/2016), Malawi (1972/2016), Mali (1971/2016), Mozambique (1973/2015), Niger (1971/2016), Nigeria (1971/2013), Rwanda (1971/2016), Sao Tome and Principe (1971/2016), Senegal (1971/2016), Sierra Leone (1971/2016), Swaziland (1971/2015), Tanzania (1971/2013), and Zimbabwe (1971/2013)
Arab fuel-endowed countries: Algeria (1971/2011), Bahrain (1971/2016), Kuwait (1971/2015), Oman (1973/2016), Qatar (1971/2016), and UAE (1973/2016)
Non-Arab fuel-endowed countries: Brunei Darussalam (1971/2016), Iran (1971/2015), Norway (1971/2016), and Venezuela (1971/2016)
Arab Mediterranean: Egypt (1971/2016), Jordan (1971/2014), Lebanon (1971/2016), Morocco (1971/2012), Syria (1971/2013), and Tunisia (1971/2016)
Rest of non-Arab world: Afghanistan (1971/2015), Albania (1976/2016), Antigua and Barbuda (1972/2015), Argentina (1971/2015), Austria (1971/2016), Bangladesh (1973/2016), Barbados (1971/2016), Belarus (1971/2016), Belgium (1971/2015), Bhutan (1971/2016), Bolivia (1971/2016), Bulgaria (1971/2016), Canada (1971/2016), Chile (1971/2016), China (1976/2013), Colombia (1971/2016), Costa Rica (1971/2016), Cuba (1972/2015), Cyprus (1971/2015), Czech Republic (1971/2015), Dominica (1973/2015), Ecuador (1971/2016), El Salvador (1971/2016), Fiji (1972/2012), Finland (1971/2016), France (1971/2015), Greece (1971/2015), Grenada (1971/2016), Guatemala (1971/2016), Guyana (1971/2012), Hungary (1971/2016), Iceland (1971/2015), India (1971/2016), Indonesia (1971/2016), Ireland (1971/2016), Israel (1973/2016), Italy (1971/2015), Jamaica (1973/2016), Japan (1971/2015), Korea (Rep.) (1971/2015), Lao PDR (1971/2016), Luxembourg (1971/2015), Malaysia (1971/2016), Malta (1971/2016), Mauritius (1971/2016), Mexico (1971/2016), Mongolia (1974/2016), Myanmar (1971/2014), Nepal (1972/2016), Netherlands (1971/2016), New Zealand (1971/2016), Pakistan (1971/2016), Panama (1971/2015), Papua New Guinea (1974/2012), Paraguay (1971/2012), Peru (1971/2016), Poland (1972/2016), Portugal (1971/2016), Romania (1971/2016), Samoa (1975/2016), Seychelles (1971/2016), Solomon Islands (1971/2012), Spain (1971/2016), Sri Lanka (1976/2016), St. Lucia (1972/2016), St. Vincent and the Grenadines (1971/2016), Suriname (1971/2015), Sweden (1971/2015), Thailand (1971/2015), Tonga (1971/2014), Turkey (1971/2015), United Kingdom (1971/2015), United States (1972/2015), and Vanuatu (1971/2015)

Latin America: Argentina (1971/2015), Bolivia (1971/2016), Chile (1971/2016), Colombia (1971/2016), Costa Rica (1971/2016), Cuba (1972/2015), Ecuador (1971/2016), El Salvador (1971/2016), Guatemala (1971/2016), Mexico (1971/2016), Panama (1971/2015), Paraguay (1971/2012), and Peru (1971/2016)

Southern Europe: Greece (1971/2015), Italy (1971/2015), Malta (1971/2016), Portugal (1971/2016), and Spain (1971/2016)

For tertiary education:

Arab sub-Saharan Africa: Comoros (2014), Djibouti (2011), Mauritania (2016), Sudan (2014), and Yemen (2011)

Non-Arab sub-Saharan Africa: Angola (2015), Benin (2016), Botswana (2016), Burkina Faso (2016), Burundi (2014), Cameroon (2015), Central African Republic (2012), Chad (2014), Congo (Dem. Rep.) (2013), Congo (Rep.) (2013), Cote d'Ivoire (2015), Ethiopia (2014), Gambia (2012), Ghana (2016), Guinea (2014), Lesotho (2015), Liberia (2012), Madagascar (2015), Malawi (2011), Mali (2015), Mozambique (2016), Niger (2012), Nigeria (2011), Rwanda (2016), Sao Tome and Principe (2015), Senegal (2016), South Africa (2014), Swaziland (2013), Tanzania (2015), Togo (2016), Uganda (2014), Zambia (2012), and Zimbabwe (2015)

Arab fuel-endowed countries: Bahrain (1971/2016), Kuwait (1971/2013), Qatar (1976/2016), and Saudi Arabia (1971/2016)

Non-Arab fuel-endowed countries: Iran (1971/2016) and Norway (1971/2016)

Arab Mediterranean: Egypt (1971/2016), Jordan (1971/2016), Lebanon (1971/2014), Morocco (1971/2016), Syria (1971/2016), and Tunisia (1971/2016)

Rest of non-Arab world: Afghanistan (1972/2014), Albania (1971/2016), Argentina (1971/2015), Australia (1971/2016), Austria (1971/2016), Bangladesh (1972/2016), Barbados (1971/2011), Belgium (1971/2015), Belize (1971/2016), Bulgaria (1971/2016), Cambodia (1972/2015), Chile (1971/2016), China (1974/2016), Colombia (1974/2016), Costa Rica (1971/2016), Cuba (1971/2016), Cyprus (1971/2015), Czech Republic (1971/2015), Denmark (1971/2016), Dominican Republic (1971/2016), Ecuador (1971/2015), El Salvador (1973/2016), Finland (1971/2016), Greece (1971/2014), Guatemala (1971/2015), Guyana (1971/2012), Honduras (1974/2015), Hungary (1971/2016), Iceland (1971/2015), India (1971/2016), Indonesia (1972/2016), Ireland (1971/2015), Israel (1971/2016), Italy (1971/2015), Jamaica (1971/2015), Japan (1971/2015), Korea (Rep.) (1971/2015), Lao PDR (1971/2016), Luxembourg (1971/2015), Malta (1972/2016), Mauritius (1971/2015), Mexico (1971/2016), Myanmar (1972/2012), Nepal (1976/2016), Netherlands (1971/2016), New Zealand (1971/2016), Pakistan (1971/2016), Panama (1971/2015), Philippines (1971/2014), Poland (1971/2016), Portugal (1971/2016), Romania (1971/2016), Russian Federation (1971/2016), Spain (1971/2016), Sri Lanka (1971/2016), Sweden (1971/2015), Thailand (1976/2015), Turkey (1971/2015), United Kingdom (1971/2015), and Vietnam (1976/2016)

Latin America: Argentina (1971/2015), Chile (1971/2016), Colombia (1974/2016), Costa Rica (1971/2016), Cuba (1971/2016), Dominican Republic (1971/2016), Ecuador (1971/2015), El Salvador (1973/2016), Guatemala (1971/2015), Honduras (1974/2015), Mexico (1971/2016), and Panama (1971/2015)

Southern Europe: Greece (1971/2014), Italy (1971/2015), Malta (1972/2016), Portugal (1971/2016), and Spain (1971/2016)

## Table 5.2

Arab sub-Saharan Africa: Comoros, Djibouti, Mauritania, Somalia, Sudan, and Yemen
Non-Arab sub-Saharan Africa: Angola, Benin, Botswana, Burkina Faso, Burundi, Cameroon, Central African Republic, Chad, Congo (Dem. Rep.), Congo (Rep.), Cote d'Ivoire, Equatorial Guinea, Ethiopia, Gabon, Gambia, Ghana, Guinea, Guinea-Bissau, Kenya, Lesotho, Liberia, Madagascar, Malawi, Mali, Mozambique, Namibia, Niger, Nigeria, Rwanda, Sao Tome and Principe, Senegal, Sierra Leone, South Africa, South Sudan, Swaziland, Tanzania, Togo, Uganda, Zambia, and Zimbabwe
Arab fuel-endowed countries: Algeria, Bahrain, Iraq, Kuwait, Libya, Oman, Qatar, Saudi Arabia, and UAE
Non-Arab fuel-endowed countries: Brunei Darussalam, Iran, Norway, Trinidad and Tobago, and Venezuela
Arab Mediterranean: Egypt, Jordan, Lebanon, Morocco, Syria, and Tunisia
Rest of non-Arab world: Afghanistan, Albania, Argentina, Armenia, Australia, Austria, Azerbaijan, Bahamas, Bangladesh, Barbados, Belarus, Belgium, Belize, Bhutan, Bolivia, Bosnia and Herzegovina, Brazil, Bulgaria, Cambodia, Canada, Chile, China, Colombia, Costa Rica, Croatia, Cuba, Cyprus, Czech Republic, Denmark, Dominican Republic, Ecuador, El Salvador, Estonia, Fiji, Finland, France, Georgia, Germany, Greece, Guatemala, Guyana, Haiti, Honduras, Hungary, Iceland, India, Indonesia, Ireland, Israel, Italy, Jamaica, Japan, Kazakhstan, Korea (Rep.), Kyrgyz Republic, Lao PDR, Latvia, Lithuania, Luxembourg, Macedonia (FYR), Malaysia, Maldives, Malta, Mauritius, Mexico, Moldova, Mongolia, Montenegro, Myanmar, Nepal, Netherlands, New Zealand, Nicaragua, Pakistan, Panama, Papua New Guinea, Paraguay, Peru, Philippines, Poland, Portugal, Romania, Russian Federation, Samoa, Serbia, Singapore, Slovak Republic, Slovenia, Solomon Islands, Spain, Sri Lanka, St. Lucia, St. Vincent and the Grenadines, Suriname, Sweden, Switzerland, Tajikistan, Thailand, Timor-Leste, Tonga, Turkey, Turkmenistan, Ukraine, United Kingdom, United States, Uruguay, Uzbekistan, Vanuatu, and Vietnam
Latin America: Argentina, Bolivia, Brazil, Chile, Colombia, Costa Rica, Cuba, Dominican Republic, Ecuador, El Salvador, Guatemala, Honduras, Mexico, Nicaragua, Panama, Paraguay, Peru, and Uruguay
Southern Europe: Greece, Italy, Malta, Portugal, and Spain

## Table 5.3

Arab countries, Iran, Turkey: Algeria, Bahrain, Comoros, Djibouti, Egypt, Iran, Iraq, Jordan, Kuwait, Lebanon, Libya, Mauritania, Morocco, Oman, Qatar, Saudi Arabia, Somalia, Sudan, Syria, Tunisia, Turkey, UAE, and Yemen
Other Muslim-majority countries: Afghanistan, Albania, Azerbaijan, Bangladesh, Brunei Darussalam, Burkina Faso, Chad, Gambia, Guinea, Indonesia, Kazakhstan, Kyrgyz Republic, Malaysia, Maldives, Mali, Niger, Pakistan, Senegal, Sierra Leone, Tajikistan, Turkmenistan, and Uzbekistan
Non-Muslim majority countries: Angola, Argentina, Armenia, Australia, Austria, Bahamas, Barbados, Belarus, Belgium, Belize, Benin, Bhutan, Bolivia, Bosnia and Herzegovina, Botswana, Brazil, Bulgaria, Burundi, Cambodia, Cameroon, Canada,

Central African Republic, Chile, China, Colombia, Congo (Dem. Rep.), Congo (Rep.), Costa Rica, Cote d'Ivoire, Croatia, Cuba, Cyprus, Czech Republic, Denmark, Dominican Republic, Ecuador, El Salvador, Equatorial Guinea, Estonia, Ethiopia, Fiji, Finland, France, Gabon, Georgia, Germany, Ghana, Greece, Guatemala, Guinea-Bissau, Guyana, Haiti, Honduras, Hungary, Iceland, India, Ireland, Israel, Italy, Jamaica, Japan, Kenya, Korea (Rep.), Lao PDR, Latvia, Lesotho, Liberia, Lithuania, Luxembourg, Macedonia (FYR), Madagascar, Malawi, Malta, Mauritius, Mexico, Moldova, Mongolia, Montenegro, Mozambique, Myanmar, Namibia, Nepal, Netherlands, New Zealand, Nicaragua, Nigeria, Norway, Panama, Papua New Guinea, Paraguay, Peru, Philippines, Poland, Portugal, Romania, Russian Federation, Rwanda, Samoa, Sao Tome and Principe, Serbia, Singapore, Slovak Republic, Slovenia, Solomon Islands, South Africa, South Sudan, Spain, Sri Lanka, St. Lucia, St. Vincent and the Grenadines, Suriname, Swaziland, Sweden, Switzerland, Tanzania, Thailand, Timor-Leste, Togo, Tonga, Trinidad and Tobago, Uganda, Ukraine, United Kingdom, United States, Uruguay, Vanuatu, Venezuela, Vietnam, Zambia, and Zimbabwe

## Table 5.5

Non-Arab sub-Saharan Africa: Burkina Faso (2010), Cameroon (2011), Central African Republic (2006), Chad (2010), Cote d'Ivoire (2012), Equatorial Guinea (2011), Ethiopia (2002), Gabon (2012), Ghana (2008), Kenya (2009), Liberia (2007), Malawi (2010), Mali (2013), Mozambique (2011), Namibia (2002), Nigeria (2013), Rwanda (2010), Sierra Leone (2013), South Africa (1998), Tanzania (2010), Uganda (2011), Zambia (2007), and Zimbabwe (2011)
Arab Mediterranean: Egypt (2005), Jordan (2012), Morocco (2010), and Tunisia (2010)
Rest of non-Arab world: Albania (2013), Australia (2003), Austria (2014), Azerbaijan (2006), Bangladesh (2011), Belgium (2014), Brazil (2003), Bulgaria (2014), Cambodia (2005), Canada (2009), Colombia (2005), Costa Rica (2003), Croatia (2014), Cyprus (2014), Czech Republic (2014), Denmark (2014), Dominican Republic (2007), Ecuador (2004), El Salvador (2008), Estonia (2014), Fiji (2011), Finland (2014), France (2014), Georgia (2010), Germany (2014), Greece (2014), Guatemala (2009), Haiti (2012), Honduras (2012), Hungary (2014), Iceland (2008), India (2006), Ireland (2014), Italy (2014), Jamaica (2009), Japan (2003), Kiribati (2008), Korea (Rep.) (2013), Kyrgyz Republic (2012), Latvia (2014), Lithuania (2014), Luxembourg (2014), Maldives (2006), Malta (2014), Mexico (2011), Moldova (2010), Nepal (2011), Netherlands (2014), New Zealand (2002), Nicaragua (2007), Pakistan (2013), Paraguay (2008), Peru (2013), Philippines (2013), Poland (2014), Portugal (2014), Romania (2014), Samoa (2000), Serbia (2003), Singapore (2009), Slovak Republic (2014), Slovenia (2014), Spain (2014), Sweden (2014), Switzerland (2003), Tajikistan (2012), Thailand (2005), Timor-Leste (2010), Tonga (2009), Turkey (2014), Ukraine (2007), United Kingdom (2014), United States (2011), Vanuatu (2009), and Vietnam (2010)
Latin America: Brazil (2003), Colombia (2005), Costa Rica (2003), Dominican Republic (2007), Ecuador (2004), El Salvador (2008), Guatemala (2009), Honduras (2012), Mexico (2011), Nicaragua (2007), Paraguay (2008), and Peru (2013)
Southern Europe: Greece (2014), Italy (2014), Malta (2014), Portugal (2014), and Spain (2014)

## Table 6.1

Arab sub-Saharan Africa: Comoros (2013), Djibouti (2013), Mauritania (2014), Sudan (2009), and Yemen (2014)
Non-Arab sub-Saharan Africa: Angola (2008), Benin (2015), Botswana (2009), Burkina Faso (2014), Burundi (2013), Cameroon (2014), Central African Republic (2008), Chad (2011), Congo (Dem. Rep.) (2012), Congo (Rep.) (2011), Cote d'Ivoire (2015), Ethiopia (2015), Gabon (2005), Gambia (2015), Ghana (2012), Guinea (2012), Guinea-Bissau (2010), Kenya (2005), Lesotho (2010), Liberia (2014), Madagascar (2012), Malawi (2010), Mali (2009), Mozambique (2014), Namibia (2009), Niger (2014), Nigeria (2009), Rwanda (2013), Sao Tome and Principe (2010), Senegal (2011), Sierra Leone (2011), South Africa (2014), South Sudan (2009), Swaziland (2009), Tanzania (2011), Togo (2015), Uganda (2012), Zambia (2015), and Zimbabwe (2011)
Arab fuel-endowed countries: Algeria (2011) and Iraq (2012)
Non-Arab fuel-endowed countries: Iran (2014), Norway (2015), Trinidad and Tobago (1992), and Venezuela (2006)
Arab Mediterranean: Egypt (2015), Jordan (2010), Lebanon (2011), Morocco (2006), Syria (2004), and Tunisia (2010)
Rest of non-Arab world: Albania (2012), Argentina (2016), Armenia (2016), Australia (2010), Austria (2015), Azerbaijan (2005), Bangladesh (2016), Belarus (2016), Belgium (2015), Belize (1999), Bhutan (2012), Bolivia (2016), Bosnia and Herzegovina (2015), Brazil (2015), Bulgaria (2014), Canada (2013), Chile (2015), China (2012), Colombia (2016), Costa Rica (2016), Croatia (2015), Cyprus (2015), Czech Republic (2015), Denmark (2015), Dominican Republic (2016), Ecuador (2016), El Salvador (2016), Estonia (2015), Fiji (2013), Finland (2015), France (2015), Georgia (2016), Germany (2015), Greece (2015), Guatemala (2014), Guyana (1998), Haiti (2012), Honduras (2016), Hungary (2015), Iceland (2014), India (2011), Indonesia (2013), Ireland (2014), Israel (2012), Italy (2014), Jamaica (2004), Japan (2008), Kazakhstan (2015), Kiribati (2006), Korea (Rep.) (2012), Kyrgyz Republic (2016), Lao PDR (2012), Latvia (2015), Lithuania (2015), Luxembourg (2014), Macedonia (FYR) (2014), Malaysia (2009), Maldives (2009), Malta (2014), Mauritius (2012), Mexico (2016), Micronesia (2013), Moldova (2016), Mongolia (2016), Montenegro (2014), Myanmar (2015), Nepal (2010), Netherlands (2015), Nicaragua (2014), Pakistan (2013), Panama (2016), Papua New Guinea (2009), Paraguay (2016), Peru (2016), Philippines (2015), Poland (2015), Portugal (2015), Romania (2016), Russian Federation (2015), Samoa (2008), Serbia (2015), Seychelles (2013), Slovak Republic (2015), Slovenia (2015), Solomon Islands (2013), Spain (2015), Sri Lanka (2016), St. Lucia (1995), Suriname (1999), Sweden (2015), Switzerland (2014), Tajikistan (2015), Thailand (2013), Timor-Leste (2014), Tonga (2009), Turkey (2016), Turkmenistan (1998), Ukraine (2016), United Kingdom (2015), United States (2016), Uruguay (2016), Uzbekistan (2003), Vanuatu (2010), and Vietnam (2014)
Latin America: Argentina (2016), Bolivia (2016), Brazil (2015), Chile (2015), Colombia (2016), Costa Rica (2016), Dominican Republic (2016), Ecuador (2016), El Salvador (2016), Guatemala (2014), Honduras (2016), Mexico (2016), Nicaragua (2014), Panama (2016), Paraguay (2016), Peru (2016), and Uruguay (2016)

272 APPENDIX

Southern Europe: Greece (2015), Italy (2014), Malta (2014), Portugal (2015), and Spain (2015)

## Table 7.2

Arab sub-Saharan Africa: Djibouti, Mauritania, and Sudan
Non-Arab sub-Saharan Africa: Angola, Benin, Botswana, Burkina Faso, Burundi, Cameroon, Cote d'Ivoire, Ethiopia, Gabon, Gambia, Ghana, Guinea, Kenya, Lesotho, Liberia, Madagascar, Malawi, Mali, Mozambique, Namibia, Niger, Nigeria, Rwanda, Senegal, Sierra Leone, South Africa, Swaziland, Tanzania, Uganda, Zambia, and Zimbabwe
Arab fuel-endowed countries: Algeria, Bahrain, Kuwait, Libya, Oman, and UAE
Non-Arab fuel-endowed countries: Brunei Darussalam, Iran, Norway, Trinidad and Tobago, and Venezuela
Arab Mediterranean: Egypt, Jordan, Lebanon, Morocco, and Tunisia
Rest of non-Arab world: Afghanistan, Albania, Andorra, Antigua and Barbuda, Argentina, Armenia, Australia, Austria, Azerbaijan, Bahamas, Bangladesh, Barbados, Belarus, Belgium, Bhutan, Bolivia, Bosnia and Herzegovina, Brazil, Bulgaria, Cambodia, Canada, Chile, China, Colombia, Costa Rica, Croatia, Cyprus, Czech Republic, Denmark, Dominica, Dominican Republic, Ecuador, Estonia, Fiji, Finland, France, Georgia, Germany, Greece, Grenada, Guatemala, Guyana, Haiti, Honduras, Hungary, Iceland, India, Indonesia, Israel, Italy, Jamaica, Japan, Kazakhstan, Korea (Rep.), Kyrgyz Republic, Lao PDR, Latvia, Liechtenstein, Lithuania, Luxembourg, Macedonia (FYR), Malaysia, Maldives, Malta, Marshall Islands, Mauritius, Mexico, Micronesia, Moldova, Monaco, Mongolia, Montenegro, Nepal, Netherlands, New Zealand, Nicaragua, Pakistan, Palau, Panama, Papua New Guinea, Paraguay, Peru, Philippines, Poland, Portugal, Romania, Russian Federation, Samoa, San Marino, Serbia, Seychelles, Singapore, Slovak Republic, Slovenia, Solomon Islands, Spain, Sri Lanka, St. Vincent and the Grenadines, Suriname, Sweden, Switzerland, Tajikistan, Thailand, Tonga, Turkey, Turkmenistan, Ukraine, United Kingdom, United States, Uruguay, Uzbekistan, Vanuatu, and Vietnam
Latin America: Argentina, Bolivia, Brazil, Chile, Colombia, Costa Rica, Dominican Republic, Ecuador, Guatemala, Honduras, Mexico, Nicaragua, Panama, Paraguay, Peru, and Uruguay
Southern Europe: Andorra, Greece, Italy, Malta, Portugal, San Marino, and Spain

## Table 7.3

Arab sub-Saharan Africa: Comoros, Djibouti, Mauritania, Somalia, Sudan, and Yemen
Non-Arab sub-Saharan Africa: Angola, Benin, Botswana, Burkina Faso, Burundi, Cameroon, Central African Republic, Chad, Congo (Dem. Rep.), Congo (Rep.), Cote d'Ivoire, Equatorial Guinea, Ethiopia, Gabon, Gambia, Ghana, Guinea, Guinea-Bissau, Kenya, Lesotho, Liberia, Madagascar, Malawi, Mali, Mozambique, Namibia,

Niger, Nigeria, Rwanda, Sao Tome and Principe, Senegal, Sierra Leone, South Africa, South Sudan, Swaziland, Tanzania, Togo, Uganda, Zambia, and Zimbabwe
Arab fuel-endowed countries: Algeria, Iraq, and Libya
Non-Arab fuel-endowed countries: Iran and Venezuela
Arab Mediterranean: Egypt, Jordan, Lebanon, Morocco, Syria, and Tunisia
Rest of non-Arab world: Afghanistan, Albania, Antigua and Barbuda, Argentina, Armenia, Azerbaijan, Bangladesh, Belarus, Belize, Bhutan, Bolivia, Bosnia and Herzegovina, Brazil, Bulgaria, Cambodia, Chile, China, Colombia, Costa Rica, Cuba, Dominica, Dominican Republic, Ecuador, El Salvador, Fiji, Georgia, Grenada, Guatemala, Guyana, Haiti, Honduras, India, Indonesia, Jamaica, Kazakhstan, Kiribati, Kyrgyz Republic, Lao PDR, Latvia, Lithuania, Macedonia (FYR), Malaysia, Maldives, Marshall Islands, Mauritius, Mexico, Micronesia, Moldova, Mongolia, Montenegro, Myanmar, Nepal, Nicaragua, Pakistan, Palau, Panama, Papua New Guinea, Paraguay, Peru, Philippines, Romania, Russian Federation, Samoa, Serbia, Seychelles, Solomon Islands, Sri Lanka, St. Lucia, St. Vincent and the Grenadines, Suriname, Tajikistan, Thailand, Timor-Leste, Tonga, Turkey, Turkmenistan, Ukraine, Uruguay, Uzbekistan, Vanuatu, and Vietnam
Latin America: Argentina, Bolivia, Brazil, Chile, Colombia, Costa Rica, Cuba, Dominican Republic, Ecuador, El Salvador, Guatemala, Honduras, Mexico, Nicaragua, Panama, Paraguay, Peru, and Uruguay

## Table 7.4

Arab sub-Saharan Africa: Comoros, Djibouti, Mauritania, Somalia, Sudan, and Yemen
Non-Arab sub-Saharan Africa: Angola, Benin, Botswana, Burkina Faso, Burundi, Cameroon, Central African Republic, Chad, Congo (Dem. Rep.), Congo (Rep.), Cote d'Ivoire, Equatorial Guinea, Ethiopia, Gabon, Gambia, Ghana, Guinea, Guinea-Bissau, Kenya, Lesotho, Liberia, Madagascar, Malawi, Mali, Mozambique, Namibia, Niger, Nigeria, Rwanda, Sao Tome and Principe, Senegal, Sierra Leone, South Africa, South Sudan, Swaziland, Tanzania, Togo, Uganda, Zambia, and Zimbabwe
Arab fuel-endowed countries: Algeria, Bahrain, Iraq, Kuwait, Libya, Oman, Qatar, Saudi Arabia, and UAE
Non-Arab fuel-endowed countries: Brunei Darussalam, Iran, Norway, Trinidad and Tobago, and Venezuela
Arab Mediterranean: Egypt, Jordan, Lebanon, Morocco, Syria, and Tunisia
Rest of non-Arab world: Afghanistan, Albania, Andorra, Antigua and Barbuda, Argentina, Armenia, Australia, Austria, Azerbaijan, Bahamas, Bangladesh, Barbados, Belarus, Belgium, Belize, Bhutan, Bolivia, Bosnia and Herzegovina, Brazil, Bulgaria, Cambodia, Canada, Chile, China, Colombia, Costa Rica, Croatia, Cuba, Cyprus, Czech Republic, Denmark, Dominica, Dominican Republic, Ecuador, El Salvador, Estonia, Fiji, Finland, France, Georgia, Germany, Greece, Grenada, Guatemala, Guyana, Haiti, Honduras, Hungary, Iceland, India, Indonesia, Ireland, Israel, Italy, Jamaica, Japan, Kazakhstan, Kiribati, Korea (Rep.), Kyrgyz Republic, Lao PDR, Latvia, Lithuania, Luxembourg, Macedonia (FYR), Malaysia, Maldives, Malta, Mauritius, Mexico, Micronesia, Moldova, Monaco, Mongolia, Montenegro, Myanmar, Nepal, Netherlands, New Zealand, Nicaragua, Pakistan, Panama, Papua New Guinea,

Paraguay, Peru, Philippines, Poland, Portugal, Romania, Russian Federation, Serbia, Seychelles, Singapore, Slovak Republic, Slovenia, Solomon Islands, Spain, Sri Lanka, St. Lucia, St. Vincent and the Grenadines, Suriname, Sweden, Switzerland, Tajikistan, Thailand, Timor-Leste, Turkey, Turkmenistan, Ukraine, United Kingdom, United States, Uruguay, Uzbekistan, Vanuatu, and Vietnam

Latin America: Argentina, Bolivia, Brazil, Chile, Colombia, Costa Rica, Cuba, Dominican Republic, Ecuador, El Salvador, Guatemala, Honduras, Mexico, Nicaragua, Panama, Paraguay, Peru, and Uruguay

Southern Europe: Andorra, Greece, Italy, Malta, Portugal, and Spain

## Table 7.5

Arab sub-Saharan Africa: Comoros, Djibouti, Mauritania, Sudan, and Yemen

Non-Arab sub-Saharan Africa: Angola, Benin, Botswana, Burkina Faso, Burundi, Cameroon, Central African Republic, Chad, Congo (Dem. Rep.), Congo (Rep.), Cote d'Ivoire, Equatorial Guinea, Ethiopia, Gabon, Gambia, Ghana, Guinea, Guinea-Bissau, Kenya, Lesotho, Liberia, Madagascar, Malawi, Mali, Mozambique, Namibia, Niger, Nigeria, Rwanda, Sao Tome and Principe, Senegal, Sierra Leone, South Africa, South Sudan, Swaziland, Tanzania, Togo, Uganda, Zambia, and Zimbabwe

Arab fuel-endowed countries: Algeria, Bahrain, Iraq, Kuwait, Libya (2011), Oman, Qatar, Saudi Arabia, and UAE

Non-Arab fuel-endowed countries: Brunei Darussalam, Iran, Norway, Trinidad and Tobago, and Venezuela

Arab Mediterranean: Egypt, Jordan, Lebanon, Morocco, and Tunisia

Rest of non-Arab world: Afghanistan, Albania, Antigua and Barbuda, Argentina, Armenia, Australia, Austria, Azerbaijan, Bahamas, Bangladesh, Barbados, Belarus, Belgium, Belize, Bhutan, Bolivia, Bosnia and Herzegovina, Brazil, Bulgaria, Cambodia, Canada, Chile, China, Colombia, Costa Rica, Croatia, Cyprus, Czech Republic, Denmark, Dominica, Dominican Republic, Ecuador, El Salvador, Estonia, Fiji, Finland, France, Georgia, Germany, Greece, Grenada, Guatemala, Guyana, Haiti, Honduras, Hungary, Iceland, India, Indonesia, Ireland, Israel, Italy, Jamaica, Japan, Kazakhstan, Kiribati, Korea (Rep.), Kyrgyz Republic, Lao PDR, Latvia, Lithuania, Luxembourg, Macedonia (FYR), Malaysia, Maldives, Malta, Marshall Islands, Mauritius, Mexico, Micronesia, Moldova, Mongolia, Montenegro, Myanmar, Nepal, Netherlands, New Zealand, Nicaragua, Pakistan, Palau, Panama, Papua New Guinea, Paraguay, Peru, Philippines, Poland, Portugal, Romania, Russian Federation, Samoa, Serbia, Seychelles, Singapore, Slovak Republic, Slovenia, Solomon Islands, Spain, Sri Lanka, St. Kitts and Nevis, St. Lucia, St. Vincent and the Grenadines, Suriname, Sweden, Switzerland, Tajikistan, Thailand, Timor-Leste, Tonga, Turkey, Turkmenistan, Ukraine, United Kingdom, United States, Uruguay, Uzbekistan, Vanuatu, and Vietnam

Latin America: Argentina, Bolivia, Brazil, Chile, Colombia, Costa Rica, Dominican Republic, Ecuador, El Salvador, Guatemala, Honduras, Mexico, Nicaragua, Panama, Paraguay, Peru, and Uruguay

Southern Europe: Greece, Italy, Malta, Portugal, and Spain

## Table 8.3

Arab sub-Saharan Africa: Djibouti, Mauritania, Sudan, and Yemen
Non-Arab sub-Saharan Africa: Angola, Benin, Botswana, Burkina Faso, Burundi, Cameroon, Central African Republic, Chad, Congo (Dem. Rep.), Congo (Rep.), Cote d'Ivoire, Equatorial Guinea, Ethiopia, Gabon, Gambia, Ghana, Guinea, Guinea-Bissau, Kenya, Lesotho, Liberia, Madagascar, Malawi, Mali, Mozambique, Namibia, Niger, Nigeria, Rwanda, Sao Tome and Principe, Senegal, Sierra Leone, South Africa, Swaziland, Tanzania, Togo, Uganda, and Zambia
Arab fuel-endowed countries: Algeria, Bahrain, Iraq, Kuwait, Libya, Oman, Qatar, Saudi Arabia, and UAE
Non-Arab fuel-endowed countries: Brunei Darussalam, Iran, Norway, Trinidad and Tobago, and Venezuela
Arab Mediterranean: Egypt, Jordan, Lebanon, Morocco, and Tunisia
Rest of non-Arab world: Afghanistan, Albania, Antigua and Barbuda, Argentina, Armenia, Australia, Austria, Azerbaijan, Bahamas, Bangladesh, Barbados, Belarus, Belgium, Belize, Bhutan, Bolivia, Bosnia and Herzegovina, Brazil, Bulgaria, Cambodia, Canada, Chile, China, Colombia, Costa Rica, Croatia, Cyprus, Czech Republic, Denmark, Dominica, Dominican Republic, Ecuador, El Salvador, Estonia, Fiji, Finland, France, Georgia, Germany, Greece, Grenada, Guatemala, Guyana, Honduras, Hungary, Iceland, India, Indonesia, Ireland, Israel, Italy, Jamaica, Japan, Kazakhstan, Korea (Rep.), Kyrgyz Republic, Lao PDR, Latvia, Lithuania, Luxembourg, Macedonia (FYR), Malaysia, Maldives, Malta, Mauritius, Mexico, Moldova, Mongolia, Montenegro, Myanmar, Nepal, Netherlands, New Zealand, Nicaragua, Pakistan, Panama, Paraguay, Peru, Philippines, Poland, Portugal, Romania, Russian Federation, Serbia, Seychelles, Singapore, Slovak Republic, Slovenia, Solomon Islands, Spain, Sri Lanka, St. Kitts and Nevis, St. Lucia, St. Vincent and the Grenadines, Suriname, Sweden, Switzerland, Tajikistan, Thailand, Timor-Leste, Tonga, Turkey, Turkmenistan, Ukraine, United Kingdom, United States, Uruguay, Uzbekistan, Vanuatu, and Vietnam
Latin America: Argentina, Bolivia, Brazil, Chile, Colombia, Costa Rica, Dominican Republic, Ecuador, El Salvador, Guatemala, Honduras, Mexico, Nicaragua, Panama, Paraguay, Peru, and Uruguay
Southern Europe: Greece, Italy, Malta, Portugal, and Spain

## Table 8.5

For 2010:
Arab sub-Saharan Africa: Yemen
Non-Arab sub-Saharan Africa: Angola, Botswana, Burkina Faso, Cameroon, Central African Republic, Chad, Congo (Dem. Rep.), Congo (Rep.), Cote d'Ivoire, Ethiopia, Gabon, Ghana, Guinea-Bissau, Kenya, Lesotho, Liberia, Madagascar, Malawi, Mali, Mozambique, Namibia, Niger, Nigeria, Rwanda, Senegal, Sierra Leone, South Africa, South Sudan, Swaziland, Tanzania, Togo, Uganda, Zambia, and Zimbabwe
Arab fuel-endowed countries: Algeria, Bahrain, Iraq, Kuwait, Oman, Qatar, Saudi Arabia, and UAE

Non-Arab fuel-endowed countries: Brunei Darussalam, Iran, Norway, Trinidad and Tobago, and Venezuela
Arab Mediterranean: Egypt, Jordan, Lebanon, Morocco, and Tunisia
Rest of Non-Arab world: Afghanistan, Albania, Argentina, Armenia, Australia, Austria, Azerbaijan, Bangladesh, Belarus, Belgium, Belize, Bolivia, Bosnia and Herzegovina, Brazil, Bulgaria, Cambodia, Canada, Chile, China, Colombia, Croatia, Cuba, Cyprus, Czech Republic, Denmark, Dominican Republic, Ecuador, El Salvador, Estonia, Fiji, Finland, France, Georgia, Germany, Greece, Guatemala, Guyana, Honduras, Hungary, Iceland, India, Indonesia, Ireland, Israel, Italy, Jamaica, Japan, Kazakhstan, Korea (Rep.), Kyrgyz Republic, Lao PDR, Latvia, Lithuania, Luxembourg, Macedonia (FYR), Malaysia, Malta, Mauritius, Mexico, Moldova, Mongolia, Montenegro, Nepal, Netherlands, New Zealand, Nicaragua, Pakistan, Papua New Guinea, Paraguay, Peru, Philippines, Poland, Portugal, Romania, Russian Federation, Serbia, Seychelles, Singapore, Slovak Republic, Slovenia, Spain, Sri Lanka, Sweden, Switzerland, Tajikistan, Thailand, Timor-Leste, Turkey, Ukraine, United Kingdom, United States, Uruguay, and Vietnam
Latin America: Argentina, Bolivia, Brazil, Chile, Colombia, Cuba, Dominican Republic, Ecuador, El Salvador, Guatemala, Honduras, Mexico, Nicaragua, Paraguay, Peru, and Uruguay
Southern Europe: Greece, Italy, Malta, Montenegro, Portugal, and Spain
Arab sub-Saharan Africa: Mauritania, Somalia, and Sudan

For 2015:
Non-Arab sub-Saharan Africa: Angola, Benin, Botswana, Burkina Faso, Burundi, Cameroon, Chad, Congo (Dem. Rep.), Cote d'Ivoire, Ethiopia, Gabon, Gambia, Ghana, Guinea, Guinea-Bissau, Kenya, Lesotho, Liberia, Madagascar, Malawi, Mali, Mozambique, Namibia, Nigeria, Rwanda, Senegal, Sierra Leone, South Africa, South Sudan, Swaziland, Tanzania, Togo, Uganda, Zambia, and Zimbabwe
Arab fuel-endowed countries: Algeria, Bahrain, Iraq, Kuwait, Oman, and Saudi Arabia
Non-Arab fuel-endowed countries: Brunei Darussalam, Iran, Norway, and Trinidad and Tobago
Arab Mediterranean: Egypt, Jordan, Lebanon, Morocco, and Tunisia
Rest of non-Arab world: Afghanistan, Albania, Argentina, Armenia, Australia, Austria, Azerbaijan, Bangladesh, Belarus, Belgium, Belize, Bolivia, Bosnia and Herzegovina, Brazil, Bulgaria, Cambodia, Canada, Chile, China, Colombia, Croatia, Cuba, Cyprus, Czech Republic, Denmark, Dominican Republic, Ecuador, El Salvador, Estonia, Fiji, Finland, France, Georgia, Germany, Greece, Guatemala, Guyana, Honduras, Hungary, India, Indonesia, Ireland, Israel, Italy, Jamaica, Japan, Kazakhstan, Korea (Rep.), Kyrgyz Republic, Latvia, Lithuania, Luxembourg, Macedonia (FYR), Malaysia, Malta, Mauritius, Mexico, Moldova, Mongolia, Montenegro, Myanmar, Nepal, Netherlands, New Zealand, Nicaragua, Pakistan, Papua New Guinea, Paraguay, Peru, Philippines, Poland, Portugal, Romania, Russian Federation, Serbia, Seychelles, Singapore, Slovak Republic, Slovenia, Spain, Sri Lanka, Sweden, Switzerland, Tajikistan, Thailand, Timor-Leste, Turkey, Ukraine, United Kingdom, United States, Uruguay, and Vietnam
Latin America: Argentina, Bolivia, Brazil, Chile, Colombia, Cuba, Dominican Republic, Ecuador, El Salvador, Guatemala, Honduras, Mexico, Nicaragua, Paraguay, Peru, and Uruguay

APPENDIX 277

Southern Europe: Greece, Italy, Malta, Montenegro, Portugal, and Spain

## Table 8.6

For 1990:
Non-Arab sub-Saharan Africa: Benin, Burkina Faso, Cameroon, Central African Republic, Chad, Cote d'Ivoire, Ethiopia, Ghana, Guinea, Kenya, Madagascar, Malawi, Mali, Mozambique, Namibia, Niger, Nigeria, Rwanda, Senegal, South Africa, Tanzania, Uganda, Zambia, and Zimbabwe
Non-Arab fuel-endowed countries: Iran
Rest of Non-Arab world: Antigua and Barbuda, Argentina, Bangladesh, Bolivia, Brazil, China, Colombia, Dominican Republic, Guatemala, Haiti, India, Indonesia, Mexico, Mongolia, Nepal, Nicaragua, Pakistan, Peru, Philippines, Turkey, and Vietnam
Latin America: Argentina, Bolivia, Brazil, Colombia, Dominican Republic, Guatemala, Mexico, Nicaragua, and Peru
For 2005 and 2014:
Non-Arab sub-Saharan Africa: Angola, Benin, Burkina Faso, Burundi, Cameroon, Central African Republic, Chad, Congo (Dem. Rep.), Congo (Rep.), Cote d'Ivoire, Equatorial Guinea, Ethiopia, Gabon, Gambia, Ghana, Guinea, Guinea-Bissau, Kenya, Lesotho, Madagascar, Malawi, Mali, Mozambique, Namibia, Niger, Nigeria, Rwanda, Senegal, Sierra Leone, South Africa, Tanzania, Togo, Uganda, Zambia, and Zimbabwe
Non-Arab fuel-endowed countries (2005 only): Iran, Trinidad and Tobago, Venezuela
Rest of non-Arab world: Argentina, Bangladesh, Bolivia, Brazil, Cambodia, China, Colombia, Costa Rica, Dominican Republic, Ecuador, Guatemala, Guyana, Haiti, Honduras, India, Indonesia, Lao PDR, Mexico, Mongolia, Myanmar, Nepal, Pakistan, Panama, Peru, Philippines, Suriname, Thailand, Turkey, and Vietnam
Latin America: Argentina, Bolivia, Brazil, Colombia, Costa Rica, Dominican Republic, Ecuador, Guatemala, Honduras, Mexico, Panama, and Peru

## Table 8.7

Arab sub-Saharan Africa: Djibouti (2013), Mauritania (2014), Sudan (2014), and Yemen (2013)
Non-Arab sub-Saharan Africa: Angola (2010), Benin (2016), Botswana (2010), Burkina Faso (2009), Burundi (2014), Cameroon (2016), Central African Republic (2011), Congo (Dem. Rep.) (2013), Congo (Rep.) (2009), Cote d'Ivoire (2016), Ethiopia (2015), Gabon (2009), Gambia (2006), Ghana (2013), Guinea (2016), Guinea-Bissau (2006), Kenya (2013), Lesotho (2016), Madagascar (2013), Malawi (2014), Mali (2016), Mozambique (2007), Namibia (2014), Nigeria (2014), Rwanda (2011), Senegal (2014), South Africa (2007), South Sudan (2014), Swaziland (2016), Tanzania (2013), Togo (2016), Uganda (2013), Zambia (2013), and Zimbabwe (2016)
Arab fuel-endowed countries: Iraq (2011)
Non-Arab fuel-endowed countries: Trinidad and Tobago (2010) and Venezuela (2010)

Arab Mediterranean: Egypt (2016), Jordan (2013), Lebanon (2013), Morocco (2013), and Tunisia (2013)

Rest of non-Arab world: Afghanistan (2014), Albania (2013), Antigua and Barbuda (2010), Armenia (2013), Azerbaijan (2013), Bahamas (2010), Bangladesh (2013), Barbados (2010), Belarus (2013), Belize (2010), Bhutan (2015), Bosnia and Herzegovina (2013), Brazil (2009), Bulgaria (2013), Cambodia (2016), Chile (2010), China (2012), Colombia (2010), Costa Rica (2010), Croatia (2013), Czech Republic (2013), Dominica (2010), Dominican Republic (2016), El Salvador (2016), Estonia (2013), Fiji (2009), Georgia (2013), Grenada (2010), Guatemala (2010), Guyana (2010), Honduras (2016), Hungary (2013), India (2014), Indonesia (2015), Israel (2013), Jamaica (2010), Kazakhstan (2013), Kyrgyz Republic (2013), Lao PDR (2016), Latvia (2013), Lithuania (2013), Macedonia (FYR) (2013), Malaysia (2015), Mauritius (2009), Mexico (2010), Micronesia (2009), Moldova (2013), Mongolia (2013), Montenegro (2013), Myanmar (2016), Nepal (2013), Nicaragua (2016), Pakistan (2013), Panama (2010), Papua New Guinea (2015), Philippines (2015), Poland (2013), Romania (2013), Russian Federation (2012), Samoa (2009), Serbia (2013), Slovak Republic (2013), Slovenia (2013), Solomon Islands (2015), Sri Lanka (2011), St. Kitts and Nevis (2010), St. Lucia (2010), St. Vincent and the Grenadines (2010), Suriname (2010), Tajikistan (2013), Thailand (2016), Timor-Leste (2015), Tonga (2009), Turkey (2013), Ukraine (2013), Uzbekistan (2013), Vanuatu (2009), and Vietnam (2015)

Latin America: Brazil (2009), Chile (2010), Colombia (2010), Costa Rica (2010), Dominican Republic (2016), El Salvador (2016), Guatemala (2010), Honduras (2016), Mexico (2010), Nicaragua (2016), and Panama (2010)

Southern Europe: None

## Tables 9.1 and 9.2

Arab sub-Saharan Africa: Mauritania, Sudan, and Yemen

Non-Arab sub-Saharan Africa: Angola, Benin, Botswana, Burkina Faso, Burundi, Cameroon, Central African Republic, Chad, Congo (Rep.), Cote d'Ivoire, Ethiopia, Ghana, Guinea, Kenya, Lesotho, Madagascar, Malawi, Mali, Mozambique, Namibia, Niger, Nigeria, Rwanda, Sao Tome and Principe, Senegal, Sierra Leone, South Africa, Tanzania, Togo, Uganda, Zambia, and Zimbabwe

Arab fuel-endowed countries: Algeria, Iraq, Kuwait, Oman, Saudi Arabia, and UAE

Non-Arab fuel-endowed countries: Iran, Norway, and Venezuela

Arab Mediterranean: Egypt, Jordan, Lebanon, Morocco, Syria, and Tunisia

Rest of non-Arab world: Afghanistan, Albania, Argentina, Armenia, Australia, Austria, Azerbaijan, Bangladesh, Belarus, Belgium, Bhutan, Bolivia, Bosnia and Herzegovina, Brazil, Bulgaria, Cambodia, Canada, Chile, China, Colombia, Costa Rica, Croatia, Czech Republic, Denmark, Dominican Republic, Ecuador, El Salvador, Estonia, Fiji, Finland, France, Georgia, Germany, Greece, Guatemala, Guyana, Haiti, Honduras, Hungary, Iceland, India, Indonesia, Ireland, Israel, Italy, Jamaica, Japan, Kazakhstan, Kiribati, Korea (Rep.), Kyrgyz Republic, Lao PDR, Latvia, Lithuania, Macedonia (FYR), Malaysia, Maldives, Marshall Islands, Mauritius, Mexico, Micronesia, Moldova, Mongolia, Nepal, Netherlands, New Zealand, Nicaragua, Pakistan, Palau,

Panama, Papua New Guinea, Paraguay, Peru, Philippines, Poland, Portugal, Russian Federation, Samoa, Serbia, Singapore, Slovak Republic, Slovenia, Solomon Islands, Spain, Sri Lanka, Sweden, Switzerland, Thailand, Tonga, Turkey, Ukraine, United Kingdom, United States, Uruguay, Uzbekistan, Vanuatu, and Vietnam

Latin America: Argentina, Bolivia, Brazil, Chile, Colombia, Costa Rica, Dominican Republic, Ecuador, El Salvador, Guatemala, Honduras, Mexico, Nicaragua, Panama, Paraguay, Peru, and Uruguay

Southern Europe: Greece, Italy, Portugal, and Spain

# References

Acemoglu, Daron; Hassan, Tarek; and Tahoun, Ahmed. 2018. "The Power of the Street: Evidence From Egypt's Arab Spring." *Review of Financial Studies* 31(1): 1–42.

Acemoglu, Daron; Johnson, Simon; and Robinson, James. 2001. "The Colonial Origins of Comparative Development: An Empirical Investigation." *American Economic Review* 91(5): 1369–1401.

Adams, Richard H. Jr.; and Page, John. 2003. "Poverty, Inequality and Growth in Selected Middle East and North Africa Countries, 1980–2000." *World Development* 31(12): 2027–2048.

Aitken, Brian; and Harrison, Ann. 1999. "Do Domestic Firms Benefit from Direct Foreign Investment? Evidence from Venezuela." *American Economic Review* 89(3): 605–618.

Aizenman, Joshua; and Jinjarak, Yothin. 2009. "Globalization and Developing Countries—A Shrinking Tax Base?" *Journal of Development Studies* 45(5): 653–671.

Al Sayyad, Nezar. 2011. *Cairo: Histories of a City* (Cambridge, MA: Harvard University Press).

Angrist, Joshua; and Lavy, Victor. 1997. "The Effect of a Change in Language of Instruction on the Returns to Schooling in Morocco." *Journal of Labor Economics* 15(1): S48–S76.

Asea, Patrick K.; and Lahiri, Amartya. 1999. "The Precious Bane." *Journal of Economic Dynamics and Control* 23: 823–849.

Assaad, Ragui; and Zouari, Sami. 2003. "Estimating the Impact of Marriage and Fertility on the Female Labor Force Participation When Decisions Are Interrelated: Evidence from Urban Morocco." *Proceedings of the Middle East Economic Association* 5 (September).

Atkin, David; Khandelwal, Amit; and Osman, Adam. 2017. "Exporting and Firm Performance: Evidence from a Randomized Experiment." *Quarterly Journal of Economics* 132 (May): 551–615.

Balassa, Bela. 1980. "The Process of Industrial Development and Alternative Development Strategies." Princeton University International Finance Section, Essays in International Finance No. 141 (December).

Bardhan, Pranab K. 1971. "On Optimum Subsidy to a Learning Industry: An Aspect of the Theory of Infant Industry Protection." *International Economic Review* 12: 54–70.

Bassiouney, Reem. 2009. *Arabic Sociolinguistics: Topics in Diglossia, Gender, Identity, and Politics* (Washington, DC: Georgetown University Press).

Beck, Thorsten; Demirgüç-Kunt, Asli; and Merrouche, Ouarda. 2013. "Islamic vs. Conventional Banking: Business Model, Efficiency, and Stability." *Journal of Banking and Finance* 37(2): 433–447.

Bhagwati, Jagdish N. 1984. "Why Are Services Cheaper in the Poor Countries?" *Economic Journal* 94 (June): 279–286.

Bloom, David E.; and Williamson, Jeffrey G. 1998. "Demographic Transitions and Economic Miracles in Emerging Asia." *World Bank Economic Review* 12(3): 419–455.

Bloom, Nicholas; Eifert, Benn; Mahajan, Aprajit; McKenzie, David; and Roberts, John. 2013. "Does Management Matter? Evidence from India." *Quarterly Journal of Economics* 128(1): 1–51.

Branstetter, Lee; Lima, Francisco; Taylor, Lowell J.; and Venâncio, Ana. 2014. "Do Entry Regulations Deter Entrepreneurship and Job Creation? Evidence from Recent Reforms in Portugal." *Economic Journal* 124(577): 805–832.

Bulos, Nabih. 2017. "It's a Bird! It's a Plane! Therein Lies the Problem at Lebanon's International Airport." *Los Angeles Times* (January 22). www.latimes.com/world/middleeast/la-fg-lebanon-airport-birds-2017-story.html.

Bursztyn, Leonardo; González, Alessandra L.; and Yanagizawa-Drott, David. 2018. "Misperceived Social Norms: Female Labor Force Participation in Saudi Arabia." National Bureau of Economic Research Working Paper No. 24736 (June).

Chamlou, Nadereh; Muzi, Silvia; and Ahmed, Hanane. 2016. "The Determinants of Female Labor Force Participation in the MENA Region." In Nadereh Chamlou and Massoud Karshenas, eds., *Women, Work and Welfare in the Middle East and North Africa* (London: Imperial College Press).

Collier, Paul; and Gunning, Jan Willem. 1999. "Why Has Africa Grown Slowly?" *Journal of Economic Perspectives* 13(3): 3–22.

Das Gupta, Monica. 1987. "Selective Discrimination against Female Children in Rural Punjab, India." *Population and Development Review* 13(1): 77–100.

Dell, Melissa; and Olken, Benjamin. 2017. "The Development Effects of the Extractive Colonial Economy: The Dutch Cultivation System in Java." National Bureau of Economic Research Working Paper No. 24009 (November).

Delpech, Annette; Girard, François; Robine, Gérard; and Roumi, Muhammad. 1997. *Les Norias de L'Oronte* (Damascus: Institut Français de Damas).

Dettling, Lisa J. 2017. "Broadband in the Labor Market: The Impact of Residential High-Speed Internet on Married Women's Labor Force Participation." *ILR Review* 70(2): 451–482.

Devarajan, Shanta; and Mottaghi, Lili. 2017. "Meeting the Development Challenge for Refugees in Middle East and North Africa." *Middle East and North Africa Economic Monitor* (October). Washington, DC: World Bank.

Diop, Ndiame; and Ghali, Sofiane. 2012. "Are Jordan and Tunisia's exports becoming more technologically sophisticated? Analysis using highly disaggregated export databases." Middle East and North Africa Working Paper Series, no 54. Washington, DC: World Bank.

Diwan, Ishac; Keefer, Philip; and Schiffbauer, Marc. 2018. "Pyramid Capitalism: Cronyism, Regulation, and Firm Productivity in Egypt." *Review of International Organizations* (forthcoming).

Djankov, Simeon; La Porta, Rafael; Lopez-di-Silanes, Florencio; and Shleifer, Andrei. 2002. "The Regulation of Entry." *Quarterly Journal of Economics* 117(1): 1–37.

Duflo, Esther. 2001. "Schooling and Labor Market Consequences of School Construction in Indonesia: Evidence from an Unusual Policy Experiment." *American Economic Review* 91(4): 795–813.

Easterly, William. 2001. "The Middle Class Consensus and Economic Development." *Journal of Economic Growth* 6(4): 317–335.

Easterly, William; and Levine, Ross. 1997. "Africa's Growth Tragedy: Policies and Ethnic Divisions." *Quarterly Journal of Economics* 112(4): 1203–1250.

Ebenstein, Avraham. 2010. "The 'Missing Girls' of China and the Unintended Consequences of the One Child Policy." *Journal of Human Resources* 45(1): 87–115.

Egan, Mary Lou; and Mody, Ashoka. 1992. "Buyer-Seller Links in Export Development." *World Development* 20(3): 321–334.

Enami, Ali; Lustig, Nora; and Taqdiri, Alireza. 2016. "Fiscal Policy, Inequality, and Poverty in Iran: Assessing the Impact and Effectiveness of Taxes and Transfers on the Poor in the Developing World." Center for Global Development Working Paper No. 442 (November).

Engerman, Stanley L.; and Sokoloff, Kenneth L. 2002. "Factor Endowments, Inequality, and Paths of Development Among New World Economies." *Economia* 3 (Fall): 41–110.

Evans, David K.; and Popova, Anna. 2017. "Cash Transfers and Temptation Goods." *Economic Development and Cultural Change* 65(2): 189–221.

Faccio, Mara. 2006. "Politically Connected Firms." *American Economic Review* 96(1): 369–386.

Fajgelbaum, Pablo D.; and Gaubert, Cecile. 2018. "Optimal Spatial Policies, Geography and Sorting." National Bureau of Economic Research Working Paper No. 24632 (May).

Fakih, Ali; and Ghazalian, Pascal L. 2015. "Female Employment in MENA's Manufacturing Sector: the Implications of Firm-Related and National Factors." *Economic Change and Restructuring* 48(1): 37–69.

Feng, Ying; Lagakos, David; and Rauch, James E. 2018. "Unemployment and Development." National Bureau of Economic Research Working Paper No. 25171 (October).

Fields, Gary S.; and Fei, John C. H. 1978. "On Inequality Comparisons." *Econometrica* 46 (March): 303–316.

Fisman, Raymond; and Wang, Yongxiang. 2015. "The Mortality Cost of Political Connections." *Review of Economic Studies* 82(4): 1346–1382.

Frey, Bruno S.; and Stutzer, Alois. 2002. "What Can Economists Learn from Happiness Research?" *Journal of Economic Literature* 40(2): 402–435.

Gallup, John Luke; and Sachs, Jeffrey D. 2000. "Agriculture, Climate, and Technology: Why Are the Tropics Falling Behind?" *American Journal of Agricultural Economics* 82 (August): 731–737.

Gallup, John Luke; and Sachs, Jeffrey. 2001. "The Economic Burden of Malaria." *American Journal of Tropical Medicine and Hygiene* 64(1, 2)S: 85–96.

Gelb, Alan H. 1988. *Oil Windfalls: Blessing or Curse?* (New York: Oxford University Press).

Glewwe, Paul; and Muralidharan, Karthik. 2016. "Improving School Education Outcomes in Developing Countries: Evidence, Knowledge Gaps, and Policy Implications." In Eric Hanushek, Stephen Machin, and Ludger Woessmann, eds., *Handbook of the Economics of Education*, Vol. 5 (Amsterdam: North-Holland).

Grossman, Michael. 2006. "Education and Nonmarket Outcomes." In Eric Hanushek and Finis Welch, eds., *Handbook of the Economics of Education*, Vol. 1 (Amsterdam: North-Holland).

Gylvason, Thorvaldur. 2001. "Natural Resources, Education, and Economic Development." *European Economic Review* 45: 847–859.

Harrigan, Jane; and El-Said, Hamed. 2009. *Economic Liberalisation, Social Capital and Islamic Welfare Provision* (London: Palgrave Macmillan).

Henderson, Vernon. 2002. "Urban Primacy, External Costs, and Quality of Life." *Resource and Energy Economics* 24: 95–106.
International Monetary Fund. 2013. *Energy Subsidy Reform: Lessons and Implications* (Washington, DC: International Monetary Fund).
International Monetary Fund. 2017. "If Not Now, When? Energy Price Reform in Arab Countries." http://www.imf.org/en/Publications/Policy-Papers/Issues/2017/06/13/if-not-now-when-energy-price-reform-in-arab-countries.
Iqbal, Zafar; and Lewis, Mervyn K. 2014. "*Zakat* and the Economy." In M. Kabir Hassan and Mervyn K. Lewis, eds., *Handbook on Islam and Economic Life* (Cheltenham, UK: Edward Elgar).
Javorcik, Beata Smarzynska. 2004. "Does Foreign Direct Investment Increase the Productivity of Domestic Firms? In Search of Spillovers through Backward Linkages." *American Economic Review* 94(3): 605–627.
Jayachandran, Seema; and Lleras-Muney, Adriana. 2009. "Life Expectancy and Human Capital Investments: Evidence from Maternal Mortality Declines." *Quarterly Journal of Economics* 124(1): 349–397.
Kapiszewski, Andrezj. 2006. "Arab Versus Asian Migrant Workers in the GCC Countries." UN Department of Economic and Social Affairs, May 22. http://www.un.org/esa/population/meetings/EGM_Ittmig_Arab/P02_Kapiszewski.pdf.
Khwaja, Asim Ijaz; and Mian, Atif. 2005. "Do Lenders Favor Politically Connected Firms? Rent Provision in an Emerging Financial Market." *Quarterly Journal of Economics* 120(4): 1371–1411.
Klasen, Stephan; and Wink, Claudia. 2003. "'Missing Women': Revisiting the Debate." *Feminist Economics* 9(2–3): 263–299.
Kremer, Michael. 2002. "Pharmaceuticals and the Developing World." *Journal of Economic Perspectives* 16 (Fall): 67–90.
Lelieveld, Jos; et al. 2014. "Model Projected Heat Extremes and Air Pollution in the Eastern Mediterranean and Middle East in the Twenty-First Century." *Regional Environmental Change* 14: 1937–1949.
Lewis, W. Arthur. 1950. "The Industrialization of the British West Indies." *Caribbean Economic Review* (May).
Lewis, W. Arthur. 1978. *The Evolution of the International Economic Order* (Princeton, NJ: Princeton University Press).
Lleras-Muney, Adriana. 2005. "The Relationship between Education and Adult Mortality in the United States." *Review of Economic Studies* 72(1): 189–221.
Malthus, Thomas R. 1798. *An Essay on the Principle of Population* (London: J. Johnson).
Márquez-Ramos, Laura; and Martínez-Zarzoso, Inmaculada. 2014. "Trade in Intermediate Goods and Euro-Med Production Networks." *Middle East Development Journal* 6(2): 215–231.
Mason, Charles F.; and Polasky, Stephen. 2005. "What Motivates Membership in Non-Renewable Resource Cartels? The Case of OPEC." *Resource and Energy Economics* 27: 321–342.
Montenegro, Claudio E.; and Patrinos, Harry Anthony. 2014. "Comparable Estimates of Returns to Schooling Around the World." World Bank Policy Research Working Paper No. 7020 (September).
Murphy, Kevin M.; Shleifer, Andrei; and Vishny, Robert W. 1989. "Income Distribution, Market Size, and Industrialization." *Quarterly Journal of Economics* 104 (August): 537–564.

Naufal, George S. 2015. "The Economics of Migration in the Gulf Cooperation Council Countries." In Barry R. Chiswick and Paul W. Miller, eds., *Handbook of the Economics of International Migration* (Amsterdam: North-Holland).

Ponticelli, Jacopo; and Alencar, Leonardo S. 2016. "Court Enforcement and Firm Productivity: Evidence from a Bankruptcy Reform in Brazil." *Quarterly Journal of Economics* 131(3): 1365–1413.

Pritchett, Lant. 1997. "Divergence, Big Time." *Journal of Economic Perspectives* 11 (Summer): 3–17.

Psacharopoulos, George. 1991. *The Economic Impact of Education: Lessons for Policymakers* (San Francisco: ICS Press).

Rahman, Md. Mizanur. 2015. "Migrant Indebtedness: Bangladeshis in the GCC Countries." *International Migration* 53(6): 205–219.

Ranis, Gustav. 1984. "Typology in Development Theory: Retrospective and Prospects." In Moshe Syrquin, Lance Taylor, and Larry E. Westphal, eds., *Economic Structure and Performance* (Orlando, FL: Academic Press).

Rauch, James E. 1993. "Productivity Gains from Geographic Concentration of Human Capital: Evidence from the Cities." *Journal of Urban Economics* 34 (November): 380–400.

Rauch, James E. 2001. "Business and Social Networks in International Trade." *Journal of Economic Literature* 39 (December): 1177–1203.

Rauch, James E. 2005. "Getting the Properties Right to Secure Property Rights: Dixit's *Lawlessness and Economics*." *Journal of Economic Literature* 43 (June): 480–487.

Rauch, James E.; and Evans, Peter B. 2000. "Bureaucratic Structure and Bureaucratic Performance in Less Developed Countries." *Journal of Public Economics* 75 (January): 49–71.

Ravallion, Martin; Chen, Shaohua; and Sangraula, Prem. 2009. "Dollar a Day Revisited." *World Bank Economic Review* 23(2): 163–184.

Read, Jen'nan G. 2004. "Cultural Influences on Women's Labor Force Participation: The Arab-American Case." *International Migration Review* 38(1): 52–77.

Reynolds, Lloyd G. 1983. "The Spread of Economic Growth to the Third World." *Journal of Economic Literature* 21 (September): 941–980.

Rhee, Yung Whee; Ross-Larson, Bruce; and Pursell, Garry. 1984. *Korea's Competitive Edge: Managing the Entry into World Markets* (Baltimore: Johns Hopkins University Press).

Riedl, Arno; and Smeets, Paul. 2017. "Why Do Investors Hold Socially Responsible Mutual Funds?" *Journal of Finance* 72(6): 2505–2550.

Rijkers, Bob; Baghdadi, Leila; and Raballand, Gael. 2017. "Political Connections and Tariff Evasion: Evidence from Tunisia." *World Bank Economic Review* 31(2): 459–482.

Rodrik, Dani; Subramanian, Arvind; and Trebbi, Francesco. 2004. "Institutions Rule: The Primacy of Institutions Over Geography and Integration in Economic Development." *Journal of Economic Growth* 9(2): 131–165.

Salehi-Isfahani, Djavad. 2016. "Family Planning and Female Empowerment in Iran." In Nadereh Chamlou and Massoud Karshenas, eds., *Women, Work and Welfare in the Middle East and North Africa* (London: Imperial College Press).

Schoellman, Todd. 2012. "Education Quality and Development Accounting." *Review of Economic Studies* 79(1): 388–417.

Sen, Amartya. 1992. "Missing Women." *British Medical Journal* 304(March 7): 586–587.

Silva, Joana; Levin, Victoria; and Morgandi, Matteo. 2013. *Inclusion and Resilience: The Way Forward for Safety Nets in the Middle East and North Africa* (Washington, DC: World Bank).

Tybout, James R. 2000. "Manufacturing Firms in Developing Countries: How Well Do They Do, and Why?" *Journal of Economic Literature* 38(1): 11–44.

United Nations. 2015. *The World's Women 2015: Trends and Statistics*. Sales No. E.15. XVII.8, Statistical Annex, Annex Table 6.1. (New York: United Nations, Department of Economic and Social Affairs, Statistics Division).

United Nations Development Fund for Women. 2004. *Progress of Arab Women 2004*. http://www.unifem.org/attachments/products/Progress.Arab.Women__Chapter.3.pdf.

UN-Habitat. 2010. *Global Report on Human Settlements 2003*. Chapter 1, Revised and Updated Version (April). https://unhabitat.org/wp-content/uploads/2003/07/GRHS_2003_Chapter_01_Revised_2010.pdf.

van Wijnbergen, Sweder. 1984. "The 'Dutch Disease': A Disease After All?" *Economic Journal* 94(373): 41–55.

Versteegh, Kees. 2001. *The Arabic Language* (Edinburgh: Edinburgh University Press).

Voigtländer, Nico; and Voth, Hans-Joachim. 2013. "Gifts of Mars: Warfare and Europe's Early Rise to Riches." *Journal of Economic Perspectives* 27(4): 165–186.

United Nations Conference on Trade and Development. 2012. *Investment Country Profiles: Turkey*.

Wahba, Jackline. 2007. "Returns to Overseas Work Experience: The Case of Egypt." In Çaglar Özden and Maurice Schiff, eds., *International Migration, Economic Development and Policy* (Washington, DC: World Bank and Palgrave Macmillan).

Wahba, Jackline. 2014. "Immigration, Emigration, and the Labor Market in Jordan." In Ragui Assaad, ed., *The Jordanian Labour Market in the New Millennium* (Oxford: Oxford University Press).

World Bank. 1993. *World Development Report 1992: Development and the Environment* (Washington, DC: World Bank).

World Bank. 2004. *Unlocking the Employment Potential in the Middle East and North Africa* (Washington, DC: World Bank).

World Bank. 2007a. *Doing Business 2008* (Washington, DC: World Bank).

World Bank. 2007b. *Making the Most of Scarcity: Accountability for Better Water Results in the Middle East and North Africa* (Washington, DC: World Bank).

World Bank. 2012. *World Development Report 2013: Jobs* (Washington, DC: World Bank).

World Bank. 2013a. *Investing in Turbulent Times*. https://openknowledge.worldbank.org/handle/10986/20562.

World Bank. 2013b. *Jobs for Shared Prosperity: Time for Action in the Middle East and North Africa* (Washington, DC: World Bank).

World Bank. 2013c. *Opening Doors: Gender Equality and Development in the Middle East and North Africa* (Washington, DC: World Bank).

World Bank. 2014. *Turn Down the Heat: Confronting the New Climate Normal* (Washington, DC: World Bank).

World Bank. 2017. *Beyond Scarcity: Water Scarcity in the Middle East and North Africa*. MENA Development Series (Washington, DC: World Bank).

Yergin, Daniel. 1991. *The Prize: The Epic Quest for Oil, Money, and Power* (New York: Simon and Schuster).

Yoshino, M. Y.; and Lifson, Thomas B. 1986. *The Invisible Link: Japan's* Sogo Shosha *and the Organization of Trade* (Cambridge, MA: MIT Press).
Yousef, Tarik M. 2004. "The Murabaha Syndrome in Islamic Finance: Laws, Institutions, and Politics." In Clement M. Wilson and Rodney Wilson, eds., *The Politics of Islamic Finance* (Edinburgh: Edinburgh University Press).
Zhang, Junjie; and Mu, Quan. 2018. "Air Pollution and Defensive Expenditures: Evidence from Particulate-Filtering Facemasks." *Journal of Environmental Economics and Management*, in press.
Zhang, Xuelei; et al. 2016. "A Systematic Review of Global Desert Dust and Associated Human Health Effects." *Atmosphere* 7(12).

# Index

Note: Page numbers followed by *f*, *t*, and *b* refer to figures, tables, and boxes respectively.

ability bias, and rate of return to education, 98*b*
abortions
   difficulty of obtaining in Arab countries, 135
   sex-selective, 133–35
Acemoglu, Daron, 47*b*, 238–41, 240*t*
Adams, Richard, 147–49, 148*t*, 151, 152–53, 170
Afghanistan
   missing women in, 133, 134*t*
   refugees from, 161*t*
agricultural productivity
   climate differences and, 44–46, 45*f*
   high, as prerequisite for industrialization, 44, 47–48
agriculture
   income distribution, climate and, 47–48
   and water scarcity, 175–76
   *See also* land, arable, limited supply of
Ahmed, Hanane, 130
air pollution, 180–84
   GDP per capita and, 171, 180–82, 181*f*
   health effects of, 172, 180, 182–83, 183*t*, 252
   individuals' protective measures against, 183–84
   lack of success in reducing, 172
   measurement of, 180
   over-consumption of fuel and, 188–90, 207*b*, 210, 252, 253
   sources of, 180
air pollution, desert dust and, 180–81
   countries with high levels, 180–81
   difficulty of reducing, 183
   health effects of, 172, 182
   individuals' protective measures against, 183–84
   lack of success in reducing, 172
   policy recommendations on, 253
   as unrelated to GDP, 180
Aitken, Brian, 84–85
Aizenman, Joshua, 198, 199*f*
Alencar, Leonardo, 233
Algeria
   and air pollution, 180–81
   and Arab Spring, 29–32
   date of independence, 5*t*
   *de facto* workplace discrimination against women in, 129–30
   economic diversification efforts, 81–83
   education, instruction in colonial language, 102*t*, 103
   education quality in, 96*f*, 97
   energy subsidies in, 206*t*, 209*t*
   former colonial power in, 5*t*
   fuel reserves and GDP per capita, 80–81, 80*t*
   GDP per capita, 81–82
   GDP per capita changes, pre- and post-Arab Spring, 29–32, 31*t*
   and global warming, 192–93, 192*t*
   global warming damage, expected, 172–73
   greenfield FDI by sector, 89*t*
   greenfield FDI by source, 87*t*
   intensive growth, greater share of oil rents and, 76
   intensive growth, late onset of, 54, 55, 76
   life expectancy changes, pre- and post-Arab Spring, 30*t*
   as member of fuel-endowed countries group, 19–20
   military spending as share of GDP, 211*t*, 212–13
   missing women in, 133, 134*t*
   official name, 5*t*
   and OPEC, 78
   perceived corruption in, 226–27
   population, 21*t*
   population living in slums, 217*t*
   poverty headcount ratio in, 147–48
   share of fuel in merchandise exports, 80*t*, 81
   shrinking of public sector in, 130–31
   slow GDP per capita growth, causes of, 81–83
   water scarcity in, 173*t*
Anderson, Lisa, 131
Angola, and OPEC, 78–79, 79*t*
Angrist, Joshua, 101
Arab countries
   data on, scarcity before 1960, 35
   and desert climate, 171
   disaggregation of, need for, 17–18
   and Industrial Revolution, effect of, 35–36
   *See also* Arab Mediterranean countries; fuel-endowed Arab countries; sub-Saharan Arab countries
Arabic language
   as defining feature of Arab League countries, 1
   regional dialects, 3*b*
   spread of, 1–3
Arab League, member states, 1, 34*t*

Arab Mediterranean countries
  and Arab Spring, 30t, 31t, 32, 33
  births per woman, 1970-2016, 113-14, 114t
  carbon dioxide emissions in, 188-90, 190t
  characteristics of countries in group, 20-21
  contract enforcement efficiency in, 235, 235t
  countries included in group, 19f, 20-22, 34t
  denser population in, 21-22
  domestic violence in, 137-38, 137t
  electrical outages, 220-21, 220t
  electricity access, 219
  energy subsidies in, 195-96, 204-5, 206t, 208, 218-19
  Euro-Mediterranean Association Agreements with EU, 22, 68
  GDP per capita changes, 1970-2010, 26-28, 27t
  GDP per capita changes before vs. after Arab Spring, 29, 31t, 32-33
  gender gap in labor force participation, 125, 126t
  Gini index vs. comparison countries, 143-44, 144t
  GNI per capita, range of, 20t, 21
  greenfield FDI by destination and sector, 86-87, 88, 89t
  greenfield FDI by destination and source, 86-87, 87t
  and greenhouse gases, 190-91, 191t
  growing importance of exports to economy, 64-65
  growth rate, 1970-2010, 26-28, 27t
  infrastructure quality for business in, 196, 220t
  intensive growth, government aid in creating, 56
  intensive growth sources, 55
  and ISI, turn from, 66
  life expectancy, changes 1970-2010, 24-25, 25t, 28
  life expectancy, changes before vs. after Arab Spring in, 29, 30t
  manufactured exports, upgrading of, 82-83
  markets for export, 67, 67t
  military spending as share of GDP, 211t, 213
  non-oil manufacturing as share of greenfield FDI, 88, 89t
  percent of Arab land area, 21-22
  population of, 21-22, 21t
  population, changing dependency ratios in, 117-18, 118t, 119
  population growth, 1970-2016, 113-14, 113t
  population living in slums, 196, 216, 217t, 218-19
  population projections for 2020-2066, 114-15, 115t
  potential benefits of manufacturing FDI for, 88-90
  progress 1970-2010, 28
  shift to manufactures exports, 82-83
  starting a business, time and cost of, 231t, 232
  tariffs, lowering of, 198
  transition to exporter of manufactures, 66
  urbanization in, 197, 197t
  water scarcity in, 173t, 220t
  water tariffs vs. comparison countries, 174-75, 175t
  and WTO, 63-64
  *See also* education in Arab Mediterranean countries; health in Arab Mediterranean countries; import-substituting industrialization in Arab Mediterranean and Turkey (ISI); industrialization through international trade in Arab Mediterranean and Turkey
Arabs, ethnic, 1-2
Arab Spring
  and Arab Mediterranean countries, 30t, 31t, 32, 33
  in Bahrain, 29-32
  and break in socioeconomic development trends, 6
  effect on HDI, 29, 30t, 31t, 33
  and fuel-endowed Arab countries, 29-32, 30t, 31t, 33
  and Human Development Indices, 29, 30t, 31t, 33
  in Libya, 29-32
  and sub-Saharan Arab countries, 29, 30t, 31t, 33
Arab state boundaries, establishment of, 4
Arab UN member states
  names, official and short versions, 4, 5t
  population of, 1, 21t
Arab world
  boundaries of, 2-3
  population of, 1
  range of HDI vs. Latin America, 17, 17t, 21
  states included in, 1, 2f
Armenians, and trade diasporas, 41
artisanal core(s)
  development of, in era of extensive growth, 40
  in Fez, Morocco, 40f, 40
Asea, Patrick, 82
Assaad, Ragui, 130-31
al-Assad, Bashar, 6
Atkin, David, 70-71
automobile industry
  required network of suppliers for, 62-63
  in Turkey, lack of necessary domestic suppliers for, 63

backward linkages from foreign subsidiaries, in manufacturing vs. resource extraction and processing, 86t
Baghdadi, Leila, 246-49, 248t

INDEX    291

Bahrain
    and abortion, 135
    and air pollution, 180–81
    and Arab Spring, 29–32
    date of independence, 5t
    education in, instruction in colonial
        language, 102t
    energy subsidies in, 206t, 209t
    failure of price levels to rise with income, 14
    former colonial power in, 5t
    fuel reserves and GDP per capita, 80t
    GDP per capita changes, pre- and post-Arab
        Spring, 29–32, 31t
    greenfield FDI by sector, 86t, 89t
    greenfield FDI by source, 87t
    and greenhouse gases, 188, 189f
    intensive growth, sources of, 55
    life expectancy changes, pre- and post-Arab
        Spring, 30t
    as member of fuel-endowed countries
        group, 19–20
    migrant residents, 156, 156t, 157t
    military spending as share of GDP, 211t
    official name of, 5t
    and OPEC, 79t
    population of, 21t
    share of fuel in merchandise exports, 80t, 81
    water desalination in, 174
    water scarcity in, 173t
Balassa, Bela, 62–63
Bangladesh
    migrants to GCC countries, 156–57
    missing women in, 134t
banks, Islamic, 164–66b
Barcelona Process, 22
Bardhan, Pranab, 60
Bassiouney, Reem, 103
Beck, Thorsten, 165–66b
Ben Ali, Zine El Abidine, 246–47, 249
Bhagwati, Jagdish, 11–12
Bill and Melinda Gates Foundation, 108
Bloom, David, 119
Bloom, Nicholas, 75
BP Statistical Review, 19–20
Branstetter, Lee, 232–33, 246
Brunei, and OPEC, 79t
Bulos, Nabih, 186–87b
bureaucracies
    competent staffing, need for, 223
    and difficulty of controlling corruption, 249
    See also corruption
bureaucracy in fuel-endowed Arab countries
    bloating of, 226
    and bureaucratic toll booths, 226, 228b
    inefficiency of, as perceived corruption, 223–
        24, 226, 228b
bureaucratic inefficiency
    decline with increased GDP per capita, 226–27
    as perceived corruption, 223–24, 226, 228b

bureaucratic toll booths
    in Egypt, 246
    in fuel-endowed Arab countries, 226, 228b
Bursztyn, Leonardo, 255–56
business. See contract enforcement efficiency;
    Doing Business ranking (World Bank);
    infrastructure quality for business; starting
    a business, time and cost of

cancers, DALY per 100,000 population,
    103–6, 105t
capital equipment
    Arab Mediterranean countries ongoing need
        to import, 57–58
    exports to pay for, in industrialization
        through international trade, 57–58
carbon dioxide emissions
    efforts to reduce, 187–88
    GDP per capita and, 188–90, 189f, 190t
    over-consumption of fuel and, 252
cartel
    definition of, 78
    OPEC as, 78
cash payments
    benefits of replacing subsidies with, 163, 252–53
    logistics of delivering, 252–53
Chad
    income gap with industrialized countries,
        53f, 54
    as refugee host, 159t, 160
Chamlou, Nadereh, 130
charity in Muslim countries
    social services provided by religious
        organizations, 166
    zakat, 164b, 164
Chen, Shaohua, 145
child mortality rate, urbanization and,
    201–3, 202t
China
    air pollution in, 182–84
    and greenhouse gas emissions, 188–90
    missing women in, 133–35, 134t
    One Child Policy, 133–35
city growth. See urbanization
climate
    and agricultural productivity, 44–46, 45f
    and distribution of agricultural
        income, 47–48
Collier, Paul, 18
Colombia, and OPEC, 79t
colonial rule in Arab world, 4, 5t
    and Arab state boundaries, 4
    decolonization, 4
    and education, language of instruction in,
        102–3, 102t
Comoros
    as Arab League member, 1
    date of independence, 5t
    domestic violence in, 137t

Comoros (*cont.*)
    education in, instruction in colonial language, 102t
    former colonial power in, 5t
    GDP per capita changes, pre- and post-Arab Spring, 31t
    intensive growth, lack of, 55
    life expectancy changes, pre- and post-Arab Spring, 30t
    as member of sub-Saharan Arab countries group, 18
    official name, 5t
    population of, 21t
    population living in slums, 217t
    tourism in, 71–72
    water scarcity in, 173t
constant base-year units, 15b
constant returns to scale, 36
consumers, high-income, demand for high-quality goods, 68
contract enforcement efficiency, 233–36, 235t
    economic importance of, 233
    limited improvement in, 235
    vs. reputation, as check on businesses' misbehavior, 235–36
controlling interest, definition of, 84
corruption
    definition of, 224–25
    difficulty of controlling, 249
    measurement of, 224–25
    strategies to control, 223
corruption, perceived
    bureaucratic inefficiency as factor in, 223–24, 226–27, 227f, 228b
    GDP per capita and, 223–24, 226–27, 227f
    high levels in Arab countries, 223–24, 225f, 225–26
    measurement of, 224–25
    prevalence of politically connected firms and, 237
Corruption Perceptions Index (CPI), 224–25
    vs. GDP per capita, 225f, 225–26
country groups, 33, 34t
    *See also* Arab Mediterranean countries; fuel-endowed Arab countries; Gulf Cooperation Council (GCC); Middle East and North Africa (MENA); sub-Saharan Arab countries
CPI. *See* Corruption Perceptions Index
current units of account, 15b

Dell, Melissa, 52
Demirgüç-Kunt, Asli, 165–66b
demographic transition
    and decline in labor force participation, 127
    definition of, 112–13
    fall in birth rates, theories on, 115–17
    incomplete, definition of, 112–13

demographic transition in Arab countries, 112–19
    and age structure changes, 117–19, 118t
    and demographic dividend, 119
    and dependency ratio changes, 117–19, 118t
    as incomplete, 113–14
dependent variable, in multiple regression analysis, 148–49b
desalination, 174
desert dust. *See* air pollution, desert dust and
Dettling, Lisa, 131
Devarajan, Shanta, 160–61
developing countries, non-MENA, FDI in MENA countries, 87–88, 87t
developmental lag of Arab countries, 35–44
    capture of mineral resource earnings by foreigners and, 35–36
    lack of capacity for primary product exports, 52
    and lack of necessary prerequisites for industrialization, 35–36, 42–51
    limited supply of arable land and, 35–36
    as result of later and slower intensive growth, 54
difference-in-difference technique, 92–93b, 92t, 101, 116–17, 232–33
Diop, Ndiame, 71
Disability Adjusted Life Years (DALY)
    DALY in Arab countries per 100,000 population, by disease, 103–6, 105t, 107t
    definition and calculation of, 104–5b
    for unsafe water and sanitation, 178, 179t
diseases, tropical, and agricultural productivity, 44–45
diseases, tropical, in sub-Saharan Arab countries
    as drag on socioeconomic performance, 18, 103–4
    as health problem, 103–6, 105t
    success in controlling, vs. non-Arab sub-Saharan countries, 103–4, 105–6
Diwan, Ishac, 241–46, 244t
Djankov, Simeon, 229, 230f, 232
Djibouti
    and air pollution, 180–81
    date of independence, 5t
    education, instruction in colonial language, 102t
    energy subsidies in, 206t, 208, 209t
    former colonial power in, 5t
    GDP per capita changes, pre- and post-Arab Spring, 31t
    and global warming, 192t
    infrastructure quality for business, 220t
    intensive growth, lack of, 55
    Islamic banking in, 165b
    life expectancy changes, pre- and post-Arab Spring, 30t
    low malaria index, 18
    as member of sub-Saharan Arab countries group, 18
    official name, 5t

population, 21t
population living in slums, 217t
urban primacy in, 203, 204
water scarcity in, 173t
*Doing Business* ranking (World Bank)
   and bureaucratic inefficiency as perceived corruption, 226–27, 227f, 228b
   data on contract enforcement efficiency, 233–36
   data on time and cost of starting a business, 229–33
   *See also* contract enforcement efficiency; starting a business, time and cost of
domestic violence, 136–38, 137t
   scarcity of data on, 121–22
drinking water services, basic
   ability of Arab countries to provide, 172, 176f, 176–77
   World Bank definition of, 176–77
   *See also* water, safe, access to
Dubai, economic diversification efforts, 81
Duflo, Esther, 92–93b, 92t
Dutch Disease, 82–83

Easterly, William, 18, 143–44
Ebenstein, Avraham, 133–35
economics, as dismal science, 37–38b
Ecuador, and OPEC, 78–79, 79t
education
   as contributor to human development, 93–94
   effect on per capita incomes, 93–94
   and health, as mutually reinforcing, 111–12b, 256
   as investment in human capital, 93–94
   tertiary, cost and social return vs. secondary or primary education, 98b
   *See also* female school enrollment
education, language of instruction in Arab countries, 100–3
   and bilingualism as goal, 102–3
   and English or French as language of business, 101
   before independence, 100
   instruction in colonial language, 102–3, 102t
   switch to Arabic, effect on return to education, 100–1
education, rate of return to, 94–97
   adjusting for ability bias, 98b
   for Arab countries and comparison groups, 94–95, 94t, 97
   definition of, 94
   effect of switch to Arabic instruction on, 100–3
   and private vs. social returns, 98b
   questionable precision of values, 99b
   separation of basic quality and country-specific level of rewards, 95–97, 96f
   social return, and human capital externality, 98b
education in Arab countries
   lack of data after 2010, 29
   regional Arabic dialects as issue in, 3b
   success in increasing access to, 91
   *See also* schooling
education in Arab countries, tertiary level
   high cost vs. secondary or primary education, 98b
   low rate of return to education vs. comparison groups, 94–95, 94t
   male-female enrollment ratios in, 122, 123t, 124–25
   need for higher student costs in, 99–100
   over-production of graduates, 95, 97
   overspending on, 91, 99–100
   policy recommendations on, 253–54
   technical subjects, language of instruction for, 103
education in Arab Mediterranean countries
   average years of schooling, 1970-2010, 25–26, 26t, 28
   instruction in colonial language, 102–3, 102t
   male-female enrollment ratios, 122–25, 123t
   mean years of schooling, 20t, 21
   quality of, 96f, 97
   rate of return to education vs. comparison groups, 94–95, 94t, 97
   spending ratios by level, 99, 100t
education index of HDI, 6
   measures used in, 7
   *See also* schooling
education in fuel-endowed Arab countries
   average years of schooling, 1970-2010, 25–26, 26t, 28
   instruction in colonial language, 102t
   male-female enrollment ratios, 122–25, 123t
   mean years of schooling, 20t, 21
   quality of, 91, 96f, 97
   rate of return to education vs. comparison groups, 97
   spending ratios by level, 99, 100t
education in Iran
   quality of, 91
   spending ratios by level, 100t
   success in increasing access to, 91
education in sub-Saharan Arab countries
   average years of schooling, 1970-2010, 25–26, 26t, 28
   instruction in colonial language, 102–3, 102t
   male-female enrollment ratios, 122–25, 123t
   mean years of schooling, 20t, 21
   quality of, 91, 96f, 97
   rate of return to education vs. comparison groups, 94–95, 94t, 97
   spending ratios by level, 99, 100t
education in Turkey
   quality of, 91, 96f, 97
   rate of return to education vs. comparison groups, 94–95, 94t, 100t
   spending ratios by level, 99, 100t
   success in increasing access to, 91

education quality
  correlation with productivity level of country, 96–97
  measure by returns to schooling of immigrants, 95–97, 96f
Egan, Mary Lou, 69
Egypt
  air pollution in, 180–81, 181f, 182–83, 184f
  Arab-owned hotels in, small number of, 75
  and Arab Spring, 6, 16b, 16t, 32
  bureaucratic toll booths in, 246
  date of independence, 5t
  *de facto* workplace discrimination against women in, 129–30
  domestic violence in, 137t, 138
  education, free tuition as constitutional right, 99–100
  education, instruction in colonial language, 102t
  education quality in, 96f, 97
  energy subsidies in, 206t, 209t, 210
  energy subsidy preferential treatment for politically connected firms, 243–45, 244t
  expected global warming damage in, 172–73
  exports of manufactures relative to GDP, 64–65, 65t, 66
  and female genital mutilation, 135–36
  female labor force participation in, 129–30, 255–56
  foreign aid from GCC countries, 152
  former colonial power in, 5t
  and global warming, 192–93, 192t, 193t
  government promotion of first stage ISI, 59
  greenfield FDI by sector, 88, 89t
  greenfield FDI by source, 87t
  HDI, calculation of, 7–9
  HDI data, 2015, 7, 7t
  HDI rating, 10–11
  and health, increased awareness of, 110–11, 111f
  import-substituting industrialization in, 61–62, 63
  infrastructure quality for business, 220t
  intensive growth, as product of industrialization, 55, 61–62
  intensive growth, late onset of, 54, 55
  life expectancy changes, pre- and post-Arab Spring, 30t, 32
  and manager-entrepreneurs, shortage of, 75
  manufacturing assistance from foreign buyers, effect of, 70–71
  markets for exports, 67, 67t
  as member of Arab Mediterranean countries group, 20–21
  migrants from, countries hosting, 152, 153t
  migrants from, return with skills and contacts, 153, 154t
  military spending as share of GDP, 211t
  missing women in, 133, 134t
  non-tariff measures (NTMs), selective enforcement of, 242–43, 244t, 245, 246
  official name, 5t
  and OPEC, 79t
  population, 21t
  population living in slums, 216, 217t
  poverty headcount ratio in, 147–48
  price indices, 2008-2014, 16b, 16t
  primary product exports, 52
  ranking by HDI vs. GNI per capita, 10–11
  remittances, sources of, 151–52, 153t
  remittances received, ratio to GDP, 151, 151t
  shrinking of public sector in, 130–31
  slums in, 214
  tariff reductions in, 242–43
  tourism as proportion of exports, 72t
  tourism receipts vs. manufactures exports, 72, 73t
  tourism to, Arab Spring and, 73–75, 74f
  urbanization in, 197, 197t, 203–4
  urban primacy, as excessive, 195, 203–4
  urban primacy, policy recommendations on, 254–55
  water scarcity in, 173t
  *See also* politically connected firms in Egypt
Egyptian GDP per capita
  changes, pre- and post-Arab Spring, 31t, 32–33
  decline after Arab Spring, 16b, 16t
  growth in, 249
  real vs. current, 2008-2014, 16b, 16t
Eifert, Benn, 75
electrical outages, 219–21, 220t
El-Said, Hamed, 166
Enami, Ali, 208–9
energy subsidies, 204–10
  computing of, 205, 207b
  for electricity, 195–96, 204–5, 206t, 208
  as large share of government spending, 195–96
  and lost government revenue, 205–8, 218–19
  means of paying for, 205–8
  and opportunity costs, 207b
  and over-consumption, 207b, 210, 252, 253
  as percent of GDP, 204–5, 206t, 208, 209t
  as percent of government revenues, 204–5, 206t
  for petroleum, 188–90, 195–96, 204–5, 206t, 208
energy subsidies, reduction of
  benefits of, 252, 253
  Iranian strategy for, 195–96, 252
  political difficulty of, 195–96, 208–9, 252
Engel's Law, 47
Engerman, Stanley, 47–48, 143–44
environmental problems, three types of, 171–72
  *See also* air pollution; greenhouse gases; municipal wastes; sanitation access; water, safe, access to

INDEX 295

Equatorial Guinea, and OPEC, 78
Erdoğan, Recep, 63
Esfahan, Iran, cathedral ceiling in new Julfa
    Quarter, 41, 42f
Ethiopia
    income gap with industrialized countries,
        53f, 54
    as refugee host, 159t, 160
Euro-Mediterranean Association
    Agreements, 22, 68
    and "rules of origin" (RoOs), 68
European Union
    as market for Arab Mediterranean and
        Turkish manufactures, 67, 67t
    migrants in, source countries of, 152, 153t
    as source of FDI in MENA, 86t
    as source of remittances, 151–52, 153t
Evans, David, 163
explanatory variable, in multiple regression
    analysis, 148–49b
extensive growth, definition of, 36
extensive growth in preindustrial
    economies, 36–42
    development of specialization, 39–40
    development of states to ensure
        security, 40–41
    development of towns and artisanal
        cores, 40–41
    increased total factor productivity required
        for, 36–37
    and limited supply of high-quality
        land, 36–38
    and long-distance trade, development of, 41
    and Malthusian equilibrium, 37–38b
    and preconditions for Industrial
        Revolution, 42
    and technological innovation, 38–39b, 38

Fajgelbaum, Pablo, 254–55
Faccio, Mara, 236–37
factory production, large market needed for
    industrialization, 48f, 48–49
Fakih, Ali, 129–30
FDI. See foreign direct investment
female genital mutilation (FGM), 135–36, 136f
female health issues
    domestic violence, 136–38, 137t
    female genital mutilation (FGM),
        135–36, 136f
    health care neglect vs. males, 133–35
    obesity rates, 108–11, 110t, 256
    survival gap (missing women), 132–35, 134t
female labor force participation (FLFP), 125–32
    benefits of, 132
    and child care services, 130–31
    definition of, 125
    demographic transition and, 127
    gap vs. comparison countries, 125–27, 126t
    gender gap in, 125–28, 126t, 128t
    increased school enrollment and, 127
    Islam and, 127–29, 128t
    for married vs. single women, 129, 130–32
    overall increase in, 126t, 127
    policy recommendations on, 255–56
    and public sector reductions, 130–31
    in public vs. private sector, 130–31
    social pressure and, 129–30, 131–32,
        255–56
    and telecommuting, 131
    workplace discrimination and, 129–30
female school enrollment
    benefits of, 132
    gender gaps in, 122–25, 123t
    and reduced female labor force
        participation, 127
female survival gap (missing women), 121–22,
    132–35, 134t
Feng, Ying, 166–70
fertility
    births per woman in Arab countries, 1970-
        2016, 113–14, 114t
    drops in, and closing of gender gaps, 121
FGM. See female genital mutilation
FLFP. See female labor force participation
food production
    increased total factor productivity required
        for increase in, 36–37
    and limited supply of high-quality
        land, 36–38
    and Malthusian equilibrium, 37–38b
    necessary increase with population, 36–37
    preindustrial technological innovations,
        36–38, 38–39b
food subsidies
    benefits of replacing with cash payments, 163
    and obesity, 110–11, 163, 252
foreign direct investment (FDI)
    benefits for domestic businesses, 84–85
    definition of, 84
    manufacturing technical support
        accompanying, 84–85
    and total factor productivity, 84–85
foreign direct investment in fuel-endowed Arab
    countries, 84–90
    and capital and technology to initiate oil and
        gas exports, 84
    FDI benefits for non-oil manufacturing vs.
        resource and oil-manufacturing, 86t
    greenfield FDI by destination and sector, 89t
    greenfield FDI by destination and source,
        86–87, 87t
    oil and gas production as largest purpose for
        developed countries, 87–88
    ongoing interest in, 84
France
    colonial rule in Arab world, 4
    time and cost of starting a business in,
        229, 230f

fuel-endowed Arab countries
 and Arab Spring, 29–32, 30t, 31t, 33
 births per woman, 1970-2016, 113–14, 114t
 carbon dioxide emissions in, 188–90, 190t
 characteristics of countries in group, 18–20
 contract enforcement efficiency in, 235, 235t
 countries included in group, 19f, 19–20, 21–22, 34t
 economic diversification efforts, 81–82, 159
 electrical outages, 219–21, 220t
 electricity access, 219
 energy subsidies in, 204–5, 206t, 208, 218–19
 fuel exports before World War I, 52
 fuel reserves and GDP per capita, 80–81, 80t
 GDP per capita, causes of slow growth in, 82–83
 GDP per capita changes, 1970-2010, 26–28, 27t
 GDP per capita changes before vs. after Arab Spring, 29, 31t
 gender gap in labor force participation, 125, 126t, 127
 Gini index vs. comparison countries, 143–44, 144t
 GNI per capita, range of, 20t, 21
 greenfield FDI by sector, 88, 89t
 and greenhouse gases, 187–88, 190–91, 191t
 growth rate, 1970-2010, 26–28, 27t
 high incomes without HDI increase, 10–11
 intensive growth, as result of capture of rents from oil and gas, 55
 intensive growth, fuel reserves as source of, 80–81
 intensive growth, government aid in creating, 56
 life expectancy, changes 1970-2010, 24–25, 25t, 28
 life expectancy, changes before vs. after Arab Spring in, 29–32, 30t
 migrant workers in, and average income, 29–32
 migrant workers in, and price levels, 14
 military spending as share of GDP, 211t, 212–13
 negotiation of shared oil rents, 77
 non-oil manufacturing as share of greenfield FDI, 88, 89t
 and oil curse, 18, 226
 oil rents, reason for large size of, 77
 perceived corruption in, 223–24, 225f, 225–26, 228b
 population of, 21–22, 21t
 population, changing dependency ratios in, 117–18, 118t, 119
 population growth, 1970-2016, 113–14, 113t
 population living in slums, 196, 216, 217t
 population projections for 2020-2066, 114–15, 115t
 progress 1970-2010, 28

rents on oil-bearing lands, capture by foreigners prior to 1950, 52
 services as promising sector for, 81
 slow economic growth in, 27t, 28
 starting a business, time and cost of, 231t, 232
 urbanization in, 196, 197t
 water scarcity in, 173–74, 173t, 220t
 water tariffs vs. comparison countries, 174–75, 175t
 *See also* bureaucracy in fuel-endowed Arab countries; education in fuel-endowed Arab countries; foreign direct investment in fuel-endowed Arab countries; health in fuel-endowed Arab countries; intensive growth in fuel-endowed Arab countries and Iran
fuel exports, as source of intensive growth, 56

Gabon, and OPEC, 78–79, 79t
Gallup, John Luke, 18, 44–45, 47b
Gaubert, Cecile, 254–55
GCC. *See* Gulf Cooperation Council
GDP
 as better reflection of productivity than GNI, 13–14, 22–23
 defined, 13–14
 and GNI, close tracking of, 13–14
GDP per capita
 and air pollution, 171, 180–82, 181f
 as average that conceals inequality, 139
 and greenhouse gases, 171–72, 188–90, 189f, 190t
 growth rate, difficulty of increasing, 251
 measuring in constant vs. current units, 14–16b
 and municipal wastes, 171–72, 185f, 185
 nominal (not adjusted for inflation), 14–16b
 and perceived corruption, 223–24, 225f, 225–27, 227f
 price level by, 9–10b, 13f
 vs. price levels (2015), 13f, 13–14
 and safe water access, 171, 176f, 176–77
 and sanitation access, 171, 177f, 177–78
 slow growth in sub-Saharan countries, 18
GDP per capita, real, 14–16b
 base year for, 15b
 as better indication of living standard, 14–15b
 conversion from nominal GDP to, 15–16b
GDP per capita changes 1970-2010 (before Arab Spring)
 in Arab Mediterranean countries, 26–28, 27t
 in fuel-endowed Arab countries, 26–28, 27t
 in sub-Saharan Arab countries, 26–28, 27t
GDP per capita changes before vs. after Arab Spring
 in Arab Mediterranean countries, 29, 31t, 32–33
 in fuel-endowed Arab countries, 29, 31t
 in sub-Saharan Arab countries, 29, 31t

gender gaps
  in female labor force participation, 125–28, 126t, 128t
  in female survival rates, 121–22
  fertility decline as opportunity to close, 121
  in school enrollment, 122–25, 123t
gender parity index, 122
General Agreement on Tariffs and Trade (GATT), 63–64
Germany, as refugee host, 159t, 160
Ghali, Sofiane, 71
Ghazalian, Pascal, 129–30
Gini indices
  for Arab countries, Turkey and Iran vs. comparison groups, 143–44, 144t
  calculation of, 142–43b, 142f, 143
  as measure of income inequality, 139, 141
  scale of 1-100, 141
Glewwe, Paul, 253–54
global warming, 191–94
  and heat waves, 172–73, 193–94, 193t
  public's poor understanding of, 171–72
  and sea level rise, 172–73, 192–93, 192t
  uncertainty in forecasts of, 191
GNI (Gross National Income)
  calculation of, 7
  and GDP, close tracking of, 13–14
  GDP as better reflection of productivity than, 13–14, 22–23
  as measure of income index of HDI, 7
GNI per capita
  for Arab Mediterranean countries, 20t, 21
  Arab world vs. Latin America, 17, 17t, 21
  country ranking by, vs. ranking by HDI, 10–11
  for fuel-endowed countries, 20t, 21
  for sub-Saharan Arab countries, 20t, 21
González, Alessandra, 255–56
goods, equalized price across countries, 11–12, 12–13b
goods arbitrage, international, 12b
government
  difference-in-difference technique of evaluating interventions by, 92–93b, 92t, 101, 116–17
  responsibilities of, 223
  See also bureaucracies; corruption
government revenue
  income taxes and, 198–200, 199f
  new sources, transition to, 195, 198–200, 199f
  seigniorage (inflation tax) and, 198–200, 199f
  tariffs and, 198–200, 199f
  value-added tax (VAT) and, 198–200
government role in creating intensive growth
  and costs of second-stage ISI, 63
  legal regimes friendly to high-quality manufacturing, 68–69
  by renegotiation of oil and gas contracts, 56
  subsidies in, 60–61
  by tariffs protecting domestic industries, 56, 59–61
government spending
  demands on, 195
  energy subsidies as large share of, 195–96, 197–98
  military spending as large share of, 195–96, 197–98
  urbanization and, 197–98, 200–1
  See also energy subsidies; military spending; urban primacy
Great Britain, and Industrial Revolution, 35–36, 42–43, 44
greenhouse gases, 187–91
  carbon dioxide as, 187–88
  efforts to reduce, 187–88
  GDP per capita and, 171–72, 188–90, 189f, 190t
  and global warming, 187–88
  relatively small contribution of Arab countries to, 190–91, 191t
  See also global warming
Gross National Income. See GNI
growth, extensive vs. intensive, 36
growth rate, 1970-2010 (before Arab Spring)
  in Arab Mediterranean vs. Latin American countries, 26–28, 27t
  in fuel-endowed Arab countries, 26–28, 27t
  in sub-Saharan Arab countries vs. other sub-Saharan countries, 26–28, 27t
Gulf Cooperation Council (GCC)
  and air pollution, 181–82
  countries in, 33, 34t
  economic diversification efforts, 159
  failure of price levels to rise with income, 14
  FDI in Arab Mediterranean countries, 88–90
  FDI in MENA countries, 87–88
  foreign aid to Arab countries, 152
  greenfield FDI by destination and sector, 86–87, 89t
  greenfield FDI by destination and source, 86–88, 87t
  and greenhouse gases, 172, 188, 189f
  as group with fuel-endowed countries, 21
  high standard of living in, 81–82
  and income inequality, difficulty of comparing, 143–44
  as market for Jordan's exports, 67
  military spending as share of GDP, 212–13
  native residents, employment largely in public sector, 157–58, 158f, 170
  population living in slums, 218–19
  tourism to Lebanon, 72–73
Gulf Cooperation Council, migrant residents in
  employment largely in private sector, 157–58, 158f
  large number of, 143–44, 156, 156t
  remittances from, 151–52, 153t
  sources of, 152, 153t, 156, 157t

Gunning, Jan Willem, 18
Gupta, Monica Das, 133–35
Gylvason, Thorvaldur, 82

Hariri, Rafiq, 155b, 155f
Harrigan, Jane, 166
Harrison, Ann, 84–85
Hassan, Tarek, 238–41, 240t
HDI. See Human Development Index
health
   air pollution and, 172, 180, 182–83, 183t, 252
   and education, as mutually reinforcing, 111–12b, 256
   global warming and, 193, 194
   See also sanitation access; water, safe, access to
health in Arab countries, 103–11
   DALY per 100,000 population, by disease, 104–6, 105t, 107t
   improvements in, and demographic transition, 112–13
   increased awareness of, 110–11, 111f
   pharmaceutical availability and, 106–8, 109t
health in Arab Mediterranean countries
   DALY per 100,000 population, by disease, 103–6, 105t, 107t
   disease burden from unsafe water and sanitation, 178, 179t
   health effects of air pollution in, 182, 183t
   heart disease and, 108–10
   obesity and, 108–10, 110t
   success in reducing infectious and parasitic diseases, 106
   See also life expectancy in Arab Mediterranean countries
health index of HDI, 6
   life expectancy as measure of, 7
   See also life expectancy
health in fuel-endowed Arab countries
   DALY per 100,000 population, by disease, 103–6, 105t, 107t
   disease burden from unsafe water and sanitation, 178, 179t
   health effects of air pollution in, 182–83, 183t
   heart disease and, 106
   obesity and, 108–10, 110t
   See also life expectancy in fuel-endowed Arab countries
health in Iran
   air pollution and, 182, 183t
   DALY per 100,000 population, by disease, 103–6, 105t, 107t
   heart disease and, 105–6, 108–10
   infectious and parasitic diseases and, 106
   obesity and, 108–10, 110t
health in sub-Saharan Arab countries
   DALY per 100,000 population, by disease, 103–6, 105t, 107t
   disease burden from unsafe water and sanitation, 178, 179t

   health effects of air pollution in, 182–83, 183t
   obesity and, 110t
   pharmaceutical availability and, 106–8, 109t
   tropical diseases and, 103–6, 105t
   See also diseases, tropical, in sub-Saharan Arab countries; life expectancy in sub-Saharan Arab countries
health in Turkey
   air pollution and, 182, 183t
   DALY per 100,000 population, by disease, 103–6, 105t, 107t
   disease burden from unsafe water and sanitation, 178, 179t
   heart disease and, 105–6, 108–10
   infectious and parasitic diseases and, 106
   obesity and, 108–10, 110t
heart disease in Arab countries
   DALY per 100,000 population, 103–6, 105t
   as greater problem than in comparison groups, 105–6
   obesity and, 108–11
heat wave days, global warming and, 172–73, 193–94, 193t
Henderson, Vernon, 197–98, 201–3
human capital, education and, 93–94, 98b
Human Development Index (HDI), 6–15
   and Arab Spring, effect of, 29, 30t, 31t, 33
   calculation of, 7–9
   changes 1970-2010, in Arab Mediterranean countries, 22, 24–28, 25–27t
   changes 1970-2010, in fuel-endowed Arab countries, 24–28, 25–27t
   changes 1970-2010, in sub-Saharan Arab countries, 24–28, 25–27t
   changes 1970-2010, methodology, 22–23
   country ranking, vs. ranking by GNI per capita, 10–11
   development and purpose of, 6
   indices of, as averages that conceal inequality, 140–41
   measurement of indices, 7
   population-weighted averages in, 23–24b, 23
   range for Arab world, 17, 17t, 21
   range from 0 to 1, 8–9
   rankings from low to very high, 9
   three indices of, 6
   use of geometric rather than arithmetic average in, 8–9
   See also education index of HDI; health index of HDI; income index of HDI
Human Development Reports (2016), 8–9, 10b

ICP. See International Comparison Program
IDPs. See internally displaced persons (IDPs)
IMF. See International Monetary Fund
Immigration restriction Act of 1901 (Australia), 51–52
import-substituting industrialization in Arab Mediterranean and Turkey (ISI), 58f
   Arab Mediterranean countries' turn from, 66

INDEX    299

first stage of, 58f, 59–61
government role in developing, 59–61
and infant-industry argument, 59–61
as initial stage of Arab industrialization, 56
second stage of, 58f, 61–64
tourism industry and, 75–76
turn to exporting, 61
income elasticity of demand, for food, and industrialization, 47–48
income index of HDI, 6
GDP per capita as more available measure of, 13–14, 22–23
GNI per capita as measure of, 7
use of natural logarithm of GNI, 7–8, 10b
See also GDP per capita
income inequality
and absolute poverty, 145
concealment by income averages, 140–41
and poverty headcount ratios, 145–49, 146f, 147f, 148t
income inequality measurement
data collection and, 141
Gini index and, 139, 141
and Lorenz curve, 141–43b, 142f
See also Gini indices
income per capita, persistent differences by climate areas, since 16th century, 45f, 45–46
India
air pollution in, 182–83
migrants to GCC countries, 156
missing women in, 133, 134t
Indonesia, and OPEC, 78–79, 79t
industrialization
as source of intensive growth, 56
through foreign-operated domestic factories, 50
industrialization, export-driven
barriers to, 49
as impractical in 1850–1914 period, 50–51
Japan's success in, 49–50
industrialization through international trade in Arab Mediterranean and Turkey
barriers to, 61
exports to pay for capital equipment, 57–58
first stage of import-substituting industrialization, 58f, 59–61
government role in, 59–61
and growing importance of exports to economy, 58f, 63–66, 65t
and infant-industry argument, 59–61
and manufactured exports to high-income consumers, 67–71
pre-industrialization stage of, 58f, 58–59
second stage of import-substituting industrialization, 58f, 61–64
turn to, 61
See also import-substituting industrialization in Arab Mediterranean and Turkey (ISI); manufactured exports to high-income consumers in Arab Mediterranean and Turkey

Industrial Revolution
and intensive growth, 36
and machine power, 35–36, 43–44, 48–49
Industrial Revolution, and global industrial–non-industrial divide, 35–36, 42–51
barriers to export-driven industrialization and, 49
competing theories on causes of, 43
and divergence in standards of living, 51–54
high agricultural productivity needed for industrialization, 44, 47–48
large domestic market needed for industrialization, 44, 45f, 47–49, 50–51
and secure property rights needed for industrialization, 46–47b
single-cause theories, weakness of, 47–48
industrial sector, as term, 43–44
infant-industry argument, 59–61
infectious and parasitic diseases
burden of, on Arab countries, 106, 107t
pharmaceutical availability and, 106–8, 109t
infectious diseases, DALY per 100,000 population, 103–6, 105t
inflation, adjustment for, in GDP per capita, 16b, 16t
infrastructure quality for business, 196, 219–21, 220t
intensive growth
definition of, 36
and Malthusian equilibrium, 37–38b
as product of Industrial Revolution, 36
See also government role in creating intensive growth
intensive growth in Arab world
benefits of independence for, 56
as later and slower, 54
as product of international trade, 56
intensive growth in fuel-endowed Arab countries and Iran, 76–84
capture of greater share of oil rents and, 76
negotiation of shared oil rents and, 77
OPEC price increases and, 78, 80
internally displaced persons (IDPs), 160
International Comparison Program (ICP), 11
international dollars (P$)
conversion of dollars to, 7–8, 11
and GNI, 7
reason for use of, 11
international goods arbitrage, 12b
International Monetary Fund (IMF), 204–5, 208, 210
international trade
intensive growth in Arab world as product of, 56
See also import-substituting industrialization in Arab Mediterranean and Turkey (ISI)
intimate partner violence (domestic violence), 136–38, 137t
Iqbal, Zafar, 164b, 164

Iran
  air pollution in, 183
  births per woman, 1970-2016, 113–14, 114t
  births per woman, contraception program and, 116f, 116–17, 117t
  carbon dioxide emissions in, 188–90, 190t
  contract enforcement efficiency in, 234–35, 235t
  developmental lag, causes of, 35–36
  disease burden from unsafe water and sanitation, 178, 179t
  as eastern boundary of Arab world, 2–3
  economic diversification efforts, 81–83
  education in, male-female enrollment ratios, 122–25, 123t
  education quality in, 96f, 97
  electricity access, 219
  energy subsidies in, 206t, 208
  energy subsidies, strategy for reducing, 195–96, 252
  and female labor force participation, 130–31
  fuel exports before World War I, 52
  fuel reserves, and GDP per capita, 80t
  GDP per capita, 81–82
  gender gap in labor force participation, 125, 126t, 127
  Gini index vs. comparison countries, 143–44, 144t
  and global warming, 193–94, 193t
  greenfield FDI by sector, 89t
  greenfield FDI by source, 87t
  and greenhouse gases, 172, 188, 189f, 190–91, 191t
  HDI of, 9
  historical and cultural ties to Arab world, 2–3
  intensive growth, late onset of, 54, 55, 76
  intensive growth, sources of, 55, 56, 76
  Islamic banks in, 165b
  as member of fuel-endowed countries group, 21–22
  military spending as share of GDP, 211t, 213
  missing women in, 134t
  negotiation of shared oil rents, 77
  non-oil manufacturing as share of greenfield FDI, 88, 89t
  official name, 5t
  and OPEC, 78, 79t
  perceived corruption in, 225f, 225–26
  population, 21–22, 21t
  population, changing dependency ratios in, 117–18, 118t, 119
  population growth, 1970-2016, 113–14, 113t
  population living in slums, 217t, 218
  population projections for 2020-2066, 114–15, 115t
  poverty headcount ratio in, 147–48
  public sector, shrinking of, 130–31
  public sector workers, high share of, 170
  quality of education in, 97
  as refugee host, 161t
  refugees from, 160
  rents on oil-bearing lands, capture by foreigners prior to 1950, 52
  and safe water access, 176f, 176–77
  share of fuel in merchandise exports, 80t, 81
  slow GDP per capita growth, causes of, 81–83
  starting a business, time and cost of, 231t, 232
  unemployment in, 168–70, 169f
  urbanization in, 197, 197t
  water tariffs vs. comparison countries, 174–75, 175t
  See also health in Iran; intensive growth in fuel-endowed Arab countries and Iran
Iraq
  air pollution in, 180–81
  and Arab Spring, effect of, 29–32
  date of independence, 5t
  economic diversification efforts, 81–83
  education in, instruction in colonial language, 102t
  education quality in, 96f, 97
  electrical outages, 220–21
  energy subsidies in, 206t, 209t
  and female genital mutilation, 135–36
  former colonial power in, 5t
  fuel reserves and GDP per capita, 80–81, 80t
  GDP per capita, 81–82
  GDP per capita changes, pre- and post-Arab Spring, 29–32, 31t
  and global warming, 193t
  greenfield FDI by sector, 89t
  greenfield FDI by source, 87t
  infrastructure quality for business, 220t
  intensive growth, late onset of, 54, 55, 76
  intensive growth, sources of, 55, 76
  internally displaced persons in, 160
  life expectancy changes, pre- and post-Arab Spring, 30t
  as member of fuel-endowed countries group, 19–20
  military spending as share of GDP, 211t, 212–13
  official name, 5t
  and OPEC, 78, 79t
  perceived corruption in, 225f, 225–26
  population, 21t
  population living in slums, 216, 217t
  poverty headcounts ratio in, 146f, 146–47, 147f
  ranking by HDI vs. GNI per capita, 10–11
  rate of return to education vs. comparison groups, 94–95, 94t
  refugees from, 32–33, 159t, 160
  and safe water access, 176f, 176–77
  and sanitation access, 177–78
  share of fuel in merchandise exports, 80t, 81
  slow GDP per capita growth, causes of, 81–83
  unemployment in, 168–70, 169f

war damage in, 216–18, 220–21
water scarcity in, 173t
ISI. *See* import-substituting industrialization
Islam
 and female labor force participation, 127–29, 128t
 and spread of Arabic language, 1–2
 *zakat* obligation in, 164b, 164
Islamic banks, 164–66b
Islamic Financial Services Board, 165b

Japan
 export-driven industrialization in, 49–50
 *sogo shosha* trading companies in, 49–50
Javorcik, Beata, 84–85
Jayachandran, Seema, 112b
Jews, and trade diasporas, 41
Jinjarak, Yothin, 198, 199f
Johnson, Simon, 47b
joint investment, as type of foreign direct investment, 84
Jordan
 date of independence, 5t
 *de facto* workplace discrimination against women in, 129–30
 disease in, and refugee influx, 160–61
 domestic violence in, 137t, 138
 education, instruction in colonial language, 102t
 education, refugee influx and, 160–61
 education quality in, 96f, 97
 energy subsidies in, 206t, 209t
 exports of manufactures relative to GDP, 64–66, 65t
 female labor force participation in, 129–31, 255–56
 former colonial power in, 5t
 free trade agreements, 68
 GDP per capita changes, pre- and post-Arab Spring, 31t, 32–33
 and global warming, 193t
 greenfield FDI by sector, 89t
 greenfield FDI by source, 87t
 HDI of, 10–11
 infrastructure quality for business, 220t
 intensive growth, as product of foreign aid, 55
 and Iraqi refugees, 32–33
 Islamic banking in, 165b
 life expectancy changes, pre- and post-Arab Spring, 30t, 32
 manufactures as share of exports, 63–64, 64f
 markets for exports, 67, 67t
 as member of Arab Mediterranean countries group, 20–21
 migrants from, countries hosting, 152, 153t
 migrants from, skill levels of, 152–53, 154f
 military spending as share of GDP, 211t, 213
 non-oil manufacturing as share of greenfield FDI, 88, 89t

 official name, 5t
 Palestinian refugees in, 156
 population, 21t
 population growth 2004-2010, 32–33
 population growth post-Arab Spring, 32–33
 population living in slums, 217t
 poverty headcount ratio in, 147–48
 protests against subsidy removals, 252
 ranking by HDI vs. GNI per capita, 10–11
 as refugee host, 159t, 160–61, 161t
 remittances, ratio to GDP, 151, 151t
 remittances, sources of, 151–52, 153t
 share of manufactures in exports, 64f, 66
 shrinking of public sector in, 130–31
 and Syrian refugees, 32–33
 tourism, Arab Spring and, 73–75, 74f
 tourism as proportion of exports, 72t
 tourism receipts vs. manufactures exports, 72, 73t
 water scarcity in, 173t

Kazakhstan, and OPEC, 79t
Keefer, Philip, 241–46, 244t
Kenya, as refugee host, 159t, 160
Khandelwal, Amit, 70–71
Klasen, Stephan, 133, 135
knowledge. *See* education
Korean manufacturers, manufacturing assistance from foreign buyers, 69
Kremer, Michael, 106–8
Kuwait
 and air pollution, 180–81
 and Arab Spring, 29–32
 date of independence, 5t
 education, instruction in colonial language, 102t
 education quality in, 96f, 97
 energy subsidies in, 206t, 209t
 failure of price levels to rise with income, 14
 foreign aid to Arab countries, 152
 former colonial power in, 5t
 fuel reserves and GDP per capita, 80–81, 80t
 GDP per capita changes, pre- and post-Arab Spring, 29–32, 31t
 and global warming, 193t
 greenfield FDI by sector, 86t, 89t
 greenfield FDI by source, 87t
 and greenhouse gases, 188, 189f
 intensive growth, sources of, 55
 Islamic banking in, 165b
 life expectancy changes, pre- and post-Arab Spring, 30t
 as member of fuel-endowed countries group, 19–20
 migrant residents, 156, 156t, 157t
 military spending as share of GDP, 211t
 official name, 5t
 and OPEC, 78, 79t
 perceived corruption in, 225f, 225–26

Kuwait (*cont.*)
  population, 21*t*
  ranking by HDI vs. GNI per capita, 10–11
  share of fuel in merchandise exports, 80*t*, 81
  urban primacy in, 203, 204
  water desalination in, 174
  water scarcity in, 173*t*

labor force participation
  decline in, with demographic transition, 127
  definition of, 125
  male, worldwide decrease in, 126*t*, 127
  *See also* 121
Lagakos, David, 166–70
Lahiri, Amartya, 82
land, arable, limited supply of
  in Arab lands, and developmental lag, 35–36
  in Arab lands, and relative income equality, 143–44
  and extensive growth in preindustrial economies, 36–38
landfills, 171–72
La Porta, Rafael, 229, 230*f*, 232
Lavy, Victor, 101
law of one price, 12*b*
learning-by-doing, 39–40, 60
learning-by-exporting, 70–71
Lebanon
  civil war in, 216–18
  date of independence, 5*t*
  *de facto* workplace discrimination against women in, 129–30
  disease in, and refugee influx, 160–61
  education in, and refugee influx, 160–61, 161*f*
  education in, instruction in colonial language, 102–3, 102*t*
  education quality in, 96*f*, 97
  effects of war in, 216–18
  energy subsidies in, 206*t*, 209*t*
  exports of manufactures relative to GDP, 64–65, 65*t*, 66
  former colonial power in, 5*t*
  GDP per capita changes, pre- and post-Arab Spring, 31*t*, 32–33
  and global warming, 193*t*
  greenfield FDI by sector, 89*t*
  greenfield FDI by source, 87*t*
  infrastructure quality for business, 220*t*
  intensive growth, as product of tourism, 55
  life expectancy changes, pre- and post-Arab Spring, 30*t*, 32
  as member of Arab Mediterranean countries group, 20–21
  migrants from, countries hosting, 152, 153*t*
  migrants from, skill levels of, 152–53, 154*f*
  migrants from, success of, 155*b*
  military spending as share of GDP, 211*t*, 213
  municipal wastes in, 172, 186–87*b*, 186*f*, 186
  official name, 5*t*
  Palestinian refugees in, 216–18
  population, 21*t*
  population growth 2010-2016, 32–33
  population living in slums, 216–18, 217*t*
  as refugee host, 159*t*, 160–61, 161*t*
  remittances, sources of, 151–52, 153*t*
  remittances received, ratio to GDP, 151, 151*t*
  and Syrian refugees, 32
  tourism as proportion of exports, 72*t*, 73–74
  tourism receipts, Arab Spring and, 73–75, 74*f*
  tourism receipts vs. manufactures exports, 72–73, 73*t*
  tourist attractions in, 72–73
  water scarcity in, 173*t*
  and WTO, 63–64
Lelieveld, Jos, 193–94, 193*t*
Lesotho, malaria index in, 18
Levin, Victoria, 162*f*, 162, 164
Levine, Ross, 18
Lewis, Arthur W., 43*f*, 43–44, 47–48, 49, 50, 51–52, 59
Lewis, Mervyn, 164*b*, 164
Libya
  and Arab Spring, 6, 17, 29–32, 33
  civil war in, 29, 160
  date of independence, 5*t*
  energy subsidies in, 206*t*
  former colonial power in, 5*t*
  fuel reserves and GDP per capita, 80*t*
  GDP per capita changes, pre- and post-Arab Spring, 29–32, 31*t*
  and global warming, 192, 192*t*, 193*t*
  greenfield FDI by sector, 89*t*
  greenfield FDI by source, 87*t*
  intensive growth, as result of capture of rents from oil and gas, 55
  internally displaced persons in, 160
  life expectancy changes, pre- and post-Arab Spring, 29–32, 30*t*
  as member of fuel-endowed countries group, 19–20
  official name, 5*t*
  and OPEC, 78, 79*t*
  population, 21*t*
  population living in slums, 217*t*
  share of fuel in merchandise exports, 80*t*, 81
  water scarcity in, 173*t*
life expectancy, for Arab world vs. Latin America, 17, 17*t*, 21
life expectancy in Arab Mediterranean countries
  changes 1970-2010, 24–25, 25*t*, 28
  changes before vs. after Arab Spring, 29, 30*t*
  improved medical technology and, 103–4
  increases in, 103–4
  range of, 20*t*, 21
life expectancy in fuel-endowed Arab countries
  changes 1970-2010, 24–25, 25*t*, 28

changes before vs. after Arab Spring, 29–32, 30t
improved medical technology and, 103–4
increases in, 103–4
range of, 20t, 21
life expectancy in sub-Saharan Arab countries
changes 1970-2010, 24–25, 25t, 28, 103–4
changes before vs. after Arab Spring, 29, 30t
improved medical technology and, 103–4
increase in, 103–4
as lower than other Arab countries, 103–4
range of, 20t, 21
tropical diseases and, 103–4
Lifson, Thomas B., 49–50
Lima, Francisco, 232–33, 246
Lleras-Muney, Adriana, 112b
logarithms
benefits of, for graphing change in income, 9–10b
as term, 10b
logarithms, natural
vs. common, 10b
in income index of HDI, 7–8, 10b
use by UN Development Program, 10b
Lopez-di-Silanes, Florencio, 229, 230f, 232
Lorenz curve, 141–43b, 142f
Lustig, Nora, 208–9

Mahajan, Aprajit, 75
malaria
elimination from most of Arab World, Iran and Turkey, 44–45
as ongoing problem in sub-Saharan Africa, 44–45
and poor socioeconomic performance of sub-Saharan countries, 18, 47b
Malaysia, and OPEC, 79t
Malthus, Thomas, 37–38b
Malthusian equilibrium, 37–38b
Mamluk empire, 41
manufactured exports to high-income consumers in Arab Mediterranean and Turkey, 67–71
assistance from foreign buyers, 69–71
ease of rejection of faulty good, importance of, 68
education improvements required by, 68
importance of government role in, importance of, 68–69
intensive growth from, 71
markets for export, 67–68, 67t
quality improvements required by, 68, 71
market failure, and infant-industry argument, 59–60
markets, foreign, cost of gathering information on, 49–50
Márquez-Ramos, Laura, 68
Martínez-Zarzoso, Inmaculada, 68

masks, particulate-filtering, and air pollution, 183–84, 253
Mason, Charles, 78–79
Mauritania
and air pollution, 180–81
date of independence, 5t
education in, instruction in colonial language, 102–3, 102t
energy subsidies in, 206t, 208, 209t
former colonial power in, 5t
GDP per capita, 10b, 13f
GDP per capita changes, pre- and post-Arab Spring, 31t
infrastructure quality for business, 220t
intensive growth, lack of, 55
life expectancy changes, pre- and post-Arab Spring, 30t
as member of sub-Saharan Arab countries group, 18
military spending as share of GDP, 211t, 212
official name, 5t
population, 21t
population living in slums, 217t
and safe water access, 176f, 176–77
water scarcity in, 173t
McKenzie, David, 75
MENA. See Middle East and North Africa
Merrouche, Ouarda, 165–66b
Mexico, and OPEC, 79t
Middle East, as market for Arab Mediterranean and Turkish manufactures, 67, 67t
Middle East and North Africa (MENA)
countries in, 33, 34t
female labor force participation in, 131–32
greenfield FDI by destination and sector, 89t
greenfield FDI by destination and source, 86–88, 87t
greenfield FDI by source and sector, 85–86, 86t, 87–88
poverty rates in, 126t, 149–50
remittances received, ratio to GDP, 151
social safety net programs (SSNs), 162f, 162–63
unemployment rates in, 166–67
migrant workers
costs of migration, 156–57
effect on poverty levels, 152–53
and failure of price levels to rise with income, 14
in fuel-endowed Arab countries, and average income, 29–32
in fuel-endowed Arab countries, and price levels, 14
in GCC countries, large number of, 143–44
return of, and transfer of skills and contacts, 153, 154t
skill levels of, 152–53, 154f
See also remittances

military spending, 210–13
  in Arab countries vs. comparison
    groups, 195–96
  items included in, 210
  as large share of government
    spending, 195–96
  reasons for, 210, 212–13
  and reduced capacity for infrastructure
    spending, 210, 218–19
  as share of GDP, 210–13, 211*t*
  strain on public finance from, 213
mineral resource earnings, capture by
    foreigners, and developmental delay in
    Arab countries and Iran, 35–36
mobile phones, ubiquity in Arab
    countries, 252–53
Modern Standard Arabic (MSA)
  development of, 3–4*b*
  as language in Arab schools, 3–4*b*
  as language in government and media, 4*b*
Mody, Ashoka, 69
Montenegro, Claudio, 94–95
Morgandi, Matteo, 162*f*, 162, 164
Morocco
  and air pollution, 180–81
  date of independence, 5*t*
  *de facto* workplace discrimination against
    women in, 129–30
  domestic violence in, 137*t*, 138
  education, language of instruction, 101,
    102–3, 102*t*
  education quality, 96*f*, 97
  energy subsidies in, 206*t*, 209*t*
  expected global warming damage in, 172–73
  exports of manufactures relative to GDP,
    64–66, 65*t*
  female labor force participation in, 130–31
  former colonial power in, 5*t*
  free trade agreements, 68
  and GATT, 63–64
  GDP per capita changes, pre- and post-Arab
    Spring, 31*t*
  and global warming, 192–93, 192*t*
  greenfield FDI by sector, 89*t*
  greenfield FDI by source, 87*t*
  infrastructure quality for business, 220*t*
  intensive growth, late onset of, 54, 55
  intensive growth, sources of, 55
  life expectancy changes, pre- and post-Arab
    Spring, 30*t*, 32
  manufactures as share of exports, 63–64, 64*f*
  markets for exports, 67, 67*t*
  as member of Arab Mediterranean countries
    group, 20–21
  migrants from, countries hosting, 152, 153*t*
  military spending as share of GDP, 211*t*
  mineral resource exports, 86*t*
  as nation-state in extensive growth
    period, 40–41

non-oil manufacturing as share of greenfield
    FDI, 88, 89*t*
official name, 5*t*
population, 21*t*
population living in slums, 216, 217*t*
poverty headcount ratio in, 147–48
remittances, sources of, 151–52, 153*t*
remittances received, ratio to GDP, 151, 151*t*
and sanitation access, 177–78
share of manufactures in exports, 64*f*, 66
shrinking of public sector in, 130–31
tourism as proportion of exports, 72*t*
tourism receipts vs. manufactures exports,
    72, 73*t*
tourism to, Arab Spring and, 73–75, 74*f*
unemployment in, 166–67, 168–70, 169*f*
water scarcity in, 173*t*
Mottaghi, Lili, 160–61
MSA. *See* Modern Standard Arabic
Mu, Quan, 183–84
Mubarak, Hosni, 238–39, 241–42, 249
multiple regression analysis, 148–49*b*, 228*b*
  standard errors in, 149*b*
municipal wastes, 185–87
  GDP per capita and, 171–72, 185*f*, 185
  as growing problem, 187
  health effects of, 187
  landfills and, 171–72, 185–86
  in Lebanon, as crisis, 172, 186–87*b*, 186*f*,
    186
  recycling and, 185–86
  urbanization and, 201–3, 202*t*
Muralidharan, Karthik, 253–54
Murphy, Kevin, 48–49
Mursi, Mohammed, 240–41
Muslim empires, development of, 40–41
Muzi, Silvia, 130

national price indices (ICP)
  calculation of, 11
  vs. GDP per capita (2015), 13*f*, 13–14
Naufal, George, 157–58
Nepal, missing women in, 134*t*
New Zealand, time and cost of starting a
    business in, 229, 230*f*, 232
Nigeria, and OPEC, 78, 79*t*
non-governmental organizations (NGOs), and
    pharmaceuticals for Arab countries, 108
non-tariff measures (NTMs), in Egypt, selective
    enforcement of, 242–43, 244*t*, 245, 246
Norway, and OPEC, 79*t*
NTMs. *See* non-tariff measures

obesity in Arab countries
  food subsidies and, 110–11, 163, 252
  and heart disease, 108–11
  rates, by gender, 110*t*
Official Development Assistance (ODA), from
    GCC countries, 152

oil and gas production, and suppression of manufacturing sector (Dutch Disease), 82–83
oil and gas reserves, ranking of countries based on, 19–20
oil curse, 18
  causes of, 82
  and corruption, 226
  fuel-rich Arab countries and, 81–82
oil rent, definition of, 77
oil-rich countries. *See* fuel-endowed Arab countries
Olken, Benjamin, 52
Oman
  and air pollution, 180–81
  and Arab Spring, effect of, 29–32
  date of independence, 5t
  *de facto* workplace discrimination against women in, 129–30
  education in, instruction in colonial language, 102t
  energy subsidies in, 206t, 209t
  failure of price levels to rise with income, 14
  former colonial power in, 5t
  fuel reserves and GDP per capita, 80–81, 80t
  GDP per capita changes, pre- and post-Arab Spring, 29–32, 31t
  greenfield FDI by sector, 89t
  greenfield FDI by source, 87t
  intensive growth, as result of capture of rents from oil and gas, 55
  life expectancy changes, pre- and post-Arab Spring, 30t
  as member of fuel-endowed countries group, 19–20
  migrant residents, 156t, 157t
  military spending as share of GDP, 211t, 212–13
  official name, 5t
  and OPEC, 78–79, 79t
  perceived corruption in, 225f, 225–26
  population, 21t
  population living in slums, 217t
  share of fuel in merchandise exports, 80t, 81
  water scarcity in, 173t
OPEC
  as cartel, 78
  founding members, 78
  and higher prices, negative effect on consumers, 78–79
  implied probability of membership, by country, 78–79, 79t
  member countries, 78
  and oil revenue increases for fuel-endowed Arab countries and Iran, 78–79
Osman, Adam, 70–71
Ottoman Empire
  defeat in World War I, 4
  development of, 40–41
  rule over most of Arab world, 4

P$. *See* international dollars
Page, John, 147–49, 148t, 151, 152–53, 170
Pakistan
  migrants to GCC countries, 156
  missing women in, 133, 134t
Palestine, 1
Palestinian refugees, 160
Paris climate accord, and fossil fuel market, 81
Patrinos, Harry, 94–95
Persia, adoption of Islam without Arab identity, 2–3
Persian Empire, and spread of Arabic language, 1–2
Persian language, script of, 2–3
pharmaceuticals, availability in Arab world, and disease, 106–8, 109t
Polasky, Stephen, 78–79
policy recommendations, 251–56
  on desert dust mitigation, 253
  on female labor force participation, 255–56
  on reducing subsidies, 163, 251–53
  on tertiary education, 253–54
  on tourism in Arab Mediterranean countries, 75–76, 254
  on urban primacy in Egypt and Sudan, 254–55
political independence, economic benefits of, 4
politically connected firms
  countries with large number of, 237
  definition of, 236
  economic consequences of preferential treatment for, 249
  Faccio data on, 236–37
  identification of, 236, 237–38, 241–42, 246–47
  as larger than unconnected firms, 237, 247
  limited data on, 249
  and perceived corruption, 237
politically connected firms in Egypt
  availability of data on, 238, 241–42
  economic consequences of special treatment for, 245–46
  effect of Arab Spring on, 32–33
  identification of, 238–39, 241–42
  preferential treatment for, 241–46, 244t
  stock fluctuations with political fortunes, 238–41, 240t
politically connected firms in Tunisia
  availability of data on, 238, 246–47
  tariff evasion by, 32–33, 246–49, 248t
Ponticelli, Jacopo, 233
poor countries
  and equalized price of goods across countries, 11–12, 12–13b
  low price of services in, 11–12, 12–13b
Popova, Anna, 163

population
  of Arab UN member states, 21–22, 21*t*
  growth, increased food production necessary for, 36–37
  *See also* demographic transition;
population growth in Arab countries
  1970-2016, 113–14, 113*t*
  projections for 2020-2066, 114–15, 115*t*
population-weighted averages
  formula for, 24*b*
  in HDI changes 1970-2010, 23
  need for use of, 23–24*b*, 23*t*
portfolio investment, vs. foreign direct investment, 84–85
poverty
  absolute, 145
  absolute, income inequality and, 145
  lower levels in Arab countries, 145
  relative, 145
  World Bank standard for, 145–47, 146*f*, 147*f*
poverty headcount ratios
  and income inequality, 145–49, 146*f*, 147*f*, 148*t*
  and remittances, 148*t*, 150, 152–53
poverty rates in Arab countries
  low income inequality and, 145–49, 146*f*, 147*f*, 148*t*
  low levels vs. comparison countries, 143–44, 144*t*, 145, 146–47
  out-migration of poor workers and, 152–53
  remittances and, 148*t*, 150, 152–53
poverty reduction spending. *See* charity in Muslim countries; social safety net programs (SSNs)
preindustrial economies. *See* extensive growth in preindustrial economies
price levels in Arab countries
  failure to rise with income, 14
  vs. GDP per capita in 2015, 13*f*, 13–14
  government subsidies and, 14
price levels vs. GDP per capita, 9–10*b*, 13*f*
Pritchett, Lant, 52–54, 53*f*
productivity, correlation with education quality, 97
property rights
  and institutions, 46–47*b*
  secure, as prerequisite for industrialization, 46–47*b*
Psacharopoulos, George, 98*b*
public sector, high shares of workers employed in, in Arab Countries, 157–58, 158*f*, 170
purchasing power parity dollars. *See* international dollars
Pursell, Garry, 69

Qatar
  and air pollution, 180–81
  and Arab Spring, 29–32
  date of independence, 5*t*
  education in, instruction in colonial language, 102*t*
  energy subsidies in, 206*t*, 209*t*
  failure of price levels to rise with income, 14
  former colonial power in, 5*t*
  fuel reserves and GDP per capita, 80–81, 80*t*
  GDP per capita changes, pre- and post-Arab Spring, 29–32, 31*t*
  and global warming, 192
  greenfield FDI by sector, 86*t*, 89*t*
  greenfield FDI by source, 87*t*
  intensive growth, sources of, 55
  Islamic banking in, 165*b*
  life expectancy changes, pre- and post-Arab Spring, 30*t*
  as member of fuel-endowed countries group, 19–20
  migrant residents, 156, 156*t*, 157*t*
  military spending as share of GDP, 211*t*
  official name, 5*t*
  and oil curse, escape from, 18
  and OPEC, 78, 79*t*
  perceived corruption in, 226–27
  population, 21*t*
  ranking by HDI vs. GNI per capita, 10–11
  share of fuel in merchandise exports, 80*t*, 81
  water desalination in, 174
  water scarcity in, 173*t*
quality, as barrier to export, 61
*Qur'an*, and spread of Arabic language, 1–2

Raballand, Gael, 246–49, 248*t*
Rahman, Md. Mizanur, 156–57
randomized control trials, of effects of export opportunities, 70–71
Ranis, Gustav, 57–58
Rauch, James, 41, 98*b*, 166–70
Ravallion, Martin, 145
Read, Jen'nan, 128–29
refugees from war, 159–61
  impact on host countries, 160–61
  number, by country of origin, 159, 159*t*
remittances
  and poverty rates in Arab countries, 148*t*, 150, 152–53
  remittances received, ratio to GDP, 151, 151*t*
  source regions for, 151–52, 153*t*
  to South and Southeast Asia from GCC countries, effect of, 156–57
rent (economic rent), definition of, 76–77
Reynolds, Lloyd, 36, 54, 55, 76
Rhee, Yung Whee, 69
Ricardo, David, 76–77
Rijkers, Bob, 246–49, 248*t*
Roberts, John, 75
Robinson, James, 47*b*
Rodrik, Dani, 46–47*b*
Roman Empire, and spread of Arabic language, 1–2

INDEX 307

Ross-Larson, Bruce, 69
"rules of origin" (RoOs), and Euro-
 Mediterranean Association Agreements, 68
Russia, and OPEC, 79t

Sachs, Jeffrey, 18, 44–45, 47b
Safavid empire, wealth from taxation, 41
Salehi-Isfahani, Djavad, 116f, 116–17, 117t
Sangraula, Prem, 145
sanitation access
 and definition of slum, 213–14
 GDP per capita and, 171, 177f, 177–78
 health consequences of lack of, 178, 179t
 success of Arab countries in providing, 172, 179
 urbanization and, 197–98
sanitation services, basic, World Bank definition of, 177–78
Saudi Arabia
 and air pollution, 180–81
 and Arab Spring, effect of, 29–32
 date of independence, 5t
 education, instruction in colonial language, 102t
 education quality, 96f, 97
 energy subsidies in, 206t, 209t
 failure of price levels to rise with income, 14
 foreign aid to Arab countries, 152
 former colonial power in, 5t
 fuel reserves and GDP per capita, 80–81, 80t
 GDP per capita changes, pre- and post-Arab Spring, 29–32, 31t
 and global warming, 193t
 greenfield FDI by sector, 86t, 89t
 greenfield FDI by source, 87t
 and greenhouse gases, 188, 189f
 intensive growth, sources of, 55
 Islamic banking in, 165b
 life expectancy changes, pre- and post-Arab Spring, 30t
 as member of fuel-endowed countries group, 19–20
 migrant residents, 156, 156t, 157t
 military spending as share of GDP, 211t, 212–13
 negotiation of shared oil rents, 77
 official name, 5t
 and OPEC, 78, 79t
 perceived corruption in, 226–27
 population, 21t
 population living in slums, 216–18, 217t
 private sector employment share for migrants vs. citizens, 157–58, 158f
 share of fuel in merchandise exports, 80t, 81
 views on female labor force participation in, 255–56
 water scarcity in, 173t
Schiffbauer, Marc, 241–46, 244t
Schoellman, Todd, 95–97, 96f
schooling, average years of
 Arab progress in, 25–26
 oil curse and, 82
schooling, changes in average years of, 1970-2010
 in Arab Mediterranean countries, 25–26, 26t, 28
 in fuel-endowed Arab countries, 25–26, 26t, 28
 in sub-Saharan Arab countries, 25–26, 26t, 28
schooling, mean years of
 for Arab Mediterranean countries, range of, 20t, 21
 for fuel-endowed Arab countries, 20t, 21
 in Indonesia, 92–93b, 92t
 range for Arab world vs. Latin America, 17, 17t, 21
 for sub-Saharan Arab countries, 20t, 21
sea level rise from global warming, 172–73, 192–93, 192t
seigniorage (inflation tax)
 reduction of, 198–200
 as source of government revenue, 198, 199f
Sen, Amartya, 133
settlers, high mortality rates, and establishment of extractive institutions, 47b
sex ratios, actual vs. expected, 132–35, 134t
sex-selective abortions, 133–35
Shleifer, Andrei, 48–49, 229, 230f, 232
Silva, Joana, 162f, 162, 163, 164
slums
 causes of, 218–19
 defining characteristics of, 213–14, 215b
 definition of, 196
 lack of infrastructure in, 195, 196, 213–15, 215b, 218–19
 percentage of population living in, 196, 216–19, 217t
social safety net programs (SSNs), 162f, 162–63
 non-subsidy programs, 162f, 162–63
 See also subsidies
sogo shosha trading companies in Japan, 49–50
Sokoloff, Kenneth, 47–48, 143–44
Somalia
 as Arab League country, 1
 date of independence, 5t
 education quality, 96f, 97
 former colonial power in, 5t
 intensive growth, lack of, 55
 internally displaced persons in, 160
 life expectancy changes, pre- and post-Arab Spring, 30t
 as member of sub-Saharan Arab countries group, 18
 military spending as share of GDP, 211t, 212
 official name, 5t
 population, 21t
 population living in slums, 217t
 refugees from, 159t, 160
 water scarcity in, 173t

South Africa, malaria index in, 18
South Asia
  migrants to GCC countries, 156, 157t
  remittances from GCC countries, effect of, 156–57
Southeast Asia
  migrants to GCC countries, 156, 157t
  remittances from GCC countries, effect of, 156–57
Southern Sudan, as refugee host, 159t, 160
South Korea
  contract enforcement efficiency in, 234–35
  missing women in, 134t
  and *sogo shosha* trading company model, 49
specialization, development of, in era of extensive growth, 39–40
Sri Lanka, missing women in, 134t
standard errors, in multiple regression analysis, 149b
standard of living
  Arab countries' closing of gap in, 27–28
  divergence in, between industrialized and non-industrialized countries, 51–54
  *See also* income index of HDI
starting a business, time and cost of, 229–33
  in Arab countries, Iran and Turkey, 229–32, 231t
  data collection on, 229
  in France, 229, 230f
  low, economic benefits of, 232–33
  in New Zealand, 229, 230f, 232
  in Portugal, 232–33
  in Southern Europe, 231t, 232
states, development of, in era of extensive growth, 40–41
Subramanian, Arvind, 46–47b
sub-Saharan Arab countries
  and Arab Spring, 29, 30t, 31t, 33
  births per woman, 1970-2016, 113–14, 114t
  carbon dioxide emissions in, 188–90, 190t
  characteristics of countries in group, 18
  contract enforcement efficiency in, 235, 235t
  countries included in group, 18, 19f, 34t
  electrical outages, 220–21, 220t
  electricity access, 219
  energy subsidies in, 195–96, 204–5, 206t, 208, 218–19
  HDI indicators, as below those of other Arab countries, 21
  GDP per capita changes, 1970-2010, 26–28, 27t
  GDP per capita changes before vs. after Arab Spring in, 29, 31t
  gender gap in labor force participation, 125–27, 126t
  Gini index vs. comparison countries, 143–44, 144t
  GNI per capita, range of, 20t, 21
  growth rate, 1970-2010, 26–28, 27t
  infrastructure quality for business in, 196, 220t
  intensive growth, late onset of, 54
  intensive growth, mixed results for, 55
  life expectancy, changes 1970-2010, 24–25, 25t, 28, 103–4
  life expectancy, changes before vs. after Arab Spring, 29, 30t
  low HDI rating of all countries in, 28
  military spending as share of GDP, 211t, 212, 213
  population of, 21–22, 21t
  population, changing dependency ratios, 117–19, 118t
  population growth, 1970-2016, 113–14, 113t
  population living in slums, 196, 216, 217t
  population projections for 2020-2066, 114–15, 115t
  progress 1970-2010, 28
  slow economic growth in, 27t, 28
  starting a business, time and cost of, 231t, 232
  urbanization in, 196, 197t
  water scarcity in, 173–74, 173t, 220t
  water tariffs vs. comparison countries, 174–75, 175t
  *See also* diseases, tropical, in sub-Saharan Arab countries; education in sub-Saharan Arab countries; health in sub-Saharan Arab countries
sub-Saharan countries
  malaria and, 18
  missing women in, 134t
  poor socioeconomic performance of, 18
subsidies
  benefits of reducing, 251–52, 253
  benefits of replacing with cash payments, 163, 252–53
  and infant-industry argument, 60–61
  definition of, 204–5
  as one type of aid, 162
  political difficulty of removing, 252
  and price levels, 14
  strategy for reducing, 195–96, 252
  *See also* energy subsidies; food subsidies; water utility subsidies
Sudan
  and air pollution, 180–81
  date of independence, 5t
  education in, instruction in colonial language, 102t
  education quality in, 96f, 97
  energy subsidies in, 206t, 209t
  former colonial power in, 5t
  fuel exports, and GDP growth, 83–84
  GDP per capita changes, pre- and post-Arab Spring, 31t
  infrastructure quality for business, 220t
  intensive growth, late onset of, 54, 55, 83–84
  internally displaced persons in, 160

Islamic banks in, 165b
life expectancy changes, pre- and post-Arab Spring, 30t
as member of sub-Saharan Arab countries group, 18
military spending as share of GDP, 211t, 212
official name, 5t
perceived corruption in, 225f, 225–26
policy recommendations on urban primacy in, 254–55
population, 21t
population living in slums, 217t
primary product exports, 52
refugees from, 159t, 160
and safe water access, 176f, 176–77
and South Sudan independence, 83–84
urban primacy in, 203, 204
water scarcity in, 173t
survival rate, gender gap in, 121–22
Swaziland, low malaria index, 18
Syria
and Arab Spring, 6, 17, 32
civil war in, 29, 32, 213
date of independence, 5t
*de facto* workplace discrimination against women in, 129–30
education, instruction in colonial language, 102t
education quality in, 96f, 97
former colonial power in, 5t
GDP per capita changes, pre- and post-Arab Spring, 32
and global warming, 193t
government promotion of first stage ISI, 59
greenfield FDI by sector, 88, 89t
greenfield FDI by source, 87t
import-substituting industrialization in, 61–62, 63
intensive growth, sources of, 55, 61–62
internally displaced persons in, 160
life expectancy changes, pre- and post-Arab Spring, 30t, 32
markets for exports, 67, 67t
as member of Arab Mediterranean countries group, 20–21
missing women in, 134t
official name, 5t
population, 21t
population living in slums, 216, 217t
public sector, increase in, 130–31
refugees from, 32–33, 159, 159t, 160, 161t, 216–18
tourism as proportion of exports, 72t
tourism receipts vs. manufactures exports, 72, 73t
tourism to, Arab Spring and, 73–75, 74f
water scarcity in, 173t
water-wheels (norias) of Hama, 38–39b, 39f
and WTO, 63–64
Syronics, 63

Tahoun, Ahmed, 238–41, 240t
Taiwan, missing women in, 134t
Taqdiri, Alireza, 208–9
tariffs
evasion by politically connected firms in Tunisia, 32–33, 246–49, 248t
lowering of, 198–200, 199f, 242–43, 246
replacement by NTMs, in Egypt, 242–43
on silk and spice trade, wealth from, 41
as source of government revenue, 198
Taylor, Lowell, 232–33, 246
temperate countries of recent European settlement, restriction of immigration to maintain wage levels, 51–52
terrorist attacks, and Arab Mediterranean tourism decline, 73–74
TOBB. *See* Turkish Union of Chambers and Commodity Exchanges
total factor productivity
FDI and, 84–85
increase in, required for increased food production, 36–37
tourism, international, as source of intensive growth, 56
tourism in Arab Mediterranean countries and Turkey, 71–76
and Arab hotel ownership, low levels of, 75–76, 254
changes after Arab Spring, 32–33, 73–75, 74f
expected rebound of, 75
Great Recession of 2008 and, 73–74
importance in, 20–21, 32–33
policy recommendations on, 75–76, 254
as proportion of exports, 71–72, 72t
as service export to pay for capital equipment import, 57–58
tourism receipts vs. manufactures exports, 72, 73t
trade, long-distance
development of in era of extensive growth, 41
and trade diasporas, 41
*See also* industrialization through international trade in Arab Mediterranean and Turkey
trade diasporas, 41
Transparency International (TI), 224–25
transportation costs, as barrier to export-driven industrialization, 49, 50–51
Trebbi, Francesco, 46–47b
tropical economies relying on primary product exports
capture of mineral rents by foreigners, 51–52
education improvements in, 52
income gap with industrialized countries, 52–54, 53f
income inequality in, 143–44
later and slower intensive growth in, 54
price suppression by Chinese and Indian migrants, 51

tropical economies relying on primary product exports (*cont.*)
  socioeconomic development in, 52
  water supply improvements in, 52
Tunisia
  and abortion, 135
  and air pollution, 180–81
  and Arab Spring, 6, 32
  date of independence, 5*t*
  domestic violence in, 137*t*, 138
  education, instruction in colonial language, 102–3, 102*t*
  energy subsidies in, 206*t*, 209*t*
  exports of manufactures relative to GDP, 64–66, 65*t*
  former colonial power in, 5*t*
  and GATT, 63–64
  GDP per capita, 10*b*, 13*f*, 249
  GDP per capita changes, pre- and post-Arab Spring, 31*t*, 32–33
  and global warming, 192–93, 192*t*
  government promotion of first stage ISI, 59
  greenfield FDI by sector, 89*t*
  greenfield FDI by source, 87*t*
  import-substituting industrialization in, 61–62
  infrastructure quality for business, 220*t*
  intensive growth, as product of industrialization, 55, 61–62
  life expectancy changes, pre- and post-Arab Spring, 30*t*, 32
  manufactures as share of exports, 63–64, 64*f*
  manufacturing of car parts for EU, 71
  markets for exports, 67, 67*t*
  as member of Arab Mediterranean countries group, 20–21
  migrants from, countries hosting, 152, 153*t*
  military spending as share of GDP, 211*t*, 213
  mineral resource exports, 85–86
  missing women in, 134*t*
  non-oil manufacturing as share of greenfield FDI, 88, 89*t*
  official name, 5*t*
  population, 21*t*
  population living in slums, 217*t*
  poverty headcount ratio in, 147–48
  protests against subsidy removals, 252
  remittances, sources of, 151–52, 153*t*
  remittances received, ratio to GDP, 151, 151*t*
  share of manufactures in exports, 64*f*, 66
  shrinking of public sector in, 130–31
  success with manufactures exports, 65–66, 65*t*
  tariff evasion by politically connected firms in, 32–33, 246–49, 248*t*
  tariffs, lowering of, 246
  tourism as proportion of exports, 72*t*
  tourism receipts vs. manufactures exports, 72, 73*t*
  tourism to, Arab Spring and, 73–75, 74*f*
  water scarcity in, 173*t*

Turkey
  and abortion, 135
  air pollution in, 183
  automobile industry in, 63
  births per woman, 1970-2016, 113–14, 114*t*
  carbon dioxide emissions in, 188–90, 190*t*
  contract enforcement efficiency in, 235, 235*t*
  developmental lag, causes of, 35–36
  domestic violence in, 137–38, 137*t*
  education in, male-female enrollment ratios, 122–25, 123*t*
  electrical outages, 221
  electricity access, 219
  energy subsidies in, 206*t*, 218–19
  exports of manufactures relative to GDP, 64–65, 65*t*, 66
  FDI in, 88–90
  free trade agreements, 68
  gender gap in labor force participation, 125, 126*t*
  Gini index vs. comparison countries, 143–44, 144*t*
  and global warming, 193*t*
  government promotion of first stage ISI, 59
  and greenhouse gases, 190–91, 191*t*
  growing importance of exports to economy, 64–65
  HDI of, 9
  high share of workers employed in public sector, 170
  historical and cultural ties to Arab world, 2–3
  import-substituting industrialization in, 61–62, 63
  infrastructure quality for business in, 196, 220*t*
  intensive growth, late onset of, 54, 55
  intensive growth, sources of, 55, 56, 61–62
  large consumer market in, 63
  manufactures as share of exports, 63–64, 64*f*
  markets for exports, 67, 67*t*
  as member of Mediterranean countries group, 21–22
  military spending as share of GDP, 211*t*, 213, 218–19
  missing women in, 134*t*
  as more-developed than Arab Mediterranean countries, 35
  as northern boundary of Arab world, 2–3
  official name, 5*t*
  population, 21–22, 21*t*
  population, changing dependency ratios, 117–18, 118*t*, 119
  population growth, 1970-2016, 113–14, 113*t*
  population living in slums, 196, 216, 217*t*
  population projections for 2020-2066, 114–15, 115*t*
  as refugee host, 159*t*, 160, 161*t*
  share of manufactures in exports, 64*f*, 66
  shift to manufactures exports, 82–83
  and *sogo shosha* trading company model, 49

starting a business, time and cost of, 231t, 232
tariffs, lowering of, 198
tourism as proportion of exports, 72, 72t, 73t
transition to exporter of manufactures, 66
unemployment in, 168–70, 169f
urbanization in, 197, 197t
urban primacy in, 203, 204
water tariffs vs. comparison countries, 174–75, 175t
and WTO, 63–64
Turkish language, script of, 2–3
Turkish Union of Chambers and Commodity Exchanges (TOBB), 63
Tybout, James, 75

unemployment rates, 166–70
  business cycles and, 166
  in developing countries, issues in measurement of, 166–67
  increase in ratio of unemployment for less- to more-educated with GDP per capita, 167–68, 169f, 170
  increase in unemployment with GDP per capita, 167–68, 169f
  as lower in poor than in rich countries, 167–68
  measurement of, 167
  in MENA, as persistently high, 166–67, 168–70
  sustained differences across countries, causes of, 166–67
UN-Habitat. *See* United Nations Human Settlement Programme
UNHCR. *See* United Nations High Commission for Refugees
United Arab Emirates (UAE)
  and air pollution, 180–81
  and Arab Spring, 29–32
  date of independence, 5t
  economic diversification efforts, 81
  education, instruction in colonial language, 102t
  employed, by nationality and sector, 157–58, 158f
  energy subsidies in, 206t, 209t
  failure of price levels to rise with income, 14
  FDI in MENA countries, 87–88
  foreign aid to Arab countries, 152
  former colonial power in, 5t
  fuel reserves and GDP per capita, 80–81, 80t
  GDP per capita changes, pre- and post-Arab Spring, 29–32, 31t
  and global warming, 192
  greenfield FDI by sector, 86t, 89t
  greenfield FDI by source, 87t
  intensive growth, as result of capture of rents from oil and gas, 55
  Islamic banking in, 165b
  life expectancy changes, pre- and post-Arab Spring, 30t
  as member of fuel-endowed countries group, 19–20
  migrant residents, 156, 156t, 157t
  military spending as share of GDP, 211t
  official name, 5t
  and OPEC, 78, 79t
  population, 21t
  ranking by HDI vs. GNI per capita, 10–11
  share of fuel in merchandise exports, 80t, 81
  water desalination in, 174
  water scarcity in, 173t
United Kingdom, colonial rule in Arab world, 4
United Nations, on domestic violence, 136–38, 137t
United Nations Development Program, 10b
United Nations High Commission for Refugees (UNHCR), 159, 160
United Nations Human Settlement Programme (UN-Habitat), 213–14, 215b, 216–18
United States, as market for Arab Mediterranean and Turkish manufactures, 67, 67t
  as source of FDI in MENA, 86t
United States and Canada
  migrants in, source countries of, 152, 153t
  as source of remittances, 151–52, 153t
urban infrastructure
  government inability to provide in slums, 195, 196, 213–15, 215b, 218–19
  increased need for, with urbanization, 197–98, 200–4, 202t
  military spending as drain on spending for, 210
  public sector as most common supplier of, 197–98
urbanization, 196–200
  and child mortality rate, 201–3, 202t
  and increased share of public investment in GDP, 197–98, 201–3
  and infrastructure demand, 197–98, 200–4, 202t
  limits to, 200–1
  rate of, 196–97, 197t
urban primacy, 200–4
  causes of, 201
  and child mortality, 202t
  and increase in public investment share of GDP, 201–3
  policy recommendations on, 254–55
  by population, 203, 204
  problems caused by, 195, 201–4
  and urban infrastructure, 201–4, 202t
urban primacy hypothesis, 201

Venâncio, Ana, 232–33, 246
Venezuela
  FDI in, 84–85
  introduction of shared oil rents, 76, 77
  and OPEC, 78, 79t
Versteegh, Kees, 3b
Vishny, Robert, 48–49

Wahba, Jackline, 152–53
water, safe, access to, 173–77
   and definition of slum, 213–14, 215*b*
   desalination and, 174
   GDP per capita and, 171, 176*f*, 176–77
   health consequences of lack of, 178, 179*t*
   success of Arab countries in providing, 172, 176*f*, 176–77
   urbanization and, 197–98, 202*t*
water scarcity in Arab countries, 173–74, 173*t*, 220*t*
   and cost of supplying water, 174
   and sophistication in water management, 175–76
   tariff increases and, 175–76
   water utility subsidies and, 172, 174–75, 175*t*, 252
water utility subsidies, and water scarcity, 172, 174–75, 175*t*, 252
water-wheels (*norias*), 38–39*b*, 38, 39*f*
West Bank and Gaza (Palestine), as MENA country, 33
   and non-subsidy programs, 162–63
Williamson, Jeffrey, 119
Wink, Claudia, 133, 135
women. *See* female
workplace discrimination, and female labor force participation, 129–30
World Bank
   on air pollution, 171, 180
   basic sanitation, definition of, 177–78
   country codes, 33, 34*t*
   definition of basic drinking water services, 176–77
   *Development and the Environment* (1993), 171, 180–81
   Enterprise Surveys, 219
   on environmental problem types, 171–72
   on FDI, 85–86, 86–89*t*
   gender parity index of, 122
   on global warming, 192
   on high employment in public sector in Arab countries, 170
   on income inequality, 143
   poverty measures, 145–47, 146*f*, 147*f*
   poverty reduction study, 162–63
   on public sector employment rates, 170
   on unemployment rates, 166–67
   on water scarcity, 174, 175–76
   *zakat* study, 164
   See also *Doing Business* ranking (World Bank)
World Development Indicators, 11, 143
world economic boom, first, and growth of development gap, 42–43, 54
World Health Organization (WHO)
   on air pollution, 182
   on disease burden from unsafe water and sanitation, 178–79, 179*t*
   and pharmaceuticals for Arab countries, 108
World Trade Organization (WTO)
   Arab countries belonging to, 63–64
   and constraints on Arab Mediterranean countries' policies, 66
   and international free trade, 12*b*

Yanagizawa-Drott, David, 255–56
Yemen
   and air pollution, 180–81
   and Arab Spring, 6, 17, 29, 33
   civil war in, 29, 160
   date of independence, 5*t*
   *de facto* workplace discrimination against women in, 129–30
   education in, instruction in colonial language, 102*t*
   education quality in, 96*f*, 97
   energy subsidies in, 206*t*
   female labor force participation in, 129–30, 255–56
   former colonial power in, 5*t*
   fuel exports, and GDP growth, 83–84
   GDP per capita changes, pre- and post-Arab Spring, 29, 31*t*
   infrastructure quality for business, 220*t*
   intensive growth, late onset of, 55, 83–84
   internally displaced persons in, 160
   Islamic banking in, 165*b*
   life expectancy changes, pre- and post-Arab Spring, 29, 30*t*
   malaria index in, 18
   as member of sub-Saharan Arab countries group, 18
   migrants from, countries hosting, 152, 153*t*
   military spending as share of GDP, 211*t*, 212
   official name, 5*t*
   and OPEC, 79*t*
   population, 21*t*
   population living in slums, 217*t*
   poverty headcount ratio in, 146*f*, 146–48, 147*f*
   as refugee host, 159*t*, 160
   remittances, sources of, 151–52, 153*t*
   remittances received, ratio to GDP, 151, 151*t*
   and sanitation access, 177–78
   water scarcity in, 173*t*
Yergin, Daniel, 76–77
Yoshino, M. Y., 49–50
Yousef, Tarik, 165–66*b*

*zakat*, 164*b*, 164
Zhang, Junjie, 183–84
Zhang, Xuelei, 182
Zouari, Sami, 130–31